The Gnostic Bible
The Pistis Sophia Unveiled

The Gnostic Bible

The Pistis Sophia Unveiled

The Translated Coptic Text
and Accompanying Explanation
of the Gnostic Doctrine

by

Samael Aun Weor

2011

The Pistis Sophia Unveiled
A Glorian Publishing Book
Second Edition (English)

Originally published in Spanish as "El Pistis Sophia Develado" (1983, posthumous)

Print ISBN 978-1-934206-81-2
Ebook ISBN 978-1-934206-64-5
Library of Congress Control Number: 2005902954

Glorian Publishing (formerly Thelema Press) is a non-profit organization delivering to humanity the teachings of Samael Aun Weor. All proceeds go to further the distribution of these books. For more information, visit:

gnosticteachings.org

Contents

A Third Book

A Fourth Book

A Sixth Book

List of Illustrations

Publisher's Note

The Pistis Sophia was dictated by Jesus of Nazareth to his disciples. Since that time, it has enjoyed a mysterious history, only becoming known to scholars in the 18th century, and being made publicly available some years later. Perhaps the most widely known edition is a translation by G.R.S. Mead, the former secretary of H. P. Blavatsky.

The origins of the original text remain unknown to scholars, although speculation has poured forth for many years. Two centuries of debate and discussion about *The Pistis Sophia* has brought forth no real knowledge, and the same can be said of the many "interpretations" of the text offered by scholars, priests, and religious leaders. This is true because *The Pistis Sophia*—like all the great scriptures—is a work of awakened consciousness, and can only be understood by the awakened consciousness. The mind—trapped within its cage of beliefs and theories—cannot see the truth. Humanity, asleep and dreaming of spirituality, remains in darkness until the consciousness is awakened.

Before beginning his commentary on *The Pistis Sophia,* Samael Aun Weor had already written more than sixty books about Gnosis and the path of the self-realization of the Being, and he had millions of students throughout the world. He was approaching the final moments of the most severe levels of internal initiation, and had completely eliminated all the subjective elements from his mind; in short, he had eliminated his ego, awakened his consciousness, and was preparing for the death of his physical body.

When the time came for him to write this work, the only available editions of *The Pistis Sophia* were in English. So one of his disciples brought him a copy of the text (as translated by G.R.S. Mead) and translated it into Spanish for him. And thus, section by section, Samael Aun Weor wrote his commentaries. Yet, due to the nature of the ordeals he was facing, he did not complete the entire portion of the book he planned to comment upon. So, the book remained unfinished, and after the death of his physical body, the G.R.S. Mead translation of *The Pistis Sophia* was translated into Spanish, and the commentaries by Samael Aun Weor were compiled and published as *El Pistis Sophia Develado.*

Over twenty years later, the first English edition of *The Pistis Sophia Unveiled* was published. In spite of many people's interest in a new translation of the original Coptic texts, we chose to obey the injunction at the end of the book which forbids adulteration of the text, and we keep the text as it was prepared by Samael Aun Weor. Therefore, we present to you the same translation (by G.R.S. Mead) that Samael Aun Weor heard (in Spanish) from the lips of his disciple.

It is worth mentioning at this point that the chapter divisions and descriptions were added by Mead and do not occur in the original text. We leave them intact. The only changes we have made to the Mead version are small typographical corrections and the occasional clarification of certain words; for example, where Mead used "righteousness," Samael Aun Weor used "virtue." We have retained the terms as used by Samael Aun Weor. Furthermore, it is also interesting to note that the original manuscript is arranged into four divisions, which are further divided into six books. This arrangement appears to be the result of the accumulation of these various writings, which represent only a portion of the materials that were originally composed.

Our single interest in publishing this work is to give to all who read it the opportunity for their consciousness to comprehend the meaning of the scripture. Within these pages, the reader will discover a form of wisdom that completely obliterates the speculations of scholars and intellectuals. Those who merely seek to compare these writings with what they have been told in the past will surely be disappointed. Here, you will find something completely new and without precedence in the theories and dogmas of men. Here, you will find the actual wisdom teachings of the universal Cosmic Christ, that wisdom that has been expressed throughout all ages and times, and which has given birth to every religion in the world. Here you will find the pure and complete knowledge that every soul requires in order to discover its true nature. In the Gnostic tradition, we understand that "all religions are precious pearls on the golden string of divinity," and in their heart-essence all religions teach the same wisdom. Where there is discord or disagreement among religions is where there has been adulteration by the minds of men. Here, in this text, one can find the pure expression of that eternal wisdom that leads the soul toward the emancipation of Sophia (wisdom) from the cage of the subjective mind. Yet, let it be understood clearly: without moment-to-moment application of the techniques and practices that awaken the consciousness, there can be no entrance into the living wisdom contained in these pages. Those who merely fill their minds with the information provided herein will remain like a dark and stuffy cellar, filled with dry pages of theory, and lacking the light and music of the soul. Thus, to understand what is written here, you must put it into action from moment to moment.

The Pistis Sophia Unveiled can be understood and applied by people of all races, religions, cultures, and of either sex. It is a message for all humankind, in every corner of the world. With great happiness and joy we humbly offer this precious scripture to this suffering humanity, in hopes that all souls may come to realize the nature of their own suffering, and seek to change in a radical and revolutionary way.

May all beings be happy!
May all beings be joyful!
May all beings be in peace!

A Liturgical Note

Certain works in the Gnostic tradition require the presence of *The Pistis Sophia Unveiled* opened to a particular page number. In this edition, that page is 291, "The Note of a Scribe."

Prologue of the Original Spanish Edition

We, the Forty-two Judges of Karma, exhort the Gnostic people to be united in these moments in which humanity is found at the crossroads of, "To be or not to be." We speak, reunited in full council, with the just authorization of Yew, Patriarch of the Supreme Hierarchy, and the whole White Fraternity to which we belong.

We send our blessings to all humans beings, without distinction of sex, creed, race or color. We yearn for the revolution of the Christic consciousness to accelerate its steps in order for Christ to descend into you. Thus, the light of the Divine Logos will make the igneous rose of spirituality flourish on the giant cross of the galaxy.

We, reunited in the heart temple of the Earth by the supreme order of the heart temple of the Sun and its Hierarchies, and with the powers that have been conferred to us, have decided that until further order, the direction of the Gnostic institutions of the world must be directed by the venerable Master Litelantes [deceased 6/2/1998].

We have authorized the publication of this book, *The Gnostic Bible, The Pistis Sophia Unveiled*, in which all of our sacred mysteries are concretely found, because the precise moment has arrived in which it must encounter humanity.

The ascending periplus, with all the published books of the venerable Master Samael Aun Weor, has accomplished its commendable mission with the unveiling of this sacred work. Now, the mission of the venerable Master Litelantes has begun, as the headmaster of the Gnostic Movement with her outright esoteric hierarchy, for the good of humanity.

This book fills one of the greatest necessities of the world. It is the forefather of a new civilization, of a new culture and the re-establishment of the holy Gnostic Church on the face of the Earth.

You are close to the great cataclysm. The times of the end have already arrived. The struggle of the elements will begin to break loose in diverse places on our planet. Be aware as a watchman in the epoch of war. You must put an end to the Kundabuffer organ, and with it, the "I," the ego, will definitely be destroyed, and the Being will be born.

Thus, you will achieve the inner Self-realization. The seed of the angel is within the sanctuarium of each one of you. Its germination will be possible through the perfect matrimony and the Three Factors, which you already know.

Drink of its pure and crystalline waters so that you can ascend on the wings of pleroma.

Foreword by Samael Aun Weor

The Hebrew Bible clearly connotes the word of the Eternal One. However, we, the Gnostics, also have our very special Bible. I want to emphatically declare that this is *The Pistis Sophia,* whose original is in Coptic. It was found underground in Egypt, the land of the Pharaohs.

The Pistis Sophia contains all the words of the adorable Savior of the world. It was written by the Apostles. Thus, all the esoteric Christic instructions that Jesus Christ gave to his disciples on the Mount of Olives and other holy places is written within this book. This book had been conserved in secret for many centuries. In this book, the Adorable One left an extraordinary, formidable body of doctrine.

Samael Aun Weor, who is my real Being within me—that is to say, my profound real inner Being—has commented on each paragraph of the Nazarene's doctrine. My inner God Samael unveiled each paragraph, in order to explain it correctly. We are delivering this work precisely in these despairing moments. Thus, this is how we will be able to give to humanity the unveiled and explained *Pistis Sophia:* the body of doctrine of the adorable Savior of the world, Jesus Christ.

Humanity will undoubtedly be surprised because the doctrine of the Nazarene is formidable. It is hidden wisdom in the most transcendental sense of the word. Therefore, all Gnostics must study *The Pistis Sophia.* This book must always be on the Gnostic altars. This book reveals to us the word of the Master, of the Lord, of Christ. We, the Gnostics, must venerate His work.

I do not want to underestimate the Hebrew Bible, since it is an extraordinary and marvellous book. However, we, the Gnostics, have our own specific book: The Gnostic Bible—*The Pistis Sophia,* which is the written word of Christ.

Obviously all religions, schools and beliefs will be shaken to their very roots, because the word of the Adorable One is extraordinary.

And Jesus said to his disciples: "I am come forth out of that First Mystery, which is the last mystery, that is the four and twentieth mystery."

Engraving by Gustave Doré

THE PISTIS SOPHIA UNVEILED

The First Book

This image of a sacred Mayan seal was given to Samael Aun Weor by a Master of the Mayan tradition. This seal was placed in the beginning and ending of the commentary written by Samael Aun Weor.

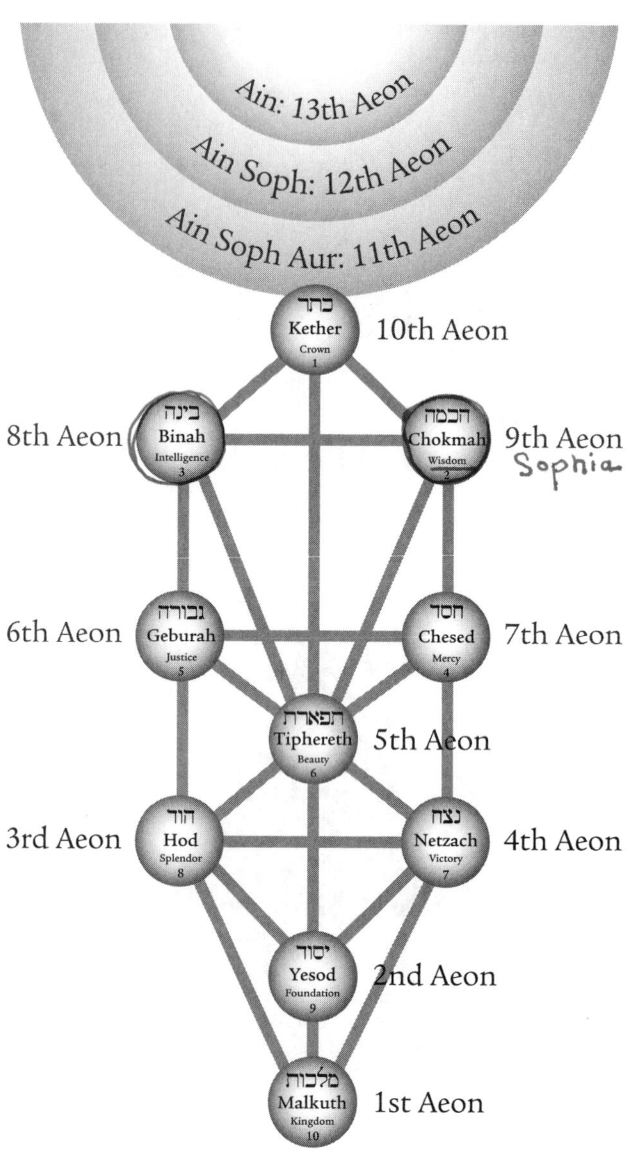

Ain: 13th Aeon
Ain Soph: 12th Aeon
Ain Soph Aur: 11th Aeon
כתר
Kether
Crown
1
10th Aeon
בינה
Binah
Intelligence
3
8th Aeon
חכמה
Chokmah
Wisdom
2
9th Aeon
Sophia
גבורה
Geburah
Justice
5
6th Aeon
חסד
Chesed
Mercy
4
7th Aeon
תפארת
Tiphereth
Beauty
6
5th Aeon
הוד
Hod
Splendor
8
3rd Aeon
נצח
Netzach
Victory
7
4th Aeon
יסוד
Yesod
Foundation
9
2nd Aeon
מלכות
Malkuth
Kingdom
10
1st Aeon

Chapter 1

Jesus hitherto instructeth his disciples only up to the regions of the First Mystery

It came to pass, when Jesus had risen from the dead, that he passed eleven years discoursing with his disciples, and instructing them only up to the regions of the First Commandment and up to the regions of the First Mystery, that within the Veil, within the First Commandment, which is the four and twentieth mystery without and below—those (four and twenty) which are in the second space of the First Mystery which is before all mysteries, the Father in the form of a dove.

> *"Joyful in hope, suffering in tribulation, be thou constant in thy prayer."*

The kings of sexual fire work with patience in the Great Work.

The inner Christ instructs the mind and the heart.

The First Commandment is: "*To love God above all things, and thy neighbor as thyself.*"

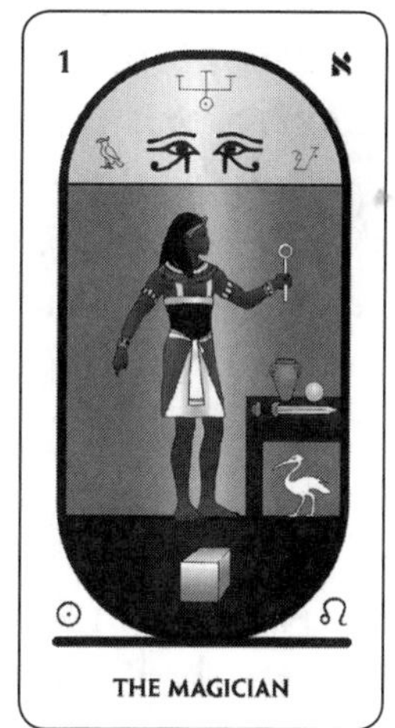

The First Mystery is Kether, the Ancient of Days. You know this.

When the devotee comprehends the First Commandment, he then easily understands the Four-and-twentieth Mystery.

The Four-and-twentieth Mystery is hidden within the loom of God.

> *"My loom is weaving net after net, a cloth for my honour and cloths to honour."*

The Ancient of Days is always hidden within his own loom, within his own creation.

To understand the Four-and-twentieth Mystery is not possible without previously comprehending the Sixth Mystery.

> *"Thou art giving me labour, O Lord, and fortitude with it."*

The Sixth Mystery explains with complete clarity the Four-and-twentieth Mystery.

The Spirit is strong, but the flesh is weak. Do not fall into temptation.

The soul, sex, temptation, downfall and regeneration, are found hidden within the Sixth Mystery.

The Ancient of Days, the Father who is in secret, is found in the First Space.

Nature, which is explainable only with the Sixth Mystery, is found within the Second Space.

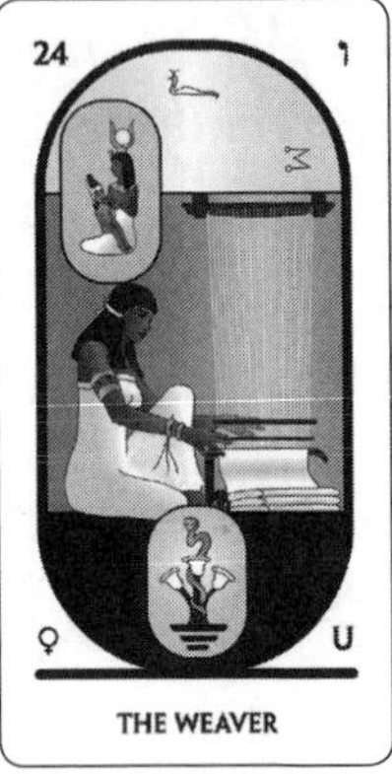

What the First Mystery surroundeth

And Jesus said to his disciples: "I am come forth out of that First Mystery, which is the last mystery, that is the four and twentieth mystery." And his disciples have not known nor understood that anything existeth within that mystery; but they thought of that mystery, that it is the head of the universe and the head of all existence; and they thought it is the completion of all completions, because Jesus had said to them concerning that mystery, that it surroundeth the First Commandment and the five Impressions and the great Light and the five Helpers and the whole Treasury of the Light.

The inner Jesus comes forth out of the First Mystery. Considering that the Son is one with the Father, and the Father is one with the Son, whosoever has seen the Son has seen the Father.

The First Mystery is the Mystery of the Father, and this is why it is also the Last Mystery. The Ancient of Centuries is the First and the Last of the Mysteries.

The Four-and-twentieth Mystery, which is explainable by the Sixth Mystery, hides within its womb the First Mystery.

The First Mystery, which is explainable by the Four-and-twentieth Mystery, and which is synthesized in the Sixth Mystery, is the very head of the universe.

The First Mystery, which is also the Four-and-twentieth Mystery, infolds the First Commandment, although the commandments of the law of God are twenty-two.

The First Commandment also surrounds the five Impressions of the great Light, and the five Helpers, and the whole Treasury of the Light.

> *I have heard of thee by the hearing of the ear: but now mine eye seeth thee, and my heart feeleth thee.*

Even though the First Commandment, the five Impressions of the Great Light, the five Helpers, and the entire Treasury of the Light are under the law of the scale, they are contained within the First Mystery in their final synthesis.

The five Impressions of the Great Light are found represented in the esoteric Pentagram.

The Gnostic Pentagram is the human figure with four limbs, and one single apex which is the head.

The sign of the Pentagram is also called the sign of the Microcosm. It represents what the Kabbalist Rabbis of the book *Zohar* call the Microprosopos.

When the superior point of the Pentagram is aiming upwards towards the sky, it represents the Savior of the world.

When the two inferior points of the Pentagram are aiming upwards towards the sky, it represents the male goat of the Witches' Sabbath.

A human figure with the head aiming downwards obviously represents a demon, that is to say, an intellectual subversion, disorder, or madness.

The Pentagram, which in the Gnostic schools is known as the Flaming Star, is the sign of magic omnipotence.

The five Impressions of the Great Light, and the five Helpers, are contained within the Flaming Star.

The five Helpers are the five Genii: Gabriel, Raphael, Uriel, Michael, and Samael.

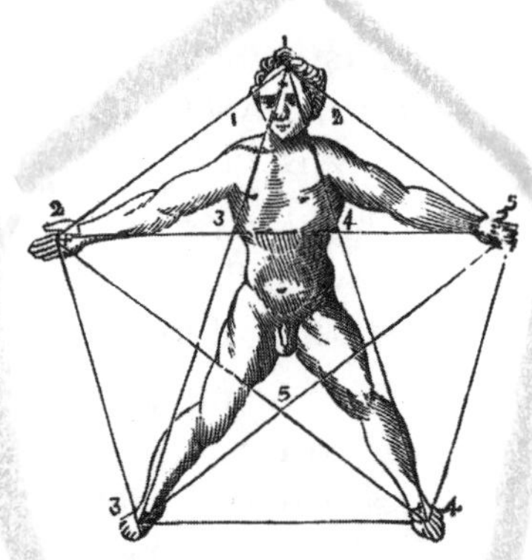

The entire Treasury of the Light is contained within the Pentagram, and this allegorizes the human being.

The comprehension of the magic Pentagram is the key of the two Spaces.

The sign of the Pentagram must be composed of the seven metals, or at least traced in pure gold upon white virgin marble.

The seven metals are as follows: silver, mercury, copper, gold, iron, tin and lead.

The Pentagram, with its superior ray aiming upwards, forces the columns of demons to scatter.

The Pentagram, with the two inferior rays aiming upwards, attracts the tenebrous ones.

When the Pentagram is traced with charcoal on the floor of the threshold (entrance) of the room, with its two inferior rays aiming towards the outside of the room, it does not permit the entrance of the tenebrous ones.

The Pentagram must be consecrated with the four elements, while reciting the exorcisms of fire, air, water and earth.

Five breaths must be blown upon the magical figure of the Pentagram.

The Flaming Star must be sprinkled five times with ritual water.

The figure of the Pentagram must be dried with the smoke of five perfumes: frankincense, myrrh, aloe, sulphur, and camphor.

Afterwards, the Pentagram is placed on the floor, alternating it successively to the North, South, East and West.

The name of א Aleph and the sacred name of ת Tav must be uttered, united in the Kabbalistic name of Azoth.

While blowing the five breaths upon the Flaming Star, the five magic Helpers Gabriel, Raphael, Uriel, Michael, and Samael must be invoked.

Do not forget that the Golden Fleece is the Treasury of the Light.

Unquestionably, the Golden Fleece is contained in the First Mystery.

No adept can take possession of the Golden Fleece if he has not previously comprehended the First Commandment and the First Mystery.

The First Mystery is found contained within the Four-and-twentieth Mystery which is the loom upon which our own fate is woven and unwoven.

The loom of God, the Great Work, functions only with the Sixth Mystery.

The Sixth Mystery is the Lover, the mystery of love.

The transcendental sexual electricity is that marvellous force which originates all motion in the loom of God.

Those who never transmute the sacred sperm into transcendental sexual electricity leave the loom of God in suspense.

Those who leave the loom of God in suspense are not working within the Great Work.

It is necessary to worship יהוה Iod-Heve.

Nevertheless, if the worshipper does not continue his work in the Great Work, he becomes stagnant.

When one does not possess a Hermetic Glass, then one must attain it in order to work in the Great Work.

Often moral codes, prejudgments, and fears constitute a great obstacle to the acquisition of a Hermetic Glass.

A damaged or destroyed Hermetic Glass does not serve the alchemist for his work in the Great Work.

The Hermetic Glass is the feminine yoni; you know this.

The key of all power is found in the wise connection of the generator lingam with the feminine yoni.

Those who spill the Mercury do not obtain the generation of the transcendental sexual electricity. Thus, they fail in the Great Work.

Spilling the Hermetic Glass is equivalent to paralyzing all the activities of the Four-and-twentieth Mystery.

The cowards that are influenced by prejudgments and absurd fears never obtain a Hermetic Glass. Thus, they lamentably fail.

Those who, for absurd considerations and false moral postulates, adhere themselves to a destroyed or damaged Hermetic Glass and do not dare take a new one, leave the Great Work paralyzed. Thus, they lamentably fail.

The Treasury is for courageous workers.

If the Gods do not want their physical body to degenerate and die, then they must feed themselves with the nectar of immortality.

The nectar of immortality is contained within the Holy Grail.

The Holy Grail is the feminine sexual yoni.

The Regions of the great Invisible

And moreover Jesus had not told his disciples the total expansion of all the regions of the great Invisible and of the three triple-powers and of the four and twenty invisibles, and all their regions and their aeons and their orders, how they are extended those which are the emanations of the great Invisible and their ungenerated and their self-generated and their generated and their light givers and their unpaired and their rulers and their authorities and their lords and their archangels and their angels and their decans and their servitors and all the houses of their spheres and all the orders of every one of them.

The outcome of the total expansion of all the regions of the Great Invisible, in the dawn of any cosmic creation becomes extraordinary.

The adept must know about all of the supra-sensible Regions of Nature and the cosmos, and the way in which they are expanded in the dawn of creation.

The Aeons and their sacred Orders, which are the emanations of the Unknowable and Unmanifested Divinity, dwell in those regions.

The thirty pleromatic Aeons shine when emerging in successive and orderly emanations, and in pairs, from the Forefather.

The thirty Aeons emerge in the dawn of creation.

The Triple-powers, the Law of Three, the three primary forces of Nature and the cosmos are indispensable in order to create and create anew.

The three forces are: Holy Affirmation, Holy Negation, and Holy Conciliation; Father, Son, and Holy Spirit; positive force, negative force and neutral force.

When these three forces flow in different directions, creation cannot be achieved.

In order for a new creation to emerge, these three primary forces must reunite at a given point.

The Triple-powers and the Four-and-Twenty Invisibles are present in the dawn of any cosmic creation.

Positive, negative and neutral forces, and intensive work in the Great Work, form a single whole.

Thus, the Four-and-Twenty Elders work intensely in the Zodiac, within which our solar system is palpitating.

> From the effulgency of light—the Ray of the Ever-Darkness—sprung in space the reawakened energies on the Dawn of the Great Day. The One from the Egg, the Six and the Five, then the Three, the One, the Four, the One, the Five, the Twice Seven, the Sum Total. And these are the Essences, the Flames, the Elements, the Divine Builders, the Numbers, those who have not a body and those who have a body, the Divine Man, the Sum Total.
>
> And from the Divine Man emanated the Forms, the Sparks, the Sacred Animals, and the Messengers of the Sacred Powers within the Holy Four.

This is how it always happens on the dawn of every cosmic creation.

Those who are "ungenerated" by themselves, which means, those who still have not reached the Second Birth, also emanate from the Great Invisible.

The "self-generated," those who have worked in the mysteries of sex and who have reached the Second Birth, emanate from the Great Invisible.

The disciples of the "self-generated" also emanate generated from the Great Invisible.

The disciples of those generated by means of their own Self, and the Light Givers, and their Unpaired, and their Rulers, and their Authorities, and their Lords, and their Archangels, and their Angels, and their Decans, and their Liturgists, and all the houses of their respective Spheres, and all the Esoteric Orders of each one of them, emanate from the Great Invisible.

The Treasury of the Light

And Jesus had not told his disciples to total expansion of the emanations of the Treasury, nor their orders, how they are extended; nor had he told them their saviours, according to the order of every one, how they are; nor had he told them what guard is at every (gate) of the Treasury of the Light; nor had he told them the region of the Twin-saviour, who is the Child of the Child; nor had he told them the regions of the three Amens, in what regions they are expanded; nor had he told them into what regions the five Trees are expanded; nor as to the seven Amens, that is the seven Voices, what is their region, how they are expanded.

The Treasury is the Philosophical Stone, the resurrected King within each one of us.

Emanations, Mystic Orders that are extended, Saviors, etc. emerge from the Treasury.

In each temple, there is always a Guardian at every gate.

At every gate of the Treasury of the Light there is always a Guardian.

The Treasury of the Light is possessed only by the resurrected Master.

The Twin Savior is the Son of Man.

The Twin Savior is Tiphereth, the Causal Man, within whom the Logos, the Christ is manifested.

The Twin Savior is certainly the Child of the Child.

The regions of the three Amens are symbolized by the triangle of the three Supernals, which are found separated from the rest of the universe by that abyss through which the intellectual humanoid can never pass.

The Ancient of Days is the first activity of manifestation and movement, which is a state of pure becoming.

Christ, the Logos, is the Second Primordial, which is gleaming in the Zodiacal belt.

The Serpent that bites its tail with its mouth, which is the Third Primordial, emerges from the Logos.

The three Amens are the three Primordial Forces from Nature and the cosmos.

The three Primordial Forces are: Holy Affirmation, Holy Negation, and Holy Conciliation.

Three Witnesses in heaven exist: the Father, the Logos, and the Holy Spirit. Three Witnesses on Earth exist: the Breath, the Blood, and the Water.

The five Trees are the Prodigies, the Bewitchments, the Jinns, the most hidden powers, the law, the karma, the orders of the lords of the law.

The seven Amens are the seven Weors, the seven Spirits before the Throne of the Lamb, the seven Planetary Spirits, the seven Regions.

The seven Voices are the seven Spirits before the Throne of the Lamb.

The seven Genii are: Gabriel, Raphael, Uriel, Michael, Samael, Zachariel, Orifiel.

The Light-world

And Jesus had not told his disciples of what type are the five Helpers, nor into what region they are brought; nor had he told them how the great Light hath expanded itself, nor into what region it hath been brought; nor had he told them of the five impressions, nor as to the First Commandment, into what region they have been brought. But he had discoursed with them generally, teaching that they exist, but he had not told them their expansion and the order of their regions, how they are. For this cause they have not known that there were also other regions within that mystery.

And he had not told his disciples: "I have gone forth out of such and such regions until I entered into that mystery, and until I went forth out of it"; but, in teaching them, he said to them: "I am come forth from that mystery." For this cause then they thought of that mystery, that it is the completion of completions, and that it is the head of the universe and that it is the total Fullness. For Jesus had said to his disciples: "That mystery surroundeth that universe of which I have spoken unto you from the day when I met with you even unto this day." For this cause then the disciples thought there is nothing within that mystery.

The five Helpers are part of the seven Spirits who stand before the Throne of the Lamb. They are brought into manifestation and later brought into the Absolute.

The Light is expanded in the dawn of every creation, and then gathered into the bosom of the Absolute at the end of every creation.

The five Impressions are related with the First Commandment. They are brought to the cosmos when the day of every creation is dawning.

The order of their diverse cosmic regions is explained perfectly in the Tree of Life.

Unquestionably, Jesus departed from the First Mystery.

The First Mystery is the completion of completions, the Head of the universe, and the total Fullness.

Chapter 2

Jesus and his disciples are seated on the Mount of Olives

It came to pass then when the disciples were sitting together on the Mount of Olives, speaking of these words and rejoicing in great joy, and exulting exceedingly and saying one to another: "Blessed are we before all men who are on the earth, because the Saviours hath revealed this unto us, and we have received the Fullness and total completion", —they said this to one another, while Jesus sat a little removed from them.

A great light-power descendeth on Jesus

And it came to pass then, on the fifteenth day of the moon in the month Tybi, which is the day on which the moon is full, on that day then, when the sun had come forth in his going, that there came forth behind him a great light-power shining most exceedingly, and there was no measure to the light conjoined with it. For it came out of the Light of lights, and it came out of the last mystery, which is the four and twentieth mystery, from within without, —those which are in the orders of the second space of the First Mystery. And that light-power came down over Jesus and surrounded him entirely, while he was seated removed from his disciples, and he had shone most exceedingly, and there was no measure for the light which was on him.

The fifteenth day of the Moon is related to Lucifer.

The code of Lucifer is the Arcanum A.Z.F., the sexual force.

Unquestionably, the creative power of the Logos is in the creative organs.

The splendorous, interior, profound Sun shines on the path of the initiate.

The luminous sexual force shines most exceedingly in the aura of the Christified Ones.

In the final synthesis, the sexual force comes from the Light of Lights, which is precisely the Logos.

Unquestionably, this Light comes from the Last and First Mystery, which in reality is the Four-and-twentieth Mystery, the Mystery of the Great Work, the Mystery of the work in the great laboratory of the universe.

All that we have said in these paragraphs is completely understandable to the well qualified Hermetic Artists.

Indubitably, the Hermetic Artists belong to the Esoteric Orders who work in the Second Space of the First Mystery.

It is understandable that the Second Space of the First Mystery is the region in which the Hermetic Sages are dwelling.

The Ancient of Days dwells within the First Space of the First Mystery, and the First of the Twenty-two Commandments of the Law of God correspond to Him.

It surroundeth him entirely

And the disciples had not seen Jesus because of the great light in which he was, or which was about him; for their eyes were darkened because of the great light in which he was. But they saw only the light, which shot forth many light-rays. And the light-rays were not like one another, but the light was of diverse kind, and it was of diverse type, from below upwards, one (ray) more excellent than the other,......., in one great immeasurable glory of light; it stretched from under the earth right up to heaven. And when the disciples saw that light, they fell into great fear and great agitation.

Within the inner Jesus Christ of each one of us, the creative energy shines marvelously.

The Logos is the Perfect Multiple Unity. In the world of the Logos, diversity is unity.

The inner Christ within each one of us is beyond individuality, personality, and the "I."

All beings are indeed one in the Lord.

Many rays bud in the "Christ-Light," and from the "Christ-Light."

Each Logoic ray is of a diverse type and distinct class. However, all the rays in themselves constitute the Logos.

Each ray is the living expression of this or that adept, or of this or that Christified One.

Every Logoic ray serves as a foundation for this or that Hierophant.

The existence of any adept would be inconceivable, if we exclude from the depth of his Being his corresponding ray of Light.

In the final synthesis, all the rays of Light are reduced to one, which stretches itself into one immeasurable Glory of Light, from the Abyss right up to heaven.

Chapter 3

Jesus ascendeth into heaven

It came to pass then, when that light-power had come down over Jesus, that it gradually surrounded him entirely. Then Jesus ascended or soared into the height, shining most exceedingly in an immeasurable light. And the disciples gazed after him and none of them spake, until he had reached unto heaven; but they all kept in deep silence. This then came to pass on the fifteenth day of the moon, on the day on which it is full in the month Tybi.

Unquestionably the ascension of the inner Christ within each one of us can be attained by means of the Fifteenth Mystery, which is the mystery of Typhon Baphomet.

The mystery of Baphomet is solved with the Sixth Mystery; you know this.

The Hermetic figure of the Baphomet was never absent from the houses of the old alchemists of the Middle Ages.

Lucifer-Baphomet grants us the sexual impulse, through which the realization of the Great Work is possible.

When we wound Baphomet to death with the lance of Longinus, we transmute lead into gold.

Sexual transmutation is fundamental for Christification. This is the mystery of Baphomet.

Indubitably, if we spill the Hermetic Glass, then metallic transmutation is absolutely impossible.

Those who learn how to utilize the sexual impulse intelligently can perform the Great Work.

The ascension of the inner Christ within us is absolutely possible when we have comprehended the Fifteenth Mystery, which is the same mystery of Lucifer-Baphomet.

The confusion of the powers and the great earthquake

It came to pass then, when Jesus had reached the heaven, after three hours, that all the powers of the heaven fell into agitation, and all were set in motion one against the other, they and all their aeons and all their regions and all their orders, and the whole earth was agitated and all they who dwell thereon. And all men who are in the world fell into agitation, and also the disciples, and all thought: Peradventure the world will be rolled up.

And all the powers in the heavens ceased not from their agitation, they and the whole world, and all were moved one against the other, from the third hour of the fifteenth day of the moon of Tybi until the ninth hour of the morrow. And all the angels and their archangels and all the powers of the height, all sang praises to the interiors of the interiors, so that the whole world hear their voices, without their ceasing till the ninth hour of the morrow.

The ascension of the intimate Jesus Christ is a sexual mystery of practical and transcendental Alchemy.

The ascension of the intimate Jesus Christ within us is certainly clear by means of the wise combination of the three Amens. I am emphatically referring to the three fundamental forces of Nature and the cosmos.

The three forces, positive, negative, and neutral, when wisely combined in the flaming forge of Vulcan, originate the human transformation, the ascension of Christ within us.

Stella Maris, the Divine Mother Kundalini, guides the navigator within the boisterous ocean.

The victorious inner Christ is the Red Christ.

The revolutionary Christ, the rebel Christ, causes all the powers of good and evil to be agitated.

The Red Christ can never be comprehended by the powers of good and evil.

All the powers of heaven are in agitation and set into motion, one against the other, in the presence of the strange procedures of the revolutionary Logos.

Indeed, all the Beings, all the Aeons, and all the Regions of the Tree of Life and their Orders are in agitation in the presence of the Red Christ.

The Red Christ is the Christ who worked in the flaming forge of Vulcan; the intimate Savior Christ; the Christ who became victorious in the hour of temptation; the Christ who ejected all the merchants of the interior temple; the Christ who killed the disloyal ones; the Christ dressed with the purple of the kings.

The profound inner Christ must fight a tremendous battle against the eternal enemies of the night who are within us here and now.

These enemies are the disloyal ones, the diverse psychic aggregates that personify our psychological defects.

The ascension of Christ within us is a sexual problem.

The powers of light and the powers of darkness are in agitation, and revolve when the resurrection and ascension of the inner Christ occurs within us.

The inner Christ must fight against the powers of good and evil.

The inner Christ is beyond good and evil.

The inner Christ grasps the sword of cosmic justice.

The powers of good and evil fight amongst themselves while in the presence of the Christic events.

The three primary forces of Nature and of the cosmos must be crystallized within the human being.

The Sacred Absolute Sun wants to crystallize the three primary forces within each one of us.

The initiate is developed under the constellation of the Whale.

The inner Self-realization of the Being would be impossible without Lucifer-Baphomet.

Lucifer originates the sexual impulse within each one of us.

If we control the sexual impulse and transmute the sacred sperm, then we rise from degree to degree.

All the work of the Great Work is performed in the Ninth Sphere.

The Ninth Sphere is sex.

Those who spill Hermes' Glass fail in the Great Work.

The Hierarchies of the Fire worship the Interiors of the Interiors.

The Interiors of the Interiors are the Beings of the Beings.

The Interiors of the Interiors are the Real of the Real.

The Seer of the Seer is the intimate God of the Seer; you know this.

Chapter 4

But the disciples sat together in fear and were in exceedingly great agitation and were afraid because of the great earthquake which took place, and they wept together, saying, "What will then be? Peradventure the Saviour will destroy all regions?" Thus saying, they wept together.

All of the great, divine cosmic events are always announced with great earthquakes.

Indubitably, great earthquakes also exist within the Superior Worlds.

Obviously, the adepts of Christ prostrate with amazement in the presence of these great events.

Jesus descendeth again

While they then said this and wept together, then, on the ninth hour of the morrow, the heavens opened, and they saw Jesus descend, shining most exceedingly, and there was no measure for his light in which he was. For he shone more (radiantly) than at the hour when he had ascended to the heavens, so that men in the world cannot describe the light which was on him; and it shot forth light-rays in great abundance, and there was no measure for its rays, and its light was not alike together, but it was of diverse kind and of diverse type, some (rays) being more excellent than others...; and the whole light consisted together.

The nature of his glory

It was of threefold kind, and the one (kind) was more excellent than the other... The second, that in the midst, was more excellent than the first which was below, and the third, which was above them all, was more excellent than the two which were below. And the first glory, which was placed below them all, was like to the light which had come over Jesus before he had ascended into the heavens, and was like only itself in its light.

And the three light-modes were of diverse light-kinds, and they were of diverse type, one being more excellent than the other....

In the ninth hour the heavens are opened and the inner Christ descends, shining most exceedingly.

Those who understand the ninth hour comprehend the twelve hours of Apollonius.

The mysteries of Chokmah correspond to the ninth hour.

No adept can experience the ninth hour unless he has previously resurrected.

The resurrection of the inner Christ within us takes place in the eighth hour.

The twelve hours of Apollonius are related with the twelve works of Hercules.

The multiple rays of the Logos are of a diverse class and diverse type. Some rays are more excellent than others.

However, the Logos is a Perfect Multiple Unity.

The light of the Cosmic Christ harmonizes in union.

In itself and by itself, the Logos has three aspects.

The Father, the Son, and the Holy Spirit are the three Logoic aspects.

The sacred Absolute Sun wants to crystallize the three primary forces within us.

The Logoic Light is threefold, and each one is more excellent than the other.

One is the light of glory of the Holy Spirit. Another is the glory of Christ, and another the glory of the Father.

The three forms of Logoic Light are of a diverse class and diverse type, one more excellent than the other.

However, the entire Logoic Triple Light is one.

The Triple World of the Logos is the glory of Atziluth.

The world of Atziluth is derived from the omnipresent and active Okidanokh.

The active Okidanokh is the eternal incessant breath, profoundly unknowable to itself.

The active Okidanokh has its root within the sacred Absolute Sun.

Chapter 5

Jesus addresseth them

And it came to pass then, when the disciples saw this, that they feared exceedingly, and were in agitation. Then Jesus, the compassionate and tender-hearted, when he saw his disciples, that they were in great agitation, spake with them, saying: "Take courage. It is I, be not afraid."

The psychological aggregate of fear must be radically eliminated from our nature.

The existence of fear is impossible in the Logos.

Fear serves as a base for many errors.

Chapter 6

It came to pass then, when the disciples had heard this word, that they said: "Lord, if it be thou, withdraw thy light-glory into thyself that we may be able to stand; otherwise our eyes are darkened, and we are agitated, and the whole world also is in agitation because of the great light which is about thee."

The Egyptians said, "Osiris is a dark God."

Human beings are not capable of enduring the light-glory.

The light of Christ dazzles the dwellers of the Earth.

This is why Osiris-Christ is dark for the human beings.

The splendors of Christ bewilder the inhabitants of the Earth.

Indeed, the splendors of Christ are not comprehended by people.

The consciousness is asleep among the multitudes.

As long as the ego, the "I," continues to dwell within us, then unquestionably the consciousness will continue to sleep.

The awakening occurs only by annihilating the ego.

Only the awakened one can understand the Christic mysteries.

He draweth his light unto himself

Then Jesus drew to himself the glory of his light; and when this was done, all the disciples took courage, stepped forward to Jesus, fell down all together, adored him, rejoicing in great joy, and said unto him: "Rabbi, whither hast thou gone, or what was thy ministry on which thou has gone, or wherefore rather were all these confusions and all the earth-quakings which have taken place?"

The inner Christ comes time and time again, continuously, each time when it is necessary.

The Cosmic Christ is a force, as electricity is a force, or as gravity is a force, etc.

The Cosmic Christ is beyond the personality, individuality, and the "I."

Christ expresses himself through any human being who is perfectly prepared.

Nevertheless, all the Christic events are accompanied by great earthquakes and confusions.

Christic events are terrifically revolutionary.

He promiseth to tell them all things

Then Jesus, the compassionate, said unto them: "Rejoice and exult from this hour on, for I have gone to the regions out of which I had come forth. From this day on then will I discourse with you in openness, from the beginning of the Truth unto its completion; and I will discourse with you face to face without similitude. From this hour on will I not hide anything from you of the [mystery] of the height and of that of the region of Truth. For authority hath been given me through the Ineffable and through the First Mystery of all mysteries to speak with you, from the Beginning right up to the Fullness, both from within without and from without within. Hearken, therefore, that I may tell you all things.

"It came to pass, when I sat a little removed from you on the Mount of Olives, that I thought on the order of the ministry for the sake of which I was sent, that it was completed, and that the last mystery,

that is the four-and-twentieth mystery from within without, —those which are in the second space of the First Mystery, in the orders of that space, —had not yet sent me my Vesture. It came to pass then, when I had known that the order of the ministry for the sake of which I had come, was completed, and that mystery had not yet sent me my Vesture, which I had left behind in it, until its time was completed, — thinking then this, I sat on the Mount of Olives a little removed from you."

Jesus Christ, or the inner Jesus Christ within each one of us, always emerges from the world of the Solar Logos in order to be manifested to mankind.

In Kabbalah, we would say that the secret Jesus Christ emerges from Chokmah, and thus He appears in the Tree of Life.

Unquestionably, He descends from this region in order to penetrate into the womb of His Divine Mother, by the grace and work of the Holy Spirit.

Stella Maris is a Virgin before, during, and after childbirth.

The Virgin of the Sea gives birth to Her Son within the stable of the world.

The stable of Bethlehem is the physical body of the initiate.

The animals of the mind, desire, and evil will are found within the stable of Bethlehem.

The intimate Jesus Christ must eliminate all of the undesirable elements that we carry within our interior.

The Virgin of the Sea is the daughter of Her Son, and the adorable wife of the Holy Spirit.

She, Stella Maris, obeys the orders of the intimate Jesus Christ and works with Him, eliminating all the undesirable psychic elements from within us.

The intimate Jesus Christ can teach the initiates, thanks to the First Mystery, which means, thanks to the Ancient of Days, thanks to the Father of all Lights.

The Lord does not hide anything from those who are truly awakened.

The Lord teaches the Mystery of the Height, and that of the region of Truth to all the adepts.

The Lord secretly instructs us, thanks to the Ineffable, and by the grace and work of the First Mystery of all Mysteries, which is the Mystery of the Father.

He instructs us from the beginning right up to the Fullness, both from within, without and from without, within.

All of this is possible when we incarnate Him.

Whosoever knows, the Word gives power to. No one has uttered it, no one will utter it, except the one who has incarnated Him.

The Mount of the Olives is the Causal World.

The Lord descends from the World of the Solar Logos in order to live as a Causal Man.

The Lord projects Himself from the Causal World into the physical world.

The Manifested Lord acts within the regions of the Mind.

The Manifested Lord shines within the Astral Body of the one who has incarnated Him.

The Manifested Lord enters the physical body in order to live as a human amongst humans.

Every time it is necessary, the Lord comes to this valley of tears in order to help humanity.

The sleeping multitudes never know the Lord.

When He comes they always condemn Him.

The intimate Jesus Christ has been crucified many times....

On the Mount of the Olives, the inner Christ profoundly reflects.

The Last Mystery is the Four-and-twentieth Mystery.

This is counted from within to without; you know this.

The Divine Mother Kundalini works in the Four-and-twentieth Mystery, weaving Her own loom.

All of this which has been stated is comprehended by those who work in the Second Space of the First Mystery.

The Divine Mother Kundalini, Stella Maris, works within the Second Space of the First Mystery.

We find all the workers of the Great Work within the Second Space of the First Mystery.

The workers of the Great Work obey the Father in heaven as well as on the Earth.

Now you comprehend better why the Four-and-twentieth Mystery is the First Mystery.

The Divine Mother Kundalini weaves a Vesture for the adept.

The whole of this work is performed based on conscious efforts and voluntary sufferings.

Those who have lost their sacred Vesture must search for it again.

Chapter 7

How the Vesture of Light was sent unto him

"It came to pass, when the sun rose in the east, thereafter then through the First Mystery, which existed from the beginning, on account of which the universe hath arisen, out of which also I am myself now come, not in the time before my crucifixion, but now, —it came to pass, through the command of that mystery, that there should be sent me my Light-vesture, which it had given me from the beginning, and which I had left behind in the last mystery, that is the four-and-twentieth mystery from within without, —those which are in the order of the second space of the First Mystery. That Vesture then I left behind in the last mystery, until the time should be completed to put it on, and I should begin to discourse with the race of men and reveal unto them all from the beginning of the Truth to its completion, and discourse with them from the interiors of the interiors to the exteriors of the exteriors and from the exteriors of the exteriors to the interiors of the interiors. Rejoice then and exult and rejoice more and more greatly, for to you it is given that I speak first with you from the beginning of the Truth to its completion."

The Sun of Midnight guides the initiates in the Superior Worlds.

The initiates must know the symbolic movements of the Sun of Midnight.

Sunrise is equivalent to the birth, to the rising, and to the manifestation of Him, etc.

Sunset allegorizes the death of something, the descent of something, etc.

The Sun, with complete splendor in midday, allegorizes complete plenitude, complete triumph, success of such or such initiation, etc.

We are emphatically referring to the Sun-Christ, the Logos, the Astral Sun.

The mystics see the Astral Sun. He guides them along the path of the razor's edge.

When the clouds of the sky are covering the Astral Sun, this signifies that the animal ego is still very strong within the initiate.

It is necessary, it is urgent, to dissolve the animal ego, to reduce it to cosmic dust.

The Sun-Christ, ascending through the First Mystery, signifies action of the Lord by the will of the Father.

The same universe in which we live, move, and have our Being, emerged and came into existence when the Sun ascended through the First Mystery.

It was by the will of the Ancient of Days that the Sun ascended through the First Mystery.

The inner Christ comes into manifestation not in the time before the hour of His crucifixion, but now.

It is here and now that the Lord must be crucified.

The Lord is crucified within us.

The Lord must live the entire cosmic drama within us, just as it is written within the Four Gospels, here and now.

Nevertheless, it is written that we must previously incarnate Him, you know this.

However, it is necessary to make the following warning:

Take heed that no man shall deceive you.

For many shall come in my name, saying I am the Christ; and shall deceive many.

(Read Matthew 23:4-5, New Testament)

The Venustic Initiation is frightfully difficult.

The inner Christ is incarnated in the Venustic Initiation.

It is very rare to find someone who has succeeded in incarnating Him.

Nevertheless, there are some sincerely mistaken ones who think the best of themselves.

They say, "I have incarnated Him, I am the Christ."

Such people are cheating themselves, as well as others.

Then if any man shall say unto you, Lo, here is the Christ, or there; believe it not.

For there shall arise false Christs, and false prophets, and shall show great signs and wonders; insomuch that, if it were possible, they shall deceive the very elect.

Behold, I have told you before.

Wherefore, if they shall say unto you, Behold, He is in the desert go not forth: Behold, He is in the secret chambers; believe it not.

For as the lightning cometh out of the east, and shineth even unto the west; so shall also the coming of the Son of Man be.

(Read Matthew: 24:23-27)

The Vesture of Light of the inner Christ was originally granted to Him. Nevertheless, it must be elaborately woven upon the loom of God, in the Four-and-twentieth Mystery of the Great Work.

The Vesture of Light of the inner Christ, a symbol of all the powers, is in the Father's power. The Father is the First and the Last of the Mysteries.

The inner Christ, when incarnated in a simple and humble human being, will use his sacred Vesture in the Mystery.

Profane people will never know the Vesture of Light.

The inner Christ is covered by the humble personality of someone.

People can never recognize the incarnated Christ.

The inner Christ is the Instructor of the world.

The incarnated Instructor of the world must discourse with the human race, and reveal to them the beginning of the Truth until its completion.

The adept who has incarnated Him will know how to love Him within himself, and he will never say, "I am the Christ."

The Master who has incarnated Him will worship the Lord and will serve as an instrument for Him.

The incarnated Lord will discourse with the human beings from the interiors of the interiors to the exteriors of the exteriors, and from the exteriors of the exteriors to the interiors of the interiors.

All of this signifies that the Lord can help the Being of the Being and the human personality.

The incarnated Instructor of the world can instruct not only the human persons, but also the Beings of those persons, and finally, the Being of the Being.

To help the exteriors of the exteriors signifies complete help in the order of all things.

To help the interior of the interior signifies complete instruction to the Being of the Being.

The incarnated inner Christ not only helps, but moreover He helps to help.

Only the adepts of perfection have incarnated Him.

Nevertheless, I tell you, be vigilant, because in these times of the end, there are many who presume that they are adepts of perfection.

Beware of false prophets.

Of the souls of the disciples and their incarnation

"For this cause have I chosen you verily from the beginning through the First Mystery. Rejoice then and exult, for when I set out for the world, I brought from the beginning with me twelve powers, as I have told you from the beginning, which I have taken from the twelve saviours of the Treasury of the Light, according to the command of the First Mystery. These then I cast into the womb of your mothers, when I came into the world, that is those which are in your bodies today. For these powers have been given unto you before the whole world, because ye are they who will save the whole world, and that ye may be able to endure the threat of the rulers of the world and the pains of the world and its dangers and all its persecutions, which the rulers of the height will bring upon you. For many times have I said unto you that I have brought the power in you out of the twelve saviours who are in the Treasury of the Light. For which cause I have said unto you indeed from the beginning that ye are not of the world. I also am not of it. For all men who are in the world have gotten their souls out of [the power of] the rulers of the aeons. But the power which is in you is from me; your souls belong to the height. I have brought twelve powers of the twelve saviours of the Treasury of the Light, taking them out of the portion of my power which I did first receive. And when I had set forth for the world, I came into the midst of the rulers of the sphere and had the form of Gabriel the angel of the aeons; and the rulers of the aeons did not know me, but they thought that I was the angel Gabriel."

The Twelve Apostles, the Twelve Powers, are within us, here and now.

The Twelve Apostles are twelve autonomous parts of our Being.

The Twelve Powers, the Twelve, are twelve self-cognizant parts, and even independent parts of our own Being.

The Twelve Powers, which are the Twelve Apostles of the inner Christ are wisely related with the twelve faculties of the human being.

However, we must make a clear differentiation between the Twelve Powers and the twelve faculties.

Unquestionably, during the cosmic manifestation, the Being within each one of us is the multiplicity within the unity.

All of these autonomous and self-cognizant parts of the Being must work in the inner Self-realization.

The inner Self-realization of each one of the autonomous and self-cognizant parts of the Being is more than impossible, as long as all the undesirable elements that we carry within our interior are not disintegrated.

The Twelve Powers are only twelve parts of the many autonomous and self-cognizant parts of the Being.

Whosoever perfects the highest part of the Being receives for that reason the degree of Ishmesch.

It is not possible to perfect the highest part of the Being without the radical dissolution of the inhuman elements that we carry within our interior.

Within the interior of our Being, James is the blessed Master of the Great Work.

Only the Father of all the Lights, the intimate Father within each one of us, can illuminate us with wisdom through James.

James is the Mercury within each one of us.

The Mercury of the Secret Philosophy is the very foundation of the Great Work.

The inner Christ and the Twelve Powers reside within us, here and now.

Unquestionably, the Twelve Powers are poured by the inner Christ into the womb of the Divine Mother.

Each one of us has our own Divine Mother.

The Twelve Powers must dwell within our bodies.

This is possible only by disintegrating all the undesirable psychic elements that we carry within our interior.

The Twelve Apostles, the fundamental parts of the Being, are always slandered and persecuted by the perverse ones. This is known by every illuminated Master.

The historical Jesus Christ and His Twelve Apostles symbolize the inner Christ and the Twelve Powers incarnated in every true human being.

There exist Twelve Saviors who symbolize the twelve zodiacal constellations.

The Twelve Powers within each human being are related with the Redeemer of such and such constellation.

All the Masters have succeeded in engendering their Souls, or better said crystallizing them within the human person, thanks to the teachings of the Twelve Saviors.

Each one of the twelve have come to the world in order to help humanity.

It is possible to crystallize the Soul within ourselves by dissolving the animal ego.

We need to dissolve the undesirable psychological elements in order to crystallize the Soul within ourselves.

We must convert ourselves into pure Soul.

With patience you will possess your Soul.

This is possible based on conscious work and voluntary sufferings.

The Souls of the people reside in a superior level of the Being.

The Soul is the conjunction of all the forces, powers, virtues, essences, etc., that crystallize within us when the entire animal ego has been dissolved.

Each time that a psychological defect is dissolved, a virtue, a power, etc., crystallizes within our interior.

The complete dissolution of all the defects implies the integral crystallization of the Soul within ourselves.

If the water does not boil at one hundred degrees, that which must be crystallized does not crystallize, and that which must be dissolved is not dissolved.

In similar form, we say that it is necessary to pass through great emotional crisis in order to dissolve psychological defects and crystallize the Soul.

The Angel Gabriel is the regent of the Moon and is related with the Lunar Sphere.

Jesus, the inner Christ, is the divine Sun within us.

Of the incarnation of John the Baptizer

"It came to pass then, when I had come into the midst of the rulers of the aeons, that I looked down on the world of mankind, by command of the First Mystery. I found Elizabeth, the mother of John the Baptizer, before she had conceived him, and I sowed into her a power which I had received from the little IAO, the Good, who is in the Midst, that he might be able to make proclamation before me and make ready my way, and baptize with the water of the forgiveness of sins. That power then is in the body of John."

John the Baptizer is Elias reincarnated.

The great IAO is the power from the Logos itself. The little IAO is the power from the human being.

The great IAO is the power from the Super-Man. The minor IAO is the power from Man.

The inner John is inside each one of us, here and now.

Every initiate must encounter the part of his Being that is called John the Baptizer.

The encounter with John always takes place in the Second Initiation of the Fire.

The encounter with John always takes place in Eden.

John is the precursor who prepares the path to our inner Christ.

The historic John the Baptizer allegorizes the interior John the Baptizer within each one of us.

That John was Elias in a former birth

"Moreover in place of the soul of the rulers which he was appointed to receive, I found the soul of the prophet Elias in the aeons of the sphere; and I took him thence, and took his soul and brought it to the Virgin of Light, and she gave it over to her receivers; they brought it

to the sphere of the rulers and cast it into the womb of Elizabeth. So the power of the little IAO, who is in the Midst, and the soul of the Prophet Elias, they were bound into the body of John the Baptizer. For this cause then were ye in doubt afore time, when I said unto you; 'John said: I am not the Christ,' and ye said unto me: 'It standeth written in the scripture: When the Christ shall come, Elias cometh before him and maketh ready his way.' But when ye said this unto me, I said unto you: 'Elias verily is come and hath made ready all things, as it standeth written, and they have done unto him as they would.' And when I knew that ye had not understood that I had discoursed with you concerning the soul of Elias which is bound into John the Baptizer, I answered you in the discourse in openness face to face: 'If ye like to accept John the Baptizer: he is Elias, of whom I have said that he will come.'"

The Rulers of the Gnostic Church are true awakened initiates.

The Spirit of Elias is also an Aeon, which means a Master of the Great Day. You know this.

The Virgin of Light, Stella Maris, the Divine Mother Kundalini of John the Baptizer, is named by the great Kabir Jesus.

The Savior delivered the Spirit of Elias to Stella Maris of John, and She delivered Him to Her Receivers. They brought him to the sphere of the Rulers of the Light and cast Him into the womb of Elizabeth.

In this manner, the little IAO, the Divine Mother of Light, and the Spirit of Elias were bound into the body of John the Baptizer.

Elias reincarnated in John the Baptizer. Thus, John is the living reincarnation of Elias.

Chapter 8

Of his own incarnation through Mary

And Jesus continued again in the discourse and said: "It came to pass then thereafter, that at the command of the First Mystery I looked down on the world of mankind and found Mary, who is called 'my mother' according to the body of matter. I spake with her in the type of Gabriel, and when she had turned herself to the height towards me, I cast thence into her the first power which I had received from Barbelo that is the body which I have borne in the height. And instead of the soul I cast into her the power which I have received from the great Sabaoth, the Good, who is in the region of the Right."

More concerning the light-powers in the disciples

"And the twelve powers of the twelve saviours of the Treasury of Light which I had received from the twelve ministers of the Midst, I cast into the sphere of the rulers. And the decans of the rulers and their servitors thought that they were souls of the rulers; and the servitors brought them, they bound them into the body of your mothers. And when your time was completed, ye were born in the world without souls of the rulers in you. And ye have received your portion out of the power which the last Helper hath breathed into the Mixture, that [power] which is blended with all the invisibles and all rulers and all aeons, —in a word, which is blended with the world of destruction which is the Mixture. This [power], which from the beginning I brought out of myself, I have cast into the First Commandment, and the First Commandment cast a portion thereof into the great Light, and the great Light cast a portion of that which it had received, into the five Helpers, and the last Helper took a portion of that which it received, and cast it into the Mixture. And [this portion] is in all who are in the Mixture, as I have just said unto you."

The command of the First Mystery is equivalent to the command of the Father.

Mary is always Isis, the Divine Mother, whose veil no mortal has lifted.

In Hebrew, the Army of the Voice, the Host or Creative Hostess of the Elohim, receives the name of Sabaoth.

In the Old Testament, the name of Jehovah is applied to the Host of the Cosmocreators or divine Androgynes who created this universe, rather than the original name יהוה Iod-Heve.

Isis-Mary always receives the First Power, the Holy Affirmation.

The inner Christ transmits such power to the Divine Mother Kundalini.

We must never forget that there exist three primary forces: Holy Affirmation, Holy Negation, Holy Conciliation.

The Great Sabaoth, the Good, who is in the Region of the Right, is the Host of the Creator Elohim.

The inner Christ always transmits the marvellous power of the Great Sabaoth to Stella Maris.

We could not, in anyway, deny the existence of the Twelve Saviors or Avatars.

Each one of the Twelve Redeemers has within himself the Twelve Powers.

Between each Logoic Redeemer and the manifested world, there exists a corresponding Master, Spirit, who has emanated from the Redeemer in question.

Obviously, the emanated Minister is a sunderable part of the intimate Logoi.

The decans of the Rulers and their servitors often think the best of themselves. They mistakenly assume that they are the Rulers of the Light. Such an error is due to pride and ambition.

Clearly, those mistaken ones are reborn and return to the world. They are brought to this valley of tears by the servitors of the Rulers.

The Princes of the Gnostic Church never ignore the work of the Abyss.

Only those who have worked intensely in the infernal worlds achieve the state of Princes or Rulers of the Gnostic Church.

In reality, to convert oneself into a Ruler of the Light is only possible by working on oneself in the Dantesque Ninth Circle.

Every exaltation is preceded by a terrible humiliation.

Those who want to ascend must first of all descend; such is the law.

When the sincerely mistaken ones (who believe that they are Rulers, yet they are not) are reborn, rather than receiving the Spirit of the Rulers, they receive the power for the struggle in life. This Martian power is combined with the world of destruction, which is the mixture or the result of the mixture of laws and forces.

The power of the Savior of the world is found in a very superior level, in relation to the powers of the five Helpers.

The power of the Redeemer of the world is cast into the First Commandment, which states: *To love thy God above all things, and thy neighbor as thyself.*

The First Commandment, which is love, casts a portion of that power into the Great Light.

Unquestionably, the Great Light also casts a portion of the love-power into the five Helpers.

The fifth Helper, acting with great power, takes a certain quantity of the substance of love in order to cast it into the mixture, into the world.

Indubitably, this last portion of the substance of love is bestowed within the Essence.

The Essence, the consciousness, is disgracefully found bottled up within the psychic aggregates, the living interior representations of our defects of a psychological type.

The Essence is liberated and love shines by the annihilation of the psychological aggregates.

Why they should rejoice that the time of his investiture had come

This then Jesus said to his disciples on the Mount of Olives. Jesus continued again in the discourse with his disciples [and said]: "Rejoice and exult and add joy to your joy, for the times are completed for me to put on my Vesture, which hath been prepared for me from the beginning, which I left behind in the last mystery until the time of its completion. Now the time of its completion is the time when I shall be commanded through the First Mystery to discourse with you from the beginning of the Truth to the completion thereof, and from the interiors of the interiors [to the exteriors of the exteriors]. For the world will be saved through you. Rejoice then and exult, for ye are blessed before all men who are on the earth. It is ye who will save the whole world."

The inner Christ uses His Vesture, the sacred purple, when he has performed the Great Work successfully.

We must never forget that the Last Mystery is the First Mystery.

The Father has prepared the purple of the Kings for the Son.

In the hour of completion, the Son is dressed with the sacred Vesture.

The hour of completion of the Great Work within ourselves, here and now, is terribly divine.

The Twelve Powers, the Twelve Apostles, are, I repeat, twelve autonomous and self-cognizant parts of our own Being.

The Twelve Apostles under the direction of the inner Christ are expressing themselves through the initiate when he is working for this suffering humanity.

The Twelve are twelve aspects of the Being within the individual unity.

Chapter 9

It came to pass then, when Jesus had finished saying these words to his disciples, that he continued again in the discourse, and said unto them: "Lo, I have then put on my Vesture, and all authority hath been given me through the First Mystery. Yet a little while and I will tell you the mystery of the universe and the fullness of the universe; and I will hide nothing from you from this hour on, but in fullness will I perfect you in all fullness and in all perfection and in all mysteries, which are the perfection of all perfections and the fullness of all fullnesses and the gnosis of all gnoses, —those which are in my Vesture. I will tell you all mysteries from the exteriors of the exteriors to the interiors of the interiors. But hearken that I may tell you all things which have befallen me."

The inner Christ is revested with the divine purple, which is used by those who have accomplished the Great Work.

Christ said, *"Lo, I have put on my Vesture, and all authority hath been given to me through the First Mystery."*

It is well known to us that the First Mystery is the Father who is in secret. There are as many Fathers in heaven as there are creatures on Earth. Each one of us has his own Father.

The Father is the First and the Last of the Mysteries.

There are twenty-two fundamental mysteries.

The inner Christ is the Instructor of the world. He can secretly reveal to us the mystery of the universe and the plenitude contained within it.

Christ, the Solar Logos, is the Perfect Multiple Unity.

The inner Christ, within the interior profundity of the Being, can and must perfect the Twelve, the Seven, the Twenty-four, and the Four, etc...

Moreover, it is necessary to repeat that the Being is multiple during his manifestation.

The inner Christ perfects the different autonomous and self-cognizant parts of our Being by dissolving the undesirable elements that we carry within our interior.

The Being is the Being, and the reason for the Being to be, is to be the Being Himself.

We must not confuse the Being with the "I."

The "I" is composed of thousands of psychic aggregates that personify our psychological defects.

The inner Christ in ourselves and within us must dissolve all of the undesirable elements that we carry within our interior.

The inner Christ comes to instruct us in secret. He reveals all of the mysteries to us from the exteriors to the exteriors and from the interiors to the interiors.

Chapter 10

The mystery of the five words on the vesture

"It came to pass then, when the sun had risen in the east, that a great light-power came down, in which was my Vesture, which I had left behind in the four-and-twentieth mystery, as I have said unto you. And I found a mystery in my Vesture, written in five words of those from the height: ***zama zama ozza rachma ozai****, —whose solution is this..."*

Obviously, the Vesture of the Adorable One is found in the Four-and-twentieth Mystery.

The Divine Mother Kundalini weaves the Lord's Vesture on the loom of God.

The loom of God is the Four-and-twentieth Mystery.

These five magic words are written on the Lord's Vesture: ***Zama Zama Ozza Rachma Ozai***.

These are words from the language of the Light.

The solution thereof

"O Mystery, which is without in the world, for whose sake the universe hath arisen, —this is the total outgoing and the total ascent,

which hath emanated all emanations and all that is therein and for whose sake all mysteries and all their regions have arisen, —come hither unto us, for we are thy fellow-members. We are all with thyself; we are one and the same. Thou art the First Mystery, which existed from the beginning in the Ineffable before it came forth; and the name thereof are we all. Now, therefore, are we all come to meet thee at the last limit, which also is the last mystery from within; itself is a portion of us. Now, therefore, have we sent thee thy Vesture, which hath belonged to thee from the beginning, which thou has left behind in the last limit, which also is the last mystery from within, until its time should be completed, according to the commandment of the First Mystery. Lo, its time is completed; put it on [thee]."

The Ancient of Days is the First and the Last of the Mysteries within our own Being.

The Ancient of Days is the cause of the great universal arising.

The Ancient of Ancients combines causes in order to make the universe arise.

All of the mysteries have arisen by the will of the Father who is in secret.

The total outgoing of the primary universal forces and the ascension or re-entering of the three original forces are due to the First Mystery, which is also the Last of the Mysteries.

All the cosmic emanations and all that is therein, and for whose sake all the mysteries have arisen, have emanated from these ascending and descending emanations and from the re-absorption of the three primary forces.

All that takes place within the universe also takes place within the real human being.

The three primary forces come from the Great Breath. You know this.

The three primary forces in themselves and by themselves are sunderable parts of the Great Breath, which is profoundly unknowable to itself.

The Great Breath is rooted in the Sacred Absolute Sun. You know this.

The three primary forces emanate from the Great Breath, and are reabsorbed in the Great Breath.

The Great Breath emanates from the Sacred Absolute Sun, and at the end of the Great Day it is reabsorbed in the Sacred Absolute Sun.

It is not possible to create unless the Great Breath has previously unfolded into its three forces: Positive, negative and neutral.

When these three original forces, the Father, the Son, and the Holy Spirit, meet or coincide at a given point, a creation is performed.

The Holy Seven is that which corresponds to the organization of such creation.

The Holy Three creates and re-creates, but creation cannot be organized without the Holy Seven.

Any cosmos can exist thanks to the very intimate collaboration of the Three and the Seven.

The Ancient of Days is the First Mystery, which existed within the Ineffable from the beginning, before it came forth.

Come to us and within us, Divine Ancient, for we are part of Thyself.

We are really the result of the final results of the multiple, sunderable divisions of the Ancient of Days.

The Father and the Son are one; the Father is one with the Son and the Son is one with the Father. Whosoever has seen the Son has seen the Father.

We must search for the Ancient of Days within the last limits of ourselves. He is the Last Mystery from within, and He, Himself is the superior part of our Being.

When we refer to the last limit, we refer to it in the sense of cosmic manifestation. The Being is unlimited beyond cosmic manifestation.

The Sacred Absolute Sun wants to crystallize the three primary forces within us, here and now.

The Ancient of Days must create his Vesture.

The Son must create His Vesture.

The Holy Spirit must create His Vesture.

We must create the Vesture for the Father, here and now, in the forge of the Cyclops.

We must create the Vesture for the Son, here and now, in the flaming forge of Vulcan.

We must create the Vesture for the Holy Spirit, here and now, in the Ninth Sphere, in sex, and with the Mercury of the wise.

O, Ancient of Days, we will send you the Vesture which is rightfully yours from the beginning, which you left behind in the Last Limit, the one which is also the Last Mystery from within.

O, devotees, O adepts, workers of the Great Work, when your hour is consumed in accordance to the Commandments of the First Mystery, then the Ancient of Centuries will be dressed with his gleaming Vesture.

The three Vestures of the Holy Trimurti are the three bodies of glory.

Only the Gnostic alchemists know how to work in the Great Work.

The three glorious bodies can be created in the alchemist's laboratory.

The three robes of light

"Come unto us, for we all draw nigh to thee to clothe thee with the First Mystery and all his glory, by commandment of himself, in that the First Mystery hath given us it, consisting of two vestures, to clothe thee therewith, besides the one which we have sent thee, for thou are worthy of them, since thou art prior to us and existeth before us. For this cause, therefore, hath the First Mystery sent thee through us the mystery of all his glory, consisting of two vestures."

The Father is the First Mystery with all His glory.

The Father, the Son, and the Holy Spirit constitute the Trinity within the Unity of life.

If the Son and the Holy Spirit are clothed, each one with his holy Vesture, unquestionably the Ancient of Days is also clothed with those two Vestures.

The three Vestures, or the three glorious bodies, gleam in the Infinite.

The Father is prior to all that which is, has been, and will be.

He is the Existence of Existences, the Primordial Point, the White Head, the Ancient of Days, the Vast Countenance, Lux Occulta, Lux Interna and the Point within the Circle.

The Ancient of Centuries is the One who existed before there was any reflection of Himself to serve Him for an image in consciousness and set up polarity.

The Ancient of Days is concealed Intelligence.

The Ancient of Days shines in the glory of Atziluth.

The first vesture

"In the first is the whole glory of all the names of all mysteries and all emanations of the orders of the spaces of the Ineffable."

The emanations of all Orders of all the Spaces of the Ineffable shine on the Vesture of the Ancient of Days.

The names of all mysteries shine gloriously on the Vesture of the Ancient of Centuries.

The second vesture

"And in the second vesture is the whole glory of the name of all mysteries and all emanations which are in the orders of the two spaces of the First Mystery."

The name of all Lesser and Major Mysteries and all radiant emanations, which are in the Orders of the two Spaces of the First Mystery, shine in the Vesture of Christ.

The third vesture

"And in this [third] vesture, which we have just sent thee, is the glory of the name of the mystery of the Revealer, which is the First

Commandment, and of the mystery of the five Impressions, and of the mystery of the great Envoy of the Ineffable, who is the great Light, and of the mystery of the five Leaders, who are the five Helpers. There is further in this vesture the glory of the name of the mystery of all orders of the emanations of the Treasury of the Light and of their saviours, and [of the mystery] of the orders of the orders, which are the seven Amens and the seven Voices and the five Trees and the three Amens and the Twin-Saviour, that is the Child of the Child, and of the mystery of the nine guards of the three gates of the Treasury of the Light. There is further therein the whole glory of the name [of all those] which are in the Right, and of all those which are in the Midst. And further there is therein the whole glory of the name of the great Invisible, which is the great Forefather, and the mystery of the three triple-powers and the mystery of their whole region and the mystery of all their invisibles and of all those who are in the thirteenth aeon, and the name of the twelve aeons and of all their rulers and all their archangels and all their angels and of all those who are in the twelve aeons, and the whole mystery of the name of all those who are in the Fate and in all the heavens, and the whole mystery of the name of all those who are in the sphere, and of its firmaments and of all who are in them, and of all their regions."

The Revealer is always the Holy Spirit.

The gentle human, illuminated and perfect, is the concrete result of the crystallization of the Holy Spirit within us.

The Wife of the Holy Spirit is the Divine Mother Kundalini, Marah, the Great Sea, our Particular Cosmic Mother. Each one of us has his own Mother.

The Divine Mother Isis is a sunderable part of the Holy Spirit within us, a variation of our own Being.

The Mystery of the Revealer is included in the First Commandment of the Law of God.

The divine spouse and his ineffable wife constitute the Original Couple.

Love God above all things, and thy neighbor as thyself.

The Original Couple serves as a foundation for the First Commandment.

The Original Couple is the foundation of the Mystery of the Revealer.

The Arcanum A.Z.F. is the Mystery of the Revealer.

The key of the Great Mystery is the connection of the lingam-yoni, without the ejaculation of the Ens Seminis.

The mystery of the five Impressions is the Flaming Star. You know this.

The Great Envoy is the inner Christ.

The inner Christ comes to the world whenever it is necessary.

It is fundamental to incarnate the Christ within ourselves in order to perform the Great Work.

The five Leaders are the five Helpers within ourselves, here and now.

In the same manner which the five Helpers Gabriel, Raphael, Uriel, Michael, and Samael, exist in the solar system, there also exists five Helpers inside of the microcosmic human being. They are five autonomous and independent parts of the Being.

The inner five Helpers guide the initiate under the supreme direction of the Father.

The glory of the name of the occult mystery of all orders of the emanations of the Treasury of the Light shines in the Vesture of the Holy Spirit.

The Treasury of the Light is the Logos clothed with To Soma Heliakon, the body of Gold of the Solar Human.

Every authentic, Christified initiate possesses the Treasury of the Light within his interior.

Emanations, rays, radiations, etc. emerge from the Treasury of the Light.

Esoteric orders and ineffable religions emerge from the Treasury of the Light that are inside of any adept of perfection.

The glory of the name of every mystic order originally emerged from the Treasury of the Light.

The mystery of the Saviors emerges from the Treasury of the Light, which is hidden within the profundity of the illuminated adepts.

The Mystery of the Orders of the Orders emerges from the Treasury of the Light, which is hidden within the Being of the Being of every Self-realized adept.

The Orders of the Orders are constituted by the seven Amens, the seven Voices, the five Trees and the Twin Savior, who is the Child of the Child.

The nine Guards of the Great Treasury of the Light are hidden within each one of us.

The nine Guards of the Great Treasury are nine self-independent and self-cognizant parts of our own Being.

The Ninth Path is pure intelligence. The Ninth Path is Yesod, the very foundation of the Great Work.

The Ninth Path is absolutely sexual.

The Ninth Path is in the sexual organs.

The Ninth Path is guarded by the flaming sword of the Cherubim, the Mighty Ones.

Shaddai El Chai is the secret name of the Ninth Path.

The path that conduces the initiate to the final liberation is absolutely sexual.

Sex is in the Ninth Sphere. It is really the Ninth Sphere.

The three gates of the Treasury of the Light have three secret names.

Eheieh is the name of the first gate.

Yehovah is the divine name of the second gate.

Yehovah-Elohim is the sacred name of the third gate.

The first gate is in the Father.

The second gate is in the Son.

The third gate is in the Holy Spirit.

Obviously, the Treasury of the Light has three gates.

The great Gothic cathedrals have one central gate and two minor gates on either side. You know this.

The entire glory of all those who are in the Right and of all those who are in the Midst shine in the Vesture of the Holy Spirit.

The Great Invisible is the Cosmic Common Eternal Father, the Infinitude that sustains all, the Omnimerciful.

Elohim emerges from the Great Invisible.

Elohim is the Army of the Voice.

Elohim is the Creator-Verb.

Elohim is interpreted as a manifested God who emerges from within the womb of Aelohim in order to create and create anew.

Elohim is a feminine name with a plural masculine ending. Therefore, Elohim means "Gods and Goddesses."

A religion without Goddesses is found halfway upon the path of atheism because Elohim is Gods and Goddesses.

The name of the Great Invisible is Aelohim.

Let it be known, now and forever, that Aelohim is the Unknowable and Unmanifested Divinity.

The Great Invisible is the Abstract Absolute Space.

The Great Invisible is the Unmanifested One.

Elohim buds from the Great Invisible.

Elohim is both masculine and feminine.

Unquestionably, this is why men and women have the same rights. Together, they can obtain Christification.

Man could never go beyond woman, nor could she climb spiritual heights more elevated than man.

Those who affirm that women cannot Self-realize are ignorant.

Blessed be the Christified women.

The Great Invisible is the Forefather of all that has been, is, and will be.

The Three Triple Powers emanate from the Great Invisible.

The Mystery of the Three Triple Powers is explained in the human being and within the human being.

Two Triples emerge from the Thrice-One Logoi, the Father, the Son, and the Holy Spirit within every Being, who is really a human being.

The Innermost and his two Twin Souls, the Spiritual Soul who is feminine, and the Human Soul who is masculine, constitute the second Trimurti which emanates from the Logoi.

The Mental, Astral, and physical bodies constitute the Third Triple that emerges from the Logoi.

The vital base or Linga-Sarira is only the superior section of the physical body. Never forget that the physical body is tetradimensional.

The Thirteenth Aeon, which is beyond the Twelve Gates, is Ain, Sat, the Unmanifested One.

Knocking on the Thirteenth Gate is equivalent to entering the bosom of the Cosmic Common Eternal Father whose Hebraic name is Aelohim.

Every initiate must previously integrate himself with Elohim before integrating himself with Aelohim.

Each one of us has his own inner Elohim.

The inner Elohim is the Being of our Being.

The inner Elohim is our Father-Mother.

The inner Elohim is the ray that emanates from Aelohim.

Aelohim is the Omnimerciful, the Cosmic Common Eternal Father, the Abstract Absolute Space.

Every adept can perform the twelve works of Hercules if he proposes to do so. Rare is he that dares to knock on the Thirteenth Aeon.

Knocking on the Thirteenth Gate signifies the submergence within the bosom of the Infinitude that sustains all.

Absolute perfection is needed in order not to fall from the bosom of Aelohim.

Any longing, as insignificant as it may be, for a separate existence or to be someone, is enough to cause one to be self-released from Aelohim and to fall under the reign of the Demiurge Creator.

All the Rulers, Archangels, Lords and Angels of the Twelve Regions or Twelve Aeons, shine in the sacred Vesture of the Holy Spirit.

The Twelve Aeons or Twelve Cosmic Regions mutually penetrate and co-penetrate without confusion.

The total mystery of the name of all those who are in the Fate shines in the Vesture of the Holy Spirit.

Not all the Beings are in the law of Fate.

Millions of creatures are found trapped within the law of accidents.

The names of all those who dwell in the Spheres and in the Firmaments, and in the diverse Regions, shine in the Vesture of the Holy Spirit.

The thesis of the various Firmaments is the same as the thesis of the various infinities.

$\infty + \infty = \infty$

Transinfinite mathematics demonstrate the crude reality of the various infinities.

Beyond our infinity, which is perceptible with the most powerful telescopes, there exists another infinity.

It is written that much further than the infinity beyond, there is yet another infinity.

The total number of Firmaments is known only by Aelohim.

The names of all the ineffable Beings that live in the various Firmaments shine in the sacred Vesture of the Holy Spirit.

The names of all those who live in the diverse Regions sparkle in the ineffable Vesture of the Holy Spirit.

We must make a clear differentiation between Firmament and Regions.

Regions are equivalent to dimensions.

The Twelve Aeons are the twelve Regions.

The twelve hours of Apollonius are related with the twelve existing Aeons within every Firmament.

Each one of the twelve works of Hercules that the adepts must perform are found to be related to the Twelve Aeons.

The thirty Aeons that emanated as couples from within the bosom of Aelohim are something different. They are the Cosmocreators or Creator Elohim.

The day of "Come unto us"

"'Lo, therefore, we have sent thee this vesture, which no one knew from the First Commandment downwards, for the glory of its light was hidden in it, and the spheres and all regions from the First Commandment downwards [have not know it]. Haste thee, therefore, clothe thyself with this vesture and come unto us. For we draw nigh unto thee, to clothe thee by command of the First Mystery with thy two vestures [other] which existed for thee from the beginning with the First Mystery until the time appointed by the Ineffable is completed. Come, therefore, to us quickly, that we may put them on thee, until thou hast fulfilled the total ministry of the perfection of the First Mystery which is appointed by the Ineffable. Come, therefore, to us quickly, in order that we may clothe thee with them, according to the command of the First Mystery. For yet a little while, a very little while, and thou shalt come unto us and leave the world. Come, therefore, quickly, that thou mayest receive thy whole glory, that is the glory of the First Mystery.'"

The intimate Jesus Christ within each one of us has the absolute right to use His Vesture.

The Glory of the Light gleams in the Vesture of the intimate Jesus Christ.

The Multiple Cosmic Spheres and all the suprasensible Regions of the universe and universes of the First Commandment glisten in the infinite Space.

The Spheres shine from the First Commandment in the First Space.

The Father, the Ancient of Days, Mercy of Mercies, Concealed of the Concealed, is the First Mystery.

The Son is clothed at the command of the Father.

The Son is clothed with His two Vestures.

The Vesture of the Son and the one of the Child of the Child, which is the Christified Causal Body, marvelously glisten in the Lord.

The total mystery of the perfection of the First Mystery, situated in the Ancient of Centuries, is assigned by Aelohim.

Aelohim is the infinitude that sustains all.

The glory of the First Mystery is the whole glory.

The one who is integrated with the Ancient of Days, after some intimate super-efforts, could be integrated with Aelohim.

Chapter 11

Jesus putteth on his vesture

"It came to pass then, when I saw the mystery of all these words in the vesture which was sent me, that straightway I clothed myself therewith, and I shone most exceedingly and soared into the height."

The intimate Jesus Christ within each one of us is clothed with His Sacred Vesture in order to soar into the height.

The inner Christ shines while ascending.

He entereth the firmament

"I came before the [first] gate of the firmament, shining most exceedingly, and there was no measure for the light which was about me, and the gates of the firmament were shaken one over against another and all opened at once."

Normally, every initiate has the right to travel to the Central Sun Sirius.

Not a single initiate can pass beyond Sirius.

Sirius is the capital of the Milky Way.

Our whole Galaxy splendorously revolves around Sirius.

The right to pass beyond Sirius must be earned.

Only those who are integrated with the inner Christ have earned that right.

Opening the gates of the Firmament is equivalent to gaining the right to pass beyond Sirius.

The inner Christ, integrated with the adept, gloriously shines most exceedingly when passing through the gates of the Firmament.

Passing through the gates of the Firmament is equivalent to passing beyond our galaxy.

The gates of the infinite are opened before the Christified adept.

The powers of the firmament are amazed and fall down and adore Him

"And all the archons and all authorities and all angels therein were thrown all together into agitation because of the great light which was on me. And they gazed at the radiant vesture of light with which I was clad, and they saw the mystery which contains their names, and they feared most exceedingly. And all their bonds with which they were bound, were unloosed and every one left his order, and they all fell down before me, adored and said: "How hath the lord of the universe passed though us without our knowing?" And they all sang praises together to the interiors of the interiors; but me they saw not, but they saw only the light. And they were in great fear and were exceedingly agitated and sang praises to the interiors of the interiors."

The Vesture of Christ gloriously shines.

The mystery that contains the ineffable names shines in the Vesture of the inner Christ.

The Cosmic Christ, the inner Christ, is the Lord of the universe.

The initiated, devoted and sincere persons sing to the Interiors of the Interiors, but very few see the inner Christ.

The inner Christ loosens the bonds and breaks the chains. He is the Great Liberator.

The inner Christ is one hundred percent revolutionary.

Chapter 12

He entereth the first sphere

"And I left that region behind me and ascended to the first sphere, shining most exceedingly, forty-and-nine-times more brightly than I had shone in the firmament. It came to pass then, when I had reached the gate of the first sphere, that its gates were shaken and opened of themselves at once."

> *"Sweet is the work of the one who works happily, and sweet is the stillness of the one who has deserved it."*

The Christified human, the Blessed One, the Christ-Man, has the keys to all the Firmament, as does the Emperor of the cosmos.

It is fundamental to work on ourselves in order to reach Christification.

It is written:

> *"Give blessings unto the labor of thy hands, and place thy heart into thy thoughts."*

The intimate Jesus Christ passes through the suprasensible world with a suit of sparkling light and soars from sphere to sphere. All the doors have been exempted to Him. However, the Archons and Guardians of those places, who always worship Him, are frightened by Him.

Christ is worshipped in all the houses of the sphere of manifestation.

The powers of the first sphere are amazed and fall down and adore him

"I entered into the houses of the sphere, shining most exceedingly, and there was no measure to the light that was about me. And all the rulers and all those who are in that sphere, fell into agitation one against another. And they saw the great light that was about me, and they gazed upon my vesture and saw thereon the mystery of their name. And they fell into still greater agitation, and were in great fear, saying: "How hath the Lord of the universe passed through us without our knowing?" And all their bonds were unloosed and their regions and their orders; and every one left his order, and they fell down all together, adored before me, or before my vesture, and all sang praises together to the interiors of the interiors, being in great fear and great agitation."

All the Archons and all those who are in the sphere of manifestation are always agitated in the presence of the victorious Jesus Christ.

The victorious Jesus Christ gloriously shines most exceedingly within any Christified adept.

The mystery of the sacred names shine in the Vesture of the intimate Jesus Christ.

Every knee is bent in the presence of the intimate Jesus Christ.

The intimate Jesus Christ loosens the bonds, breaks the chains, and liberates.

To adore the Interiors of the Interiors signifies to become a worshipper of the inner Christ.

The Interior of the Interior is the Logos.

Chapter 13

He entereth the second sphere

"And I left that region behind me and came to the gate of the second sphere, which is the Fate. Then were all its gates thrown into agitation

and opened of themselves. And I entered into the houses of the Fate, shining most exceedingly, and there was no measure for the light that was about me, for I shone in the Fate forty-and-nine times more than in the [first] sphere."

Christ, our Lord, has power to enter the sanctum of our own zodiacal Fate.

The Zodiacal House, or the Temple of the Zodiac, has twelve sanctuaries.

Every creature that is reborn is placed under a determined zodiacal sign.

When they are reborn, the awakened initiates penetrate willfully into any of the twelve sanctuaries of the Zodiacal Temple.

Every Illuminated One has the complete right to willfully choose their zodiacal sign.

The Illuminated One waits inside of the chosen zodiacal sanctuary for the lords of the law. They bind him to the body in which he must be reborn.

The corresponding symbols shine within each one of the twelve sanctuaries of the Zodiacal cathedral.

Unquestionably, each zodiacal sign has its symbolism.

The inner Christ is the Great Liberator.

The Lord of Perfections can liberate us from zodiacal tyranny.

Christ can emancipate us from the Law of the Fate.

The powers of the second sphere are amazed and fall down and adore Him

"And all the rulers and all those who are in the Fate, were thrown into agitation and fell on one another and were in exceeding great fear on seeing the great light that was about me. And they gazed on my vesture of light and saw the mystery of their name on my vesture and fell into still greater agitation; and they were in great fear, saying; 'How hath the lord of the universe passed through us without our knowing?' And all the bonds of their regions and of their orders and

of their houses were unloosed; they all came at once, fell down adored before me and sang praises all together to the interiors of the interiors, being in great fear and great agitation."

The Blessed One also knows the mystery of the names of all those who are under the law of the Fate.

Those who live within the sphere of the Fate adore the Solar Logos.

Chapter 14

He entereth the aeons

"And I left that region behind me and ascended to the great aeons of the rulers and came before their veils and their gates, shining most exceedingly, and there was no measure for the light which was about me. It came to pass then, when I arrived at the twelve aeons, that their veils and their gates were shaken one over against the other. Their veils drew themselves apart of their own accord, and their gates opened one over against the other. And I entered into the aeons, shining most exceedingly, and there was no measure for the light that was about me, forty-and-nine times more than the light with which I shone in the houses of the Fate."

The intimate Jesus Christ can victoriously enter into the Twelve Aeons or Regions.

The victorious Christ has the power to pass through the twelve gates and to reach the Thirteenth Aeon.

The Lord has the power to penetrate into the sphere of the Houses of the Fate.

The Lord has the power to penetrate into the sphere of the Aeons.

One is the sphere of the Houses of the Fate, another is the sphere of the Aeons.

It is urgent to correctly comprehend the mystery of each sphere.

The powers of the aeons are amazed and fall down and adore him

"And all the angels of the aeons and their archangels and their archons and their gods and their lords and their authorities and their tyrants and their powers and their light-sparks and their light-givers and their unpaired and their invisibles and their forefathers and their triple-powers saw me, shining most exceedingly, and there was no measure for the light which was about me. And they were thrown into agitation the one over against the other and great fear fell upon them, when they saw the great light that was about me. And in their great agitation and their great fear they withdrew as far as the region of the great invisible Forefather, and of the three great triple-powers. And because of the great fear of their agitation, the great Forefather, he and the three triple-powers, kept on running hither and thither in his region, and they could not close all their regions because of the great fear in which they were. And they agitated all their aeons together and all their spheres and all their orders, fearing and being greatly agitated because of the great light which was about me —not of the former quality that it was about me when I was on the earth of mankind, when the light-vesture came over me, —for the world could not bear the light such as it was in its truth, else would the world at once be destroyed and all upon it, —but the light which was about me in the twelve aeons was eight-thousand-and-seven-hundred-myriad times greater than that which was about me in the world among you."

The Angels and Archangels of the Aeons, the Rulers, the ineffable Gods, and the Gods and Lords reverentially prostrate in the presence of the intimate Jesus Christ.

Their Light-Givers and their Unpaired and their Invisibles and their Forefathers and their Triple Powers adore the Lord.

The Light of the Logos is formidable, marvellous and extraordinary.

To withdraw to the Region of the great Forefather signifies praying to the Cosmic Common Eternal Father, in search of refuge within the single One.

The Aeons and their spheres and their orders are always agitated in the presence of the Cosmic Christ.

The intimate Jesus Christ, totally incarnated in any Christified adept shines gloriously.

Therefore, to obtain Christification is urgent; it cannot be delayed or postponed...

8,700 myriads of light is a symbolic quantity.

8+7+0+0 = 15.

Unquestionably, the Fifteenth Arcanum is terrific. Typhon Baphomet, Lucifer is the Fifteenth Arcanum.

Sexual transmutation is the foundation of the mystery of Baphomet.

Typhon Baphomet is the reflection of the Solar Logos within our own selves, here and now.

Lucifer Baphomet always gives the sexual impulse. If we refrain the sexual impulse in the sexual act, we obtain transmutation.

Lucifer Baphomet gives the great impulse; however, if we thrust the lance of willpower into his side we will defeat him.

Defeating temptation is equivalent to climbing on the back of Lucifer.

Lucifer is the staircase to ascend.

Lucifer is the staircase to descend.

1+5=6, the Lover, Love.

Six is the key of the Fifteenth Arcanum.

Lucifer will convert us into Archangels if we perform the mystery of Baphomet within ourselves.

The brass must be whitened.

Burn your books and whiten the brass.

Whiten the devil; convert him into Lucifer.

One whitens the devil when one transmutes the sexual energy and eliminates the ego.

People have their Lucifer converted into a devil.

When shining Lucifer integrates with the human being, then he converts us into Archangels of Light.

Within the completely Christified adept, that light is of 8,700 myriads; you know this.

Only those who have worked with Lucifer in the infernos can reach or possess such light.

Lo and behold the mystery of Baphomet and Abraxas.

Light is born from darkness, and the cosmos sprouts from the Chaos.

Chapter 15

Adamas and the tyrants fight against the light

"It came to pass then, when all those who are in the twelve aeons saw the great light which was about me, that they were all thrown into agitation one over against the other, and ran hither and thither in the aeons. And all aeons and all heavens and their whole ordering were agitated one over against the other on account of the great fear which was on them, for they knew not the mystery which had taken place. And Adamas, the great Tyrant, and all the tyrants in all the aeons began to fight in vain against the light, and they knew not against whom they fought, because they saw nothing but the over-mastering light.

"It came to pass then, when they fought against the light, that they were weakened all together one with another, were dashed down in the aeons and became as the inhabitants of the earth, dead and without breath of life."

All those who live in the Aeons are agitated in the presence of the Solar Logos.

Adamas, the great Tyrant of the Fate, and all the tyrants in all the Aeons call upon the adept.

This signifies that the lords of the law call upon the adept, time after time to yield his accounts.

The adepts, called to yield their accounts, suffer while answering to their debts, which belong to very transcendental stages.

Those who read these paragraphs must be as alert and vigilant as the watchman in the epoch of war.

He taketh from them a third of their power

"And I took from all a third of their power, that they should no more be active in their evil doings, and that, if the men who are in the world, invoke them in their mysteries those which the angels who transgressed have brought down, that is their sorceries, —in order that, therefore, if they invoke them in their evil doings, they may not be able to accomplish them."

The fallen Bodhisattvas lose their ineffable powers.

In order to Christify oneself, one must previously pay or settle karmic debts.

He changeth the motion of their spheres

"And the Fate and the sphere over which they rule, I have changed and brought it to pass that they spend six months turned to the left and accomplish their influences, and that six months they face to the right and accomplish their influences. For by command of the First Commandment and by command of the First Mystery Yew, the Overseer of the Light, had set them facing the left at every time and accomplishing their influences and their deeds."

This is how the multitudes live over this hard crust of the planet Earth, illuminated by a Sun which moves elliptically, travelling from south to north and from north to south.

This solar voyage is from right to left and from left to right.

Chapter 16

"It came to pass then, when I came into their region, that they mutinied and fought against the light. And I took the third of their power,

in order that they should not be able to accomplish their evil deeds. And the Fate and the sphere over which they rule, I have changed, and set them facing the left six months and accomplishing their influences, and I have set them turned another six months to the right and accomplishing their influences."

The humanity which is upon the planet Earth traverses within the Law of the Fate. The human beings have been set facing the left for six months and have been set turned to the right for another six months.

Chapter 17

When then he had said this to his disciples, he said unto them: "Who have ears to hear, let him hear." It came to pass then, when Mary had heard the Saviour say these words, that she gazed fixedly into the air for the space of an hour. She said: "My Lord give commandment unto me to speak in openness."

Marah, Mary, Isis, our Divine Individual Cosmic Mother, is the spouse of the Holy Spirit and the daughter of Her Son.

Marah, therefore, is a sunderable part of our own particular divine Glorian.

Isis, Mary, is a derivative of our own Being.

Isis, Mary, is God Mother in ourselves. She is the Virgin of the Sea.

Isis, Marah, is a sunderable part of the Holy Spirit in each one of us.

Mary, Isis, is our Divine Mother Kundalini.

Marah, Isis, possesses wisdom, love, and power.

Isis, Marah, Tonantzin, teaches, guides and directs us.

The Virgin of the Sea guides the alchemist. She is the Star that orientates us in the boisterous ocean.

Mary Magdalene asketh and receiveth permission to speak

And Jesus, the compassionate, answered and said unto Mary: "Mary, thou blessed one, whom I will perfect in all mysteries of those of the height, discourse in openness, thou, whose heart is raised to the kingdom of heaven more than all thy brethren."

Mary Magdalene is the repented sinner, Kundry, Gundrigia, the indispensable woman for the Great Work.

In Wagner's drama, Parsifal totally transforms the tempter Kundry after she submits to him.

A man needs a Mary Magdalene in order to work in the Ninth Sphere and in order to obtain the resurrection.

What is magnificent is to be saved, and to save Kundry, Magdalene.

Tempter Gundrigia, Magdalene, Kundry, you will be perfected in all mysteries of those of the Height, more than all your brethren.

Chapter 18

Then said Mary to the Saviour: "My Lord, the word which thou hast spoken unto us: 'Who hath ears to hear, let him hear,' thou sayest in order that we may understand the word which thou hast spoken. Hearken, therefore, my Lord, that I may discourse in openness."

Mary Magdalene may discourse in openness.

Mary interpreteth the discourse from the words of Isaiah

"The word which thou hast spoken: 'I have taken a third from the power of the rulers of all the aeons, and changed their Fate and their sphere over which they rule, in order that, if the race of men invoke them in the mysteries those which the angels who transgressed have taught them for the accomplishing of their evil and lawless deeds in

the mystery of their sorcery,' in order then that they may no more from this hour accomplish their lawless deeds, because thou hast taken their power from them and from their horoscope-casters and their consulters and from those who declare to the men in the world all things which shall come to pass, in order that they should no more from this hour know how to declare unto them any thing at all which will come to pass (for thou hast changed their spheres, and hast made them spend six months turned to the left and accomplishing their influences, and another six months facing the right and accomplishing their influences), —concerning this word then, my Lord, the power which was in the prophet Isaiah, hath spoken thus and proclaimed afore time in a spiritual similitude, discoursing on the 'Vision about Egypt': 'Where then, O Egypt, where are thy consulters and horoscope-casters and those who cry out of the earth and those who cry out of their belly? Let them then declare unto thee from now on the deeds which the lord Sabaoth will do!'

"The power then which was in the prophet Isaiah, prophesied before thou didst come, that thou wouldst take away the power of the rulers of the aeons and wouldst change their sphere and their Fate, in order that they might know nothing from now on. For this cause it hath said also: 'Ye shall then know not of what the Lord Sabaoth will do'; that is, none of the rulers will know what thou wilt do from now on, —for they are 'Egypt,' because they are matter. The power then which was in Isaiah, prophesied concerning thee afore time, saying: 'From now on ye shall then know not what the Lord Sabaoth will do.' Because of the light-power which thou didst receive from Sabaoth, the Good, who is in the region of the Right, and which is in thy material body to-day, for this cause then, my Lord Jesus, thou hast said unto us: 'Who hath ears to hear, let him hear,' in order that thou mightest know whose heart is ardently raised to the kingdom of heaven."

At this time, the solar creatures, converted into lunar creatures live as vulgar beings over the face of the Earth.

The solar creatures (by involutionary processes) transformed themselves into lunar creatures. Therefore, they lost their powers.

Those who cry out of the Earth, those who cry out of their belly, the horoscope casters and fortune tellers from street fairs or businesses, are in their majority lunar creatures.

It is written that the ancient Solar humanity degenerated, became lunar, and became vulgar.

Sabaoth will accomplish Its own Work.

Sabaoth is the Army of the Voice, the Great Word, the Verb.

The Solar Gods from the past frightfully devolved. Thus, they became lunar.

The Rulers of the Aeons and their Spheres fell, and their Fate was changed since ancient times.

The fallen Gods, converted into lunar human beings, know nothing about the occult purpose of Sabaoth.

Chapter 19

It came to pass then, when Mary had finished saying these words, that he said: "Well said, Mary, for thou art blessed before all women on the earth, because thou shalt be the fullness of the fullnesses and the perfection of all perfections."

In the cathedral of the Soul there is more happiness for one repented sinner than for a thousand righteous ones who do not need repentance.

Mary Magdalene gleams, and will gleam terribly divine.

Jesus commandeth Mary. She further questioneth him on the changing of the spheres

Now when Mary had heard the Saviour speak these words, she exulted greatly, and she came before Jesus, fell down before him, adored his feet and said unto him: "My Lord, hearken unto me, that I may question thee on this word, before that thou discoursest with us about the regions whither thou didst go."

Jesus answered and said unto Mary: "Discourse in openness and fear not; all things on which thou questionest, I will reveal unto thee."

Kundry always falls at the feet of Parsifal in order to manifest her love and obedience.

The intimate Jesus Christ reveals the mysteries to Magdalene.

Chapter 20

She said: "My Lord, will all the men who know the mystery of the magic of all the rulers of all the aeons of the Fate and of those of the sphere, in the way in which the angels who transgressed have taught them, if they invoke them in their mysteries, that is in their evil magic, to the hindering of good deeds,—will they accomplish them henceforth from now on or not?"

The fallen Bodhisattvas of Angels, or Human Souls of Angelic Spirits know the mystery of the magic of all the Archons of all the Aeons of the Fate.

Let it be understood that a Bodhisattva is a seed, a germ, with the possibility of transcendental, divine development by means of pressure coming from the Height.

Jesus explaineth further the conversion of the spheres

Jesus answered and said unto Mary: "They will not accomplish them as they accomplished them from the beginning, because I have taken away a third of their power; but they will raise a loan from those who know the mysteries of the magic of the thirteenth aeon. And if they invoke the mysteries of the magic of those who are in the thirteenth aeon, they will accomplish them well and surely, because I have not taken away power from that region, according to the command of the First Mystery."

The fallen Bodhisattvas have lost a third of their power.

This signifies that in no way do they possess the crystallization of the three primary forces of Nature and the cosmos.

Only with the powers of the Thirteenth Aeon is it possible for the fallen Gods to once again become Solar.

The mysteries of the magic of the Thirteenth Aeon lead us to the Buddhist Annihilation.

Redemption is obtained by the death of the ego, by omitting its existence.

We can and must invoke Isis in the flaming forge of Vulcan.

Those who invoke the serpent in the Ninth Sphere will be assisted.

The Divine Mother Kundalini is reinforced with sexual power.

The Cosmic Mother can reduce any undesirable psychic element to cosmic dust when we invoke Her during the moment of the chemical copulation.

If we work in the Ninth Sphere, then all the undesirable psychic aggregates can be disintegrated.

Those who spill Hermes' Glass never disintegrate the animal ego.

If the fallen Gods work in the Ninth Sphere, then they will be redeemed.

The mysteries of the Thirteenth Aeon signify: "Radical death of the ego."

When the Angels fornicate, they fall; then the ego resurrects.

The fallen Angels can rise again if they annihilate the ego.

The ego must be annihilated in the Ninth Sphere, sex. You know this.

Chapter 21

And it came to pass, when Jesus had finished saying these words, that Mary continued again and said: "My Lord, will not then the horoscope-casters and consulters from now on declare unto men what will come to pass for them?"

And Jesus answered and said unto Mary: "If the horoscope-casters find the Fate and the sphere turned towards the left, according to their first extension, their words will come to pass, and they will say what is to take place. But if they chance on the Fate or the sphere turned to the right, they are bound to say nothing true, for I have changed their influences and their squares and their triangles and their octagons; seeing that their influences from the beginning onwards were continuously turned to the left and their squares and their triangles and their octagons. But now I have made them spend six months turned to the left and six months turned to the right. He who then shall find their reckoning from the time when I change them, setting them so as to spend six months facing towards their left and six months facing their right path,—he who then shall observe them in this wise, will know their influences surely and will declare all things which they will do. In like manner also the consulters, if they invoke the names of the archons and chance on them facing the left, will tell [men] with accuracy all things concerning which they shall ask their decans. On the contrary, if the consulters invoke their names when they face to the right, they will not give ear unto them, because they are facing in another form compared with their former position in which Yew had established them; seeing that other are their names when they are turned to the left and other their names when they are turned to the right. And if they invoke them whey they are turned to the right, they will not tell them the truth, but they will confound them with confusion and threaten them with threatening. Those then who do not know their path, when they are turned to the right, and their triangles and their squares and all their figures, will find nothing true, but will be confounded in great confusion and will find themselves in great delusion, because I have now changed the works which they effected afore time in their squares, when turned to the left ,and in their triangles and in their octagons, in which they were busied continuously turned to the left; and I have made them spend six months forming all their configurations turned to the right, in order that they may be confounded in confusion in their whole range. And moreover I have made them spend six months turned to the left and accomplishing the works of their influences and all their configurations, in order that the archons who are in the aeons and in their spheres and in their heavens and in all their regions, may be confounded in confusion and deluded in delusion, so that they may not understand their own paths."

Diviners and soothsayers can forecast what will occur to human beings only if the fate of these persons has not been altered.

Fate can be altered when the Logos or Christ wants to do so.

Karma is an oriental word that signifies action and consequence.

Karma is a Sanskrit term that indicates the law of cause and effect.

Every cause has its effect. A cause does not exist without an effect, neither does an effect exist without a cause.

Those who know the law of return and recurrence comprehend the law of karma.

Those who know the law of reincarnation know the law of karma.

The bad actions of former lives must be canceled, here and now.

Not only do we pay karma for the evil that we do, but also for the good that we should do but we do not do.

However, karma can be negotiated.

Karma can also be forgiven.

Kamaduro is another Sanskrit term that indicates karma that can neither be negotiated nor forgiven.

There is also the law of Katancia, the superior karma of Gods and adepts.

The law of Katancia also allows negotiations and forgiveness.

The lion of the law must be fought with the scale.

Perform good deeds in order to pay your debts.

Whosoever has capital in order to pay, then pays and does well in his affairs. Whosoever does not have capital in order to pay will then have to pay with pain.

All types of sins can be forgiven, except the sins against the Holy Spirit.

Sex, the sexual force, is the power of the Holy Spirit.

Adultery, fornication, and any sexual fault or crime is a sin against the Holy Spirit.

Therefore, the phrase of Christ is clarified. It states, *"If the horoscope-casters find the Fate and the sphere turned towards the left, according to their first extension, their words will come to pass, and they will say what is to take place. But if they chance on the Fate or the sphere turned to the right, they are bound to say nothing true, for I have changed their influences and their squares and their triangles and their octagons."*

The horoscope-casters, consulters, prophets, and sages can forecast the fate and karma of someone. Yet, they could be right or wrong.

It is right when karma has not been forgiven.

The horoscope-caster or consulter is wrong when karma has been negotiated or forgiven.

It is written, *"When an inferior law is transcended by a superior law, the superior law washes away the inferior law."* The Cosmic Christ has made karmic negotiations possible for the good of this suffering humanity.

Chapter 22

Philip questioneth Jesus

It came to pass then, when Jesus had finished saying these words, while Philip sat and wrote all the words that Jesus spake, —thereafter then it came to pass that Philip came forward, fell down and adored the feet of Jesus, saying: "My Lord and Saviour, grant me authority to discourse before thee and to question thee on this word, before thou discoursest with us concerning the regions whither thou didst go because of thy ministry."

And the compassionate Saviour answered and said unto Philip: "Authority is given thee to bring forward the word which thou willest."

And Philip answered and said unto Jesus: "My Lord, on account of what mystery hast thou changed the binding of the rulers and their aeons and their Fate and their sphere and all their regions, and made them confounded in confusion on their path and deluded in their course? Hast thou then done this unto them for the salvation of the world or has thou not?"

If the intimate Lord had not made forgiveness and negotiations possible, many who could have been saved would have sunk.

Negotiations and forgiveness were made possible for the salvation of the world.

The Great Compassionate One loves this entire suffering humanity.

Chapter 23

Why the path of the aeons was changed

And Jesus answered and said unto Philip and to all the disciples together: "I have changed their path for the salvation of all souls. Amen, amen, I say unto you: If I had not changed their path, a host of souls would have been destroyed, and they would have spent a long time, if the archons of the aeons and the archons of the Fate and of the sphere and of all their regions and all their heavens and all their aeons had not been brought to naught; and the souls would have continued a long time here outside, and the completion of the number of perfect souls would have been delayed, which [souls] shall be counted in the Inheritance of the Height through the mysteries and shall be in the Treasury of the Light. For this cause then I have changed their path, that they might be deluded and fall into agitation and yield up the power which is in the matter of their world and which they fashion into souls, in order that those who shall be saved, might be quickly purified and raised on high, they and the whole power, and that those who shall not be saved, might be quickly destroyed."

Unquestionably, the inner Christ has made forgiveness and negotiations possible in order that those who shall be saved might be quickly purified and raised on high.

The Lord has made possible all types of negotiations and forgiveness so that people might define themselves, and that those who shall not be saved might be quickly destroyed.

Chapter 24

Mary questioneth him again

It came to pass then, when Jesus had finished saying these words unto his disciples, that Mary, the fair in her discourse and the blessed one, came forward, fell at the feet of Jesus and said: "My Lord, suffer me that I speak before thee, and be not wroth with me, if oft I give thee trouble questioning thee."

The Saviour, full of compassion, answered and said unto Mary: "Speak the word which thou willest, and I will reveal it to thee in all openness."

Mary answered and said unto Jesus: "My Lord, in what way will the souls have delayed themselves here outside, and in what type will they be quickly purified?"

The Souls have delayed themselves here outside, due to the inhuman elements which constitute the ego, the "I."

Unquestionably, the Essence is found bottled up within multiple, inhuman psychic aggregates.

Such aggregates personify our psychological defects: anger, greed, lust, envy, pride, laziness, gluttony, etc.

In Egypt, such undesirable elements were known as the red demons of Seth.

Each demon of Seth is an "I" in itself. This is irrefutable and indisputable.

As long as the psychic Essence continues to be bottled up within the red demons of Seth, the consciousness will process itself by virtue of its own embottlement.

Indubitably, the bottled up consciousness sleeps profoundly.

People live asleep, unconscious. This is how they exist, work, and suffer. Nevertheless, they think that they are awake.

Those who annihilate the red demons of Seth will liberate their consciousness. They will radically awaken it.

The annihilation of the psychic aggregates can be made possible only by radically comprehending our errors through meditation and by the evident Self-reflection of the Being.

The mind can never annihilate a psychological defect. The mind can hide the psychological defect from itself, justifying it, condemning it, hiding it from the others, and labelling it with distinct names. However, it can never fundamentally alter the defect.

If we want to atomically disintegrate the psychic aggregates which we carry within our interior, then we need a power that is superior to the mind.

Fortunately, we have Devi Kundalini inside.

Unquestionably, she is Stella Maris, the Virgin of the Sea, the igneous serpent of our magical powers.

Obviously, Stella Maris is a flaming power of our own Being. She is our own Being, but a derivative.

Stella Maris is Isis, Insobertha, Mary, Rhea, Cybele, Tonantzin, Marah, Diana, etc.

Our own Goddess Mother within ourselves can reduce any undesirable element of our psyche to cosmic dust, with the condition that it has been previously comprehended.

The Divine Woman-Serpent possesses terribly divine powers.

Isis is our particular Divine Cosmic Mother. Each one of us has his own Isis.

The Divine Mother Kundalini-Isis assists and helps us, with the condition that we have upright behavior.

The power of Isis is reinforced by the electric sexual power in the flaming forge of Vulcan.

The forge of Vulcan is in sex.

The transcendental sexual electricity intensifies the power of Isis.

We can invoke Isis-Marah during the chemical copulation. We will then receive help.

If we invoke the Divine Mother-Serpent, Isis, Adonia, in the Ninth Sphere, that is to say, if we invoke her during sex, during the moment of the chemical coitus, then She can disintegrate any psychological defect.

Chapter 25

And Jesus answered and said unto Mary: "Well said, Mary: thou questionest finely with thy excellent question, and thou throwest light on all things with surety and precision. Now, therefore, from now on will I hide nothing from you, but I will reveal unto you all things with surety and openness. Hearken then, Mary, and give ear, all ye disciples: Before I made proclamation to all the archons of the aeons and to all the rulers of the Fate and of the sphere, they were all bound in their bonds and in their spheres and in their seals, as Yew, the Overseer of the Light, had bound them from the beginning; and every one of them remained in his order, and every one journeyed according to his course, as Yew, the Overseer of the Light, had established them."

Yew, the profoundly sacred name, is related with the light and clairvoyance.

It is written that Jesus, the great Kabir, chanted a song of praise in the great Name.

It is written that He pronounced the profoundly sacred name Yew and He blew in their eyes saying, *"Ye are now clairvoyant."*

Unquestionably, Yew is a mantric word or magic key related to clairvoyance.

The word Yew appears in the Gnostic Mass.

The coming of Melchizedek

"And when the time of the number of Melchizedek, the great Receiver of the Light, came, he was wont to come into the midst of the aeons and of all the archons who are bound in the sphere and in the Fate, and he carried away the purification of the light from all the rulers of the aeons and from all the archons of the Fate and from those of the sphere —for he carried away then that which brings them into agitation and he set in motion the hastener who is over them, and made them turn their circles swiftly, and he [sc. the hastener] carried away their power which was in them and the breath of their mouth and the tears [lit. waters] of their eyes and the sweat of their bodies."

Melchizedek is the planetary Genie of the Earth, of whom Jesus, the great Kabir gave testimony.

Melchizedek is the great Receiver of the Cosmic Light.

Melchizedek has a physical body. He is a Man, or better said, he is a Super-Man.

The Kingdom of Agharti is found in the subterranean caverns of the Earth.

The Earth is hollow and the network of caverns constitute Agharti.

The Genie of the Earth lives in Agharti with a group of survivors from Lemuria and Atlantis.

The Goros, powerful lords of life and death work with Melchizedek.

The whole ancient wisdom of the centuries has been recorded on stone within the Kingdom of Agharti.

When Abraham returned from the slaughter of the kings of Sodom and Gomorra, with whom he had fought, he found Melchizedek.

Melchizedek lived in a fort situated in the place where Jerusalem, the beloved city of the Prophets, was raised at a later time.

Abraham gave to Melchizedek his tithes and his goods, as the law commands.

Melchizedek has an immortal physical body.

It is stated that Melchizedek and his people, and Abraham and his people, celebrated the holy Gnostic Unction with the distribution of bread and wine in that time.

It was then when Melchizedek delivered the Holy Grail to Abraham.

Much later in time, this chalice was carried by the Queen of Sheba to King Solomon.

The Queen of Sheba submitted Solomon to many ordeals before she surrendered this divine jewel.

The great Kabir Jesus celebrated the Last Supper with the sacred chalice.

Joseph of Arimathaea filled the chalice with the blood that flowed from the body of the Adorable One on the Mount of the Skulls.

The Roman Senator hid the chalice and the lance with which Longinus wounded the side of the Lord.

When the Roman police entered the home of the Senator Joseph of Arimathaea, they found neither the chalice nor the lance.

Joseph of Arimathaea was enclosed within a prison for a long time for such reason.

After leaving the jail, Joseph of Arimathaea took the sacred relics (chalice and lance) and went to Rome.

He found Nero disgracefully persecuting the Gnostic Christians there.

He travelled along the Mediterranean, and one night, in his dreams, he was approached by an Angel who told him, "That chalice has great power because it contains the blood of the Redeemer of the World. Keep it there." The Angel then showed him the Temple of Monserrat, in Cataluña, Spain.

Joseph of Arimathaea hid the chalice and the lance within that temple.

Therefore, the Holy Grail and the lance of Longinus, the Roman Centurion, are found in the Castle of the Grail in transcendental Monsalvat.

It is necessary to emphatically affirm that the Temple of the Grail is found in Jinn state.

The chalice symbolizes the feminine yoni. The lance allegorizes the phallus of Greek mysteries.

The mysteries of lingam-yoni are found hidden in the chalice and the lance.

The path that leads to the inner Self-realization of the Being is absolutely sexual.

Melchizedek, in the midst of the Aeons and the Rulers, always carries away that which he must carry away, for the good of this suffering humanity.

The Genie of the Earth, in constant manner, continuously overtakes the purified Light, absorbs it and attracts it towards our Earth world, in order to help the Souls.

We must not forget that the Aeons and Archons are banished to the Sphere and to the Fate.

It is possible, individually speaking, to settle the affairs of the law with the Rulers and the Aeons of the Fate and the Sphere, by means of forgiveness and negotiations.

So, this is what is signified by, *"to carry away the purification of the light from all the Rulers of the Aeons and from all the Archons of the Fate and from those of the sphere."*

That is why it is stated that Melchizedek *"carried away their power which was in them and the breath of their mouth and the tears of their eyes and the sweat of their bodies."*

Melchizedek, in ourselves and for ourselves, as Lord of this planetary abode in which we live, put in motion the hastener who is over them, and made them turn their circles swiftly.

This means that the acceleration of our inner Self-realization is always possible based on conscious works, voluntary sufferings, negotiations, and forgiveness.

Melchizedek answers for all the Souls of the Earth.

Jesus, the Great Kabir, was made a High Priest forever, in accordance with the order of Melchizedek.

> *For this Melchizedek, King of Salem, priest of the most high God, who met Abraham returning from the slaughter of the Kings, and blessed him;*
>
> *To whom also Abraham gave a tenth part of all; first being by interpretations King of justice, and after that also King of Salem, which is, King of peace."*
>
> *Without* (earthly) *Father, without* (earthly) *Mother, without descent, having neither beginning of days nor end of life; but made like unto the Son of God abideth a priest continually.* - Hebrews 7:1-3

Of the fashioning of the souls of men

"And Melchizedek, the Receiver of the Light, purifieth those powers and carrieth their light into the Treasury of the Light, while the servitors of all the archons gather together all matter from them all; and the servitors of all the rulers of the Fate and the servitors of the sphere which is below the aeons, take it and fashion it into souls of men and cattle and reptiles and wild-beasts and birds, and send them down into the world of mankind. And further the receivers of the sun and the receivers of the moon, if they look above and see the configurations of the paths of the aeons and the configurations of the Fate and those of the sphere, then they take from them the light-power; and the receivers of the sun get it ready and deposit it, until they hand it over to the receivers of Melchizedek, the Light-purifier. And their material refuse they bring to the sphere which is below the aeons, and fashion it into [souls of] men, and fashion it also into souls of reptiles and of cattle and of wild-beasts and of birds, according to the circle of the rulers of that sphere and according to all the configuration of its revolution, and they cast them into this world of mankind, and they become souls in this region, as I have just said unto you."

Time after time, Melchizedek, the Genie of the Earth, must purify the powers of this world with sacrifices and terrible transformations.

Great cataclysms are necessary.

Thus, this is how Melchizedek must purify the powers of the soul of the world and carry its light to the Treasury of the Light.

An exact parallel indicates to us that the same must occur within the microcosmic human, when he wants to attain the inner Self-realization of the Being.

The workers of the Great Work intensely work on themselves and on the universe. This is specified in every religion's Genesis.

It is imperative for us to perform within ourselves what the Army of the Word performed within the Macrocosm.

The Servitors of all the Rulers gathered and gather together all matter from them all.

This refers to the gathering of Salt, Sulphur, and Mercury for the Great Work.

The Great Work is created by means of wisely combining Salt, Sulphur, and Mercury.

Those who have performed the Great Work present it to the Receivers of Melchizedek.

Those who have performed the Great Work enter into the Sacred Order of Melchizedek.

The material refuse is cast into the infernal worlds, which means, into the submerged sphere which is below the Aeons, the region of the beasts, which personify our psychological defects.

These frightful things emerge from the abyss, according to the circle of the Rulers of that Sphere and according to all the configuration of its revolution, and the Rulers cast them into this world of mankind.

In the final synthesis, we can crystallize the Soul within ourselves by means of Buddhist and Christic annihilation, meaning by disintegrating psychic aggregates, or Dry Mercury.

The Receivers of the Sphere, who are below the Aeons, perform marvellous works that are not even remotely suspected by people.

The Receivers of the Sphere can fashion the material refuse which falls in the Sphere that is below the Aeons.

They can fashion such material refuse into souls of reptiles and wild-beasts, and birds, according to all the configurations of its revolution, and they cast them into this world of mankind, and they become souls in this region, as I have just said unto you.

The Receivers of the Sphere can and must direct the involuted process of wild-beasts, reptiles, cattle, furious bulls and demons with crocodile faces within the submerged sphere which is below the Aeons.

Such beasts from the Averno are psychic aggregates that personify psychological defects, the inferno's own spawns, egos that come from human organisms.

The Rulers of the Sphere, which are below the Aeons, have power over life and death.

The Rulers of that submerged Sphere direct the tides of life and death.

Concretely, we shall say that the Rulers of the infernal submerged Sphere, which is below the Thirteen Aeons, have power in order to work with the living creatures that dwell on the surface of the Earth, and power in order to work with the beasts of the abyss.

The psychic aggregates which constitute the ego have animal forms.

Those who enter the infernal worlds devolve within time, until the Second Death.

The Soul is liberated through the Second Death. The Essence then enters into Eden in order to restart, or reinitiate new evolving processes that must emerge from within the mineral kingdom, continuing in the plant kingdom, and proceeding in the animal kingdom, until conquering once again the human state which was lost in the past.

All of this work with souls of men and beasts on the surface of the world, and in the Sphere which is below the thirteen Aeons, is directed by the Rulers of the Averno.

Chapter 26

"This then they accomplished continuously before their power was diminished in them and they waned and became exhausted, or powerless. It came to pass then, when they became powerless, that their power began to cease in them, so that they became exhausted in their power, and their light, which was in the region, ceased and their kingdom was destroyed, and the universe became quickly raised up.

"It came to pass then, when they had perceived this at the time, and when the number of the cipher of Melchizedek, the Receiver [of the Light], happened, then had he to come out again and enter into the midst of the archons of all the aeons and into the midst of all the archons of the Fate and of those of the sphere; and he threw them into agitation, and made them quickly abandon their circles. And forthwith they were constrained, and cast forth the power out of themselves, out of the breath of their mouth and the tears of their eyes and the sweat of their bodies."

Unquestionably, when the Solar Gods fell into animal generation, they then converted themselves into lunar Gods.

When the Solar Gods became lunar, their power began to cease within them, so that they became exhausted in their power. Thus, without energies, they fell.

Then, the number of the cipher of Melchizedek, the Receiver of the Light, took place. Hence, the Great Being entered into action.

Melchizedek, in action and with a strong hand, governs the Archons of all the Aeons, and the Rulers of the Fate, and those Rulers of the Sphere.

Melchizedek, in action, makes these Hierarchies quickly abandon their respective circles when they commit the error of falling into animal generation.

Therefore, from that moment, these Lords find themselves constrained to search for their power outside of themselves, in the vain world.

Indubitably, the Solar Gods, when converted into lunar creatures, suffer terribly, as anyone else does.

The rulers devour their matter so that souls may not be fashioned

"And Melchizedek, the Receiver of the Light, purifieth them, as he doth continually; he carrieth their light into the Treasury of the Light. And all the archons of the aeons and the archons of the Fate and those of the sphere turn to the matter of their refuse; they devour it and do not let it go and become souls in the world. They devour then their matter, so that they may not become powerless and exhausted and their power cease in them and their kingdom become destroyed, but in order that they may delay and linger a long time until the completion of the number of the perfect souls who shall be in the Treasury of the Light."

Notwithstanding, Melchizedek, the Genie of the Earth, the Receiver of the Light, shows the way of purification to the fallen Gods through his adepts.

Melchizedek can carry the light of the Souls to the Treasury of the Light.

We have previously stated that the Golden Fleece, the Treasury of the Light, is found within the profundities of oneself.

Unquestionably, the Archons of the Fate and the Rulers of the Aeons and those of the Sphere turn to the matter of their refuse. They subdue it, devour it, subjugate it, govern it, and do not let it go to become Souls in the world.

This means that they, the Rulers, maintain the elemental Essences in their respective kingdoms.

Such elemental Essences are governed by the Archons.

However, while the elemental Essences develop, they pass from one kingdom to another, according to the law.

Every elemental Essence can convert itself into a human Soul, at its time and hour, and according to the law.

The completion of the number of the perfect Souls who shall be in the Treasury of the Light will be in the day of "Be with us," which is at the end of the Great Cosmic Day.

Chapter 27

"It came to pass then, when the archons of the aeons and those of the Fate and those of the sphere continued to carry out this type, — turning on themselves, devouring the refuse of their matter, and not allowing souls to be born into the world of mankind, in order that they might delay in being rulers, and that the powers which are in their powers, that is the souls, might spend a long time here outside, — they then persisted doing this continually for two circles.

"It came to pass then, when I wished to ascend for the ministry for the sake of which I was called by command of the First Mystery, that I came up into the midst of the tyrants of the archons of the twelve aeons, with my light-vesture about me, shining most exceedingly, and there was no measure for the light which was about me."

May the Sun that illuminates you shine within you, and may the tyrants that enslave you be reborn as human beings, in order to teach and illuminate you perpetually.

Thus, they will devour the refuse of the matter, liberating those who must be liberated.

The lords of the law will continue to be Rulers as long as their human persons respect the law.

This is easily comprehended when we know that the lords of the law are also reincarnating, and for that reason, they possess a human body.

The term "tyrants" is merely symbolic or allegoric, or simply seen from another angle; it is a symbolic term from the point of view of the "super-human."

The powers of the Rulers are within our own Soul.

The Laws of the Archons of the Aeons and of the Fate, and of those from the sphere of action in which we move ourselves, are within our own Soul.

We always spend a long time here outside, in this valley of tears, for a duration of two circles or in two circles, the external and the internal, the exoteric and the esoteric, and the visible and the occult.

Finally, the real Human Being is Christified and victoriously ascends in order to practice the ministry which was appointed to him by order of the Father of all the Lights, the Ancient of Days.

The Christified adept must rise up into the midst of the Tyrants of the Rulers of the Twelve Aeons, with his Vesture of Light shining most exceedingly.

Adamas and the tyrants fight against the light-vesture

"It came to pass then, when those tyrants saw the great light which was about me, that the great Adamas, the Tyrant, and all the tyrants of the twelve aeons, all together began to fight against the light of my vesture, desiring to hold it fast among them, in order to delay in their rulership. This then they did, not knowing against whom they fought."

Adamas, the "Tyrant," and all the "tyrants" of the law of karma who govern the Twelve Aeons oppose the step of the human being who marches towards the final liberation.

"Tyrants" is an allegoric matter. The lords of the law are just, and they collect the debts from those who march towards their liberation.

Obviously, we must convert ourselves into an "adeptus exentus."

Jesus taketh from them a third of their power and changeth their course

"When then they mutinied and fought against the light, thereon by command of the First Mystery I changed the paths and the courses of

their aeons and the paths of their fate and of the sphere. I made them face six months towards the triangles on the left and towards the squares and towards those in their aspect and towards their octagons, just as they had formerly been. But their manner of turning, or facing, I changed to another order, and made them other six months face towards the works of their influences in the squares on the right and in their triangles and in those in their aspect and in their octagons. And I made them to be confounded in great confusion and deluded in great delusion —the archons of the aeons and all the archons of the Fate and those of the sphere; and I set them in great agitation, and thence on they were no longer able to turn towards the refuse of their matter to devour it, in order that their regions may continue to delay and they [themselves] may spend a long time as archons.

"But when I had taken away a third of their power, I changed their spheres, so that they spend a time facing to the left and another time facing to the right. I have changed their whole path and their whole course, and I have made the path of their course to hurry, so that they may be quickly purified and raised up quickly. And I have shortened their circles, and made their path more speedy, and it will be exceedingly hurried. And they were thrown into confusion in their path, and from then on were no more able to devour the matter of the refuse of the purification of their light."

It is not unjust to collect the debts from those who owe.

However, the one who fights for his liberation suffers immensely, and feels that the agents of the law are tyrants.

The inner Christ, by command of the First Mystery, can change within us the paths and courses of the Fate and the sphere in which we live, with the purpose that we may obtain our Christification.

Unquestionably, we must learn how to walk with two feet if we want to reach Christification.

We must walk intensely with the Sixth Mystery, towards the triangles on the left.

The Four-and-twentieth Mystery cannot function without the Sixth Mystery.

The First Mystery is hidden within the Four-and-twentieth Mystery.

The squares of upright behavior and the octagons of the Eightfold Path, in the diverse aspects, are the foundation of the Great Work.

The squares to the right and the triangles and their octagons in their diverse aspects serve as a foundation to the Great Work.

In synthesis, six months towards the right and six months towards the left with their triangles and squares and octagons in the diverse aspects enclose the work of the Great Work.

Triangles signify the three primary forces of Nature and the cosmos.

Squares signify upright behavior.

Octagons signify eight initiations, eight initiatic qualifications, etc.

The entire secret path that leads to the final liberation is marked with triangles squares and octagons.

Six months towards the right and six months towards the left means half light and half darkness.

The sages must work for epochs within the light, and for epochs within the darkness of no-being.

This type of Gnostic work, which is for epochs within the light and for epochs within the darkness, confuses many. Therefore, there are very few who attain the total inner Self-realization of the Being.

Remember the Sixth Arcanum—sex, love, the work in the forge of the Cyclops.

It is urgent to work within the super-obscurity and the august silence of the wise in certain epochs.

It is indispensable to work within the light during certain times.

Every ascent is preceded by a descent.

Every exaltation is preceded by a frightful and terrible humiliation.

It is necessary to live among the demons in the infernal worlds, working within triangles, squares and octagons.

It is indispensable to live within the light, working within triangles, octagons, and squares.

Light and darkness are opposed, yet they compliment each other.

At this precise moment, it is beneficial to transcribe the Hermetic foundation which is related to what we are stating.

The Emerald Tablet, by Hermes Trismegistus.

> *It is true, no lie, certain, and to be depended upon, the superior agrees with the inferior, and the inferior with the superior, to effect that one truly wonderful work. As all things owe their existence to the will of the Only One, so all things owe their origin to the One Only Thing, the most hidden, by the arrangement of the Only God.*
>
> *The Father of that One Only Thing is the Sun, its Mother is the Moon, the Wind carries it in its belly; but its nourse is a Spirituous Earth. That One Only Thing is the Father of all things in the universe, its power is perfect, after it is has been united to a Spirituous Earth.*
>
> *Separate that Spirituous Earth from the dense or crude by means of a gentle heat, with much attention. In great measure it ascends from the Earth up to Heaven, and the superior and the inferior are increased in power.*
>
> *By this thou wilt partake of the honours of the whole world. And the Darkness will fly from thee.*
>
> *This is the strength of all powers. With this thou wilt be able to overcome all things and to transmute all what is fine and what is coarse. In this manner, the world was created; the arrangements to follow this road are hidden. In this is hidden the Wisdom of the whole world.*

Without Sexual Magic and without the infernal worlds, it is impossible to comprehend the previous paragraphs of Hermes Trismegistus.

Unquestionably, the path of the Inner Self-realization of the Being is frightfully difficult.

The initiate must pass far beyond good and evil.

The adept must fight not only against the forces of evil, but moreover, he must also fight against the forces of good.

The rocky path is surrounded by frightful abysses, which are impossible to describe in words.

At times the path is lost within quicksand, at times it is cut by terrible precipices, at times we must ascend or descend towards the darkness of no-being.

At times, a beautiful virtue which has no evil can convert itself into an insurmountable obstacle that stops the march of the walker.

The descent into the darkness of no-being used to scare the walkers of the lonely path.

The virtuous ones slander the walkers who descend into the abode of Pluto.

Nevertheless, we must never mistake a fall with a descent.

In all of this are terrible confusions.

The Rulers of the Fate and the Archons of the Aeons, and those of the sphere in which we live, whose powers are within our own Soul, become terribly confused.

They are agitated within the Soul of the walker.

The matter of the refuse does not attract those who march along the difficult path. They already do not consume garbage and they only feed themselves with sepulchral food offered to the Gods.

It is not very pleasing to continue as Rulers of undesirable things.

The inner Christ does not change the sphere of the Rulers within ourselves, so that the Rulers may equilibrate their work between light and darkness.

This is how we can purify ourselves rapidly, so that we can be elevated.

In this way the circles remain abbreviated and the path is quickly completed.

The Buddhist Annihilation is fundamental for the radical Christification.

The Rulers of the Aeons and those of the Fate and those of the sphere of action in which we live, who are within ourselves and who are autonomous and conscious parts of our own Being, want the radical elimination of the animal ego.

It is not possible to establish correct relations in the diverse parts of our own Being unless we previously eliminate the psychic aggregates.

The entire ensemble of psychic aggregates, which are living personifications of our psychological defects, constitutes the ego, the "I."

Disgracefully, the Essence, the consciousness, is found bottled up within these psychic aggregates. Thus, the consciousness processes itself by virtue of its own embottlement.

Now we better comprehend why humanity is found in such a hypnotic state, unconscious and asleep.

The correct relation with oneself is not possible as long as the animal ego continues to thrive within us.

They no more have the power of devouring their matter

"And moreover I have shortened their times and their periods, so that the perfect number of souls who shall receive the mysteries and be in the Treasury of the Light, shall be quickly completed. For had I not changed their courses, and had I not shortened their periods, they would not have let any soul come into the world, because of the matter of the refuse which they devoured, and they would have destroyed many souls. For this cause I said unto you afore time: 'I have shortened the times because of my elect; otherwise no soul would have been able to be saved.' And I have shortened the times and the periods because of the perfect number of the souls who shall receive the mysteries, that is to say, the 'elect'; and had I not shortened their periods, no material souls would have been saved, but they would have perished in the fire which is in the flesh of the rulers. This then is the word on which thou dost question me with precision."

It came to pass then, when Jesus had finished speaking these words unto his disciples, that they fell down all together, adored him and said to him: "Blessed are we before all men, for unto us thou hast revealed these great exploits."

The diverse, autonomous and self-cognizant parts of our Being are represented within our own Soul by the Rulers of the Aeons and of those of the Fate and those of the Sphere. They do not desire to devour the matter of the refuse of the purification of their light.

Christ, our Lord, reduces times and periods in order that we may quickly receive the mysteries and be in the Treasury of the Light.

Nevertheless, we must work on ourselves intensely if we wish to receive help from the inner Christ.

Strike with thy rod while thou beg to thy God.

Without death, there is no resurrection.

If you do not die, then you will not be resurrected.

The death which we refer to in these paragraphs is not the death of the physical body. Resurrection is not necessary for the death of the physical body.

The immortal Soul does not need the resurrection of the physical body.

The terrible judgment of the Lord is necessary before resurrection.

Obviously we must be judged and we must die before the profound inner resurrection.

The tyrant, the ego that we carry within ourselves, must die, if we truly long for the resurrection of Christ within ourselves.

We will continue to be unconscious and perverse, submerged in pain, as long as the Being is not resurrected.

The death of the ego and the resurrection of the Being within ourselves must occur during life.

The Being and the ego are incompatible.

The Being and the ego are like water and oil. They can never be mixed.

Only the resurrected Souls will be in the Treasury of the Light.

Total illumination is only for the resurrected Beings, for the perfect Souls.

The inner Christ within ourselves changes courses and shortens periods, with the objective that the Soul may crystallize within our human personality.

Each psychic aggregate within ourselves is the living personification of a psychological defect.

It is unquestionable that when a psychological defect is disintegrated, it is replaced with a virtue, power, force or law, which crystallizes within our human personality.

This is how we crystallize the Soul little by little.

Obviously, even the physical body must be converted into Soul.

Therefore, the Soul is the whole assembly of forces and spiritual powers that must be crystallized within ourselves.

This is how the Soul enters this world. This is how the Souls arrive to the Earth.

However, if the water does not boil at one hundred degrees, that which must be crystallized does not crystallize, and that which must be eliminated is not eliminated.

Similarly, we affirm that we must pass through great emotional crises before attaining the disintegration of any psychic aggregate.

It is not enough to comprehend a defect. It is necessary to eliminate it.

It is urgent to know how to meditate, in order to comprehend any psychic aggregate, or in other words, any psychological defect.

It is indispensable to know how to work with all our heart and with all our soul, if we want the elimination to occur.

When we beseech Stella Maris, the Virgin of the Sea, we are assisted.

The Divine Mother Kundalini, the igneous serpent of our magical powers, can and must eliminate the psychic aggregates.

Each one of us has his individual, particular Cosmic Mother.

Stella Maris is reinforced by the transcendental sexual electricity in the forge of the Cyclops.

Obviously, this is why it is preferable to invoke the igneous serpent of our magical powers while in the flaming forge of Vulcan, during the precise moment of metaphysical copulation.

This is how we can and must precipitate the death of the tyrant we carry within.

In this way the Souls can rapidly come to Earth.

The matter of refuse, the psychic aggregates, the living representations of our psychological defects impede the arrival of the Souls into the world.

This is why it is absolutely necessary to eliminate defects and to crystallize the Soul.

The perfect number of Souls who will receive the mysteries of the light is ineffable.

If Christ would not have shortened the periods within ourselves, then no Soul would have been able to be saved.

In other words, this signifies that the crystallization of the Soul within human persons would have been unsuccessful.

The fire of the abominable Kundabuffer organ, the negative fire that burns in the atomic infernos of the intellectual animal (mistakenly called the human being), would have annulled every intent of psychic crystallization.

Thus, it would have been impossible for the Souls to arrive on the Earth.

In the former verses, psychic crystallization, or the arrival of the Souls is perceived as a synonym or something similar.

Chapter 28

The powers adore the light-vesture

And Jesus continued again in his discourse and said unto his disciples: "Hearken concerning the things which befell me among the rulers of the twelve aeons and all their rulers and their lords and their authorities and their angels and their archangels. When then they had seen the vesture of light which was about me, they and their unpaired, then every one of them saw the mystery of his name, that it was on my vesture of light, which was about me. They fell down all together, adored the vesture of light which was about me and cried out all together, saying: 'How hath the lord of the universe passed through us without our knowing it?' And they all sang praises together to the interiors of the interiors. And all their triple-powers and their great forefathers and their ungenerated and their self-generated and their generated and their gods and their light-sparks and their light-bearers —in a word all their great ones —saw the tyrants of their region, that their power was diminished in them. And they were in weakness and themselves fell into great and immeasurable fear. And they gazed on the mystery of their name on my vesture, and they had set out to come and adore the mystery of their name which was on my vesture, and they could not because of the great light which was about me; but they adored a little removed from me, and they adored the light of my vesture and all cried out together, singing praises to the interiors of the interiors."

The Archons of the Twelve Aeons, their Lords and their Authorities, their Angels and their Archangels, are represented within ourselves by the distinct autonomous and self-cognizant parts of our own Being.

The powers of the Rulers of the Aeons, and those of the Fate and those of the Sphere are found within our own Soul.

In the depth of our own Being, we must find the inner Christ and His Vesture of Light.

The mystery of the mystic name that each one of us carries within our own Being must be read on the Vesture of the inner Christ.

Our mystic name has its profound significance in the inner Christ.

The inner Christ has passed through the distinct corners of our Microcosmic universe many times without us knowing it.

The distinct, independent parts of our own Being sing praises to the inner Christ.

The Triple-powers of the Being and their forefathers and their Ungenerated and their Self-generated and their Gods and their Light-sparks and their Light-bearers, whose powers are found within our own Soul, know very well that the tyrants, whom we carry within, succumb in front of the Lord.

All the divine, inner powers adore the inner Christ.

This is repeated in the universe and in the human being, in the Macrocosm and in the Microcosm.

The tyrants become as the dead

"It came to pass then, when this befell among the tyrants who are below these rulers, that they all lost power and fell down to the ground in their aeons and became as the dead world-dwellers with no breath in them, as they became in the hour when I took from them their power.

"It came to pass then thereafter, when I left those aeons, that every one of all those who were in the twelve aeons, was bound to their order all together, and they accomplished their works as I have established them, so that they spend six months turned to the left and accomplishing their works in their squares and their triangles and in those which are in their aspect, and that further they spend another six months facing to the right and towards their triangles and their squares and those which are in their aspect. Thus then will those who are in the Fate and in the sphere travel."

The Twelve Aeons are within us, here and now.

The Twelve Aeons are atomic.

The Twelve Aeons are related with the twelve Zodiacal orders.

Leo is the most exalted among the twelve orders.

Let us remember the "Lions of Fire," the "Lions of Life," the "Igneous Shapeless Breaths," the Triple Divine Powers, who emanated from the active, omnipenetrant and omniscient Okidanokh.

These "Lions of Fire" are Kether, Chokmah, and Binah, true Dragons of Wisdom.

The ten Sephiroth or emanations, plus the Ain Soph Aur and the Ain Soph, are in reality the Twelve Aeons.

The Twelve Aeons are in reality twelve Regions.

The Thirteenth Aeon is terribly divine.

Each one of the Rulers of the Aeons is bound to its order. All the Rulers of the Aeons work in the Macrocosm and within the Microcosmic human being, in accordance with the Solar Logos.

Part of the work must be performed in the light, and part within the super-obscurity and the august silence of the wise.

We must not ever forget that the inferno and paradise exist right here, and not in any other world.

The inferno is found situated within ourselves and within the womb of the Earth.

Paradise is found situated within the Being and in the superior dimensions of the world.

We can gain the right to enter into paradise only by working in the flaming forge of Vulcan, which is situated in the inferno and within the august darkness of no-being.

The inferno is the womb of heaven.

All the works within light or darkness must be performed within triangles, octagons, and squares.

We must clothe ourselves with the boots of the God Mercury. Thus, we, who are in the Fate and in the sphere, will then travel.

Chapter 29

Jesus entereth the thirteenth aeon and findeth Pistis Sophia

"It came to pass then thereafter that I ascended to the veils of the thirteenth aeon. It came to pass then, when had I arrived at their veils, that they drew apart of their own accord and opened themselves for me. I entered in into the thirteenth aeon and found Pistis Sophia below the thirteenth aeon all alone and no one of them with her. And she sat in that region grieving and mourning, because she had not been admitted into the thirteenth aeon, her higher region. And she was moreover grieving because of the torments which Self-willed, who is one of the three triple-powers, had inflicted on her. But this, —when I shall come to speak with you respecting their expansion, I will tell you the mystery, how this befell her."

The Thirteenth Aeon reminds us of the thirteen heavens of the Aztecs or Nahuas from ancient Mexico.

There are also thirteen Katuns among the Mayas of Yucatan, Palenque, and Central America in general.

These are the thirteen prophetic Katuns, thirteen periods of time for each human race.

Obviously, the prophecies for each one of the past Katuns of our Aryan Root Race were exactly fulfilled.

Presently, we are approaching the Thirteenth Katun.

The Mayas say that between the years 2040 and 2043, the Thirteenth Katun will enter into activity.

The great catastrophe that will destroy this present humanity that lives on the five continents of the world will occur during the Thirteenth Katun.

Our solar system has thirteen worlds, which are as follows: Earth, Mercury, Venus, Sun, Mars, Jupiter, Saturn, Uranus, Neptune, Pluto, Vulcan, Persephone, and Clarion.

The thirteen Katuns, the thirteen worlds, the thirteen heavens of Anahuac, are related with the thirteen Sephiroth of Hebraic Kabbalah, as follows:

Ain, Ain Soph, Ain Soph Aur.

Kether, Chokmah, Binah, Chesed, Geburah, Tiphereth, Netzach, Hod, Yesod, Malkuth.

These are the thirteen Aeons or supra-sensible atomic Regions, which are mutually penetrating and co-penetrating without confusion.

The Unmanifested Absolute is beyond these thirteen Aeons.

Inside the human being, the inner Christ ascends within the resurrected adept up to the terrific mysteries of the Thirteenth Aeon.

The mysteries of the Thirteenth Aeon are opened in the presence of the Christified and resurrected adept.

Pistis Sophia is a compound word.

Pistis Sophia signifies power-wisdom.

Pistis signifies "power." *Sophia* means "wisdom."

Unquestionably, the power is in the Fohat, which means in the fire.

The authentic wisdom is converted into fire.

There exists the Fire of the fire, the Flame of the flame, which is the astral signature of the Fire.

Obviously, Christ-Wisdom is the astral signature of the fire.

The terrific mysteries of Pistis Sophia are within the Thirteenth Aeon.

Obviously, Pistis Sophia emerged from within the bosom of the Cosmic Common Eternal Father.

Clearly, Pistis Sophia emerged from within the Unmanifested Absolute and remained cast within the Thirteenth Aeon.

We must pass through the Buddhist Annihilation if we wish to be betrothed with Pistis Sophia.

Those who worship their "beloved ego" will never find Pistis Sophia.

Only through death comes newness. If the seed does not die, then the plant is not born.

Pistis Sophia is found latent within each one of us, within our interior universe.

Only the death of the ego will permit us to be betrothed with Pistis Sophia in order to ascend to the Thirteenth Aeon.

Unquestionably, averted Eros or misguided Cupid, who is one of the three Triple-powers, is what inflicts the worst damage on Pistis Sophia.

However, we will never proclaim ourselves against Eros, Shiva, the Holy Spirit, or against Cupid-Eros because we know very well that the key of all power is found within the Tantric mysteries of lingam-yoni.

Chaos-Gae, Eros, the Greek Trinity, invites us to reflect.

Markedly, we only proclaim ourselves against averted Eros or misguided Cupid, which is fornication, adultery and sexual abuse.

Sophia and her fellow-powers behold the light

"It came to pass then, when Pistis Sophia saw me shining most exceedingly and with no measure for the light which was about me, that she was in great agitation and gazed at the light of my vesture. She saw the mystery of her name on my vesture and the whole glory of its mystery, for formerly she was in the region of the height, in the thirteenth aeon, —but she was wont to sing praises to the higher light, which she had seen in the veil of the Treasury of the Light.

"It came to pass then, when she persisted in singing praises to the higher light, that all the rulers who are with the two great triple-powers, and her invisible who is paired with her, and the other two-and-twenty invisible emanations gazed [at the light], —in as much as Pistis Sophia and her pair, they and the other two-and-twenty emanations make up four-and-twenty emanations, which the great invisible Forefather and the two great triple-powers have emanated."

Pistis Sophia, the divine Wisdom-Power, shines within the Christic mysteries and in great agitation she palpitates and shakes within the Logoic Vestures.

The mystery of the name of Pistis Sophia is hidden in the Solar Logos.

This is why it was always said to us that Christ is the Instructor of the world.

> *The supreme personality of God said: Many, many births both you and I have passed. I can remember all of them, but you cannot, O subduer of the enemy!*
>
> *Although I am unborn and My transcendental body never deteriorates, and although I am the Lord of all sentient beings, I incarnate dominating my Prakriti and appear in My original transcendental form; serving My Self of My own maya.*
>
> *Whenever and wherever there is a decline in religious practice, O descendant of Bharata, and a predominant rise of irreligion—at that time I descend Myself.*
>
> *To deliver the pious and to annihilate the miscreants, as well as to reestablish the principles of religion, I advent Myself millennium after millennium.*
>
> *One who knows the transcendental nature of my appearance and activities does not, upon leaving the body, take his birth again in this material world, but attains My external abode, O Arjuna!*

This quotation is from the *Bhagavad-Gita*, the Hymn of the Lord.

The reincarnated Christ expresses himself through every authentic Avatar.

Pistis Sophia gloriously shines within the Lord. The entire glory of the mystery of Pistis Sophia is within Christ.

Pistis Sophia descends from the Thirteenth Aeon and returns into the Thirteenth Aeon.

Shining unmistakably within the Prophets, Pistis Sophia sings praises to the highest Light that exists within the mysteries of the Treasury of the Light.

Pistis Sophia utters with the sacred Verb of the great Hierophants.

Pistis Sophia, Wisdom-Power made flesh within the incarnated Gods, gloriously shines.

Chapter 30

Mary desireth to hear the story of Sophia

It came to pass then, when Jesus has said this unto his disciples, that Mary came forward and said: "My Lord, I have heard thee say afore time: 'Pistis Sophia is herself one of the four-and-twenty emanations,' —how then is she not in their region? But thou hast said: 'I found her below the thirteenth aeon.'"

Marah, Ram-Io, Isis, Tonantzin, etc., is a variation of our own Being, but a derivative.

Therefore, Marah, Diana, Isis, is our Divine Mother Kundalini, an autonomous and self-cognizant part of our Being.

Marah interrogates the inner Christ within us about Pistis Sophia.

Obviously, Sophia, divine wisdom, Gnosis, emerges from the holy and mysterious Tetragrammaton, and is attained with the resurrection.

At one time, in my rank of adept, I invoked Minerva, the Goddess of wisdom, inside of a Lumisial. In the center of the Lumisial there was a triangular stone which was sustained by a column.

The invocation was performed according to all the rules of Iamblicus' High Theurgy.

Suddenly the stone shone, and within it appeared the blue eyes of Minerva.

The potent voice of Minerva, the one with blue eyes, resounded within the Lumisial.

"I am Minerva, the Goddess of wisdom. What do you want from me?"

I then answered firmly, *"Wisdom!"*

"What do you want wisdom for?" She asked.

"In order to help humanity." I answered.

Minerva remained in absolute silence.

Silence is the eloquence of wisdom.

When Minerva left, the triangular stone that was held up upon the mysterious column remained there as an answer.

Obviously, the three ingredients of the Holy Triamatzikamno emerge from the active omnipresent and omnipenetrant Okidanokh.

In other words, we state that the three primary forces of Nature and of the cosmos emerge from the Great Breath, profoundly unknowable to itself.

Unquestionably, the Great Breath has its roots in the Sacred Absolute Sun.

The Sacred Absolute Sun wants to crystallize the three primary forces within us, here and now.

When the three primary forces crystallize in us and within us, we then obtain wisdom.

Thus, when integrated with Sophia, we ascend to the Thirteenth Aeon.

If we do not learn how to perform the will of the Father in the superior worlds as well as in the physical world, then we cannot crystallize the first force within ourselves.

If we do not disintegrate the psychic aggregates, living personification of our psychological defects, then we cannot crystallize the second force within ourselves.

We cannot crystallize the third force in ourselves unless we previously create within ourselves the superior existential bodies of the Being.

The first force, the Holy Affirmation, is the ray of the Father.

The second force, the Holy Negation, is the ray of the Son.

The third force, the Holy Conciliation, is the ray of the Holy Spirit.

These are the three forces: positive, negative, and neutral. Whosoever obtains within himself the crystallization of the three primary forces of Nature, and of the cosmos, in reality will know what Sophia is.

Pistis Sophia, herself, is one of the Four-and-twenty Emanations.

The Four-and-twentieth Mystery, inside of which the First Mystery is hidden, is the loom of God.

The "Theomertmalogos" weaves and unweaves its own loom with infinite wisdom.

All of Nature is the loom of God.

The Four-and-twentieth Mystery only functions by way of the Sixth Mystery.

When Hermes' Glass is not spilled, the sacred sperm is transformed into the Mercury of the wise.

The connection of lingam-yoni, without the ejaculation of the Ens Seminis, is fundamental for the preparation of the Mercury of the wise.

The prepared Mercury ascends through the spinal medullar canal, opening centers and revolutionizing the consciousness.

The surplus of Mercury crystallizes into a superior octave, in the form of the Astral Body.

The surplus of Mercury crystallizes into a second superior octave, in the form of the Mental Body.

Then, the surplus of Mercury crystallizes into a third superior octave, in the form of the Causal Body.

The initiate who possesses the Physical, Astral, Mental and Causal bodies receives for that reason the psychic principles, and is converted into a true Human Being.

This is how the Holy Spirit crystallizes within us.

The crystallized Holy Spirit within the adept converts him into a gentleman, an illuminated gentleman (or gentlewoman).

When we pass through the Buddhist Annihilation, and when the ego is reduced to cosmic dust, then we Christify ourselves. The Lord crystallizes within us.

When we have totally surrendered to the Father, the first Force crystallizes within us.

The Divine Trimurti within us shines with Pistis Sophia.

The Story of Pistis Sophia

Sophia desireth to enter the Light-world

And Jesus answered and said unto his disciples: "It came to pass, when Pistis Sophia was in the thirteenth aeon, in the region of all her brethren the invisibles, that is the four-and-twenty emanations of the great Invisible, —it came to pass then by command of the First Mystery that Pistis Sophia gazed into the height. She saw the light of the veil of the Treasury of the Light, and she longed to reach to that region, and she could not reach to that region. But she ceased to perform the mystery of the thirteenth aeon, and sang praises to the light of the height, which she had seen in the light of the veil of the Treasury of the Light."

Pistis Sophia's center of gravity is within the Thirteenth Aeon.

The Four-and-twenty Emanations of the Great Invisible are within our own Being here and now.

The Four-and-twenty Emanations of the Great Invisible are the twenty-and-four Zodiacal Elders.

The twenty-and-four Elders gloriously shine in the Zodiacal belt.

The powers of the twenty-and-four Elders are found placed within the depth of our Soul.

The twenty-and-four autonomous and self-cognizant parts of our own Being are the twenty-and-four Elders, within our own individual Zodiac.

By command of the First Mystery, Sophia gazes at the Light. She sees the mysteries of the secret Treasury of the Light.

We have stated that the Treasury of the Light must be searched for within our own Being.

Within us, Sophia wishes to reach the region where the Treasury of the Light is found.

Sophia sings praises to the Light of the Heights, which she always sees in the light of the mysteries of the Treasury of the Light.

The Treasury of the Light is the Golden Fleece of the ancients, guarded by the Dragon that throws fire and sulphur.

The Golden Fleece, with all of its precious stones and incalculable wealth, is our own Christified and resurrected Being.

Fortunate is the one who reaches Christification.

Fortunate is the one who reaches resurrection.

Blessed be the one who defeats the Dragon and takes possession of the Golden Fleece.

The rulers hate her for ceasing in their mystery

"It came to pass then, when she sang praises to the region of the height, that all the rulers in the twelve aeons, who are below, hated her, because she had ceased from their mysteries, and because she had desired to go into the height and be above them all. For this cause then they were enraged against her and hated her, [as did] the great triple-powered Self-willed, that is the third triple-power, who is in the thirteenth aeon, he who had become disobedient, in as much as he had not emanated the whole purification of his power in him, and had not given the purification of his light at the time when the rulers gave their purification, in that he desired to rule over the whole thirteenth aeon and those who are below it."

Pistis Sophia can ascend or descend; ascend until reaching the Thirteenth Aeon or descend until reaching Tartarus.

Pistis Sophia is within us, here and now.

The Rulers of the Twelve Aeons, who are within us and who are self-independent parts of our own Being, suffer and long for the moment when Sophia is elevated to the height of the Thirteenth Aeon, the highest part of the Being.

Whosoever perfects the highest part of the Being receives for that reason the esoteric degree of "IS."

It is not possible to perfect the highest part of the Being unless we previously disintegrate the totality of the psychic aggregates that we carry within our interior.

Each one of the psychic aggregates personify one of our psychological defects.

Each aggregate specifies one or another psychological defect.

It is not possible to perfect the superior parts of our own Being unless we previously disintegrate all of those undesirable elements that we carry in our interior.

The perfection of all the autonomous and self-cognizant parts of our own Being cannot be gained in any way without the splendors of Pistis Sophia.

When Pistis Sophia ascends to the superior Aeons, the less elevated levels of the Being suffer terribly.

These are the nights of the Soul in which the diverse parts of the Being feel the absence of Sophia.

These are the deserts of the Soul, nights of the Spirit, periods of solitude, and ordeals for the aspirants.

The third triple-power—mind, desire, and sex—became independent and perverse.

Mind, desire, and sex become terribly perverse when falling into animal generation.

This is why the adulterous and fornicating intellectual animal is always frightfully malignant.

The intellectual mammal—mistakenly called the human being—hates Pistis Sophia.

Nevertheless, in the final synthesis, the third triple power comes from the Thirteenth Aeon.

In the final synthesis, all the parts of the Being emanate from the Thirteenth Aeon.

The third triple power, filled with arrogance, wants to command over the Thirteen Aeons.

When the third triple power emanates all of its millenary purifications from its power in itself, everything becomes different.

In order for the third triple power—mind, astral, and sex—to emanate millenary purifications, the Buddhist Annihilation is necessary.

As long as the ego is alive, purification is absent.

The Archons can give their purification when the psychic aggregates are annihilated.

Self-willed uniteth himself with the rulers of the twelve aeons and emanateth a lion-faced power to plague Sophia

"It came to pass then, when the rulers of the twelve aeons were enraged against Pistis Sophia, who is above them, and hated her exceedingly, that the great triple-powered Self-willed, of whom I have just now told you, joined himself to the rulers of the twelve aeons, and also was enraged against Pistis Sophia and hated her exceedingly, because she had thought to go to the light which is higher than her. And he emanated out of himself a great lion-faced power, and out of his matter in him he emanated a host of other very violent material emanations, and sent them into regions below, to the parts of the chaos, in order that they might there lie in wait for Pistis Sophia and take away her power out of her, because she thought to go to the height which is above them all, and moreover she had ceased to perform their mystery, and lamented continuously and sought after the light which she had seen. And the rulers who abide, or persist, in performing the mystery, hated her, and all the guards who are at the gates of the aeons, hated her also.

"It came to pass then thereafter by command of the First Commandment that the great triple-powered Self-willed, who is one of the three triple-powers, pursued Sophia in the thirteenth aeon, in order that she should look toward the parts below, so that she might see in that region his lion-faced light-power and long after it and go to that region, so that her light might be taken from her."

The Archons of the Twelve Aeons within us suffer because of Pistis Sophia, who is above them. They do not know what to do.

Obviously, the third triple power (mind, astral, and sex) is joined to the general discontentment of the Rulers of the Twelve Aeons.

This means that the terrestrial human suffers for Pistis Sophia. You know this.

Mind, desire, and sex are restless because of Pistis Sophia.

The violent, passionate emanations and the Lion-faced power arrive to the inferior regions.

The tenebrous powers, which dwell within the lower animal depth of the human being, want to deprive Pistis Sophia of her power. They never forgive her for illuminating the mysteries that are in the superior levels of the Being.

The Rulers are found to be displeased because Sophia does not manifest her mystery in all the parts. She hides the mysteries when they must be hidden: *"Silence is the eloquence of Wisdom."*

We must never forget that the Archons of the Aeons, and the Guardians of the same Aeons, are diverse self-cognizant parts of our own Being.

Our Being looks like an army of innocent children. Each part of the individual Being is self-cognizant and even autonomous.

Fortunate is the one who obtains the integration of the Being.

In the infernal worlds, the adept must work in order to be illuminated by Pistis Sophia.

Pistis Sophia must also be assimilated by those who work consciously in the Averno.

Pistis Sophia has her center of gravity within the Thirteenth Aeon.

The third triple power cries, prays, and asks for light to Pistis Sophia, even though she abides in the Thirteenth Aeon.

Pistis Sophia moves through all the Aeons. She ascends, descends, and also travels underneath the Aeons.

Chapter 31

Sophia taketh the lion-faced power of Self-willed for the true Light

"It came to pass then thereafter that she looked below and saw his light-power in the parts below; and she knew not that it is that of the triple-powered Self-willed, but she thought that it came out of the light which she had seen from the beginning in the height, which came out of the veil of the Treasury of the Light. And she thought to herself: I will go into that region without my pair and take the light and thereout fashion for myself light-aeons, so that I may go to the Light of lights, which is in the Height of heights."

The terrestrial, great triple-powered Self-willed has its own intellection. It is easy to mistake the light of this intellection with the Light that comes from the Treasury of the Light.

Moreover, this intellection even feels that it is very capable of stealing the light of the Great Treasury and thereout fashion for itself light-Aeons or Genii. Thus, sequentially, it hallucinates of reaching the power that permits it to reach the Light of lights, which is in the Height of heights.

Therefore, we must make a clear differentiation between Sophia and the subjective reasoning of the intellectual mammal, mistakenly called a human being.

It is better to think about objective reasoning. Yet, for this, we must know the three existing minds.

The first is the Sensual Mind.

The second is the Intermediate Mind.

The third is the Inner Mind.

The first mind elaborates its concepts with its contents, by way of the data obtained with external sensorial perceptive senses. Therefore, it cannot know anything about That which is the Reality.

The second mind is the deposit of religious beliefs.

The third mind functions only with the data of the awakened consciousness.

The leaven of the materialistic and incredulous Sadducees is in the first mind.

The leaven of the hypocritical Pharisees, who do not work on themselves, is in the second mind.

In the third mind is Sophia, Divine Wisdom, who is based on the direct and lively experience of That which is not of time.

Jesus, the great Kabir, warned us by saying, *"Take heed and beware of the leaven of the Pharisees and of the Sadducees."*

The materialistic doctrines of the Sadducees always rotate inside their vicious circle, which is their external sensorial perceptions. Therefore, they cannot know anything about That which is the Reality, about That which is beyond time.

Obviously, the Truth is beyond the body, affections and mind.

The fanatical Sadducees, materialists, and incredulous ones are born in time and they are lost in time. They do not know the Reality.

The hypocritical Pharisees believe, yet they do not know anything about That which is beyond time.

Only Pistis Sophia knows by direct mystical experience. However, she is related only with the inner mind.

Real experience of That which is the Truth is only possible with Pistis Sophia.

Nevertheless, the opening of the Inner Mind and the advent of Sophia is only possible by awakening the consciousness.

Pistis Sophia is a living experience, manifested as the objective reasoning of the Being.

The Inner Mind could never function as objective reasoning, without previously having passed through the Buddhist Annihilation.

The absolute resurrection of the Being is more than impossible without radical death.

If you do not die, then your consciousness will not be resurrected.

The awakening of the consciousness, the opening of the Inner Mind, and the advent of Sophia is made possible only by the resurrection of the Being.

Sophia is the objective reasoning of the Being, the awakened consciousness.

The complete functionalism of Pistis Sophia is within the objective reasoning of the Being.

In Gnostic Christic esotericism, we are always quoting six degrees of the conscious objective reasoning of the Being.

The degrees of development of the objective reasoning of the Being are known by the number of tridents that are shown on the horns of the individual Lucifer, who is within each one of us.

Obviously, the individual Lucifer within each one of us is a reflection of the Logos (Christ) within our interior. This is why he is referred to us as Christus-Lucifer.

Lucifer gives us the sexual impulse. Therefore, Lucifer is the staircase to ascend and the staircase to descend.

We arise, we ascend when defeating Lucifer.

Lucifer, integrated with ourselves, converts us into Archangels.

When the fourth trident appears over the horns, then the objective reasoning of the Being has been perfected up to the sacred Ternoonald. Therefore, only two gradations remain before obtaining the Anklad degree.

The reasoning of the sacred Anklad is the most transcendental and luminous gradation that any Being can attain, and it corresponds to the third degree, in relation to the absolute reasoning of the Infinitude that sustains all.

The reasoning of the sacred Podkoolad is the final gradation before the sacred Anklad.

The fifth trident over the horns indicates the degree of the sacred Podkoolad.

The sixth trident over the horns marks the degree of the sacred Anklad.

It is necessary to know about the Taurine mysteries in order not to alarm ourselves with the luminous horns of Christus-Lucifer within each one of us.

Let us remember the horns of silver of great Hierophants.

The horns of demons are the fatal antithesis of the horns of light.

The horns of the tenebrous ones grow in accordance with each evil action.

Therefore, we must not confuse the horns of the demons with the luminous horns of Christus-Lucifer.

The great triple powered (mind, desire and sex), in complete degeneration, has nothing to do with the degrees of the objective reasoning of the Being.

Therefore, the intellectual animal does not know anything about Pistis Sophia.

She descendeth to the twelve aeons and thence into the chaos

"This then thinking, she went forth from her own region, the thirteenth aeon, and went down to the twelve aeons. The rulers of the aeons pursued her and were enraged against her, because she had thought of grandeur. And she went forth also from the twelve aeons, and came into the regions of the chaos and drew nigh to that lion-faced light-power to devour it."

Sophia, departing from the Thirteenth Aeon, is something tremendous. This invites us to the evident self-reflection of the Being.

Consequently, the Thirteenth Aeon, the "13-Serpent," is frightfully divine.

The form of the cross of Saint Andrew is prominent in the crown of the "13-Woman Serpent."

The Mercury and the Sulphur being crossed and crossed throughout the Great Work take us to the "13th" Aeon.

The metallic soul of the sacred sperm is the Mercury.

Unquestionably, the Mercury of the wise must be fecundated by the Sulphur, in other words by the fire.

Salt, Sulphur, and Mercury must ascend throughout the medullar spinal canal, awakening in the human being all the powers which make him divine.

Salt, Sulphur, and Mercury are the vitriol of the wise.

The Gold for the superior existential bodies of the Being is obtained only by multiplying the vitriol.

The Spirit of the gold is the sacred sperm.

The Antimony is one part of the Being. It is the great alchemist who fastens the gold into the superior existential bodies of the Being.

The bodies of gold, mutually penetrating and co-penetrating without becoming confused, constitute "To Soma Heliakon," the body of gold of the Solar Man.

The inner Christ, revested with this metallic cover of gold, is the Philosophical Stone.

Whosoever possesses the Philosophical Stone, the Red Carbuncle, is married to Pistis Sophia. Consequently, he can reach the Thirteenth Aeon.

Woman-Serpent, numeral thirteen, indicates supreme death and supreme liberation.

Pistis Sophia descends to the Twelve Aeons when she considers it to be indispensable.

In no way do the Archons of the Aeons, who are within us, wish to remain without Sophia.

The Rulers of the Aeons feel that they are alone without Sophia when she is rising towards the Thirteenth Aeon.

Sophia can also penetrate into the Chaos. Since Pistis Sophia in essence is Logoic, she can penetrate into the Chaos.

We know very well that the "Great Abyss" of the eternal waters is found between Binah and Chesed. This is known by any Kabbalist who consults the Tree of Life.

The Divine Ray and the Chaos, Pistis Sophia and the Great Abyss, shine with pleasure when united.

Thus, the Chaos delectably sparkles when obtaining its meaning from this union with the Spirit.

When Sophia, as Divine Spirit, is associated with the Chaos, then the Protogonos, the primogenial light, emerges.

The Logoic Ray, impregnated by Sophia, fecundates the waters of life, in order for the universe to emerge.

Marah, Mary, the eternal Mother Space, is fecundated by the Logos.

Marah, Mary, conceives the universe in the dawn of creation.

Marah, Mary, the Chaos, is the Great Ocean.

Marah, Mary, as Divine Mother of the adept, is Stella Maris, the "Virgin of the Sea," Devi Kundalini.

Marah, Mary, weeps at the foot of the cross, her heart pierced with seven daggers.

The Virgin of the Sea is the wife of the Holy Spirit.

"As above so below." Sophia within us must also descend into the Chaos.

The sexual force, the creative energy, the Holy Spirit, must fecundate the chaotic waters, the sacred sperm, in order for the Solar Human to emerge, here and now.

Sophia must descend to work within the Chaos of our Being, in order for life to emerge. You know this.

The Lion-faced light-power absorbs the divine wisdom.

The emanations of Self-willed squeeze the light-powers out of Sophia

"But all the material emanations of Self-willed surrounded her, and the great lion-faced light-power devoured all the light-powers in Sophia and cleaned out her light and devoured it, and her matter

was thrust into the chaos; it became a lion-faced ruler in the chaos, of which one half is fire and the other is darkness, —that is Yaldabaoth, of whom I have spoken unto you many times. When this befell, Sophia became very greatly exhausted, and that lion-faced light-power set to work to take away from Sophia all her light-powers, and all the material powers of Self-willed surrounded Sophia at the same time and pressed her sore."

Sophia, exhausted after having been absorbed, suffers intensely.

The material powers of the Self-willed intellect surround Sophia and lamentably oppress her.

The Self-willed intellect of the Antichrist, expressing itself everywhere, looks with disregard at Sophia.

The intellectual Antichrist detests Pistis Sophia.

The intellectual Antichrist—the living manifestation of the ego—performs false miracles and deceitful prodigies everywhere: atomic bombs, supersonic airplanes, atomic submarines, teleguided atomic rockets, travel to the Moon, etc.

The hatred of the Antichrist towards Sophia is shown through all of these false miracles and marvels.

All of the people kneel in the presence of the Antichrist and say, "*Who is like unto the beast?*"

The Lion-faced, false intellectual light-power, with his dominion, laughs, usurps the place of Sophia and works in order to take away all of Sophia's luminous powers.

False doctrines are propagating everywhere, taking the eternal values from this poor suffering humanity.

The absurd materialism and the repugnant atheism want to carry away all of Sophia's powers of light.

The Antichrist of intellectualism is presumptuously seated upon the throne of Sophia in these tenebrous times of "Kali Yuga," in vespers of the "**13th Katun**." This occurs while the catastrophe is approaching, which will completely change the physiognomy of the terrestrial crust and will end the human species.

The real wisdom, Sophia, is displaced by the false assumption of knowledge of the scoundrels of the intellect.

Nevertheless, the Antichrist, the Self-willed, believes that he possesses Sophia.

The true substance of Sophia must be searched for within the Chaos.

The glory of Sophia is found within the Chaos.

Lux in tenebris lucet.

The Light shines in the darkness.

Sophia shines in the darkness.

The Starry Water, the prepared Mercury, the substance obtained in the form of white and brilliant metallic water, is the result of the Hermetic Art.

That which was found diffused within the tenebrous, gross and vile mass of the animal sperm can now shine by means of sexual transmutation.

The Light of Sophia always emerges from the sexual Chaos, and this Light shines in the darkness.

Sophia, as a Verb, is Yaldabaoth in complete action.

Chapter 32

"And Pistis Sophia cried out most exceedingly, she cried to the Light of lights which she had seen from the beginning, in which she had had faith, and uttered this repentance, saying thus..."

Pistis Sophia cries to the Light of lights, and cries out with a great voice.

Sophia converted into intellectualism is no longer Sophia. Thus, the evil thoughts emerge in sequence.

The first repentance of Sophia

1. *O Light of lights, in whom I have had faith from the beginning, hearken now then, O light, unto my repentance. Save me, O Light, for evil thoughts have entered into me.*

2. *I gazed, O Light, into the lower parts and saw there a light, thinking: I will go to that region, in order that I may take that light. And I went and found myself in the darkness which is in the chaos below and I could no more speed thence and go to my region, for I was sore pressed by all the emanations of Self-willed, and the lion-faced power took away my light in me.*

3. *And I cried for help, but my voice hath not reached out of the darkness. And I looked unto the height, that the Light, in which I had faith, might help me.*

4. *And when I looked unto the height, I saw all the rulers of the aeons, how in their numbers they looked down on me and rejoiced over me, though I had done them no ill; but they hated me without a cause. And when the emanations of Self-willed saw the rulers of the aeons rejoicing over me, they knew that the rulers of the aeons would not come to my aid; and those emanations which sore pressed me with violence, took courage, and the light which I had not taken from them, they have taken from me.*

5. *Now, therefore, O Light of Truth, thou knowest that I have done this in my innocence, thinking that the lion-faced light-power belonged to thee; and the sin which I have done is open before thee.*

6. *Suffer me no more to lack, O Lord, for I have had faith in thy light from the beginning; O Lord, O Light of the powers, suffer me no more to lack my light.*

7. *For because of thy inducement and for the sake of thy light am I fallen into this oppression, and shame hath covered me.*

8. *And because of the illusion of thy light, I am become a stranger to my brethren, the invisibles, and to the great emanations of Barbelo.*

9. *This hath befallen me, O Light, because I have been zealous for thy abode; and the wrath of Self-willed is come upon me—of him who had not hearkened unto thy command to emanate from the ema-*

nation of his power—because I was in his aeon without performing his mystery.

10. And all the rulers of the aeons mocked me.

11. And I was in that region, mourning and seeking after the light which I had seen in the height.

12. And the guards of the gates of the aeons searched for me, and all who remain in their mystery mocked me.

13. But I looked up unto the height towards thee and had faith in thee. Now, therefore, O Light of lights, I am sore pressed in the darkness of chaos. If now thou wilt come to save me, —great is thy mercy, —then hear me in truth and save me.

14. Save me out of the matter of this darkness, that I may not be submerged therein, that I may be saved from the emanations of god Self-willed which press me sore, and from their evil doings.

15. Let not this darkness submerge me, and let not this lion-faced power entirely devour the whole of my power, and let not this chaos shroud my power.

16. Hear me, O Light, for thy grace is precious, and look down upon me according to the great mercy of Light.

17. Turn not thy face from me, for I am exceedingly tormented.

18. Haste thee, hearken unto me and save my power.

19. Save me because of the rulers who hate me, for thou knowest my sore oppression and my torment and the torment of my power which they have taken from me. They who have set me in all this evil are before thee; deal with them according to thy good pleasure.

20. My power looked forth from the midst of the chaos and from the midst of the darkness, and I waited for my pair, that he should come and fight for me, and he came not, and I looked that he should come and lend me power, and I found him not.

21. And when I sought the light, they gave me darkness; and when I sought my power, they gave me matter.

22. Now, therefore, O Light of lights, may the darkness and the matter which the emanations of the Self-willed have brought upon me, be unto them for a snare, and may they be ensnared therein, and recompense them and may they be made to stumble and not come into the region of their Self-willed.

23. May they remain in the darkness and not behold the light; may they behold the chaos for ever, and let them not look unto the height.

24. Bring upon them their revenge, and may thy judgement lay hold upon them.

25. Let them not henceforth come into their region to their god Self-willed, and let not his emanations henceforth come into their regions; for their god is impious and Self-willed, and he thought that he had done this evil of himself, not knowing that, had I not been brought low according to thy command, he would not have had any authority over me.

26. But when thou hadst by thy command brought me low, they pursued me the more, and their emanations added pain to my humiliation.

27. And they have taken light-power from me and fallen again to pressing me sore, in order to take away all the light in me. Because of this in which they have set me, let them not ascend to the thirteenth aeon, the region of Justice.

28. But let them not be reckoned in the lot of those who purify themselves and the light, and let them not be reckoned with those who will quickly repent, that they may quickly receive mysteries in the Light.

29. For they have taken my light from me, and my power hath begun to cease in me and I am destitute of my light.

30. Now, therefore, O Light, which is in thee and is with me, I sing praises to thy name, O Light, in glory.

31. May my song of praise please thee, O Light, as an excellent mystery, which leadeth to the gates of the Light, which they who shall repent will utter, and the light of which will purify them.

32. Now, therefore, let all matters rejoice; seek ye all the Light, that the power of the stars which is in you, may live.

33. For the Light hath heard the matters, nor will it leave any without having purified them.

34. Let the souls and the matters praise the Lord of all aeons, and [let] the matters and all that is in them [praise him].

35. For God shall save their soul from all matters, and a city shall be prepared in the Light, and all the souls who are saved, will dwell in that city and will inherit it.

36. And the soul of them who shall receive mysteries will abide in that region, and they who have received mysteries in its name will abide therein."

The Self-willed and the Lion-faced power absorbed the reflections of Sophia.

Sophia has found herself within the obscurity.

Sophia asks for help from the darkness.

Sophia suffers inexpressibly in the darkness.

The Rulers of the Aeons show resentment towards Sophia when she changes places.

Sophia travels wherever she pleases. She can stay in the Thirteenth Aeon or in the Chaos.

In essence, Sophia, the wisdom, is a concrete result of a symbiosis of the mixture of Light with darkness.

The descent of the Logos into matter is made dialectically comprehensible by means of the cosmic drama.

The immersion of the Spirit into matter is dialectically explainable with the life, passion, death, and resurrection of Christ within us.

Sophia is the result of the descent of the Logos into the Chaos.

The Lion-faced light-power, which is the triple inferior power: mind, desire and sexual degeneration, have nothing to do with That which is beyond the body, affections and the mind; That is the Truth.

The great emanations of Barbelo, the abode of the Light, can never be comprehended by the intellectual light.

The Uncreated Light is distinct from the intellect, as water is from oil.

When the initiate lets himself fall, he then cannot enjoy the emanations of Barbelo.

There are those who, being jealous of the abode of Barbelo, fall into the darkness, where the cries and the gnashing of teeth are heard.

The Self-willed ego never obeys, and it always emanates from itself that which should never be emanated.

The Rulers of the Aeons mock the intellectualism that is blindly confused with Sophia.

In the inferior regions, the initiate is lamenting and is searching for the Light that he has seen in the heights.

The Guardians of the gates of the Aeons want to grant the initiate the right to pass, but when they see him very much alive, they realize that he is not yet prepared.

Sophia is found in the sexual Chaos, in the brute Azoth.

We must liberate Sophia from within the darkness of the Chaos.

This is possible by transmuting the sacred sperm into creative energy.

There exist two Chaos, the one from the Macrocosm and the one from the Microcosm.

The Chaos of the Microcosm is found in our sexual organs.

In the Chaos of creation, the elements and the principles, the darkness and the light are found confused, intermixed, and without the possibility of one reacting to the other.

This is the reason why the Chaos in the figure of the world, which contains in itself the materials of our Hermetic globe, has been painted by many artists.

The cosmos comes from the Chaos, and the light from the darkness.

In no way can the cosmos and the light emerge in the Macrocosm or in the Microcosm without the help of Pistis Sophia.

However, Sophia wants to ascend up to the Thirteenth Aeon.

The subjective reasoning within the intellectual animal is a type of chaos where disorder reigns.

Obviously, the chaotic disorder of the subjective reasoning also overtakes Sophia, and totally alters her.

However, it is not convenient to confuse the authentic, venerable Chaos of sex with these types of intellectual and emotional chaos of the tricerebral biped, mistakenly called a human being.

Sophia aspires to reach the Thirteenth Aeon.

Sophia does not want to be in the darkness.

Sophia awaits for the Grace of the Uncreated Light to come and give her help.

Sophia wishes the Light to turn its face towards her because she is suffering in the Chaos.

Sophia wishes for the Light to save her luminous powers.

The Archons protest for Sophia, they long for her, and at times they see themselves without her.

Nevertheless, the Rulers know that Sophia must illuminate the Chaos.

What would become of the Rulers, what would become of us, if Pistis Sophia would not enter into the Chaos?

How could we perform the "Great Work" without Pistis Sophia?

The Chaos also needs Pistis Sophia.

The Rulers need Sophia to be in the Chaos, so that they can perform the Great Work within themselves.

We had said, and we repeat again, that the Archons are the diverse, autonomous and self-cognizant parts of our own Being.

By itself, the Essence within each one of us could never perform all of the "Great Work."

It is necessary for the Rulers, which means the diverse, self-cognizant and independent parts of our own Being, to work intensely in the Great Work.

Only thus, when all the parts of the Being are working, can we reach the intimate Self-realization.

The superior part of the Being must intensely help man, because if He (the superior part of the Being) does not help him, man fails, and if man fails, the superior part or the superior parts also fail.

The initiate illuminated by Sophia looks towards the Height. He observes from the Chaos, and from the midst of the obscurity he awaits with infinite longing for his pair, for his Valkyrie, for his Spiritual Soul. However, he suffers because she has not yet arrived.

The Valkyrie, the beautiful Helen, the Buddhi, is like a fine and transparent glass of alabaster through which the flame of Prajna burns.

To integrate oneself with the Valkyrie, to be completely betrothed with the beautiful Helen, is only possible by means of resurrection.

Unquestionably, all the Christic principles are found contained within Buddhi.

When the Causal Man is integrated with Buddhi, he becomes resurrected.

Man, in his totality, becomes illuminated with this whole integration.

But, how difficult it is to obtain that integration.

In no way is such an integration possible without the previous elimination of the psychic aggregates that we carry within our interior.

The Causal Man is the true man, and the beautiful Helen is his real wife.

The Mental and Astral Bodies, and the physical vehicle with its vital base are his only vestures.

Dr. Johannes Faust, physician, enchanter and magician, was married with his pair, in other words, with the beautiful Helen of Troy.

One time, Johannes Faust made the beautiful Helen visible and tangible before a group of young students that were left in astonishment before such beauty.

The initiate, inebriated by Sophia, searches for Light, yet he receives darkness. He wants power, yet he receives matter. The Rulers punish him for his own good.

Nevertheless, the Archons also suffer from the effects of karma.

The Rulers working in the Chaos suffer inexpressibly. They want to ascend and cry.

It is obviously necessary to work in the Chaos in order to have the right to rise towards the Light.

Every ascent is preceded by a descent, and every exaltation is followed by a terrible and frightful humiliation.

The Self-willed god, the terrestrial man with the animal ego within is always impious and perverse.

Sophia does not wish for the Self-willed god to receive the advent of the Rulers.

Sophia does not wish for the radiation of the ego to affect the Archons.

Sophia knows very well what the ego is capable of. The Self-willed always feels that he is a Lord of all.

The ego feels as though he has authority over Pistis Sophia.

The Self-willed ego thinks that all that happens to Pistis Sophia is by its power, and by its authority.

The Self-willed is the triple inferior power dominated by the ego.

The ego in itself is plural. It is a sum of multiple, psychic inhuman aggregates, which are living personifications of the psychological defects that we carry within our interior.

Pistis Sophia descends into the Chaos, by the command of the Father of all Lights, and by the command of the Self-willed.

Pistis Sophia, adulterated and absorbed by the scoundrels of the intellect and converted into intellectualism is the calamity of this epoch of Kali Yuga.

Now, the Kalkian personalities of this Iron Age are abundant.

Nevertheless, the perverse ones believe that they have within their degenerated brains all the sapience of Pistis Sophia.

The perverse ones of intellectualism are precisely the ones who are against the ascension of Pistis Sophia.

The scoundrels of the intellect do not want anything to do with real spirituality.

The scoundrels of the mind do not want the ascension of Pistis Sophia to the Thirteenth Aeon.

In no way can we forget that the Thirteenth Aeon is the Region of the cosmic justice.

Obviously, the mere intellective functionalism cannot purify anyone. Before anything, it is necessary to pass through great emotional crises.

If the water does not boil at one hundred degrees, that which must be disintegrated does not disintegrate, and that which must be crystallized does not crystallize.

The disintegration of any psychic aggregate is possible only based on conscious works and voluntary sufferings.

The mysteries of the Light are possible only for those who have disintegrated within themselves the undesirable psychic elements that we carry within our interior.

Sophia, deprived of her Light, is the intellectualism of the Self-willed ego, the Antichrist.

Sophia sings praises to the Verb of the Light.

The Light purifies those who truly are repented of their errors.

Each time that an undesirable psychic element is disintegrated within us, a luminous power crystallizes in our personality.

This is how the luminous Soul is crystallizing within us.

May the power of the Stars perpetuate in each initiate. This is our greatest longing.

The luminous Beings and the luminous Being within us want to purify us.

Purification is possible only by disintegrating the undesirable elements of our psyche.

The disintegration of the undesirable elements of the psyche is never possible without the direct help of Stella Maris.

Stella Maris is the Virgin of the Sea, the igneous serpent of our magical powers.

Stella Maris is a variation of our own Being.

Stella Maris is our own Being, but a derivative.

The Light wants to purify all the Beings and persons.

The Light hears the prayer of all the Beings and persons.

May the people and the Souls praise the Lord of all Aeons, the Cosmic Common Eternal Father. This is our longing.

God will liberate the soul of all matter, and the city of Heliopolis will open its gates, in order for the perfect ones to enter through them.

They will abide in that city, and they will inherit it.

That is the new Jerusalem from *The Apocalypse* of St. John.

The initiates will abide in the city of Heliopolis, in the luminous regions of the Great Light.

Nevertheless, it is necessary to note that only those who have completed the Great Work can reside in the city of Heliopolis.

Chapter 33

It came to pass then, when Jesus had spoken these words unto his disciples, that he said unto them: "This is the song of praise which

Pistis Sophia uttered in her first repentance, repenting of her sin, and reciting all which had befallen her. Now, therefore: 'Who hath ears to hear, let him hear.'"

Mary again came forward and said: "My Lord, my indweller of light hath ears, and I hear with my light-power, and thy spirit which is with me, hath sobered me. Hearken then that I may speak concerning the repentance which Pistis Sophia hath uttered, speaking of her sin and all that befell her. Thy light-power hath prophesied thereof afore time through the prophet David in the sixty-eighth Psalm [Modern Psalm 69]."

Those who have repented of their sins sing to the Great Light.

Marah, Mary, Isis, the Virgin of the Sea, within us, hears the power of the Light, and the Spirit of the Lord dwells within Her.

God is rising within us when our Divine Mother Kundalini disintegrates and scatters the ashes of the enemies of the Eternal One.

Unquestionably, the enemies of God are the undesirable psychic elements that we carry within our interior.

Such elements personify our psychological defects: anger, greed, lust, envy, pride, laziness, gluttony, etc.

Just as the wax melts in front of the fire, the impious ones will perish in front of our profound interior God.

But the just ones—those who have completed the Great Work—will be joyful and will rejoice, and they will leap with pleasure in the presence of the Innermost God.

Sing to your profound Innermost God. Sing psalms to his Name. Exalt in He who rides over all the superior levels of the Being.

Jah is his name. Jah is the mantra through which the Ancient of Days is invoked. Each one of us has his own Ancient. He is the superior part of the Being.

"Father of Orphans and defender of Widows," is God in His holy abode.

> *"To the orphans, God gives a family to reside with, and to the captives, He gives freedom and prosperity. Yet, the rebel ones will abide on dry land."*

Mary interpreteth the first repentance from Psalm LXVIII [Modern Psalm 69]

1. Save me, O God, for the waters are come in even unto my soul.

2. I sank, or am submerged, in the slime of the abyss, and power was not. I have gone down into the depths of the sea; a tempest hath submerged me.

3. I have kept on crying; my throat is gone, my eyes faded, waiting patiently for God.

4. They who hate me without a cause are more than the hairs of my head; mighty are my foes, who violently pursued me. They required of me that which I took not from them.

5. God, thou hast known my foolishness, and my faults are not hid from thee.

6. Let not them that wait on thee, O Lord, Lord of powers, be ashamed for my sake; Let not those who seek thee be ashamed for my sake, O Lord, God of Israel, God of powers.

7. For thy sake have I endured shame; shame hath covered my face.

8. I am become a stranger to my brethren, a stranger unto the sons of my mother.

9. For the zeal of thy house hath consumed me; the revilings of them that revile thee have fallen upon me.

10. I bowed my soul with fasting, and it was turned to my reproach.

11. I put on sackcloth; I became unto them a bye-word.

12. They who sit at the gates, chattered at me; and they who drink wine, harped about me.

13. But I prayed with my soul unto thee, O Lord; the time of thy well-liking is [now], O God. In the fullness of thy grace give ear unto my salvation in truth.

14. Save me out of this slime, that I sink not therein; let me be saved from them that hate me, and from the deep waters.

15. Let not a water-flood submerge me, let not the deep swallow me, let not a well close its mouth above me.

16. Hear me, O Lord, for thy grace is good; according to the fullness of thy compassion look down upon me.

17. Turn not thy face away from thy servant, for I am oppressed.

18. Hear me quickly, give heed to my soul and deliver it.

19. Save me because of my foes, for thou knowest my disgrace, my shame and my dishonour; all my oppressors are before thee.

20. My heart awaiteth disgrace and misery; I waited for him who should sorrow with me, but I could not come at him, and for him who should comfort me, and I found him not.

21. They gave me gall for my meat; and in my thirst they gave me vinegar to drink.

22. Let their table be unto them for a trap and for a snare and for a retribution and for a stumbling block.

23. Mayest thou bend their backs at all time.

24. Pour out thy anger upon them, and let the wrath of thy anger lay hold upon them.

25. Let their encampment be desolate, let there be no dweller in their habitations.

26. For they persecuted him whom thou hast smitten, and added to the smart of their woundings.

27. They added iniquity to their iniquities; let them not come into thy justice.

28. Let them be wiped out of the book of the living, and let them not be written in among the righteous.

29. I am a poor wretch who is heart-broken too; it is the salvation of thy face which hath taken me unto itself.

30. I will praise the name of God in the ode, and exalt it in the song of thanksgiving.

31. This shall please God better than a young bull which putteth forth horns and hoofs.

32. May the wretched see and make merry; seek ye God, that your souls may live.

33. For God hath heard the wretched and despiseth not the prisoners.

34. Let heaven and earth praise the Lord, the sea and all that is therein.

35. For God will save Zion, and the cities of Judaea will be built up, and they will dwell there and inherit it.

36. The seed of his servants shall possess it, and they who love his name shall dwell therein.

Marah, Isis, Adonia, the igneous serpent of our magical powers, the "Woman Serpent," tremendously suffers within us.

Isis always suffers for Her Child in us, and within our own selves, here and now.

Each one of us makes his Divine Mother Kundalini suffer tremendously.

People spill Hermes' glass, thus they perish within the waters of life.

Moses was saved from the waters. Yet, the multitudes do not want to be saved from the waters.

Truly, only those who never spill Hermes' glass can be saved from the waters.

When submerged in the slime, Marah, Mary, suffers inexpressibly.

Evil children make their Mother suffer.

The lustful current of the evil child sinks his Mother into the profundities of the ocean of pain.

The psychic aggregates mortally hate the Divine Mother Kundalini.

The tenebrous ones violently attack all those who name the Divine Mother Kundalini within the castle of Klingsor, and in all the temples of black magic.

The Divine Mother Kundalini suffers inexpressibly for Her child.

She fights to disintegrate the undesirable psychic elements, and She answers for Her child, feeling herself one with Her child.

The divine Woman-Serpent feels shame for the sins of Her child.

It is tremendous how we make our Mother Kundalini suffer.

The initiate, fallen in the slime, suffers inexpressibly, and the injuries hurt his heart.

Those who have lost their Soul and have recovered it suffer when they see their errors.

We must repent of our errors.

The initiate must remain impassible before praise and calumny.

Truly, we are not more because they praise us, neither are we less because they condemn us, because we are always what we are.

Salvation within the Truth is radical.

"Ye shall know the truth and the truth shall make you free," said Christ.

The initiate works with the help of the Divine Mother Kundalini, illuminated by Sophia. Yet, when in pain, he asks his Father to take him out of the slime.

To be saved from the waters, as was Moses, is extraordinary.

The waters of life, the "Ens Seminis," are accustomed to being boisterous.

Rare are those who obtain real salvation.

Almost all the human beings fall into the well. They are swallowed up by the profundity.

The Great Merciful One can save us, but only if we work on ourselves.

The Lord shows His face to the serf that works on himself.

Only the inner Christ can save us.

The enemies of ourselves are within our own selves.

The secret enemies dwell within our own psyche.

They are the subjective aggregates, which are living personifications of our psychological defects.

The psychic aggregates make us abnormal creatures.

The psyche of the humanoids of the Earth is very strange. It is subjective, incoherent and abnormal.

Obviously, the psyche which is bottled up within the psychic aggregates is abnormally processed.

As long as the animal ego continues to thrive within us, we will have gall as our meat.

While the initiate continues with the undesirable elements of the "myself" inside of the psyche, he will have vinegar to drink in order to calm his thirst, and the pain will multiply until the infinite.

May bitterness be for the psychic aggregates.

The psychic aggregates are really those who must distil and drink their own poison.

The indignation of the Being must be against them, against the undesirable elements that we carry within.

May the Essence be free and may the tenebrous ones perish.

Those perverse ones that we carry within our interior always add iniquity to their iniquities.

The psychic aggregates must be disintegrated and erased from the book of the living.

The initiate feels as though he is a poor, unfortunate one, with a broken heart. Yet, the salvation of the profound Innermost Being raises him, stimulates him, keeps him straight on the real path.

It is necessary to praise the profound name of the Innermost Lord in the ode, and exalt it in the song of thanksgiving.

God hears the suffering soul and never despises the prisoners, which means, those who are paying karma.

The four elements fire, water, air, and earth are found contained within the Mercury of the wise. This is how the wise can govern the elements of Nature.

The elements of Nature are governed by the Super-Man.

The Celestial Jerusalem shines within the resurrected adept.

The Celestial Jerusalem is in the seed of the serfs of the Lord.

The ancient populace worshipped corn, wheat and rice because the sacred seed is represented by them.

Mayas and Nahuas symbolized the Mercury of the wise with corn.

The Middle East and Europe saw the blessed seed in the wheat.

China, Japan, and India saw the sacred sperm in the rice.

We transform the Ens Seminis into creative energy, which means into Mercury, only by the transmutation science.

Whosoever possesses the Mercury of the wise can create within himself the superior existential bodies of the Being.

Whosoever possesses the Mercury of the wise within himself will abide in the city of Heliopolis.

God will save Zion by virtue of the Mercury of the wise. The interior cities will be constructed, and the initiates will dwell in them and inherit them.

A City of Light, a Celestial Jerusalem, must be constructed within each human being.

This is how initiates can abide in the city of Heliopolis.

Thus, within each human being, a terribly malignant psychological city exists, which is inhabited by the demons of desire. We must destroy this city.

It is necessary to create the Mercury of the wise in order to edify the Celestial Jerusalem within us.

It is written, *"The seed of his servants shall possess it, and they who love his name shall dwell therein."*

"Know Thyself."

You, who wishes to know the Philosophical Stone, must know yourself very well. Thus, you will know it.

The key of the Philosophical Stone is within the Mercury of the wise.

The elements of Nature are joined in their precise proportion and in their natural quality within the Mercury, which is the metallic soul of the sacred sperm.

All of that which is searched for by the wise is what comes from the Mercury.

Only the Mercury has the power to dissolve, mortify, and destroy the undesirable psychic elements that we carry within our interior.

Elements transform themselves into other elements within the Mercury.

The element earth within each one of us will convert itself into water, and the water into air. Finally, the air will convert itself into fire.

Thus, the Mercury fecundated by Sulphur (fire), by way of the good duties of the sublimed Salt, will rise through the medullar canal of the aspirant in order to radically transform him.

Light shines within darkness.

Stella Maris, the Virgin of the Sea, Devi Kundalini, shines in the Mercury that ascends through the medullar canal of the initiate.

The igneous serpent of our magical powers reduces all the tenebrous dwellers of the psychological city into dust.

The Celestial Jerusalem will be raised upon the ruins of the damned city.

Therefore, the Celestial Jerusalem is something profoundly internal. It is our own interior universe.

Chapter 34

It came to pass then, when Mary had finished speaking these words unto Jesus in the midst of the disciples, that she said unto him: "My Lord, this is the solution of the mystery of the repentance of Pistis Sophia."

It came to pass then, when Jesus had heard Mary speak these words, that he said unto her: "Well said, Mary, blessed one, the fullness, or all-blessed fullness, thou who shalt be sung of as blessed in all generation."

Mary, Marah, Tonantzin, Isis, Adonia, Diana, Rhea, Insobertha, etc. is as we have previously stated, a part of our own Being, but a derivative.

Unquestionably, Marah, Mary, is the igneous serpent of our magical powers.

Therefore, Mary is the blessed one, the Divine Mother Kundalini.

The repentance of Sophia within the initiate and the Mystery of such repentance resides within the science of sexual transmutation.

It is indispensable to build the Celestial Jerusalem upon the stone of truth.

Obviously, the cubic stone of Yesod is the foundation of the city of Heliopolis.

Undoubtedly, Yesod-Mercury is found within sex.

Yesod signifies "foundation" and also Mercury, because the Mercury is the foundation of the transmutation art.

Those who reject the cubic stone of Yesod fall into the abyss of perdition.

Peter, the great Hierophant of the sexual mysteries, said:

> *...Behold, I lay in Zion a chief corner stone, elect, precious: and he that believeth on Him shall not be confounded.*
>
> *...The stone that the builders disallowed, the same is made the head of the corner.* - Peter 2:6-8

This stone is sex, which is "*... a stone of stumbling and a rock of offence.*"

The ignorant ones reject the mysteries of sex. Thus, frightfully, they fail.

Those who spill Hermes' Glass sink into the exterior darkness, where only the weeping and gnashing of teeth can be heard.

Chapter 35

The second repentance of Sophia

Jesus continued again in the discourse and said: "Pistis Sophia again continued and still sang praises in a second repentance, saying thus:

1. *Light of lights, in whom I have had faith, leave me not in the darkness until the end of my time.*

2. *Help me and save me through thy mysteries; incline thine ear unto me and save me.*

3. *May the power of thy light save me and carry me to the higher aeons; for thou wilt save me and lead me into the height of thy aeons.*

4. *Save me, O Light, from the hand of this lion-faced power and from the hands of the emanations of god Self-willed.*

5. *For it is thou, O Light, in whose light I have had faith and in whose light I have trusted from the beginning.*

6. *And I have had faith in it from the time when it emanated me, and thou thyself didst make me to emanate; and I have had faith in thy light from the beginning.*

7. *And when I had faith in thee, the rulers of the aeons mocked at me, saying: She hath ceased in her mystery. Thou art my saviour and thou art my deliverer and thou art my mystery, O Light.*

8. *My mouth was filled with glorifying, that I may tell of the mystery of thy grandeur at all times.*

9. *Now, therefore, O Light, leave me not in the chaos for the completion of my whole time; forsake me not, O Light.*

10. *For all the emanations of Self-willed have taken from me my whole light-power and have surrounded me. They desired to take away my whole light from me utterly and have set a watch on my power.*

11. *Saying one to another together: The Light have forsaken her, let us seize her and take away the whole light in her.*

12. *Therefore, then, O Light, cease not from me; turn thee, O Light, and save me from the hands of the merciless.*

13. *May they who would take away my power, fall down and become powerless. May they who would take away my light-power from me, be enwrapped in darkness and sink into powerlessness.*

"This then is the second repentance which Pistis Sophia hath uttered, singing praises to the Light."

The Father who is in secret is the Father of all Lights, and the initiate travels towards Him.

The Ancient of Days is the supreme Lord of all mysteries.

Each one of us has his own Kabbalistic Ancient.

The Ancient of Days in us can and must save us through His mysteries.

The Father of all Lights, the Ancient of Centuries within us, the superior part of the Being, can save us and take us to the highest Aeons.

The Self-willed god, the animal ego, must be reduced to cosmic dust.

The Ancient of the Light is the Concealed of the concealed, the Goodness of goodness, the Mercy of mercies.

We originally emanated from the Father who is in secret; you know this.

Essentially speaking, we as human beings, as souls, are the result of the various sunderable divisions of the Ancient of Centuries.

The Rulers of the Aeons within us mock the fallen Bodhisattva, saying, *"You have ceased in your Mystery; you are a pig that is wallowing in the mud of the Earth."*

The Bodhisattva is a seed from any sacred individual, who is placed within the sacred sperm with the possibilities of development; that is all.

Undoubtedly, if such a seed were not developed, reincarnation would then be a failure.

Fallen Bodhisattvas are always true failures.

The Ancient of Days is the Savior. He is the Redeemer. He is the Mystery of mysteries.

The inner Christ emanates from the Ancient of Days, and through Him the Father saves us.

The Son is one with the Father, and the Father is one with the Son.

Whosoever has seen the Son, has seen the Father.

The mystery of the magnificence of the Father of all Lights is the Mystery of all mysteries.

The Light buds from the Chaos. Each one of us carries the Chaos in our own self and within our own self.

Alchemically, the Chaos is the seed plot of the cosmos.

The Alchemical Chaos is found within the current creative organs.

Sophia does not wish to be left exclusively in the Chaos. She wants to ascend to the Thirteenth Aeon.

Every initiate who longs to ascend towards the Thirteenth Aeon is helped in his or her ascension by the Ancient of Days.

The ego, the Self-willed, hates Pistis Sophia. Thus, by submerging her into Chaos and into desperation the Self-willed defeats her.

The emanations of the Self-willed are the psychic aggregates that we carry within our interior.

In reality, all of those multiple aggregates are stealing the Light.

Within each psychic aggregate, there is a certain percentage of imprisoned Light.

Obviously, we are referring to a certain percentage of Essence, of consciousness, which is trapped and bottled up.

Each time that we attain the disintegration of a psychic aggregate, we liberate the corresponding percentage of Essence, of consciousness which is bottled up there.

This is how we can increase, little by little, the percentage of real consciousness within us.

Normally, humanity possesses three percent of free consciousness. If humanity had ten percent of consciousness, then wars would not exist.

During the nineteenth century and part of the twentieth century, the various adepts who sacrificed themselves for humanity enjoyed fifty percent of awakened consciousness.

Only the resurrected adepts possess one hundred percent of awakened consciousness.

The psychic aggregates multiply themselves within the intellectual animal. Thus, logically speaking, they steal the Light from him.

Each psychic aggregate has stolen a certain percentage of our consciousness.

Only the Light can save us from the hands of those merciless ones, whom we carry within our interior.

May those who steal the power fall and be reduced to cosmic dust.

This is the second repentance that Sophia sang to the Ancient of Days, to the Father who is in secret.

The initiate, filled with Pistis Sophia, sings and beseeches the Father of all Lights.

Chapter 36

Peter complaineth of Mary

It came to pass then, when Jesus had finished speaking these words unto his disciples, that he said unto them: "Do ye understand in what manner I discourse with you?"

And Peter started forward and said unto Jesus: "My Lord, we will not endure this woman, for she taketh the opportunity from us and hath let none of us speak, but she discourseth many times."

And Jesus answered and said unto his disciples: "Let him in whom the power of his spirit shall seeth, so that he understandeth what I say, come forward and speak. But now, Peter, I see thy power in thee, that it understandeth the solution of the mystery of the repentance which Pistis Sophia hath uttered. Now, therefore, Peter, speak the thought of her repentance in the midst of thy brethren."

Peter, the Hierophant of sexual mysteries, speaks with great wisdom. We must know how to listen to him.

We have previously stated that the Twelve Powers are within us.

Previously, we emphatically affirmed that the Twelve Powers are the twelve parts of our own Being.

We formerly explained that the twelve autonomous and self-cognizant parts of our own Being are the Twelve Apostles of the cosmic drama within us, here and now.

Therefore, we must comprehend that Peter, within us, is that self-cognizant part of our profound interior Being related with the mysteries of sex.

Peter's death, crucified on the inverted cross with his head towards the ground, indicates the necessity for us to descend into the Ninth Sphere, sex, in order to work with the fire and water. All white initiations begin here.

Peter makes us understand that the Woman-Serpent discourses many times.

Nevertheless, Peter and the Woman-Serpent within us are found intimately related.

The Woman-Serpent, Stella Maris, must interrogate Her son, Christ, many times during the Great Work in order to help us.

The Woman-Serpent is the wife of the Holy Spirit and the daughter of Her Son.

The Woman-Serpent is Marah, Mary, Isis, our Divine Mother Kundalini.

The inner Christ knows very well that the interior Peter of each one of us integrally comprehends the solution of the repentance that Pistis Sophia uttered.

Peter, Patar, with his radical letters, knows very well that the key of repentance is in sex.

The three radical letters of Peter, Patar, are "P-T-R."

Only the power of the Spirit can comprehend the words of the inner Christ.

It is necessary to receive the "Donum Dei" in order to comprehend all the science of the Great Work.

The true repentance has its foundation in the sexual mysteries.

Peter is the one who has to express the idea of repentance in the midst of his brethren.

The brethren of Peter are the autonomous and self-cognizant parts of our own individual Being.

Peter interpreteth the second repentance of Psalm LXX

[Modern Psalm 71]

And Peter answered and said unto Jesus: "O Lord, give ear that I may speak the thought of her repentance, of which afore time thy power prophesied through the prophet David, uttering her repentance in the seventieth Psalm:

1. O God, my God, I have trusted in thee, let me no more be put to shame for ever.

2. Save me in thy virtuousness and set me free; incline thine ear unto me and save me.

3. Be unto me a strong God and a firm place to save me; for thou art my strength and my refuge.

4. My God, save me from the hand of the sinner and from the hand of the transgressor and from the impious [one].

5. For thou art my endurance, O Lord, thou art my hope from my youth up.

6. I have trusted myself to thee from my mother's womb; thou hast brought me out of my mother's womb. My remembrance is ever in thee.

7. I have become as the crazy for many; thou art my help and my strength, thou art my deliverer, O Lord.

8. My mouth was filled with glorifying, that I may praise the glory of thy splendour the whole day long.

9. Cast me not away in the time of age; if my soul fades, forsake me not.

10. For mine enemies have spoken evil against me and they who lay in wait for my soul, have taken counsel against my soul.

11. Saying together: God hath forsaken him; pursue and seize him, for there is no saviour.

12. God, give heed to my help.

13. Let them be ashamed and destroyed who calumniate my soul. Let them be enwrapped in shame and disgrace who seek evil against me.

"This then is the solution of the second repentance which Pistis Sophia hath uttered."

The interior God of each one of us is what counts.

Only our interior God can save us from all disgrace.

The interior Lord, the superior part of the Being, hears us and helps us.

May the severity of our God save us.

May the mercy of our God protect us.

The Lord will save us from the hand of the transgressor, from the hand of the sinner, and from the impious one.

The transgressor, the sinner, and the impious ones are within us.

Verily, the transgressors, the sinners, and the impious ones are the psychic aggregates that we carry within our interior.

The intimate God is our resistance and our hope, our strength and our reality.

Whosoever has incarnated the inner Christ knows very well that he has come from the womb of his Divine Mother Kundalini.

We came from the womb of the Mother by the will of the Ancient of Centuries.

We must never forget our Father, who is in secret. Each one of us has his own Father.

For the intellectual animal, mistakenly called a human being, anything related with the Spirit is mere craziness.

We must praise the Father, who is in secret.

The Soul often fades, but if the Father fortifies us, we will be victorious.

When the child falls, when he perverts himself, then the Father withdraws.

When the Father withdraws, the child falls into disgrace.

If the Father would not withdraw, then the child would not fall into disgrace.

Whosoever is assisted by his or her Father never falls into misery.

Miserable is the wicked child who has his Father absent.

It would have been better for that child not to have been born, or it would have been better for him that a millstone were hanged about his neck and that he were drowned in the depth of the sea.

The Ancient of Centuries can give to us all, or He can withdraw from us, if this is His will.

Woe to the one who is withdrawn from the Ancient of Days.

The enemies of the night, the red demons of Seth, the living personifications of our psychological defects, have spoken evil against the Being.

Verily, verily, beloved reader, the red demons of Seth, your psychic aggregates, are waiting for your Soul. A certain percentage of psychic Essence exists within each aggregate.

The red demons of Seth take counsel against your Soul.

Woe to the one who loses his Soul.

The tenebrous ones who dwell within us exclaim, *"God hath forsaken him; pursue and seize him, for there is no Savior."*

Our interior God can help us.

May shame, disgrace, and destruction be for the red demons of Seth.

Chapter 37

Jesus promiseth to perfect the disciples in all things

The saviour answered and said unto Peter: "Finally, Peter; this is the solution of her repentance. Blessed are ye before all men on the earth, because I have revealed unto you these mysteries. Amen, amen, I say unto you: I will perfect you in all fullness from the mysteries of the interior to the mysteries of the exterior and fill you with the spirit, so that ye shall be called 'spiritual, perfected in all fullness.' And, amen, amen, I say unto you: I will give unto you all the mysteries of all the regions of my Father and of all the regions of the First Mystery, so that he whom ye shall admit on earth, shall be admitted into the Light of the height; and he whom he ye shall expel on earth, shall be expelled from the kingdom of my Father in the heaven. But hearken, therefore, and give ear attentively to all the repentance which Pistis Sophia hath uttered. She continued again and uttered the third repentance, saying..."

The inner Christ always instructs Peter.

The inner Christ reveals the mysteries to Peter.

The inner Christ has the power in order to perfect Peter in all his splendor.

The Lord gives all the mysteries of all the regions of the Father and all the regions of the First Mystery to the interior Peter within each one of us.

Consequently, the secret Peter of each one of us is interesting. He, who Peter admits on earth, shall be admitted into the Light of the height, and he who Peter expels on earth, shall be expelled from the Kingdom of the Father in heaven.

It is clear that Peter is the Hierophant of sex within us. Therefore, he has the power to open or to close the doors of heaven in ourselves and within us.

Verily, verily, I say unto you that Peter holds the keys of the Kingdom.

The secret power that opens or closes the doors of Eden is in sex.

The sexual energy, when correctly orientated, opens the doors of paradise.

The creative energy, when incorrectly orientated, closes the doors of paradise.

Sulphur and Mercury are the two keys of the kingdom.

These two keys, one of gold and the other of silver, form a cross in the hands of Peter.

The third repentance of Sophia

1. *O Light of powers, give heed and save me.*

2. *May they who would take away my light, lack and be in the darkness. May they who would take away my power, turn into chaos and be put to shame.*

3. *May they turn quickly to darkness, who press me sore and say: We have become lords over her.*

4. *May rather all those who seek the Light, rejoice and exult, and they who desire thy mystery, say ever: May the mystery be exalted.*

5. *Save me then now, O Light, for I lacked my light, which they have taken away, and I needed my power, which they have taken from me. Thou then, O Light, thou art my saviour, and thou art my deliverer, O Light. Save me quickly out of this chaos.*

The Father of all Lights attends to us and saves us. The tenebrous ones steal the Light from us. This Light is found bottled up within the tenebrous ones, who are the living personifications of our psychological defects.

The tenebrous ones believe themselves to be lords of Sophia.

The diverse parts of the Being search for the Light, and wish for the mystery of Sophia. They wish for Sophia to be exalted.

Only the Light can take Sophia away from the Chaos.

The Ancient of Days can save Sophia and conduce her away from the darkness to the Light, by means of His Son, the inner Christ, the Redeemer.

The Savior can save Sophia. He takes her from the Chaos, and carries her to the Thirteenth Aeon.

Chapter 38

And it came to pass, when Jesus had finished speaking these words unto his disciples, saying: "This is the third repentance of Pistis Sophia," that he said unto them: "Let him in whom a sensitive spirit hath arisen, come forward and speak the thought of the repentance which Pistis Sophia hath uttered."

The third repentance of Pistis Sophia is sublime.

When the sensitive Spirit arises within us, then we can speak of the third repentance of Pistis Sophia.

Martha asketh and receiveth permission to speak

It came to pass then, before Jesus had finished speaking, that Martha came forward, fell down at his feet, kissed them, cried aloud and wept with lamentation and in humbleness, saying: "My Lord, have mercy upon me and have compassion with me, and let me speak the solution of the repentance which Pistis Sophia hath uttered."

And Jesus gave his hand unto Martha and said unto her: "Blessed is every one who humbleth himself, for on him they shall have mercy. Now, therefore, Martha, art thou blessed. But proclaim then the solution of the thought of the repentance of Pistis Sophia."

Martha, within us, is that part of our Being who represents the virtue of humbleness.

Three types of relations are indispensable. First, the relation with our own body, second, the relation with the environment and third, the relation with our own Self.

If we do not know how to relate with our body wisely, then we become ill.

If we do not know how to relate with the environment which surrounds us, then we create many conflicts for ourselves.

If we do not know how to correctly relate ourselves with the distinct parts of the Being, then the true illumination is more than impossible.

The proud, the conceited, and the vain ones, can never wisely relate with the superior parts of the Being.

Only Martha, humbleness, can proclaim the solution of the repentance of Sophia.

Martha interpreteth the third repentance from Psalm LXIX [Modern Psalm 70]

And Martha answered and said unto Jesus in the midst of the disciples: "Concerning the repentance which Pistis Sophia hath uttered, O my Lord Jesus, of it thy light-power in David prophesied afore time in the sixty-ninth Psalm, saying:

1. O Lord God, give heed to my help.

2. Let them be put to shame and confounded who seek after my soul.

3. May they turn straightway and be put to shame, who say unto me: Ha, ha.

4. May all who seek thee, be joyful and exult because of thee, and they who love thy salvation, say ever, May God be exalted.

5. But I am wretched, I am poor; O Lord, help me. Thou art my helper and defence; O Lord, delay not.

"This then is the solution of the third repentance which Pistis Sophia hath uttered, singing praises to the height."

We need to be helped by the superior part of the Being.

If He would not help us, we would surely fail, and if we fail, He also fails.

Those who pursue the Soul must be put to shame.

The ensemble of inhuman elements that we carry within our interior are precisely the pursuers of the Soul.

The red demons of Seth must be put to shame, confounded, and destroyed.

Only the diverse parts of the Being search for the inner Christ.

In reality, we are poor and wretched. Nevertheless, the interior Lord can save us.

He will work from the depth of our Soul, truly experiencing all the cosmic drama.

Chapter 39

It came to pass then, when Jesus had heard Martha speak these words, that he said unto her: "Well said, Martha, and finely."

And Jesus continued again in the discourse and said unto his disciples: "Pistis Sophia again continued in the fourth repentance, reciting it before she was oppressed a second time, in order that the lion-faced power and all the material emanations with it, which Self-willed had sent into the chaos, might not take away her total light in her. She uttered then this repentance as follows..."

The Lion-faced or bestial-faced power, and its emanations, makes Pistis Sophia suffer.

Self-willed, the ego, steals the Light from Pistis Sophia.

While the multiple, undesirable elements that personify our psychological defects exist within us, it is clear that there will be pain.

It is not possible for happiness to be within each one of us, while the elements of unhappiness exist in our interior.

The Essence, bottled up within all the subjective elements of misfortune, will process itself in virtue of its own embottlement.

The subjective elements of perceptions are precisely the entire variety of inhuman psychic elements that we carry in our interior.

The marvellous, integral, unitotal, complete, illuminated perception of Reality comes when we destroy the subjective elements of perceptions. These are the living personifications of our errors.

Material emanations of the Lion-faced or bestial-faced power, and the ego, are precisely not only the variety of undesirable psychic elements, but moreover, they are also the personality.

Obviously, the personality must also be annihilated, and reduced to cosmic dust.

The personality is never homogeneous.

The personality has many heterogeneous, subjective depths.

The personality is multiple.

Karma is deposited within the personality.

The personality is Dry Mercury and Arsenic or poisonous Sulphur. This is known by the workers of the Great Work.

The personality interferes between the body and the Being.

The personality serves as an obstacle for illumination.

All subjective interference will conclude when the personality and the ego are destroyed, and the Being will resurrect within us in order to express Himself in all His plenitude.

The resurrected Being expresses Himself with wisdom, love, and power.

The Lion-faced and its emanations, Self-willed and its perversity, torture Pistis Sophia.

The fourth repentance of Sophia

1. *O Light, in whom I have trusted, give ear to my repentance, and let my voice reach unto thy dwelling-place.*

2. *Turn not away thy light-image from me, but have heed unto me, if they oppress me; and save me quickly at the time when I shall cry unto thee.*

3. *For my time is vanished like a breath and I am become matter.*

4. They have taken my light from me, and my power is dried up. I have forgotten my mystery which heretofore I was wont to accomplish.

5. Because of the voice of the fear and the power of Self-willed my power is vanished.

6. I am become as a demon apart, who dwelleth in matter and light is not in him, and I am become as a counterfeiting spirit, which is in a material body and light-power is not in it.

7. And I am become as a decan who is alone in the air.

8. The emanations of Self-willed have sore oppressed me, and my pair hath said unto himself:

9. Instead of with light which was in her, they have filled her with chaos. I have devoured the sweat of my own matter and the anguish of the tears from the matter of my eyes, so that they who oppress me may not take the rest.

10. All this hath befallen me, O Light, by thy commandment and they command, and it is thy commandment that I am here.

11. Thy commandment hath brought me down, and I am descended as a power of the chaos, and my power is numbed in me.

12. But thou, O Lord, art Light eternal, and dost visit them who are for ever oppressed.

13. Now, therefore, O light, arise and seek my power and the soul in me. Thy commandment is accomplished, which thou didst decree for me in my afflictions. My time is come, that thou shouldst seek my power and my soul, and this is the time which thou didst decree to seek me.

14. For thy saviours have sought the power which is in my soul, because the number is completed, and in order that also its matter may be saved.

15. And then at that time shall all the rulers of the material aeons be in fear of thy light, and all the emanations of the thirteenth material aeon shall be in fear of the mystery of thy light, so that the others may put on the purification of their light.

16. For the Lord will seek the power of your soul. He hath revealed his mystery,

17. So that he may regard the repentance of them who are in the regions below; and he hath not disregarded their repentance.

18. This is then that mystery which is become the type in respect of the race which shall be born; and the race which shall be born will sing praises to the height.

19. For the Light hath looked down from the height of its light. It will look down on the total matter,

20. To hear the sighing of those in chains, to loose the power of the souls whose power is bound, —

21. So that it may lay its name of the soul and its mystery in the power.

Pistis Sophia cries out within the initiate. She asks the Father of all the Lights for help.

The red demons of Seth oppress Pistis Sophia.

The Light of Pistis Sophia, identified with the inhuman elements of matter, suffers immensely.

The tenebrous ones have taken the Light and the power from Pistis Sophia.

The red demons of Seth, within us, embitter Pistis Sophia.

Thus, Sophia forgets the mystery that must be accomplished, the great mystery of the inner Self-realization.

Fear is the worst enemy of Pistis Sophia.

Men kill each other because of fear.

Nations arm themselves and go to war because of fear.

We mistrust people because of fear.

Espionage and perversity exist because of fear.

There exists thieves and prostitutes because of the fear of life.

The aspirants flee and part from the real path because of fear.

Frontiers, documents and restrictions of all types, which interrupt the journeys of people, are due to fear.

Fear is the cause of thousands of personal and collective conflicts.

The fallen initiate, lacking Light, and with Pistis Sophia within his interior, appears like a demon.

The fallen aspirant, although he has a physical body, lacks Light and power.

A decan, alone in the air, is the initiate who is fallen in the mud.

Pistis Sophia is oppressed by the ego, the Self-willed, and in general by all of its undesirable psychic elements, within which the consciousness of the initiate is found bottled up.

The Soul, wisdom, Pistis Sophia, suffers immensely.

Sophia hides the sweetness of her own Essence and the anguish of her eyes within herself, so that the tenebrous ones cannot take the rest of her Light.

How bitter is the fate of Sophia, the Soul, the Being, after the fall.

The Father of all Lights knows how we have suffered, and by His command and in accordance with the law, we are here.

We have broken the law, and we must suffer the consequences.

The human beings, devolving within the Chaos, suffer the inexpressible.

Nevertheless, Christ, the Ancient of Days, can save us.

When incarnated in the Venustic Initiation, Christ works terrifically from within the initiate, in order to liberate the fallen Soul, Pistis Sophia.

The inner Christ, the Son of the Father of all the Lights, must seek Pistis Sophia in order to save her.

The adepts of the Great Light also seek Pistis Sophia, who is hidden within the initiate, in order to help her.

By helping, the Redeemers help themselves.

Give and you shall be given. The more you give, the more you shall be given, but whosoever gives nothing, even that which he has shall be taken away from him.

The Rulers of the Aeons fear the mysteries of the Light. How difficult it is to ascend to the Thirteenth Aeon.

The fear of the Rulers in the presence of the Thirteenth Aeon is clear.

The initiate who attains the arrival to the Thirteenth Aeon is very rare.

The inner Christ will seek the power of your Soul. He will reveal the great mysteries to you, so that you can arrive at the Thirteenth Aeon.

It is not possible to arrive at the Thirteenth Aeon without previously passing through the Buddhist Annihilation.

Whosoever wishes to arrive at the Thirteenth Aeon must previously disintegrate the entire variety of undesirable psychic elements that we carry within our interior.

Pistis Sophia, bottled up within the psychic aggregates, is processed in virtue of her own bottled up state.

Whosoever wishes to arrive at the Thirteenth Aeon must disintegrate within himself not only the psychic aggregates of evil, but also the psychic aggregates of good.

We must pass beyond good and evil.

Unquestionably, the Soul can observe the repentance of the inferior parts of itself from the Thirteenth Aeon.

The inferior parts of our own Being, placed in the inferior levels, also have the right of repentance.

This is Gnosis, the Christic mystery, the fundamental doctrine that will shine gloriously in the future Sixth Great Root Race, following the great catastrophe which is approaching.

In the Golden Age, the Light will shine above the future race.

Gnosis will illuminate the consciousness and will liberate the oppressed.

The inner Christ will place His name in the Soul, and the sacred mystery in the real power.

Then, the Solar dynasties will govern the populations, and the entire Earth will be a paradise.

The future Root Race will reside in new continents, because the present continents will remain at the bottom of the seas, after being burned by ardent fire.

The gigantic planet known as Hercolubus is approaching now. It is a world thousands of times larger than the Earth.

Obviously, when Hercolubus is excessively close to the Earth, it will attract the liquid fire from the interior of the world towards the surface, and then all that which is alive will be burned.

A complete revolution of the axis of the Earth will take place upon the maximum approach of Hercolubus.

The poles will then be converted into the equator, and the equator into the poles.

The oceans will change ground, and the present continents will be on the bottom of the oceans.

A small group will be saved, so they can serve as a seed plot for the future Sixth Root Race.

This group will also be mixed with people from other worlds for their complete regeneration.

The new race of Pistis Sophia can only come from a strong and regenerated group.

Chapter 40

John asketh and receiveth permission to speak

It came to pass while Jesus spake these words unto his disciples, saying unto them: "This is the fourth repentance which Pistis Sophia hath uttered; now, therefore, let him who understandeth, understand,"

—it came to pass then, when Jesus had spoken these words, that John came forward, adored the breast of Jesus and said unto him: "My Lord, give commandment to me also, and grant me to speak the solution of the fourth repentance which Pistis Sophia hath uttered."

Jesus said unto John: "I give thee commandment, and I grant thee to speak the solution of the repentance which Pistis Sophia hath uttered."

John answered and said: "My Lord and Saviour, concerning this repentance which Pistis Sophia hath uttered, thy light-power which was in David, hath prophesied afore time in the one-hundred-and-first Psalm [Modern Psalm 102]*..."*

John, within us, is the Verb, the Word, an autonomous and self-cognizant part of our own Being.

The Light-Power that was in David, which means the Christ-power that was in David, prophesied centuries ago through the one-hundred-and-first Psalm.

Christ, the inner Christ, was also in David and within David.

Unquestionably, the inner Christ is the Instructor of the world.

Each one of the serfs of the Lord sigh for their Philosophical Stone, and they feel pity for the multitudes.

A psychological country exists within each one of us, which is populated by all of the psychic aggregates which we carry within our interior.

The people know the place in which they are situated at each given moment, yet they disgracefully ignore the psychological place in which they are situated.

There are those who live situated in brothels and taverns, or in filthy places of their psychological countries, and they lamentably ignore it.

Even though it seems incredible, the fact is that there are some very worthy and virtuous spouses who live within their homes in the physical world, yet psychologically, they are found situated in brothels.

Honest and decent gentlemen with magnificent records are found psychologically situated within the suburbs, towns, and streets of gangsters, thieves, and bandits.

All of this is due to those psychic aggregates that we carry within our interior.

By disintegrating those psychic aggregates, living personifications of our psychological defects, we will firmly establish ourselves in the heaven of our psychological country, which means, in the superior levels of our own Being, here and now.

By disintegrating the psychic aggregates is how we will make a master work of our own life.

The psychological country of each one of us fears the name of the Lord, and the Kings of the Earth. The red demons of Seth, the living personifications of our psychological defects, fear the sovereignty of the inner Christ.

The red demons of Seth know very well that the sovereignty of the Lord signifies their death.

The Lord will build Zion, which means, our interior universe, the existential superior bodies of the Being, and He will also reveal Himself in His sovereignty.

The Lord never despises the prayer of the humble one.

All of this will be understood by the future generation, the new Root Race that will be born in a newly transformed Earth, following the great cataclysm.

John interpreteth the repentance from Psalm CI [Modern Psalm 102]

1. *Lord, give ear unto my supplication, and let my voice reach unto thee.*

2. *Turn not away thy face from me; incline thine ear unto me in the day when I am oppressed; quickly give ear to me on the day when I shall cry unto thee.*

3. *For my days are vanished as smoke, and my bones are parched as stone.*

4. *I am scorched as the grass, and my heart is dried up; for I have forgotten to eat my bread.*

5. *From the voice of my groaning my bones cleaved to my flesh.*

6. *I am become as a pelican in the desert; I am become as a screech-owl in the house.*

7. *I have passed the night watching; I am become as a sparrow alone on the roof.*

8. *My enemies have reviled me all the day long, and they who honour me, have injured me.*

9. *For I have eaten ashes instead of my bread and mixed my drink with tears.*

10. *Because of thy wrath and thy rage; for thou hast lifted me up and cast me down.*

11. *My days have declined as a shadow, and I am dried up as the grass.*

12. *But thou, O Lord, thou endurest forever, and thy remembrance unto the generation of generations[s].*

13. *Arise and have mercy upon Zion, for the time is come to have mercy upon her; the proper time is come.*

14. *Thy servants have longed for her stones, and will take pity on her land.*

15. *And the nations will have fear of the name of the Lord, and the kings of the earth have fear of thy sovereignty.*

16. *For the Lord will build up Zion and reveal himself in his sovereignty.*

17. *He hath regarded the prayer of the humble and hath not despised their supplication.*

18. *This shall be recorded for another generation, and the people who shall be created will praise the Lord.*

19. Because he hath looked down on his holy height; the Lord hath looked down from the heaven on the earth,

20. To hear the sighing of those in chains, to loose the sons of those who are slain,

21. To proclaim the name of the Lord in Zion and his praise in Jerusalem."

"This, my Lord, is the solution of the mystery of the repentance which Pistis Sophia hath uttered."

The future race will understand these teachings and will praise the inner Christ.

The inner Christ helps us from within.

The Logos hears the sighing and supplications of those in chains.

The name of the Lord will shine in Zion.

The name of the Lord will glorify Jerusalem.

Zion as a real Man, and Jerusalem as a Solar Man or Super-Man, will shine in the Lord.

Chapter 41

Jesus commendeth John

It came to pass then, when John had finished speaking these words to Jesus in the midst of his disciples, that he said unto him: "Well said, John, the Virgin, who shalt rule in the kingdom of the Light."

John, the Virgin, the Verb, rules in the Kingdom of the Light.

I-E-O-U-A-N, Jeouan, John, is the Word, the Army of the Voice, the collective Host of the Creator Elohim.

> *In the beginning was the Word* (Verb), *and the Word* (Verb) *was with God, and the Word* (Verb) *was God.* - John 1:1

The Army of the Creator Elohim, the Logos, the Verb, creates with the power of the Word.

> *All things were made by Him; and without Him was not anything made that was made.* - John 1:3

The Logos sounds; this is written.

The Elohim created the universe by virtue of the Verb, and with the Verb.

The Army of the Voice, by virtue of the luminous and spermatic fiat of the first instant, created the universe.

The luminous and spermatic fiat of the first instant gave life to all that which is, has been, and will be.

Nevertheless, the emanations of the ego oppress Pistis Sophia.

The emanations of Self-willed again squeeze the light out of Sophia

And Jesus continued again in the discourse and said unto his disciples: "It came to pass again thus: The emanations of Self-willed again oppressed Pistis Sophia in the chaos and desired to take from her her whole light; and not yet was her commandment accomplished, to lead her out of the chaos, and not yet had the command reached me through the First Mystery, to save her out of the chaos. It came to pass then, when all the material emanations of Self-willed oppressed her, that she cried out and uttered the fifth repentance, saying..."

Only the command of the Ancient of Centuries can save Pistis Sophia and take her out of the Chaos.

The fifth repentance of Sophia

1. *Light of my salvation, I sing praise unto thee in the region of the height and again in the chaos.*

2. *I sing praise unto thee in my hymn with which I sang praise in the height and with which I sang praise unto thee when I was in the chaos. Let it come into thy presence, and give heed, O Light, to my repentance.*

3. *For my power is filled up with darkness, and my light hath gone down into the chaos.*

4. I am myself become as the rulers of the chaos, who are gone into the darknesses below; I am become as a material body, which hath no one in the height who will save it.

5. I am become also as matters from which their power hath been taken, when they are cast down into the chaos, —[matters] which thou hast not saved, and they are condemned utterly by thy commandment.

6. Now, therefore, have they put me into the darkness below, —in darknesses and matters which are dead and in them [is] no power.

7. Thou hast brought thy commandment upon me and all things which thou hast decreed.

8. And thy spirit hath withdrawn and abandoned me. And moreover by thy commandment the emanations of my aeon have not helped me and have hated me and separated themselves from me, and yet am I not utterly destroyed.

9. And my light is diminished in me, and I have cried up to the light with all the light in me, and I have stretched forth my hands unto thee.

10. Now, therefore, O Light, wilt thou now accomplish thy commandment in the chaos, and will not the deliverers, who come according to thy commandment, arise in the darkness and come and be disciples for thee?

11. Will they not utter the mystery of thy name in the chaos?

12. Or will they not rather utter thy name in a matter of the chaos, in which thou wilt not [thyself] purify?

13. But I have sung praises unto thee, O Light, and my repentance will reach unto thee in the height.

14. Let thy light come upon me.

15. For they have taken my light, and I am in pain on account of the Light from the time when I was emanated. And when I had looked into the height to the Light, then I looked down below at the light-power in the chaos; I rose up and went down.

16. Thy commandment came upon me, and the terrors, which thou didst decree for me, have brought me into delusion.

17. And they have surrounded me, in numbers as water, they have laid hold on me together all my time.

18. And by thy commandment thou hast not suffered my fellow-emanations to help me, nor hast thou suffered my pair to save me out of my afflictions.

"This then is the fifth repentance which Pistis Sophia hath uttered in the chaos, when all the material emanations of Self-willed had continued and oppressed her."

Pistis Sophia sings praises to the Light of salvation, as much as in the Chaos as in the Heights.

The initiate of Pistis Sophia must fulfill what the Tablet of Hermes Trismegistus literally states in the following:

> *It is true, no lie, certain, and to be depended upon, the superior agrees with the inferior, and the inferior with the superior, to affect One Truly Wonderful Work.*
>
> *As all things owe their existence to the will of the Only One, so all things owe their origin to the One Only Thing, the most hidden, by the arrangement of the Only God.*
>
> *The Father of that One Only Thing is the Sun, its Mother is the Moon, the Wind carried it in its belly; but its Nourse is a Spirituous Earth. That One Only Thing is the Father of all things in the universe. Its power is perfect, after it had been united to Spirituous Earth.*
>
> *Separate that Spirituous Earth from the dense or crude by means of gentle heat, with much attention.*
>
> *In great measure it ascends from the Earth up to Heaven, and descends again, newborn, on the Earth, and the superior and the inferior are increased in power.*

> *By this thou wilt partake of the honours of the whole world. And darkness will fly from thee.*
>
> *This is the strength of all powers. With this thou wilt be able to overcome all things, and to transmute all what is fine and what is coarse.*
>
> *In this manner the World was created; the arrangements to follow this road are Hidden. For this reason I am called Hermes Trismegistus, One in Essence, but Three in Aspect, in this Trinity is Hidden the Wisdom of the whole World.*
>
> *It is completed now, what I have said concerning the effects of the Sun.*

The initiate suffers immensely in the Chaos below, within the darknesses of the No-Being.

The darkness below is frightful.

The Rulers who are below, within the darknesses of the No-Being, know how Pistis Sophia suffers.

Many are the matters that are absolutely condemned within us.

The adept, charged with Pistis Sophia, ascends and descends when it is necessary.

At times, the initiate must remain in the abyss for a lengthy period of time, working in the super-obscurity and in the august silence of the wise.

Light emerges from darkness, and the cosmos emerges from the Chaos.

The wise, within the darkness below, live within the matters that are dead and lacking of power.

However, such matters believe themselves to be alive and powerful.

I am emphatically referring to the demons of the Averno.

The inner Christ has performed his command in the heart of the adepts who descend into the tenebrous kingdom of Pluto, in order to work in the Great Work.

When the adepts descend into the Tartarus, they remove themselves from the inner Christ, and they suffer inexpressibly.

Pistis Sophia cried for the Light when she found herself in the Averno.

The Light always fulfills its command in the Chaos.

The Deliverers are the superior parts of the Being who visit the adept in the Averno in order to instruct him.

Obviously, each ascent is anteceded by a descent, and every mystic exaltation is preceded by a frightful and terrible humiliation.

No one can ascend without previously having taken the trouble to descend.

The mystery of the secret name of each one of us is terribly divine.

Abominable matters, which are at times heroic and bountiful with many merits, exist within us. Yet, they can never purify themselves. Therefore, they must be disintegrated in the Abyss.

The initiate in the Averno, charged with Pistis Sophia, sings praises unto the Light and his repentance ascends unto the Father.

The Light must inundate the workers of the Great Work, who suffer in the tenebrous kingdom of Pluto.

May the power of the Light reach into the Chaos for the good of the wise, who work within the august, super-obscurity of the great mysteries.

May the terrors of the Abyss not confuse the wise. This is our longing.

The terrors of the infernal worlds, within the womb of the Earth, are multifaceted.

The diverse, autonomous, and self-cognizant parts of our own Being must help the adepts.

Buddhi, Dante's Beatrice, the beautiful Helen of Troy, the Spiritual Soul, must help the adept.

Fortunate is the adept who is helped by his Valkyrie.

Blessed is the adept who is helped by Guinevere, the Queen of the Jinn Knights, She, who poured wine for Lancelot into cups of Sukra and Manti.

This is the wine of transcendental sexuality, glistening within the chalice of all delights.

Chapter 42

When then Jesus had spoken these words unto his disciples, he said unto them: "Who hath ears to hear, let him hear; and let him whose spirit seetheth up in him, come forward and speak the solution of the thought of the fifth repentance of Pistis Sophia."

Philip, the Apostle of Jesus, exists within us, here and now.

Philip assists the invoker and takes him out in his Astral Body.

These invokers usually receive multiple benefits.

These types of invocations are performed when we place ourselves in normal sleep.

Philip can also take the invoker with his physical body into the Jinn state.

The key of the invocation is: *"To the little heaven, Philip."*

Repeat this phrase thousands of times.

If we wish to take the physical body, we pray to Philip for this service.

If you wish to take only the Astral Body, you pray to Philip for this service.

We must speak to Philip; we must beg Philip.

In order to go out into the astral, we need to be a little sleepy.

In order to carry the physical body into the Jinn State, less sleepiness is required, and a great deal of faith.

The reader must study our *Yellow Book*.

The historical Philip is one, yet the inner Philip is another. Each one of us has his own inner Philip.

The twelve Apostles are the Twelve Powers within us.

The twelve Apostles are the twelve parts of our own Being.

We repeat this for the good of our devotees.

Philip the scribe complaineth

And when Jesus had finished saying these words, Philip started forward, held up and laid down the book in his hand, —for he is the scribe of all the discourses which Jesus spake, and of all of that which he did, —Philip then came forward and said unto him: "My Lord, surely then it is not on me alone that thou hast enjoined to take care for the world and write down all the discourses which we shall speak and [all we shall] do? And thou hast not suffered me to come forward to speak the solution of the mysteries of the repentance of Pistis Sophia. For my spirit hath oft times seethed in me and been unloosed and constrained me to come forward and speak the solution of the repentance of Pistis Sophia; and I could not come forward because I am the scribe of all the discourses."

Philip always writes down the words of the inner Christ.

Philip is the scribe of all the discourses.

Jesus explaineth that the appointed scribes are Philip, Thomas and Matthew

It came to pass then, when Jesus had heard Philip, that he said unto him: "Hearken Philip, blessed one, that I may discourse with thee; for it is thou and Thomas and Matthew on whom it is enjoined by the First Mystery to write all the discourses which I shall speak and [all which I shall] do, and all things which ye shall see. But as for thee, the number of the discourses which thou hast to write, is so far not yet completed. When it is then completed, thou art to come forward and proclaim what pleaseth thee. Now, therefore, ye three have to write down all the discourses which I shall speak and [all things which I shall] do and which ye shall see, in order that ye may bear witness to all things of the kingdom of heaven."

Philip, Thomas, and Matthew—these three Apostles within us—obey the orders of the First Mystery and write down the discourses of the inner Christ.

Besides writing all of that which the inner Christ says, sees, and does, the three parts of the Being—Philip, Thomas and Matthew—also have the power to see and hear the things of the Lord.

Philip, Thomas, and Matthew are the three witnesses of the things of the Kingdom of Heaven.

Philip, Thomas, and Matthew are really the three parts of our own Being.

Chapter 43

Mary interpreteth the words of Jesus concerning the three witnesses

When then Jesus had said this, he said unto his disciples: "Who hath ears to hear, let him hear."

Mary started forward again, stepped into the midst, placed herself by Philip and said unto Jesus: "My Lord, my in-dweller of light hath ears, and I am ready to hear with my power, and I have understood the word which thou hast spoken. Now, therefore, my Lord, hearken that I may discourse in openness, thou who hast said unto us: 'Who hath ears to hear, let him hear.'

"Concerning the word which thou hast spoken unto Philip: 'It is thou and Thomas and Matthew on whom it hath been enjoined to you three by the First Mystery, to write all the discourses of the kingdom of the Light and thereto to bear witness'; hearken, therefore, that I may proclaim the solution of this word. This is what thy light-power prophesied afore time through Moses: 'By two or three witnesses shall every matter be established.' The three witnesses are Philip and Thomas and Matthew."

All esoteric matters will be established by virtue of three witnesses.

It would be absurd to search for the three witnesses outside of ourselves.

Obviously, we must search for the three witnesses within ourselves, here and now.

In reality, the three mentioned Apostles enjoy that which is called Self-independence within us.

The Divine Mother Kundalini gives testimony of all these things.

Philip is now given permission to speak

It came to pass then, when Jesus had heard this word, that he said: "Well said, Mary, this is the solution of the word. Now, therefore, do thou, Philip, come forward and proclaim the solution of the fifth repentance of Pistis Sophia, and thereafter take thy seat and write all the discourses which I shall speak, until the number of thy portion which thou hast to write of the words of the kingdom of the Light is completed. Then shalt thou come forward and speak what thy spirit shall understand. But do thou then now proclaim the solution of the fifth repentance of Pistis Sophia."

And Philip answered and said unto Jesus: "My Lord, harken that I may speak the solution of her repentance. For thy power hath prophesied afore time concerning it through David in the eighty-seventh Psalm [Modern Psalm 88], *saying..."*

The interior, profound Lord is our Savior.

Philip comprehends all of this.

Philip possesses luminous powers in order to understand.

Philip possesses luminous powers in order to write.

Philip interpreteth the fifth repentance from Psalm LXXXVII [Modern Psalm 88]

1. *Lord, god of my salvation, by day and by night have I cried unto thee.*

2. *Let my weeping come before thee; incline thine ear to my supplication, O Lord.*

3. *For my soul is full of evil, my life hath drawn nigh to the world below.*

4. *I am counted among them who have gone down into the pit; I am become as a man who hath no helper.*

5. *The free among the dead are as the slain who are thrown away and sleep in tombs, whom thou no more rememberest, and they are destroyed through thy hands.*

6. *They have set me in a pit below, in darkness and shadow of death.*

7. *Thy wrath hath settled down upon me and all thy cares have come upon me. (Selah.)*

8. *Thou hast put away mine acquaintances far from me; they have made me an abomination for them. They have abandoned me, and I cannot go forth.*

9. *My eye hath become dim in my misery; I have cried unto thee, O Lord, the whole day and have stretched forth my hands unto thee.*

10. *Wilt thou not surely work thy wonders on the dead? Will not surely the physicians arise and confess thee?*

11. *Will they not surely proclaim thy name in the tombs,*

12. *And thy virtuousness in a land which thou hast forgotten?*

13. *But I have cried unto thee, O Lord, and my prayer shall reach thee early in the morning.*

14. *Turn not thy face away from me.*

15. For I am miserable, I am in sorrow from my youth up. And when I had exalted myself, I humbled myself and arose.

16. Thy angers are come upon me and thy terrors have brought me into delusion.

17. They have surrounded me as water; they have seized upon me the whole day long.

18. My fellows hast thou kept far from me and my acquaintances from my misery.

"This is then the solution of the mystery of the fifth repentance which Pistis Sophia hath uttered, when she was oppressed in the chaos."

The inner Christ is the Instructor of the world.

The inner Christ is our interior Savior.

Let us repent and cry for our errors.

In truth, all of us have been drawn to the inferior world.

We are among those who have descended into the infernal worlds.

Those who even believe themselves to be free are just victims of the ego.

We suffer horribly in the pit below, in the reign of Pluto below the crust of the Earth.

Fortunate is the one who attains death in himself, here and now.

He then will not undergo the Second Death.

Pistis Sophia can be liberated only by dying within ourselves, based on conscious works and voluntary sufferings.

The initiate who passes through the annihilation of himself reaches the total illumination.

The initiate is voluntarily placed in an inferior pit. He wishes to die; he wants to die.

The Lord can perform marvels with the dead.

Fortunate are those who die because they will arise within the Lord.

The name of the Lord will be proclaimed in the tombs of those who die within themselves.

We are poor and miserable, naked and perverse. However, we believe ourselves to be holy and powerful.

The interior, profound Lord advises the initiate.

We are surrounded by evil acquaintances, yet the Lord will eject from us those evil acquaintances.

Those evil acquaintances are within us.

Those evil acquaintances are the perverse psychic aggregates, which we carry in our interior.

Those perverse fellows are destroyed, thanks to the Lord.

Pistis Sophia is liberated when our perverse fellows are dead.

It would be worthless to possess all the erudition of this world, if we did not die within ourselves.

To crush the psychic aggregates is possible, but only in the forge of the Cyclops during the moment of the chemical coitus.

Man and woman, when sexually united, are surrounded by terrific cosmic forces.

Man and woman, when sexually united, are surrounded by those terrific forces that put the universe into existence.

Man is the positive force, woman is the negative force. The neutral force conciliates both of them.

If the three forces are directed against any psychic aggregate, then it is reduced to cosmic dust.

During the moment of the chemical coitus, the man must help his wife by taking her psychic aggregates as if they were his own.

The woman must take the psychic aggregates of her husband, as if they were her own.

Thus, the positive, negative, and neutral forces perfectly united are directed against any aggregate.

This is the key in order to disintegrate psychic aggregates.

Man and woman, when sexually united, must pray to the Virgin of the Sea, Devi Kundalini, asking for the disintegration of every psychic aggregate which previously has been deeply comprehended.

If the man wants to disintegrate a psychic aggregate—whether it be hatred, lust, jealousy, etc.—he will pray to the Divine Mother Kundalini, begging Her for the disintegration of the psychic aggregate. His wife will help him with the same prayer, as if the aggregate was her own.

As well, the man will proceed with the psychic aggregates of his wife, as if they were his own.

The totality of the forces of the man and the woman during the metaphysical copulation must be directed to the psychic aggregates of the man, and to the psychic aggregates of the woman.

Thus, we will put an end to the ego.

This is the key in order to liberate Pistis Sophia.

We must not forget that when the man and the woman are united during the chemical coitus they are truly, one divine, omnipotent and terrific androgyne.

Chapter 44

Philip is commended and continueth writing

It came to pass then, when Jesus had heard Philip speak these words, that he said: "Well said, Philip, well-beloved. Now, therefore, come take thy seat and write thy portion of all the discourses which I shall speak, and [of all things which I shall] do, and of all that thou shalt see." And forthwith Philip sat down and wrote.

It came to pass thereafter that Jesus continued again in the discourse and said unto his disciples: "Then did Pistis Sophia cry to the Light. It forgave her sin, in that she had left her region and gone down into the darkness. She uttered the sixth repentance, saying thus..."

The Father of all lights forgives Pistis Sophia's sin of having fallen into the darkness of the No-Being.

Pain reigns supremely within the darkness of the No-Being.

However, the descent is necessary in order to later re-ascend victoriously.

The victorious re-ascension implies total transformation.

The Phoenix Bird resurrects more powerful than before, more omnipotent, and terribly divine.

The sixth repentance of Sophia

1. *I have sung praises unto thee, O Light, in the darkness below.*

2. *Hearken unto my repentance, and may thy light give heed to the voice of my supplication.*

3. *O Light, if thou thinkest on my sin, I shall not be able to stand before thee, and thou wilt abandon me.*

4. *For thou, O Light, art my saviour; because of the light of thy name I have had faith in thee, O Light.*

5. *And my power hath had faith in thy mystery; and moreover my power hath trusted in the Light when it was among those of the height; and it hath trusted in it when it was in the chaos below.*

6. *Let all the powers in me trust in the Light when I am in the darkness below, and may they again trust in the Light if they come into the region of the height.*

7. *For it is [the Light] which hath compassion on us and delivereth us; and a great saving mystery is in it.*

8. *And it will save all powers out of the chaos because of my transgression. For I have left my region and am come down into the chaos.*

"Now, therefore, whose mind is exalted, let him understand."

The initiate sings praises unto the Great Light, even though he is working below, within the obscurity and the august silence of the wise.

Really, we need the forgiveness of the Great Light.

If the Light always thinks on our errors, then the Light would never forgive us, and we would never advance.

The Light of his name is the name of the Light that the Being of our Being possesses.

The Mystery of mysteries is experienced by conscious faith.

The initiate trusts in the Light when he finds himself among those who dwell in the heights.

The initiate trusts in the Light when he works in the super-obscurity and within the august silence of the wise.

All the autonomous and self-cognizant parts of our own individual Being must have complete trust in the inner Light, here and now.

When we work in the Abyss, we must have complete trust in the Light, and we must not dismay.

No one can ascend without having previously descended.

We must steal the Light from the darkness.

The Light pities us and guides us.

A great mystery of salvation exists within the Light.

The Light must carry all the powers of each one of us out of the Chaos.

It is understood that the powers are each one of the independent parts of the Being that descend into the Chaos and suffer.

Obviously, each one of the independent parts of our own individual Being must be perfected.

The twelve Apostles, which means the twelve parts of our Being, the Twelve Powers, must be perfected within ourselves, here and now.

People only want to know about the twelve historical Apostles, but they do not understand anything about the twelve parts of our own individual Being.

We must search for the twelve within ourselves.

It is urgent to perfect the twelve Apostles within us.

Let us remember that twelve are the foundations of the Celestial Jerusalem, and that the name of each one of the twelve is written in each foundation.

Thus, each one of the twelve names of the twelve Apostles corresponds to his corresponding foundation.

We must destroy Babylon the Great, the mother of all fornication and abominations of the Earth.

Obviously, Babylon is our psychological city, populated by the psychic aggregates that we carry within our interior.

We must build the Celestial Jerusalem within ourselves.

Twelve are the foundations of the Celestial Jerusalem.

The perfection of the twelve is possible only by disintegrating the psychic aggregates.

Rare is he whose mind has been saved.

The wall of the Celestial Jerusalem is constructed of 144 cubits, according to the measure of a man, that is, of an Angel.

If we make the addition of the numerals 144, we get nine.

Nine is the Kabbalistic number of the Ninth Sphere.

Nine is the sexual sphere.

The total disintegration of the psychic aggregates is possible only by working in the Ninth Sphere.

We liberate the Essence and we build the Celestial Jerusalem only by disintegrating the aggregates here and now.

Chapter 45

It came to pass then, when Jesus had finished speaking these words unto his disciples, that he said unto them: "Understand ye in what manner I discourse with you?"

Andrew came forward and said: "My Lord, concerning the solution of the sixth repentance of Pistis Sophia, thy light-power prophesied afore time through David in the one-hundred-and-twenty-ninth Psalm [Modern Psalm 130], *saying..."*

Andrew and his cross are something profoundly significant.

The cross of St. Andrew on which he died crucified is alchemical.

There are terrible psychological tortures through which we must pass in order to disintegrate the Dry Mercury, in other words, the psychic aggregates, which are the living personification of our psychological defects.

The Sulphur (fire) and Mercury (water) are crossed in the form of an "X," and they cross again incessantly in the Great Work.

The Mercury of the wise is the metallic soul of the sperm.

The metallic soul of the sperm must be fecundated by the Sulphur.

Andrew and his doctrine is the struggle for the disintegration of the psychic aggregates.

Andrew, with his cross, must crystallize the Sulphur and the Mercury in the form of the existential, superior bodies of the Being.

The Sulphur and the Mercury, crossed in the first octave, crystallize in the form of the Astral Body. In the second octave, they take the form of the Mental Body, and in the third octave, they take the form of the Causal Body.

It is indispensable to possess these bodies in order to receive the psychic principles and to convert ourselves into real human beings.

The interior Andrew perfects himself when the superior existential bodies of the Being have been perfected.

It is not possible to perfect these bodies unless we have previously eliminated the psychic aggregates, the living personification of our psychological defects.

Andrew must disintegrate the Dry Mercury and the Arsenic Sulphur.

Andrew must crystallize the prepared Philosophical Mercury.

Andrew suffers when disintegrating the Dry Mercury.

Christification would not be possible without the previous disintegration of the Dry Mercury.

When the existential bodies are perfected, they become pure Gold.

Creating the bodies is only one part. To perfect them is urgent and not to be delayed.

Andrew interpreteth the sixth repentance from Psalm CXXIX [Modern Psalm 130]

1. *Out of the depths I have cried unto thee, O Lord.*

2. *Hearken unto my voice; let thine ears give heed to the voice of my supplication.*

3. *O Lord, if thou heedest my iniquities, who will be able to pass [the test]?*

4. *For pardon is in thy hands; for the sake of thy name have I waited for thee, O Lord.*

5. *My soul hath waited for thy word.*

6. *My soul hath hoped in the Lord from the morning until the evening. Let Israel hope in the Lord from the morning until the evening.*

7. *For grace standeth by the Lord and with him is great redemption.*

8. *And he will deliver Israel from all his iniquities.*

The Ordeal of the Sanctuary is very difficult. Very few human beings are capable of passing such a terrible ordeal.

The interior profound Lord knows very well what our iniquities are. We will pass the terrible Ordeal of the Sanctuary by disintegrating these iniquities.

This ordeal contains in itself all of the ordeals.

In itself this ordeal is multiple ordeals.

The Omnimerciful forgives many errors, if we truly deserve forgiveness.

The Soul always waits for the word of the Lord.

It is not enough to hear the word, we must perform the word within ourselves, here and now.

Whosoever hears the word and does not perform it is like a man who sees his reflection in the mirror and turns and walks away.

The Soul awaits the interior, profound Lord.

Israel hopes for the Lord from morning until evening.

Israel is a word that must be analyzed.

"**Is**" reminds us of Isis and the Isiac mysteries.

"**Ra**" reminds us of the Solar Logos.

Let us remember the disc of **Ra** found in the ancient Egypt of the Pharaohs.

"**El**" is "El." "El" is the interior, profound God within each one of us.

In sequence and correct etymological corollary, the people of Israel are constituted by the various parts of the Being.

All of the multiple self-cognizant and independent parts of our own individual Being constitute the people of Israel.

The grace of the interior Lord falls upon us when, in reality, we have passed through the Buddhist Annihilation.

Jesus commendeth Andrew. He promiseth that the tyrants shall be judged and consumed by the wise fire

Jesus said unto him: "Well said, Andrew, blessed one. This is the solution of her repentance. Amen, amen, I say unto you: I will perfect you in all mysteries of the Light and all gnoses from the interiors of the interiors to the exteriors of the exteriors, from the Ineffable down to the darkness of darknesses, from the Light of lights down to the... of matter, from all the gods down to the demons, from all the lords down to the decans, from all the authorities down to the servitors, from the creation of men down to [that] of the wild-beasts, of the cattle and of the reptiles, in order that ye may be called perfect, perfected in all fullness. Amen, amen, I say unto you: In the region where I shall be in the kingdom of my Father, ye will also be with me. And when the perfect number is completed, so that the Mixture shall be dissolved, I will give commandment that they bring all tyrant gods, who have not given up the purification of their light, and will give commandment to the wise fire, over which the perfect pass, to eat into those tyrants, until they give up the last purification of their light."

Obviously, Andrew will perfect himself in the mysteries of the Light with his cross in an "X" and with his complicated and terribly difficult work, which is to crystallize that which must be crystallized and to disintegrate that which must be disintegrated.

The tortures of St. Andrew are sufficient for his purification.

Nevertheless, we must not forget our individual, interior Andrew.

Each one of us has his own Andrew.

Behold here what is terribly difficult, which is to perfect him from the interiors of the interiors to the exteriors of the exteriors.

In the Great Work, Andrew, suffering on the sexual cross, must perfect himself from the Ineffable down to the darkness of darknesses, from the Light of lights down to the darkness of matter, from all the Gods down to the demons.

Andrew must perfect himself by virtue of conscious works and voluntary sufferings, from all the lords down to the decans, from all the authorities down to the servitors, etc.

Each one of the parts of the Being must reach total, integral perfection.

Andrew is one of the autonomous and self-cognizant parts.

Andrew is integrated with the Father when perfected within each one of us.

Let us remember that we need to perfect each one of the twelve within ourselves, here and now.

The perfect number within each one of us is the sum total of all the autonomous and self-cognizant parts of our own individual Being.

There are the twelve, and the twenty-four, and the seven and the four, etc..

There exists within ourselves the Twelve Powers.

There exists within ourselves the twenty-four Elders of the Zodiac.

There exists within ourselves the four Devarajas, or the four elemental Genii, etc.

The lion of the law is within us.

Obviously, the Lord of time can give back the memories of our past lives.

Within each one of us is our own particular, individual Anubis. He applies the law of karma to us, within ourselves.

The Divine Mother Kundalini within ourselves has five aspects, allegorized by the white cow with five legs.

H.P.B. really did see an authentic white cow with five legs in India. There is no doubt that it carried the fifth leg on its back and with this leg it was scaring away the flies or scratching itself with it.

H.P.B. states that this curious creature of Nature was herded by a young boy from the Sadhu sect. This virgin boy nourished himself exclusively with the milk of this mysterious cow.

Within us is Minerva, She who gives us wisdom.

The Guardian of the Threshold is within us.

The Guardian of the Threshold can never be disintegrated, because it is part of our own individual Being.

The Guardian of the Threshold is a full length mirror that shows us the psychological state in which we find ourselves at each given moment.

We have the Guardian of the Threshold in the astral, mental, and causal planes.

There are three Guardians of the Threshold, three parts of our own individual Being.

Each one of the three parts is autonomous, individual, and self-cognizant.

There is a policeman of karma within us, within our consciousness. He conduces us before the tribunals of the law when we violate the law.

The Being is a true army that must be perfected and integrated.

The whole work is sexual. There is no other way.

The independent parts of the Being are many, and we must perfect each one of them.

We have not given notice to all the parts of the Being because we would need volumes in order to talk about them and their work.

When the Being becomes integrated and the horrifying mixture of the diverse, undesirable psychic elements which we carry within our interior become dissolved, then the perverse tyrants will fall.

The tyrants that we carry within our interior are the capital factors of our abominable psychic processes.

Mary interpreteth the words of Jesus

It came to pass then, when Jesus had finished speaking these words unto his disciples, that he said unto them: "Understand ye in what manner I speak with you?"

Mary said: "Yea, Lord, I have understood the word which thou hast spoken. Concerning then the word which thou hast said: At the dissolution of the whole Mixture thou shalt take thy seat on a light-power and thy disciples, that is ourselves, shall sit on the right of thee, and thou shalt judge the tyrant gods, who have not given up the purification of their light, and the wise fire will bite into them, until they give up the last light in them, —concerning this word then thy light-power prophesied afore time through David, in the eighty-first Psalm, saying:

"'God shall sit in the assembly (synagogue) of the gods and try the gods.'"

The Divine Mother Kundalini, Marah, Mary, the Woman-Serpent, knows very well that when the undesirable psychic elements that we carry within our interior are dissolved, then the inner Christ, being all Light and power, takes his place within our Soul.

All the disciples of the inner Christ reside within ourselves. They are precisely the diverse autonomous and self-cognizant parts of our own Being.

The tyrant gods are really those autonomous and independent parts of the Being who are bottled up in lights that are not the Christic Light. Yet, they persist in purifying their light, which is not the Light of the Lord.

For example, and in order to clarify the previous paragraph, we will say that in the world there are certain religious forms that lead only to a dead-end street. However, their parishioners persist in purifying and sanctifying themselves within these cages.

We must renounce these doctrines. We must have the courage to abandon these cages.

What is important is that which is within us.

Gnosis is knowledge. In Gnosis, Self-Gnosis is Self-knowledge.

The wise Fire will bite into the tyrant gods until they renounce the many doctrines that exist in the exterior world.

We must abandon all in order to arrive to the inner Christ.

When we say abandon all, we are referring in this case to the diverse, dead religious forms.

Someone can fight for his very own purification in a completely mistaken way.

We march correctly only on the path of Self-Gnosis.

God shall sit in the assembly (synagogue) of the gods and will submit them to a trial.

Jesus said unto her, "Well said, Mary."

Chapter 46

The repentance of Sophia is not yet accepted. She is mocked by the aeons

Jesus continued again in the discourse and said unto his disciples: "It came to pass, when Pistis Sophia had finished uttering the sixth repentance for the forgiveness of her transgression, that she turned again to the height, to see if her sins were forgiven her, and to see whether they would lead her up out of the chaos. But by commandment of the First Mystery not yet was she hearkened to, so that her sin should be forgiven and she should be led up out of the chaos. When then she had turned to the height to see whether her repentance were accepted from her, she saw all the rulers of the twelve aeons mocking at her and rejoicing over her because her repentance was not accepted from her. When then she saw that they mocked at her, she grieved exceedingly and lifted up her voice to the height in her seventh repentance, saying..."

The First Mystery submits the initiate to multiple ordeals, for his own good.

The initiate is incessantly tested.

The Rulers of the Twelve Aeons comprehend the necessity of the esoteric ordeals, and they cooperate with these ordeals, for the adept's own good.

The Rulers of the Twelve Aeons are within us, here and now.

The seventh repentance of Sophia

1. *O Light, I have lifted up my power unto thee, my Light.*

2. *On thee have I had faith. Let me not be scorned; let not the rulers of the twelve aeons, who hate me, rejoice over me.*

3. *For all who have faith in thee shall not be put to shame. Let them who have taken away my power, remain in darkness; and let them not get from it any profit, but let it be taken away from them.*

4. *O Light, show me thy ways, and I shall be saved in them; and show me thy paths, whereby I shall be saved out of the chaos.*

5. *And guide me in thy light, and let me know, O Light, that thou art my saviour. On thee will I trust the whole of my time.*

6. *Give heed that thou save me, O Light, for thy mercy endureth for ever.*

7. *As to my transgression, which I have committed from the beginning in my ignorance, put it not to my account, O Light, but rather save me through thy great mystery of the forgiveness of sins because of thy goodness, O Light.*

8. *For good and sincere is the Light. For this cause will it grant me my way, to be saved out of my transgression;*

9. *And for my powers, which are diminished through the fear of the material emanations of Self-willed, will it draw near after its commandment, and will teach my powers, which are diminished because of the merciless, its gnosis.*

10. *For all gnoses of the Light are saving means and are mysteries for all who seek the regions of its Inheritance and its mysteries.*

11. *For the sake of the mystery of thy name, O Light, forgive my transgression, for it is great.*

12. *To every one who trusteth in the Light it will give the mystery which suiteth him;*

13. And his soul will abide in the regions of the Light and his power will inherit the Treasury of the Light.

14. The Light giveth power to them who have faith in it; and the name of its mystery belongeth to those who trust in it. And it will show them the region of the Inheritance, which is in the Treasury of the Light.

15. But I have ever had faith in the Light, for it will save my feet from the bonds of the darkness.

16. Give heed unto me, O Light, and save me, for they have taken away my name from me in the chaos.

17. Because of all the emanations my afflictions and my oppression have become exceedingly manifold. Save me out of my transgression and this darkness.

18. And look upon the grief of my oppression and forgive my transgression.

19. Give heed to the rulers of the twelve aeons, who have hated me through jealousy.

20. Watch over my power and save me, and let me not remain in this darkness, for I have had faith in thee.

21. And they have made of me a great fool for having had faith in thee, O Light.

22. Now, therefore, O Light, save my powers from the emanations of Self-willed, by whom I am oppressed.

"Now, therefore, who is sober, let him be sober."

When then Jesus had spoken this unto his disciples, Thomas came forward and said: "My Lord, I am sober, I am plentifully sober, and my spirit is ready in me, and I rejoice exceedingly that thou hast revealed these words unto us. But indeed I have borne with my brethren until now, so that I should not anger them; nay rather I have borne with every one that he should come before thee and speak the solution of the repentance of Pistis Sophia. Now, therefore, my Lord, concerning the solution of the seventh repentance of Pistis Sophia thy Light-power hath prophesied through the prophet David in the twenty-fourth Psalm [Modern Psalm 25], *thus...*"

We must elevate the sexual power to the Great Light.

The initiate has faith in the Great Light.

Whosoever has faith in the Great Light is never placed in shame.

The tenebrous ones who take the power away from the initiate remain in darkness.

Those tenebrous ones are the undesirable psychic aggregates, living personifications of our psychological defects.

The Great Light has its paths and its secret path.

Straight is the gate, and narrow is the way which leads to the Light, and very few there be that find it.

The path that leads to the Great Light is difficult.

Only frightful abysses are seen on either side of the path.

Many are those who begin; rare are those who attain the arrival to the goal.

At times, the path is lost within the sands of the desert.

At times, the path is cut by a dangerous abyss.

At times, we must descend in order to later re-ascend.

Not one moral code and not one ethical precept serves a purpose on the difficult path.

On this difficult path, we must always take inventory of ourselves in order to know what is excessive in us, and to know of what we are lacking.

It is necessary to eliminate what is left over in us. We must obtain what we are lacking.

At times, a beautiful maxim or precious virtue can serve as an obstacle for us on the difficult path.

It is necessary to know good from evil and evil from good, and to pass beyond good and evil.

We must liberate ourselves from the powers of good and evil.

There is the need to grasp the sword of cosmic justice.

What is believed to be good is not always good.

What is believed to be evil is not always evil.

There is a great deal of virtue in the evil ones. There is a great deal of evil in the virtuous ones.

Virtue comes from the syllable ***vir***, ***virility***.

The precious gems of virtues are obtained only with virility.

Sexual virility, sexual potency is necessary to obtain virtues in the flaming forge of Vulcan.

Each time that a psychic aggregate is dissolved a precious virtue emerges within ourselves.

The interior, profound Savior is Light and we must trust in Him.

Only the inner Christ, who is Light, can save us.

Sexual transgression occurred when we ate the fruit of which was said to us: *"You shall not eat."*

Christ, being the supreme obedience of the Father, opposes Himself to the supreme disobedience of the sinful Adam and He saves us.

The great mystery of the forgiveness of sins is related to sex.

Only the one who works in the Great Work deserves to be forgiven.

We deserve the forgiveness of these or those faults, when their corresponding inhuman elements are dissolved within us.

Certain psychic aggregates are found related to the law of karma.

Obviously, they can be disintegrated by paying their price.

Undoubtedly, these aggregates are disintegrated based on conscious works and voluntary sufferings.

In order to be saved from the great transgression, the Light gives us the manner, the way, and the system or method.

The material emanations of the ego have damaged the human faculties.

In ancient times, humanity perceived the aura of the worlds and communicated with other inhabitants of the planetary spheres.

The human beings on the Lemurian continent (located in the Pacific Ocean in previous times) perceived the mysteries of life and death directly by themselves.

We fell into animal generation with sexual transgression. Then, within each one of us the ego emerged.

The ego is a compound of diverse psychic aggregates.

The faculties of internal perception of the human being became atrophied when the Essence was kept bottled up within the psychic aggregates.

Thus, the material emanations of the Self-willed ego damaged the internal faculties.

Since then, human beings have been trapped in this painful world.

Our internal faculties will victoriously emerge by dissolving the psychic aggregates.

All of the knowledge contained in the Light corresponds to the mysteries.

The mysteries of the Light lead us to the final liberation.

The lost Inheritance is the Treasury of the Light, which is hidden within ourselves, here and now.

The mystery of the name is the very same mystery of the Verb.

Each one of us has his own sacred name.

Whosoever trusts in the great Light will receive initiation into the mysteries.

Fortunate is the one who by means of the initiations into the mysteries succeeds in converting himself into an inhabitant of the Region of the Light.

Those who submerge themselves within the Ocean of the great Light possess the power and the Treasury of the Light.

Only the Light can save our feet from the bonds of darkness.

Whosoever has faith in the Light will be saved from the darkness.

In the Chaos below, even the sacred name is forgotten.

The afflictions have become exceedingly manifold, due to the psychic aggregates.

Only the Light can save us from sin and from the darkness.

The Rulers of the Twelve Aeons are very jealous, in a spiritual sense.

In no way can they accept any psychic element within ourselves. This signifies that they are very strict within us.

Only the Great Light can save us and fortify the powers of the Soul.

The initiate has faith in the Light.

The Rulers of the Aeons mock us within ourselves, and they growl at us when we are working, or beginning to work on ourselves.

The Rulers of the Aeons say to us: "*Ah! At last you want to come to the Light? Do you want to disintegrate in an instant that which gave you pleasure for so many centuries???*" Etc., etc., etc..

"*How dare you ask to be helped to disintegrate in one moment of repentance that which you have enjoyed for so long?*"

This is how the Rulers of the Aeons speak when they mock us. This is how Pistis Sophia suffers.

Only the Great Light can save our intimate powers from the emanations of the Self-willed ego.

Being sober signifies being comprehensive, in the integral sense of the word.

Thomas is the part of the Being who is related to the intimate sense of comprehension.

A great deal of analysis, reflection, and above all, meditation and evident self-reflection of the Being are indispensable for comprehension.

Any psychological defect discovered through psychological Self-observation must be previously comprehended in all the levels of the mind before proceeding to its disintegration.

When one accepts the fact that he has his own psychological idiosyncrasy, he then begins to Self-observe himself from instant to instant.

Self-discovery is possible only through Self-observation.

Self-revelation exists in all self-discovery.

Then, Thomas is cognition, comprehension, and infinite patience.

The brothers of Thomas are eleven in number, and even more. They are all the autonomous and self-cognizant parts of the Being.

Unquestionably, all the parts of the Being are obliged to work in the inner Self-realization of the Being.

The work of Thomas is very patient, because he is obliged to provide that which is called comprehension.

Each part of the Being gives its solution to the repentance of the Soul. However, only Thomas gives the last word.

Thomas interpreteth the seventh repentance from Psalm XXIV [Modern Psalm 25]

1. *O Lord, unto thee have I lifted up my soul, O my God.*

2. *I have abandoned myself unto thee; let me not be put to shame and let not mine enemies mock at me.*

3. *For all who wait upon thee shall not be put to shame; let them be put to shame who do iniquity without a cause.*

4. *O Lord, show me thy ways and teach me thy paths.*

5. *Lead me in the way of thy truth and teach me, for thou art my God and my saviour; on thee will I wait all day long.*

6. *Call to remembrance thy mercies, O Lord, and the favours of thy grace, for they are from eternity.*

7. *Remember not the sins of my youth and those of my ignorance. Remember me according to the fullness of thy mercy because of thy goodness, O Lord.*

8. The Lord is gracious and sincere; therefore will he instruct sinners in the way.

9. He will guide the tender-hearted in the judgement and will teach the tender-hearted his ways.

10. All the ways of the Lord are grace and truth for them who seek his virtuousness and his testimonies.

11. For thy name's sake, O Lord, forgive me my sin, [for] it is exceedingly great.

12. Who is the man who feareth the Lord? For him will he establish laws in the way which he hath chosen.

13. His souls will abide in good things and his seed will inherit the land.

14. The Lord is the strength of them who fear him; and the name of the Lord belongeth to them who fear him, to make known unto them his covenant.

15. Mine eyes are raised ever unto the Lord, for he will draw my feet out of the snare.

16. Look down upon me and be gracious unto me, for I am an only-begotten; I am wretched.

17. The afflictions of my heart have increased; bring me out of my necessities.

18. Look upon my abasement and my woe, and forgive me all my sins.

19. Look upon mine enemies, how they have increased themselves and hated me with unjust hatred.

20. Preserve my soul and save me; let me not be put to shame, for I have hoped on thee.

21. The simple and sincere have joined themselves to me, for I have waited on thee, O Lord.

22. O God, deliver Israel from all his afflictions.

We must lift up the Soul unto the Lord.

We must completely deliver ourselves to our inner, profound God.

The enemies that mock us are within ourselves.

Whosoever works on himself, waiting upon the inner Lord, shall not be put to shame.

It is obvious that the interior enemies who commit iniquity shall be put to shame.

The inner Lord will show us the ways and the paths.

There are four paths:

1. The Direct Path
2. The Nirvanic Spiral Path
3. The path of those who are separate from the cosmic scenario, without having reached the level of adept
4. The path of those who fail

The Direct Path is the most magnificent. However, the sufferings are great, therefore the triumphs are also great.

On the Spiral Path, the triumphs are minor, therefore the sufferings are minor.

The inhabitants of Nirvana are rarely reincarnated.

The inhabitants of Nirvana live in constant happiness. When they take a body, they take one step ahead, and they return into happiness.

Those who renounce cosmic manifestation become submerged within the Universal Spirit of Life following the dissolution of the ego. Yet, they submerge without having built the existential superior bodies of the Being.

Nevertheless, some of those who renounce cosmic manifestation will return in the Golden Age of the future Sixth Root Race. Then, they will enter into the mysteries and they will convert themselves into adepts.

The fourth path, the ones who fail, are those who after having accomplished three thousand (3,000) cycles or periods of manifestation did not attain the level of adept.

Each cycle of manifestation contains the processes of passing through the mineral, plant, animal, and human kingdoms.

108 lives are assigned to each Soul while in the human kingdom.

It is clear that when the 108 human lives in each cycle is concluded, then the time arrives to move downwards into the infernal worlds, into involution until the Second Death.

The infernal worlds are situated within the interior of the Earth, in the submerged mineral kingdom.

Following the Second Death, the Essence emerges again to the surface.

When the Essence has emerged again, then new evolving processes begin that repeat themselves from the lowest step. The lowest step is the mineral kingdom.

Each time the cycle is repeated through the mineral kingdom, it is performed in a higher spiral, according to the spiral of life.

The laws of evolution and involution of life constitute the mechanical axis of all of Nature.

Those who fail in all of the three thousand periods of manifestation submerge themselves within the ocean of the great Light, converted into simple elementals of Nature. This is after they have followed the Second Death in their last human life of the three thousandth cycle or period.

Obviously, such failures lose all opportunity.

Nevertheless, these types of elementals know good and evil due to their lived experiences.

The fortune for those elementals is well gained, due to the infinite pain through which they had to pass in their peregrination through matter.

The laws of evolution or involution have nothing to do with the inner Self-realization of the Being.

The path of the revolution of the consciousness is the inner Self-realization of the Being. It is the path of the great rebellion.

Only our inner God can lead us to the experience of the Truth.

The favors of grace are from the inner Christ, and come from all eternity.

The Great Merciful One can have pity on us and help us.

The secret way is taught by the Merciful One, who resides within our Being.

The intimate Lord will guide our steps if we are bountiful and tender hearted.

The virtue and the testimonies that we seek are found in the ways of the Lord.

We need to be forgiven for our sins, which are exceedingly great.

The laws of the interior, profound Lord are perfect, and they must be established in the heart.

However, it is necessary to love and fear the Lord.

Fortunate is the one who remains in the Light.

The intimate Lord is the strength of all powers.

The name of the Lord—the Verb within us, the real Being of the Being—belongs to those who possess it.

Only the Christified human beings possess the incarnated Verb, the Word, the name of the Lord.

Only the Lord will draw our feet from the abyss of perdition.

Each one of us is an only-begotten and is wretched. Only the Lord can save us.

Only the Lord can liberate us from our miseries, and give us a precious balm in order to cure our painful heart.

The enemies of the Soul have increased themselves within us.

Only the inner Christ can save us and take us from the pain.

Only the one who knows how to be serene, work, and be patient can be saved.

Only the intimate Lord can deliver Israel, which means, deliver all the independent and self-cognizant parts far away from all afflictions.

Nevertheless, it is necessary to dissolve the psychic aggregates before arriving to the port of supreme happiness.

Jesus commendeth Thomas

And Jesus had heard the words of Thomas, he said unto him: "Well said, Thomas, and finely. This is the solution of the seventh repentance of Pistis Sophia. Amen, amen, I say unto you: All generations of the world shall bless you on earth, because I have revealed this unto you and ye have received of my spirit and have become understanding and spiritual, understanding what I say. And hereafter will I fill you full with the whole light and the whole power of the spirit, so that ye may understand from now on all which shall be said unto you and which ye shall see. Yet a little while and I will speak with you concerning the height without within and within without."

Jesus continued again in the discourse and said unto his disciples...

Those who pretend to reach the final liberation without having previously eliminated the multiple undesirable psychic elements that we carry within our interior, walk on the path of error.

Great hermits or anchorites were known to have lived in lonely caverns in the orient. Due to the fortitude of multiple disciplines, they reached ecstasy. However, they failed because they did not dissolve the ego.

Those anchorites were accustomed to only momentarily taking the Essence, the Buddhi, out from the bottle. They then experienced Satori and Samadhi. Yet, following that mystic experience, they returned into the bottle like the genie in Aladdin's lamp.

Some of these Saints died in complete Mahasamadhi. Nevertheless, presently such Beings have returned as vulgar, ordinary people.

They were skilled in Samadhi, yet they did not work on the ego; thus, the result is failure.

To experience the Illuminated Void does not signify the Self-realization of the Illuminated Void.

All of that which Thomas knows has been received from the inner Christ.

The abridgement or synthetic sum of the doctrine of Thomas can be summarized as this: *"Do not depend on ideals or foreign concepts because the real wisdom is within oneself."*

Nevertheless, before we can absolutely depend on our own inner Being, we must be completely obedient to our Guru.

Every authentic Guru pronounces himself against fornication and adultery.

Every authentic Guru is a Twice-born.

Every authentic Guru sacrifices himself for humanity.

To be born, to die, and to sacrifice for humanity are the three factors of the revolution of the consciousness.

The Guru who spills Hermes' glass is a false Guru, a false Prophet.

The Guru who does not teach his disciples to build the solar, existential, superior Bodies of the Being is not a proper Guru in the knowledge.

The Guru who does not guide his disciples on the path of the dissolution of the ego is a mistaken Guru or a black magician.

The Guru who does not know how to sacrifice himself for humanity is not a true Guru.

There exists space above and the internal space.

The space above is exterior in respect to the internal.

Moreover, there exists the exteriors of the exteriors and the interiors of the interiors.

Any exterior space located in one or another dimension has as its opposition, its corresponding interior space.

Chapter 47

Jesus leadeth Sophia to a less confined region, but without the commandment of the First Mystery

"It came to pass then, when Pistis Sophia had uttered the seventh repentance in the chaos, that the commandment through the First Mystery had not come to me to save her and lead her up out of the chaos. Nevertheless of myself out of compassion without commandment I led her into a somewhat spacious region in the chaos. And when the material emanations of Self-willed had noticed that she had been led into a somewhat spacious region in the chaos, they ceased a little to oppress her, for they thought that she would be led up out of the chaos altogether. When this then took place, Pistis Sophia did not know that I was her helper; nor did she know me at all, but she continued and persisted withal singing praises to the Light of the Treasury, which she had seen afore time and on which she had had faith, and she thought that it [sc. the Light] also was her helper and it was the same to which she had sung praises, thinking it was the Light in truth. But as indeed she had had faith in the Light which belongeth to the Treasury in truth, therefore will she be led up out of the chaos and her repentance will be accepted from her. But the commandment of the First Mystery was not yet accomplished to accept her repentance from her. But hearken now in order that I may tell you all things which befell Pistis Sophia."

Only the commandment of the First Mystery can conduce the initiate out of the Chaos.

The inner Christ feels compassion for the initiate, and little by little, He passes him to superior levels of the Being.

Little by little, the material emanations of the Self-willed ego are disappearing in the same measure that the initiate is dying.

It is an error of Pistis Sophia to not recognize the extra help of the inner Christ.

The Light of the interior Treasury emerges from the same Treasury, which is the Golden Fleece.

The Golden Fleece of ancient people is the inner Christ, clothed with the bodies of pure Gold. These perfected existential bodies, which are covered by the distinct parts of the Being, are terribly divine.

The Light of the Treasury is not the Treasury. However, the initiate sings praises to the Light of the Treasury.

It is necessary to search for the Treasury within the womb of the Philosophical Earth.

VITRIOL signifies: *"Visita Interiora Terrae Rectificando Invenies Occultum Lapidem."*

Many types of light exist that are not the Light of the Treasury.

Diverse types of sects, schools, or mystic orders possess a light that is not the Light of the Treasury. However, their devotees believe that this light can save them.

Those devotees are sincerely mistaken, full of magnificent intentions, but mistaken.

The true Light of the hidden Treasury is absolutely sexual.

The repentance of Pistis Sophia must be qualified.

Receiving one or another, or the whole eight Initiations of Fire is one thing; however, to pass them is a completely different thing.

Anyone can receive the eight Initiations of Fire; however, if one does not pass them, then these initiations will be worthless for the initiate.

Many who have received the eight Initiations of Fire are now terribly perverse demons.

If the dissolution of the ego is excluded, then the qualification of the eight Initiations is impossible.

Only through the Buddhist Annihilation can we qualify for each one of the eight Initiations.

We will obtain radical change by virtue of the disintegration of the ego.

We need to convert ourselves into something totally different.

We must even lose our very own personal identity.

The change must be absolute. Even our current personal identity must not continue to exist.

The emanations of the Self-willed cease for a time to oppress Sophia

"It came to pass, when I had led her unto a somewhat spacious region in the chaos, that the emanations of Self-willed ceased entirely to oppress her, thinking that she would be led up out of the chaos altogether. It came to pass then, when the emanations of Self-willed had noticed that Pistis Sophia had not been led up out of the chaos, that they turned about again all together oppressing her vehemently. Because of this then she uttered the eighth repentance, because they had not ceased to oppress her, and had turned about to oppress her to the utmost. She uttered this repentance, saying thus..."

The emanations of the Self-willed ego bother Pistis Sophia. However, these emanations cease a little when she passes into a superior level of the Being.

Every time the initiate passes through a new reevaluation of the Being, the attacks of the tenebrous ones always cease for a while so that the attacks can later restart with a new activity.

Nevertheless, in each battle, Pistis Sophia reiterates the repentance over and over again.

The eighth repentance of Sophia

1. *On thee, O Light, have I hoped. Leave me not in the chaos; deliver me and save me according to thy gnosis.*

2. *Give heed unto me and save me. Be unto me a saviour, O Light, and save me and lead me unto thy light.*

3. *For thou art my saviour and wilt lead me unto thee. And because of the mystery of thy name lead me and give me thy mystery.*

4. And thou wilt save me from this lion-faced power, which they have laid as a snare for me, for thou art my saviour.

5. And in thy hands will I lay the purification of my light; thou hast saved me, O Light, according to thy gnosis.

6. Thou art become wroth with them who keep watch over me and will not be able to lay hold of me utterly. But I have had faith in the Light.

7. I will rejoice and will sing praises that thou hast had mercy upon me and hast heeded and saved me from the oppression in which I was. And thou wilt set free my power out of the chaos.

8. And thou hast not left me in the hand of the lion-faced power; but thou hast led me into a region which is not oppressed.

According to Gnosis, the Light must guide us and save us.

The Gnostic Light must save us and lead us to the great Light.

The mystery of the name is the mystery of the Verb.

Every initiate aspires to receive the mystery of the name.

Whosoever knows, the word gives power to, no one has uttered it, no one will utter it, except the one who has incarnated it.

Christ is the Word. Fortunate is the one who has incarnated Him.

The Lion-faced power, or the face of the law, makes us suffer. However, the Lord can forgive us.

We need to purify our own light in order for the Great Light to save us, in accordance with Gnosis.

The individual, inner light must be purified by virtue of the disintegration of the psychic aggregates.

The inner Christ is severe against those who keep watch over Pistis Sophia.

Only the Christ-Light can take Sophia out of the chaos in a definitive way.

The Lion-faced power is the power of the law.

The lion of the law exists within our own Being. It is one of the parts of the Being.

At certain times, the initiate is not afflicted by the law of karma.

When Pistis Sophia rests, free from the Lion-faced power, she feels happy.

Chapter 48

The emanations of Self-willed oppress her again

When then Jesus had said this unto his disciples, he answered again and said unto them: "It came to pass then, when the lion-faced power had noticed that Pistis Sophia had not been led up altogether out of the chaos, that it came again with all the other material emanations of Self-willed, and they oppressed Pistis Sophia again. It came to pass then, when they oppressed her, that she cried out in the same repentance, saying..."

The Lion-faced power and the Self-willed ego make the initiate suffer terribly.

Obviously, karma and the emanations of the ego take the powers from the initiate.

The Archons of the Aeons and the twenty-four Elders of the Zodiac are within ourselves.

The Pair, the other Soul, cannot help us if the great law is against us.

The Spiritual Soul contemplates while the Human Soul works.

The Innermost is "Atman," the Ineffable One.

Buddhi is the Spiritual Soul.

Superior Manas is the Human Soul.

The two Souls are integrated with the resurrection of Christ within ourselves. Then, there is Light.

Buddhi is like a fine and transparent glass made of alabaster, within which the flame of Prajna burns.

Buddhi-Manas united, integrated and in fusion, confers the Light unto us.

All the powers of the Light are contained within Buddhi, as in an alabaster glass.

Obviously, with the fusion of Buddhi-Manas, the Light is established within us.

She continueth her repentance

9. Have mercy upon me, O Light, for they have oppressed me again. Because of thy commandment, the light in me is distracted and my power and my understanding.

10. My power hath begun to wane whiles I am in these afflictions, and the number of my time whiles I am in the chaos. My light is diminished, for they have taken away my power from me, and all the powers in me are tossed about.

11. I am become powerless in the presence of all the rulers of the aeons, who hate me, and in the presence of the four-and-twenty emanations, in whose region I was. And my brother, my pair, was afraid to help me, because of that in which they have set me.

12. And all the rulers of the height have counted me as matter in which is no light. I am become as a material power which hath fallen out of the rulers.

13. And all who are in the aeons said: She hath become chaos. And thereafter all the pitiless powers encompassed me together and proposed to take away the whole light in me.

14. But I have trusted in thee, O Light, and said: Thou art my saviour.

15. And my commandment, which thou hast decreed for me, is in thy hands. Save me out of the hands of the emanations of Self-willed, which oppress me and persecute me.

16. Send thy light over me, for I am as naught before thee, and save me according to thy compassion.

17. Let me not be despised, for I have sung praises unto thee, O Light. Let chaos cover the emanations of Self-willed, let them be led down into the darkness.

18. Let the mouth of them be shut up, who would devour me with guile, who say: Let us take the whole light in her, although I have done them no ill.

Really, the fallen initiates are matter without Light.

Those who believe that they can re-conquer the Light without having previously dissolved the psychic aggregates march in the way of error.

The psychic aggregates, living personifications of our psychological defects, constitute in themselves a material power which is abandoned by the Rulers.

The Soul, submerged in the interior Chaos which dwells within ourselves, has been converted into a true Chaos.

All of the impious forces surround the fallen one and intend to steal the bit of Light which remains within him.

The initiate must trust in the Light. The Light will save him.

The emanations of the Self-willed ego pursue and oppress the initiate.

We can be saved by disintegrating the ego.

The emanations of the Self-willed ego, which means, of the psychic aggregates, must be disintegrated with the weapons of Vulcan.

Dry Mercury and psychic aggregates are the same.

Only through the transcendental sexual electricity can the totality of the Dry Mercury be disintegrated. Thus, Pistis Sophia can be liberated.

Sexual Magic is urgent and not to be delayed in order to liberate Pistis Sophia.

The Woman-Serpent is reinforced within the flaming forge of Vulcan.

We know that the flaming forge of Vulcan is sex, the sexual act.

In order to work in the flaming forge of Vulcan, it is fundamental not to spill the sacred sperm.

The Woman-Serpent can perform prodigies and marvels in those instances when she is reinforced by the transcendental sexual electricity.

Devi Kundalini is the Woman-Serpent within ourselves.

Stella Maris, the Virgin of the Sea, the igneous serpent of our magical powers, can disintegrate the ego.

The Woman-Serpent has in her power the marvellous weapons of Vulcan.

The total disintegration of all the psychic aggregates is only possible in the Ninth Sphere and with the help of the Woman-Serpent.

The Ninth Sphere is sex, the metaphysical copulation, the chemical coitus.

The Woman-Serpent saves Pistis Sophia.

Man and woman sexually united are the foundation of the Luni-Solar Androgyne of "IO," Isis-Osiris.

Isolda, Parabrahatman, and Mulaprakriti are the same pure Androgyne.

The Androgilia of Ammonio Saccas, written in Latin, teaches all of this.

Ur-Anas, the primordial fire and primordial water, are within the Ninth Sphere.

The learned ignoramuses absurdly suppose that they can disintegrate the ego outside of the Ninth Sphere.

We do not deny that outside of the Ninth Sphere serious devotees can disintegrate twenty-five percent, and even fifty percent of their psychic aggregates.

Nevertheless, outside of the Ninth Sphere one hundred percent of the psychic aggregates can never be disintegrated.

Those who for some very grave reason cannot work in the Ninth Sphere must not become discouraged. They can disintegrate twenty-five percent, and even fifty percent of their psychic aggregates, by working individually on themselves.

Thus, this is how in their present existence, they will advance to the point possible for them. Then, in their future existences, they will conclude with their work.

This is not a matter of being better. It is a matter of changing radically and this is only possible by disintegrating our psychic aggregates.

Truthfully, nothing within ourselves deserves to be better. For that reason, the Buddhist Annihilation is urgent, if a total transformation is what we truly want.

It is not a matter of evolving, like the fanatics of the dogma of evolution pretend.

Obviously, the undesirable psychic elements that we carry within our interior never deserve any type of evolution.

The emanations of the Self-willed ego must be taken down towards the regions where only the weeping and gnashing of teeth are heard.

May the mouth of the tenebrous ones be shut up. They are all the monsters of darkness. They are the psychic aggregates that we carry within our interior, which make attempts against Pistis Sophia.

Chapter 49

And when Jesus had spoken this, Matthew came forward and said: "My Lord, thy spirit hath stirred me and thy light hath made me sober to proclaim this eighth repentance of Pistis Sophia. For thy power hath prophesied thereof afore time thou David in the thirtieth Psalm [Modern Psalm 31], *saying..."*

Matthew, according to science, always says terribly divine things.

Certainly, Matthew is the Apostle of pure science.

The Gospel of Matthew gives all the scientific data in order to recognize the times of the end.

Our own Matthew, the inner Matthew, is what is important for ourselves.

Unquestionably, Matthew is one of the twelve parts of our own individual Being.

Pure science is known and taught by Matthew.

The inner Christ teaches Matthew.

The Light of the Lord illuminates Matthew.

The wisdom of the inner Christ illuminates Matthew.

Matthew quotes the thirtieth Psalm.

Matthew interpreteth the eighth repentance from Psalm XXX [Modern Psalm 31]

1. *On thee, O Lord, have I hoped. Let me never be put to shame; save me according to thy righteousness.*

2. *Incline thine ear unto me, save me quickly. Be thou unto me a protecting god and a house of refuge to save me.*

3. *For thou art my support and my refuge; for thy name's sake thou wilt guide me and feed me.*

4. *And thou wilt draw me out of this snare, which they have laid privily for me; for thou art my protection.*

5. *Into thy hands I will render my spirit; thou hast redeemed me, O Lord, God of Truth.*

6. *Thou hast hated them who hold to vain emptiness; but I have trusted.*

7. *And I shall rejoice because of my Lord and make merry over thy grace. For thou hast looked down upon my humbleness and saved my soul out of my necessities.*

8. *And thou hast not shut me up in the hands of my foes; thou hast set my feet on a broad space.*

9. Be gracious unto me, O Lord, for I am afflicted; my eye is distracted in the wrath and my soul and my body.

10. For my years have wasted away in sadness and my life is wasted in sighing. My power is enfeebled in misery and my bones are distracted.

11. I am become a mockery for all my foes and my neighbours. I am become a fright for my acquaintances, and they who saw me, are fled away from me.

12. I am forgotten in their heart as a corpse, and I have become as a ruined vessel.

13. For I have heard the scorn of many who encompass me round about. Massing themselves together against me, they took counsel to take away my soul from me.

14. But I have trusted in thee. O Lord, I said: Thou art my God.

15. My lots are in thy hands. Save me from the hand of my foes and free me from my persecutors.

16. Reveal thy face over thy slave, and free me according to thy grace, O Lord.

17. Let me not be put to shame, for I have cried unto thee. Let the impious be put to shame and turn towards hell.

18. Let the crafty lips be struck dumb, which allege iniquity against the righteous in pride and scorn.

The Lord can save us, according to His justice.

To do justice within ourselves is transcendental.

The energy of the Universal Spirit is represented in the flaming sword, which corresponds to the Sun.

The scale in itself and by itself indicates the necessity of weights and proportions.

The "open book" has an extraordinary meaning in Alchemy.

Profoundly significant is the meaning of the "open book," characterized by the radical solution of the metallic body, which abandons its impurities and grants its Sulphur.

The closed book is the general symbol of all the brute bodies, minerals or metals, just as Nature provides them, or as human industry provides them for commerce.

The brute Azoth—which is the sacred sperm not yet worked with—is a closed book. We need to open that book.

From another angle, the open book is the book of law and justice.

Justice, lion, scale, and sword are found intimately associated.

The outer garment of the ermine that the Goddess Justice shows is embroidered with roses and pearls.

The Goddess Justice has a buccal crown girded upon her forehead.

The sword of justice has a pommel adorned with a radiant sun.

The peplum that completely covered her has slid down her body and is suspended by her projecting arm, and the lower part is folded.

Within us, Justice is a self-cognizant part of the Being.

Within us, Justice must be Self-realized intimately.

Within us, and as an autonomous and self-cognizant part of the Being, Minerva, daughter of Jupiter, is the cardinal virtue of justice.

Minerva is also divine wisdom and complete knowledge of all things.

Minerva, Goddess of wisdom and lady of justice is the flower of the Great Work, the mystic rose.

Justice is a virgin with a golden crown, white tunic, and a purple robe.

The Goddess Justice wears an exquisite jewel upon her chest.

The Goddess Justice rests her left foot upon a cubic stone.

We will explain the profound significance of all of this in our next book entitled *The Great Work.*

In any case, we need to intimately Self-realize the Goddess Justice within ourselves.

Our Christ-Lord within ourselves can save us according to Justice.

In no way can we intimately Self-realize Minerva within ourselves, unless we previously pass through the Buddhist Annihilation.

The intimate Lord is our protector God.

We must annihilate the psychic aggregates and find refuge within the Lord.

The Lord can save us from the merciless snare that is laid by the secret enemy.

We must place our Spirit in the hands of the inner Christ.

The Lord rejects those who latch on to vanity.

The Lord helps those who fight for the disintegration of the psychic aggregates of vanity.

In no way would it be possible to keep correct relations with the inner Lord and with all the independent and self-cognizant parts of the Being, if we do not previously annihilate all the psychic aggregates of vanity.

Vanity destroys the possibilities of illumination.

Illumination is grandiose, yet it is only possible by annihilating the psychic aggregates of vanity.

Illumination is a grace of the Lord.

Only the humble one can receive illumination by grace of the Lord.

Those who have not annihilated the psychic aggregates of pride cannot in any way reach illumination.

The Lord never shuts us up in the hands of our interior enemies.

One becomes astonished while in the presence of the craziness of anger.

The eyes of the angry one reveals complete madness.

Very devout people, apparently very simple within the temples, turn themselves into frightful creatures during attacks of anger.

Some people who study our teachings, who are dedicated to the dissolution of the undesirable psychic aggregates that we carry within our interior, suddenly become full of great anger. Within thunder and lightning, they tear apart their vestures.

The psychic aggregates of anger are multiple. There is anger because of jealousy, because of hatred, because of frustrated desires, because of selfish monetary motives, because of disputed matters, because of terror, or because of various states of spirit, mind, body, and tongue, etc.

One must Self-observe during an attack of anger, in order to truly specify the type of anger that invades us at any given moment.

At times, anger is due to self-love or hurt vanity.

At times, anger is due to hurt pride.

Anger is associated with many psychic aggregates.

The angry one fails in the Great Work of the Father.

It is necessary to aim the ray of Kundalini against any psychic aggregate of anger in order to pierce it and atomically disintegrate it.

Those who do not work on themselves waste their life in sadness or in vain pleasures which leaves only deceptions. Thus, their life is wasted away in sighs.

Those who do not work on themselves here and now, become more and more incapable. Their interior enemies, the red demons of Seth, the living personifications of their psychological defects, mock them.

Those who do not work on themselves are not only full of problems, but moreover and worst of all, they are a problem for the distinct, independent parts of the Being.

Every person who has the ego, the "I," is a hindrance everywhere; he hurts himself and he hurts others.

Whosoever has ego is a problem for himself and for his friends.

Any person who has the ego, the "I," is like a ruined vessel that sails in the ocean of life, carrying his own misery.

We must work on ourselves and deliver our Spirit to our inner God.

The inner Christ withdraws from vanity.

Vanity is a charlatan by nature and when it is hurt, it thunders with great anger.

Many are the Saints who have revested themselves with the costume of vanity.

Aristipus revested himself with an old tunic which was covered with holes and patches. He then grasped the staff of philosophy and walked down the streets of Athens.

When Socrates saw him approaching, he exclaimed: *"Oh Aristipus, your vanity is shown through the holes of your vesture."* Vanity and pride are used to being associated dangerously.

A wealthy woman could buy an antique car from the beginning of the century, in order to have it in her home. Such eccentricity is caused by dint of pride. However, because of vanity she would prefer to drive a fine new car on the streets of the city.

We would accept many things because of vanity, yet because of pride we reject them.

Anger, pride, and vanity impede the correct inner relations with the distinct, independent parts of the Being.

Our interior enemies, the red demons of Seth, take counsel in order to take our Soul away from us.

What purpose would it serve to conquer all the kingdoms of the world if we lose our Soul?

The Soul is laws, forces, divine virtues, powers, etc.

Whosoever does not crystallize the Soul within himself, loses his Soul.

We have previously stated that if the water does not boil at one hundred degrees, that which must be dissolved is not dissolved, and that which must be crystallized is not crystallized.

If, as well, we do not pass through great emotional crises, then we cannot dissolve the psychic aggregates, nor can we crystallize the Soul.

We repeat: we need to crystallize the Soul.

Each time a psychic aggregate is disintegrated, a virtue, a power, or a law, etc. is crystallized.

Thus, this is how we will reach the crystallization of the Soul. This is how we will possess our Soul.

Even the very body must convert itself into Soul.

Whosoever loses his Soul sinks himself into the infernal worlds.

We must work on ourselves and trust in our Innermost God.

Our Innermost God can save us from our interior enemies.

The Lord can reveal his face to his serf, if he is working on himself. The Lord can save us according to His grace.

The impious ones will be put to shame and turned towards the infernal worlds. The impious ones are the red demons of Seth.

The lips of the hypocrites speak against those who have performed the Goddess Justice within themselves.

The hypocrites believe themselves to be Saints and they speak against the alchemists who have performed Minerva within themselves.

The hypocrites believe themselves to be Saints and they speak of what they do not know.

The hypocrites calumniate the adept who obtains a Hermetic Glass for his work in the laboratory.

The hypocritical Pharisees tear at their vestures while thundering and striking with lightning that which they do not know.

The hypocrites believe that they know, however they do not even suspect that they do not know.

The hypocritical Pharisees of today, yesterday, and all times dare to slander and judge even the Masters of the White Lodge.

The hypocrites are as white as washed sepulchres, a perverse generation of vipers.

The hypocrites stick their noses where they do not belong. Thus, they judge what they believe they know, yet they truly do not know.

Is it perhaps a crime to obtain a Hermetic Glass when one does not have this glass?

What do the hypocritical Pharisees know about the intimate life of the wise?

Nevertheless, the Pharisees dare to attack the adepts of the Great Work.

Never has any Pharisee believed himself to be mistaken.

The Pharisees hate Christ, thus they condemn Him each time He comes to Earth.

The Pharisees arose, have arisen, and will arise in rebellion against the Lord who comes to teach them.

Christ is judged by the Pharisees who believe themselves to be wise. Thus, this is how they throw stones against Him.

The most critical is the ingratitude of the Pharisees. They attack Christ with the very same words and teachings that they learned from the Lord.

They use the words of the Lord in order to attack the Lord.

How absurd it is to judge by appearance and throw stones against Christ.

A horrible karma will befall the hypocritical Pharisees.

The hypocritical Pharisees devolve within the submerged mineral kingdom of the infernal worlds.

The Second Death and the burning lake of fire and sulphur await the hypocritical Pharisees.

The Pharisee "I" exists within each person. Woe to those who do not dissolve the Pharisee "I"!

Even the most virtuous men and women can fall into the abyss of perdition if they do not disintegrate the Pharisee "I."

Chapter 50

Jesus commendeth Matthew and promiseth his disciples that they shall sit on thrones with him

And when Jesus had heard these words, he said: "Finely [said], Matthew. Now, therefore, amen, I say unto you: When the perfect number is completed and the universe is raised hence, I will take my seat in the Treasury of the Light, and ye yourselves will sit on twelve light-powers, until we have restored all the orders of the twelve saviours to the region of the inheritances of every one of them."

And when he had said this, he said: "Understand ye what I say?"

When the reintegration of the Being has been achieved within ourselves, then the perfect number is completed.

When the total reintegration of all the autonomous and self-cognizant parts of the Being has been achieved, then the interior universe of each one of us has been completed.

The Throne of the inner Christ is precisely in the Treasury of the Light.

We have previously stated that we must search for the Treasury of the Light within the profundities of the Being.

The Treasury of the Light is of gold, diamonds, and all precious stones.

The Treasury of the Light is the Celestial Jerusalem.

The city is twelve thousand furlongs, which represent the twelve works of Hercules.

The twelve works of Hercules are performed in the Ninth Sphere.

The Ninth Sphere is one hundred percent sexual.

The Celestial Jerusalem is the same as the Philosophical Stone.

All the roads of the Celestial Jerusalem are made of pure gold.

The entire city is filled with precious stones.

The inner Christ is the luminary of the Celestial Jerusalem.

We need to destroy Babylon the great, the mother of all fornication and all abominations of the Earth.

Babylon the great is the psychological city that we carry within ourselves.

We must previously destroy the great Babylon, if we want to create the Celestial Jerusalem within ourselves.

The precious stones symbolizing virtues, gold, the twelve pearls, etc. constitute the Treasury of the Lord, the Golden Fleece of the ancient people.

Our readers must read what is written about the Celestial Jerusalem in the Apocalypse of Saint John.

It is urgent to build the Celestial Jerusalem within ourselves. We have the right to feed ourselves with the twelve fruits of the Tree of Life.

We could not build the Celestial Jerusalem without having previously disintegrated the undesirable psychic aggregates, which we carry within our interior.

The Twelve Apostles are in reality twelve parts of our own interior, profound Being, twelve Light Powers.

Let us recall that the Celestial Jerusalem has twelve gates, and at each gate there is an Angel.

These twelve Angels are twelve Light Powers, twelve parts of the Being.

Each part of the Being is ineffable and terribly divine.

The twelve gates are twelve pearls of perfection.

Only with a Golden Reed is it possible to measure the city and its gates and walls.

The Golden Reed represents the spinal column of the adept.

The Golden Reed is the Staff of Brahma, the Rod of Aaron.

The Twelve Saviors are the same as the twelve Light Powers.

The orders of the Twelve Saviors, the process of the twelve Light Powers, must be restored in the inheritances of each one of them.

The lost inheritance, the secret inheritance, exists within us.

Each one of the twelve within us has his own secret inheritance in the Great Light.

That lost inheritance is Light. It is special cosmic powers, extraordinary knowledge, which emerges from all eternities, etc..

Each of the twelve within us must re-conquer his lost inheritance.

We certainly need to comprehend the teachings of the inner Christ.

We must become serious if we truly want to reach the integration of all the autonomous and self-cognizant parts of the Being.

Many are the aspirants who believe themselves to be serious; yet, they are not.

There are many who enter our studies and then play with diverse doctrines. They are not serious.

There are many who know this doctrine; yet, they simply play with this doctrine.

The careless Gnostics who flirt with other doctrines play with Gnosis.

There are many students of Gnosis who ridicule Gnosis while playing with it.

Many clowns have infiltrated the Gnostic movement.

Those who have not declared themselves to be their own mortal enemies are not serious.

Gnostics who are not serious become fascinated with novelties. This is their problem.

These types of Gnostics—who are not serious, Gnostics who are searching and playing—definitely fail.

Only the Gnostics who work on themselves can integrally Self-realize themselves.

Mary interpreteth the words of Jesus

Mary came forward and said: "O Lord, concerning this matter thou hast said to us afore time in similitude: 'Ye have awaited with me in the trials, and I will bequeath unto you a kingdom, as my Father hath bequeathed it unto me, that ye may eat and drink at my table in my kingdom; and ye shall sit on twelve thrones and judge the twelve tribes of Israel."

He said unto her: "Well said, Mary."

Jesus continued again and said unto his disciples: "It came to pass then thereafter, when the emanations of Self-willed oppressed Pistis Sophia in the chaos, that she uttered the ninth repentance, saying..."

There are seven levels of the Being.

The first level is the instinctive human being.

The second level is the emotional human being.

The third level is the intellectual human being.

The fourth level is the equilibrated human being.

The fifth level belongs to those who have built the Astral Body.

The sixth level of human being belongs to those who have built the Mental Body.

The seventh level of human being belongs to those who have built the Causal Body.

The human beings of the first, second, and third level constitute the circle of the confusion of tongues, the Tower of Babel.

These three types of humans are the ones who have disgraced the world, the ones who provoked the first and second world wars, and the ones who will provoke the third.

These three levels of humans do not understand each other.

The instinctive level does not understand the intellectual.

The emotional level does not understand the intellectual.

The intellectual level does not understand the emotional.

The three superior levels constitute the Kingdom.

The inhabitants of the Kingdom have not provoked the two world wars.

The humans of the fourth level are not in the circle of the confusion of tongues; however, neither are they in the Kingdom.

The humans of the fourth level never identify themselves with any particular center of the human machine.

The humans of the fourth level correctly drive the five centers of the human machine.

The five centers of the human machine are: Intellect, emotion, movement, instinct and sex.

The two superior centers are the superior emotional and the superior mental. These centers can be used only by the inhabitants of the Kingdom.

Mary or Marah, the Woman-Serpent, reminds us of the Kingdom that the inner Christ promised to us.

Those who know how to suffer with patience in their trials and work on themselves will inherit the Kingdom.

Obviously, the true human beings are the ones who are the inhabitants of the Kingdom.

The inhabitants of the infernal circle of the confusion of tongues are not human beings. They are merely intellectual mammals.

Only the inhabitants of the Kingdom can eat and drink at the table of the Lord.

Only the Twelve Powers within us may sit on the twelve thrones in order to judge all of humanity, the twelve tribes of Israel.

All of humanity unfolds within the zodiacal womb, which is divided into twelve tribes represented by the zodiac.

It is clear that the integrated twelve and all the integrated parts of the Being make of the human being a God, a Super-Man.

The Super-Man can judge the twelve tribes of Israel.

We repeat, the twelve tribes of Israel is the whole of humanity.

It is important to remember that some people are born under Aries, others under Taurus, Gemini, Cancer, Leo, Virgo, Libra, Scorpio, Sagittarius, Capricorn, Aquarius, or Pisces.

The reader can now better comprehend the twelve tribes of Israel.

The emanations of the Self-willed ego incessantly oppress Pistis Sophia.

The ninth repentance of Sophia

1. *O Light, smite down them who have taken away my power from me, and take away the power from them who have taken away mine from me.*

2. *For I am thy power and thy light. Come and save me.*

3. *Let great darkness cover my oppressors. Say unto my power: I am he who will save thee.*

4. *Let all those who would take away my light from me utterly, lack their power. Let them face about unto the chaos and become powerless, who would take away my light from me utterly.*

5. *Let their power be as dust, and let Yew, thy angel, smite them.*

6. *And if they would go into the height, let darkness seize upon them and let them slip down and turn to the chaos. And let thy angel Yew pursue them and cast them down into the darkness below.*

7. *For they have set a lion-faced power as a trap for me, although I have done them no ill from which its light will be taken; and they have oppressed the power in me, which they will not be able to take away.*

8. *Now, therefore, O Light, take away the purification from the lion-faced power without its knowing it, —the thought which Self-willed hath thought, to take away my light; take away its own and let the light be taken away from the lion-faced power, which set the trap for me.*

9. But my power will exult in the Light and rejoice that he will save it.

10. And all the portions of my power shall say: There is no saviour but thee. For thou wilt save me out of the hand of the lion-faced power, which hath taken away my power from me, and thou savest me out of the hands of them who have taken away my power and my light from me.

11. For they have risen up against me, lying against me and saying that I know the mystery of the Light which is in the height, [the Light] in which I have had faith. And they have constrained me, [saying:] Tell unto us the mystery of the Light in the height, —that which I know not.

12. And they have requited me with all this ill because I have had faith in the Light of the height; and they have made my power lightless.

13. But when they constrained me, I sat in the darkness, my soul bowed down in morning.

14. And do thou, O Light —for that reason sing I praise to thee —save me. I know that thou wilt save me because I fulfilled thy will ever since I was in my aeon. I fulfilled thy will, as the invisibles who are in my region, and as my pair. And I mourned, looking unceasingly and searching for thy Light.

15. Now, therefore, have all the emanations of Self-willed surrounded me and rejoiced over me and sore oppressed me without my knowing [them]. And they have fled away and ceased from me but have had no pity upon me.

16. They have returned again and made trial of me and they have oppressed me in great oppression and ground their teeth against me, desiring to take away my light from me utterly.

17. How long, therefore, O Light, dost thou suffer them, that they oppress me? Save my power from their evil thoughts and save me from the hand of the lion-faced power; for I alone of the invisibles am in this region.

18. I will sing praises unto thee, O Light, in the midst of all who are gathered together against me, and I will cry unto thee in the midst of all who oppress me.

19. Now, therefore, O Light, let not them who hate me and desire to take away my power from me, rejoice over me —who hate me and flash their eyes against me, though I have not done anything unto them.

20. For indeed they have fawned upon me with sweet words, asking me concerning the mysteries of the Light which I know not, and have craftily spoken against me and been enraged against me, because I have had faith in the Light in the height.

21. They have opened their chops against me and said: Well indeed, we will take from her her light.

22. Now, therefore, O Light, thou hast known their guile; suffer them not and let not thy help be far from me.

23. Quickly, O Light, vindicate and avenge me.

24. And give judgment on me according to thy goodness. Now, therefore, O Light of lights, let them not take away my light from me.

25. And let them not say in their heart: Our power is glutted with her light. And let them not say: We have consumed her power.

26. But rather let darkness come upon them, and let those who long to take away my light from me, become powerless, and let them be clothed with chaos and darkness, who say there: We will take away her light and her power.

27. Now, therefore, save me that I may rejoice, for I long for the thirteenth aeon, the region of Virtuousness, and I shall say evermore: May the light of thy angel Yew shine more and more.

28. And my tongue will sing praises to thee in thy gnosis my whole time in the thirteenth aeon.

The inner Christ must take away the power from those who have taken away the power from the initiate.

The power and the Light of Christ are within Pistis Sophia.

Darkness covers the oppressors, who are the undesirable psychic elements that we carry within our interior.

Pistis Sophia as Power-Wisdom, must humble herself in the presence of the inner Christ.

The red demons of Seth take the Light away from the initiate. They steal part of the consciousness from the initiate.

The red demons of Seth, who are the psychic aggregates that we carry in our interior, must fall into the burning lake of fire and sulphur. This is the Second Death.

When the power of the ego has turned into dust, the emanations of Yew emerge.

Yew is the Illuminator, one of the self-cognizant parts of the Being.

Yew develops the sense of the psychological Self-observation within each one of us.

Moreover, Yew can pursue and cast the red demons of Seth down into the Chaos.

The power of the lion of the law is terrible and the tenebrous ones take advantage of the most difficult moments in order to embitter the life of the initiates.

The psychic aggregates oppress the power of Pistis Sophia. Yet, they will never succeed in taking the inner power away from Pistis Sophia.

The power of the lion of the law is terrible and it intends to purify us by means of pain.

Pistis Sophia wants a balm for her painful heart.

She begs for the Lion-faced to permit her to take a rest from so much bitterness.

It is necessary to take the fatal light from the Self-willed ego.

The darkness of the ego and of the Abyss are other types of light. We could say that it is light of the infrared gamut.

The light of the Lion-faced Power is Light-Justice and Pistis Sophia desperately protests against karma, against the law.

The power of Pistis Sophia exults in the Light and rejoices when saved by the Light.

The Lion-faced Power takes the power away from the initiate.

Obviously, the fallen initiate loses his powers.

The Light is our Savior. The origin of the Light is in the Fire. The Light is the Fire.

The Light, the Fire, INRI, saves us from the power of the lion of the law.

Pistis Sophia needs to be saved from the hands of those who have stolen her power.

The tenebrous ones rise against Pistis Sophia.

The mystery of the Light, which is in the Height is unknown. Rare are those who know the great mystery.

Power without Light is useless.

The Soul bows down, filled with pain in the darkness.

Only the Light can save us, if we fulfill His will at every moment.

Let us remember that the Father who is in secret is the Father of all Lights.

The profound Lord is always found in the Thirteenth Aeon.

Nevertheless, it is necessary to know that our inner Buddha is only the projection of Adi-Buddha, the Unmanifested One.

Adi-Buddha is the Unknowable and Unmanifested Lord. Each one of us has our own Adi-Buddha.

It is not possible to know the Unmanifested Adi-Buddha during the Great Cosmic Day.

Now we comprehend why Jesus, the great Kabir, always spoke of Yew, the Father of his Father.

We could not understand all the mysteries of the Light if we do not know something about the Two Ones: the manifested One and the unmanifested One.

Aelohim is the unknowable and unmanifested One.

Elohim is the manifested One.

Moses prohibited the moulding of images of Aelohim. Yet, he never prohibited the sculpting or allegorizing of the manifested Elohim.

It is impossible to symbolize or allegorize the unknowable One.

Nevertheless, the manifested One, the knowable Elohim, can be allegorized or symbolized.

The manifested Elohim is constituted by the Demiurge Creator of the universe.

The sacred fire emerges from within the womb of Aelohim.

Fohat, the fire, the intelligent flames, emerge from within the bosom of Aelohim.

The cosmic intelligence is the fire, the creators, the ineffable ones who emerge from within the womb of the unknowable One in every universe, in the beginning of the dawn of creation.

Not a single Buddha of contemplation can integrate himself with the Adi-Buddha before the cosmic night.

The mysteries of the Light are terrific, and only Adi-Buddha knows them completely.

The Invisibles who are in the region of the Thirteenth Aeon and the Pair or Twin Soul of every initiate know how to fulfill the will of the Father of all Lights.

The red demons of Seth completely oppress Pistis Sophia, without feeling any pity for her.

The inhuman psychic aggregates that we carry within our interior are processed in seven levels.

When Pistis Sophia thinks that she has been liberated, new attacks from the tenebrous ones make her suffer.

The tenebrous ones sink their teeth into Pistis Sophia, wishing to take her entire Light away from her.

The final liberation becomes almost impossible due to the precise, concrete fact that the painful process of the "I" develops in accordance with the law of seven.

The psychic aggregates within the seven levels of the Being make the liberation of Pistis Sophia almost impossible.

Only the Great Light can save Pistis Sophia from the power of the lion of the law and the power of the tenebrous ones.

We must sing praises unto the Light in the midst of all who are against us, and in the midst of all who oppress us.

The psychic aggregates hate Pistis Sophia in us and within us, here and now.

People from darkness praise the initiate with sweet words, however, thereafter they stone him.

It is clear that the tenebrous ones speak evil against the initiate because they do not understand him. The disloyal ones ignore the wisdom that is hidden behind each event of the life of the adepts.

The disloyal ones want the adepts to move themselves exclusively along the tracks of their dogmas.

The actions of the initiates provoke the anger of the demons.

The Light of the Heights, which the adepts have faith in, originates actions that the disloyal ones qualify in accordance with their torpid prejudice and preconceptions.

The disloyal ones are enraged against the adepts and say: *"We will take from him his light."*

The Light knows the guile of the tenebrous ones and helps Pistis Sophia.

The Light will vindicate Pistis Sophia.

The Light can give judgment to Pistis Sophia, according to His goodness.

The Light of lights is the Ancient of Days.

Regarding Pistis Sophia, the tenebrous ones would like to say: *"Our power is glutted with her Light."*

The tenebrous ones would like to consume the power of Pistis Sophia.

The darkness is within the tenebrous regions. The tenebrous ones are powerless in the presence of the Light.

The Chaos and the darkness envelop those who wish to take the Light and the power away from Pistis Sophia.

The first Chaos from which the cosmos emerged is between the Sephiroth Binah and Chesed.

The second Chaos, from where the fundamental principles of the human being emerged, exists within Yesod-Mercury, which is the sexual human center.

The third Chaos, the infernal worlds, exists below the Thirteenth Aeons in the region of Klipoth, in the underworld.

The region of the Thirteenth Aeon is the ineffable region of Virtue. The abode of the adepts.

Yew, the Angel of the Thirteenth Aeon, shines, giving supreme illumination to the adepts.

Yew is within the most unknowable realities of our own Being. Yew is the prince of the faces, the Angel of the Ancient of Days, one of the most elevated parts of our own Being.

The adept sings praises to the Ocean of the Great Light in the Thirteenth Aeon.

Chapter 51

It came to pass, when Jesus had finished saying these words unto his disciples, that he said unto them: "Who is sober among you, let him proclaim their solution."

James came forward, kissed the breast of Jesus and said: "My Lord, thy spirit hath sobered me, and I am ready to proclaim their solution. Concerning them indeed thy power hath prophesied afore time through David in the thirty-fourth Psalm [Modern Psalm 35], *saying thus concerning the ninth repentance of Pistis Sophia..."*

James is the blessed Master of the Great Work.

Whosoever studies the universal Epistle of James will understand the principles of the Great Work.

The Father of all Lights teaches us the mysteries of the Great Work through our own Interior James.

Therefore, James is one of the autonomous and self-cognizant parts of our own Being.

"James-Mercury" is found intimately related with the transmutation science of Yesod-Mercury.

The fundamental book of the Great Work that James carries in his hands is the Apocalypse (Revelation).

Unquestionably, the Apocalypse is the book of wisdom, which is comprehensible only by the alchemists.

Only the workers of the Great Work can comprehend the Apocalypse.

The secret science of the Apocalypse is found in superior chemistry, which is Alchemy.

The laws of superior chemistry or Alchemy, the principles, the order of the magisterium of the fire, are found placed in the Apocalypse.

I repeat, James within us is the blessed Master of the Great Work.

James is another autonomous and independent part of our own individual Being.

Each one of us has his own James.

Let it be well understood that all the powers that created the universe are found within our Being.

Christ fights against the enemies of the Soul.

The enemies of the Soul are the red demons of Seth.

May the Lord judge the red demons of Seth.

The intimate Lord fights against the red demons of Seth.

The flaming sword can never be trapped by the tenebrous ones.

The inner Christ is our salvation.

The red demons of Seth, the living personification of our psychological defects, pursue the Soul.

May the red demons of Seth be exposed to opprobrium and to humiliation.

James interpreteth the ninth repentance from Psalm XXXIV [Modern Psalm 35]

1. *Give sentence, O Lord, on them who do me injustice, and fight against them who fight against me.*

2. *Lay hand on weapon and shield and stand up to help me.*

3. *Draw forth a sword and conceal it from my oppressors. Say unto my soul: I am thy salvation.*

4. *Let them be put to shame and abashed who strive after my soul; let them fall back and be put to shame who imagine evil against me.*

5. *Let them be as chaff before the wind, and let the angel of the Lord pursue after them.*

6. *Let their way be darkness and slippery, and let the angel of the Lord oppress them.*

7. *For without cause have they hid a snare for me for their own spoiling, and they have mocked at my soul in vain.*

8. *Let a snare come upon them which they know not, and let the net which they have hid for me, catch them and let them fall into this snare.*

9. *But my soul will exult in the Lord and rejoice in its salvation.*

10. *All my bones shall say: O Lord, who can be like unto thee? —thou who settest free the wretched from the hand of him who is stronger than him; and thou savest a wretched and poor [one] from the hands of them who spoil him.*

11. *Unjust witnesses came forward and have asked me that which I knew not.*

12. They have requited me evil for good and childlessness for my soul.

13. But when they molested me, I clothed me in a sack and humbled my soul with fasting, and my prayer will return into my breast.

14. I was pleasing unto thee, as unto my neighbour and as unto my brother; and I humbled myself as one in mourning and as one who is sad.

15. They have rejoiced over me, and they are put to shame. Scourges have gathered themselves together against me and I knew not; they were cut off and were troubled.

16. They have brought me to trial and mocked me with mocking; they have ground their teeth against me.

17. O Lord, when wilt thou look upon me? Restore again my soul from their evil works and save my only one from the hands of the lions.

18. I will confess to thee, O Lord, in the great assembly, and I will sing praises to thee in the midst of a countless people.

19. Let not them who unjustly treat me as a foe, rejoice over me, who hate me without a cause and wink with their eyes.

20. For indeed they discourse with me with words of peace, though they plot wrath with craft.

21. They opened their chops wide against me and said: Well indeed, our eyes have filled our sight with him.

22. Thou hast seen, O Lord. Keep not silence, O Lord, withdraw not thyself from me.

23. Arise, O Lord, and give heed to my vindication, give heed to my vengeance, my God and my Lord.

24. Judge me, O Lord, according to thy justice; let them not rejoice over me, my God.

25. And let them not say: Well done, our soul. Let them not say: We have consumed him.

26. Let them be put to shame and be scorned who rejoice at my mischance. Let them be clothed with shame and disgrace who speak boastingly against me.

27. Let them who desire my justification, exult and rejoice and let them who desire the peace of his slave, say: May the Lord make me great and arise.

28. My tongue will exult over thy justification and over thy honour all day long.

Let those tenebrous ones who imagine evil against Pistis Sophia be damned, condemned, and dead.

The Angel of the Lord pursues the engenders of the inferno.

May the Angel of the Lord afflict the psychic aggregates.

The Angel of the Lord is another part of our own Being, in the tribunal of Truth-Justice.

The tenebrous ones set snares for Pistis Sophia and they mock the initiate.

May the snare that they, the engenders of the infernos, have set for Pistis Sophia be for them.

The Soul is exulted in the inner Christ and rejoices in His salvation.

No one is more perfect than the intimate Lord, for He saves the wretched and He helps the unhappy and the poor from the hands of them who spoil him.

Unjust witnesses pronounce themselves against the initiate.

The perverse ones requite evil for good and childlessness for the Soul.

When the red demons of Seth attack the initiate, he fasts and does penance and prays profoundly.

The initiate serves the inner Christ and the neighbor with infinite love.

The tenebrous ones rejoice over the misfortune of Pistis Sophia, but they are put to shame.

Obviously, each one of the psychic aggregates is always full of problems.

Unquestionably, the ego is the ego and it is always full of problems.

Every person with ego is filled with problems.

Whosoever does not have ego shall never have problems.

The red demons of Seth grind their teeth into Pistis Sophia.

Only the inner Christ can cure our painful heart and save us from the lions of the law.

Only the sins against the Holy Spirit become unforgivable and non-negotiable.

Fortunate are those who will confess to the Lord and will sing praises to the Lord in the midst of countless people.

Pistis Sophia is treated unjustly and is hated without cause.

All the initiates are hated by the profane and profaners.

There are many Pharisees who discourse with the adepts with words of peace, though they secretly plot against them.

The adepts are usually persecuted by their own disciples.

The adepts are praised and venerated by those who later convert themselves into their accusers and persecutors.

Terrible is the fate of the adepts. Today praised, tomorrow persecuted by their own disciples and the day after tomorrow, loved again, etc.

Certainly, the traitors exclaim: *"Well indeed, our eyes have filled our sight with him, we know him, he is perverse, etc."*

This is how the adepts suffer.

The initiate begs the inner Christ and asks Him for his help.

The Lord will arise from within his Holy Sepulchre in order to liberate Pistis Sophia.

Only the Resurrected Christ in the Spirit and in the Soul of the initiate can vindicate him.

Indubitably, the inner Lord must be born in the heart of the adept.

Unquestionably, the inner Christ must grow within the initiate.

Evidently, the Lord grows in the Soul, preaches to the multitudes and teaches with His example.

The Blessed One posteriorly performs the entire cosmic drama in the Soul and in the Spirit of the human being, as it is written in the Four Gospels.

The psychic aggregates, living personifications of our psychological defects, take the inner Christ unto Calvary.

The Lord is crucified, dies, and resurrects within the initiate.

The resurrected Lord liberates Pistis Sophia.

Only the inner Christ can judge and liberate Pistis Sophia.

The tenebrous ones want to boast about their triumph and consume the entire Light of Pistis Sophia.

Those who pronounce themselves against Pistis Sophia will be put to shame and opprobrium.

Those who desire the justification of the initiate shall be happy. Those who desire the peace of the serf will say, *"May the Lord be great and arise."*

The tongue of the initiate will exult in the justification and in the honour of the inner Christ.

Chapter 52

Jesus commendeth James and promiseth the first place unto the disciples

When James then had said this, Jesus said unto him: "Well said, finely, James. This is the solution of the ninth repentance of Pistis Sophia. Amen, amen, I say unto you: Ye shall be the first in the kingdom of heaven before all invisibles and all gods and rulers who are in the thirteenth aeon and in the twelfth aeon; and not only ye, but also every one who shall accomplish my mysteries."

> The Kingdom of Heaven is not a place as the learned ignoramuses suppose.
>
> The Kingdom of Heaven is the conscious circle of the solar humanity, which operates over the superior centers of the Being.
>
> The Kingdom of Heaven is formed by each and every one of the members of the divine humanity.
>
> All the Invisibles and all the Gods within ourselves, and all the Rulers from the Thirteenth Aeon and from the Twelfth Aeon, bow in the presence of James.
>
> Indeed, all the Invisibles and Gods and Rulers from the Twelfth and Thirteenth Aeons, are the multiple sovereign and self-cognizant parts of our own individual Being.
>
> All those who perform the Christic mysteries will one day return to the Thirteenth Aeon.
>
> The Thirteenth Aeon is Ain, Sat, the Seity.
>
> Beyond the Thirteenth Aeon is the Cosmic Common Eternal Father, and Adhi-Buddha, who is the Buddha of our individual Buddha.
>
> Adhi-Buddha is the Father of our Father, but He never comes into manifestation, because He is the unknowable divinity.
>
> Only at the end of the Mahamanvantara, after having integrated ourselves with our Father who is in secret, do we then integrate ourselves with Adhi-Buddha.
>
> This integration with Adhi-Buddha is performed in the Mahapralaya, in the Cosmic Night and within the bosom of the Absolute Abstract Space.

Mary interpreteth the words of Jesus

And when he had said this, he said unto them: "Understand ye in what manner I discourse with you?"

Mary started forward again and said: "Yea, O Lord, this is what thou didst say unto us afore time: 'The last shall be first and the first shall be last.' The first then, who were created before us, are the invisibles, for indeed they arose before mankind, they and the gods and the rulers; and the men who shall receive mysteries, will be first into the kingdom of heaven."

> *"The last shall be first and the first shall be last,"* thus says Marah, Mary, the Woman-Serpent, the Divine Mother Kundalini.
>
> Obviously, the Invisibles who were before mankind, they and the Gods and the Rulers and the Men who shall receive mysteries, will be the first in the Kingdom of Heaven.
>
> The Gods and the Rulers and the Invisibles within each one of ourselves are the basic factors of the Kingdom of Heaven.

The repentance of Sophia is accepted. Jesus is sent to help her

Jesus said unto her: "Well said, Mary."

Jesus continued again and said unto his disciples: "It came to pass then, when Pistis Sophia had proclaimed the ninth repentance, that the lion-faced power oppressed her again, desiring to take away all powers from her. She cried out again to the Light, saying:

"'O Light, in whom I have had faith from the beginning, for whose sake I have endured these great pains, help me.'"

"And in that hour her repentance was accepted from her. The First Mystery hearkened unto her, and I was sent off at his command. I came to help her, and led her up out of the chaos, because she had repented, and also because she had had faith in the Light and had endured these great pains and these great perils. She had been deluded through the god-like Self-willed, and had not been deluded through anything else, save through a light-power, because of its resemblance to the Light in which she had faith. For this cause then was I sent forth at the command of the First Mystery to help her secretly. I did not however yet go to the region of the aeons at all; but I passed down

through the midst out of them, without any single power knowing it, either those of the interior of the interior or those of the exterior of the exterior, save only the First Mystery.

"It came to pass then, when I came into the chaos to help her, that she saw me, that I was understanding and shone exceedingly and was full of compassion for her. For I was not Self-willed as the lion-faced power, which had taken away the light-power from Sophia, and had also oppressed her in order to take away from the whole light in her. Sophia then saw me, that I shone ten-thousand times more that the lion-faced power, and that I was full of compassion for her. And she knew that I came out of the Height of heights, in whose light she had had faith from the beginning. Pistis Sophia then took courage and uttered the tenth repentance saying:"

The Lion-faced Power oppressed Pistis Sophia, desiring to take away all powers from her.

It is clear that the initiate owes many debts and that the power of justice is threatening him.

Nevertheless, the inner Christ can forgive Pistis Sophia.

The Light of the lights, the Truth of the truth, the Concealed of the concealed, helps the initiate full of Pistis Sophia.

Pistis Sophia is forgiven in the ninth repentance.

It is necessary to receive and posteriorly to attain the qualification of the eight Initiations.

The Ninth Hour comes, after having passed through the eight great qualifications which correspond to the eight Initiations.

The secret number is known in the Ninth Hour. The initiate then enters the Archangelic group to which he belongs.

Now we explain why Pistis Sophia is forgiven in the Ninth Hour.

The Army of the Voice is organized in groups, and each group has its secret number according to its own form of work.

The First Mystery hears Pistis Sophia and under His commandment she is conduced out of the Chaos.

The First Mystery is the Father, the Ancient of Days. Each one of us has his own Father.

The initiate is deluded by the ego, by the Self-willed and his downfall is due to it.

The Light-Power, which resembles the primogenial Light, guides the devotee. Nevertheless, the important thing is the Light of the lights.

Christ, obedient to the Father, always comes secretly to help the initiate.

The inner Christ helps us interiorly.

The inner Christ incarnates in the initiate and helps him in the Great Work.

Christ passes through the Aeons in order to come into the incarnation.

The Incarnated Christ works remarkably when disintegrating the engenders of the inferno.

The inner Christ, in the presence of the initiate, shines ten thousand times more than the lions of the law.

The inner Lord is above the lions of the law.

The inner Christ descends in order to internally help Pistis Sophia.

The Light of the lights, the Intelligence of the intelligence, always hears the sincerely repented one.

The cunning threats and the unjust, lawless lips are always conjuring against the initiates of the rocky path which leads towards the final liberation.

The Light that the initiate has must be taken to the Father of all Lights.

The tenth repentance of Sophia

1. *I have cried unto thee, O Light of lights, in my oppression and thou hast hearkened unto me.*

2. *O Light, save my power from unjust and lawless lips and from crafty traps.*

3. The light which was being taken from me in crafty snaring, will not be brought unto thee.

4. For the traps of Self-willed and the nooses of the merciless [one] are spread out.

5. Woe unto me, that my dwelling was far off, and I was in the dwellings of the chaos.

6. My power was in regions which are not mine.

7. And I entreated those merciless [ones]; and when I entreated them, they fought against me without a cause.

It is obvious that the Self-willed ego and the snares of the unmerciful are everywhere.

The Self-willed animal ego that dwells within us, and the snares of the unmerciful, lie in wait for the initiate.

Pistis Sophia's dwelling-place is the Thirteenth Aeon. However, when she is fallen she lives within the inferior Chaos.

The regions of Pistis Sophia are in the Thirteenth Aeon and never in the abysses of perdition.

The tenebrous ones do not feel pity for the initiates. On the contrary, they attack them.

Chapter 53

When Jesus had said this unto his disciples, he said unto them: "Now, therefore, let him whom his spirit stirreth, come forward and speak the solution of the tenth repentance of Pistis Sophia."

Peter answered and said: "O Lord, concerning this thy light-power prophesied afore time through David in the one-hundred-and-nineteenth Psalm [Modern Psalm 120], *saying..."*

Peter, within each one of ourselves is the part of the Being that is related to the mysteries of sex.

In the cosmic drama, Peter died crucified, with his head pointing downwards.

The inverted cross of Peter indicates that we must work in the Ninth Sphere, sex.

Mars descends into the Ninth Sphere in order to re-temper his sword, as does Hercules in order to clean the stables of Augias, as does Perseus in order to cut the head of Medusa with his flaming sword.

The descent into the Ninth Sphere is the maximum ordeal for the Hierophant.

Buddha, Jesus, Dante, Zarathrustra, Hermes, Quezalcoatl, etc., had to pass through this terrible ordeal.

For as long as this terrible ordeal is not passed, only theories exist within the mind.

Peter interpreteth the tenth repentance from Psalm CXIX [Modern Psalm 120]

1. *I cried unto thee, O Lord, in my oppression and thou hearkened unto me.*
2. *O Lord, save my soul from unjust lips and from crafty tongues.*
3. *What will be given unto thee or what will be added unto thee with a crafty tongue?*
4. *The arrows of the strong [one] are made sharp with the coal of the desert.*
5. *Woe unto me, that my dwelling is far off, and I dwelt in the tents of Kedar.*
6. *My soul hath dwelt in many regions as a guest.*
7. *I was peaceful with them who hate peace; if I spake unto them, they fought against me without a cause.*

"This is now, therefore, O Lord, the solution of the tenth repentance of Pistis Sophia, which she hath uttered when the material emana-

tions of Self-willed oppressed her, they and his lion-faced power, and when they oppressed her exceedingly."

The Lord hears the one who implores Him.

The unjust lips and the crafty tongues always calumniate the Hierophants of sex.

The perverse ones can never comprehend the sexual mysteries and vociferate against the wise.

The crafty tongue that speaks of what it does not even remotely know will fall into the abyss of perdition.

Those who calumniate the Hierophants of sex devolve within the womb of the Earth until the Second Death.

Speaking against the mysteries of sex implies an attack against the inner Peter, who is the autonomous and self-cognizant part of our own Being related with sex.

Strong is the one who strengthens himself in Sexual Magic.

The one who has never worked in the forge of the Cyclops is frightfully weak.

The sexual energy is the mighty strength of all powers.

Life is a desert for the initiate. Rare is the one who can live in the desert of the wise.

The arrows of the mighty one are sharpened with the fire of sexual life and flaming, erotic coals.

Pistis Sophia's dwelling-place is far off from the tents of Kedar.

Our beloved readers must not forget that the CXIX Psalm, cited by the Hierophant Peter, corresponds to the specific functions of our intimate Peter and to the mysteries of sex. Similarly, each one of the personages of Pistis Sophia is one of the parts of our own Being.

Obviously, each one of the twelve parts and every one of the parts of our own Being has his documentation in the sacred scriptures.

Now our readers will comprehend the reason why each one of the personages of the *Pistis Sophia* cites a paragraph of the *Holy Bible.*

Therefore, Peter and the mysteries of sex are not an exception.

Our readers are advised about the intimate relationship between the personages of *Pistis Sophia* and the Biblical paragraphs cited by them.

Obviously, the Biblical paragraphs cited by them specify the functions of each one of them in ourselves and within us, here and now.

Pistis Sophia is certainly not a book to be mechanically read, but should be studied and profoundly meditated upon, during the entire lifetime.

The CXIX Psalm, cited by Peter, continues saying:

"My soul has dwelt in many regions as a guest." This invites us to meditate.

The great Kabir Jesus said: *"In my Father's house are many mansions."*

The adulterers and fornicators will fall into the infernal worlds where only weeping and the gnashing of teeth are heard.

We must distinguish between a downfall and a descent.

The one who wishes to ascend must first of all descend.

No one can ascend without previously having taken the trouble to descend.

Every exaltation is preceded by a frightful and terrible humiliation.

Peter has the keys of the Kingdom.

The two crossed keys are the Sulphur and the Mercury of the wise.

The Sulphur is the sexual fire.

The Mercury is the metallic soul of the sacred sperm.

The Sulphur must fecundate the Mercury of the wise before initiating the ascension of the Sulphured Mercury through the medullar spinal canal.

Sulphur and Mercury open the doors of the distinct regions of the universe.

Sulphur and Mercury, although opposites, become conciliated by the virtue of the sublimated Salt.

Sulphur and Mercury are the parents of the Philosophical Stone.

The red demons of Seth hate peace. They are the ones who fight against the Being without a cause.

The psychic aggregates and the lion of the law always oppress Pistis Sophia exceedingly.

Peter, the Hierophant of sex, always gives the solution of the repentance of Pistis Sophia.

The true repentance of the Soul has a sexual foundation.

Jesus commendeth Peter

Jesus said unto him: "Well said, Peter, and finely. This is the solution of the tenth repentance of Pistis Sophia."

Chapter 54

Jesus continued again in the discourse and said unto his disciples: "It came to pass then, when this lion-faced power saw me, how I drew nigh unto Pistis Sophia, shining very exceedingly, that it grew still more furious and emanated from itself a multitude of exceedingly violent emanations. When this then befell, Pistis Sophia uttered the eleventh repentance, saying..."

Karmic debts must be paid as we advance along the rocky path that leads to final liberation.

The eleventh repentance of Sophia

1. *Why hath the mighty power raised up itself in evil?*

2. *Its plotting taketh away the light from me all the time, and as sharp iron have they taken away power from me.*

3. *I chose to descend into the chaos rather than to abide in the thirteenth aeon, the region of Virtuousness.*

4. And they desired to lead me craftily, in order to consume my whole light.

5. For this cause then will the Light take away their whole light, and also their whole matter will be made naught. And it will take away their light and not suffer them to abide in the thirteenth aeon, their dwelling-place, and will not have their name in the region of those who shall live.

6. And the four-and-twenty emanations will see what hath befallen thee, O lion-faced power, and will be afraid and not be disobedient, but give the purification of their light.

7. And they will see thee and will rejoice over thee and say: Lo, an emanation which hath not given the purification of its light, so that it may be saved, but boasted itself in the abundance of the light of its power, because it did not emanate from the power in it, and hath said: I will take away the light from Pistis Sophia, which will now be taken from it.'

"Now, therefore, let him in whom his power is raised, come forward and proclaim the solution of the eleventh repentance of Pistis Sophia."

The Mighty Power has always raised itself up in evil, because evil fortifies it against its will.

The sharp iron takes away the power from Pistis Sophia under the tenebrous plot of the Averno.

The region of Virtuousness is ineffable, yet Pistis Sophia descends into the inferior Chaos in order to transform herself and victoriously re-ascend.

The Theomertmalogos was altered in the dawn of the Mahamanvantara, by a contact of the Geneotriamatzikamnian type.

This signifies that the sublime Theomertmalogos suffered a certain alteration when it made contact with the primogenial manifestation of the cosmos.

Similarly, Pistis Sophia passes through a certain transformation when she makes contact with the inferior Chaos.

The tenebrous ones within the Chaos always want to consume all the light of Pistis Sophia.

The Light will take away from the tenebrous ones their negative and fatal light.

The matter of the tenebrous ones will be reduced to dust. This is the Second Death.

The tenebrous ones will never ascend to the Thirteenth Aeon.

There exist the Rulers of the Light and the Tenebrorum Rulers. The Rulers of the Light have their name written in the great book of life. Yet, the Tenebrorum Rulers shall not have their name written in the great book of life.

The Four-and-twenty Emanations are the twenty-four Elders, who are the living personification of the Microcosmic Zodiac within us.

The twenty-four Elders, or twenty-four autonomous and self-cognizant parts of our own Being, will see what has befallen in front of the lion of the law. Thus, they will be afraid and will not be disobedient, but will give the purification of their Light.

A divine, ineffable purification irradiates from their Light.

The emanation that does not give the purification of its Light can never be saved.

Each part of our own Being must be perfected. The perfection of each part is possible only with the elimination of the undesirable psychic elements.

The most elevated parts of the Being are demanding. Therefore, no one can perfect them without having eliminated the totality of the undesirable psychic elements.

The one who perfects the most elevated parts of the Being receives the degree of Ishmech.

If the emanation, or the part of the Being does not give its Light of perfection, it is because it remains bottled up within a psychic aggregate.

It is obvious that when any part of the Being is bottled up, it boasts of itself, it becomes egotistical.

It is a crime to boast about the power and the Light, which does not emanate from ourselves, but from the Being.

The Light and the real wisdom emanates from the Being of the Being, not exclusively from some of the parts.

Any part of the Being which is bottled up in one or another psychic aggregate, a living personification of a psychological defect, intends to boast of itself and believes itself to be sovereign.

Those who pretend to have the totality of the light of Pistis Sophia ignore that they ignore.

Salome interpreteth the repentance from Psalm LI [Modern Psalm 52]

Then Salome came forward and said: "My Lord, concerning this thy light-power prophesied afore time through David in the fifty-first Psalm [Modern Psalm 52], *saying..."*

1. *Why doth the mighty [one] boast himself in his wickedness?*

2. *Thy tongue hath studied unrighteousness all the day long; as a sharp razor hast thou practised craft.*

3. *Thou lovedst wickedness more than goodness; thou lovedst to speak unrighteousness more than righteousness.*

4. *Thou lovedst all words of submerging and a crafty tongue.*

5. *Wherefor will God bring thee to naught utterly, and will uproot thee and drag thee out from thy dwelling-place, and will root out thy root and cast it away from the living. (Selah.)*

6. *The righteous will see and be afraid, and they will mock at him and say:*

7. *Lo, a man who made not God for his helper, but trusted to his great riches and was mighty in his vanity.*

8. *But I am as a fruit-bearing olive-tree in the house of God. I have trusted in the grace of God from all eternity.*

9. *And I will confess unto thee, for thou hast dealt faithfully with me; and I will wait on thy name, for it is auspicious in the presence of thy holy [ones].*

"This then is now, therefore, my Lord, the solution of the eleventh repentance of Pistis Sophia. While thy light-power hath roused me, I have spoken it according to thy desire."

Psalm LI specifies the functions of Salome within us, here and now.

Obviously, none of the personages of *Pistis Sophia* are outside of ourselves.

Unquestionably, all the personages of *Pistis Sophia* are autonomous and self-cognizant parts of our own Being.

With the Olooestesnokhnian type of vision, the Being appears like an army of children. This is how we, the "brethren in service," perceive Him.

An entire Hooltampanas of the universe can be perceived with this vision.

An entire Hooltampanas is equivalent to 5,764,801 tonalities of the universal cosmic color.

No one can possess this type of sight of the sacred Olooestesnokhnian without having previously passed through the Buddhist Annihilation.

Salome as virtue and virtues, law and laws, knows very well why the mighty (one) boasts and vaunts himself in his wickedness.

The tongue of the perverse one becomes like a sharp razor for evil.

The perverse one loves evil, for the love of the same evil.

The lying words and crafty tongue characterizes the perverse one.

Salome knows good from evil and evil from good.

Each part of our own Being has his sacred ministry.

Above and below, in the Macrocosm and in the Microcosmic human being, the creative powers are esoterically divided into seven, three, and four, within the twelve great cosmic orders, which bring to mind the zodiacal signs in the Macrocosm and in the Microcosm.

The lions of fire, or "lions of life" of the zodiacal sign of Leo, are constituted as the most elevated group in the Macrocosm and within the Microcosmic human being.

Moreover, it is important to remember that just as the zodiacal belt exists in the firmament, likewise, the flames of the constellation of Leo exist within the human being. The hierarchy of the fire is the most important hierarchy in the Macrocosm and in the Microcosmic human being.

Following these short paragraphs, which are necessary in order to clarify concepts, let us continue with the biblical verses cited by Salome and their corresponding commentary.

God abandons the one who marches on the path of perdition.

When the son falls, then the Father withdraws.

When the Father withdraws, then the son falls in disgrace.

The one who does not trust in the help of God, but in his material wealth and who has developed the psychic aggregate of vanity, falls into the abyss of perdition.

The aggregate or psychic aggregate of vanity impedes the correct relationship with the superior parts of the Being.

Vanity is a relative of pride.

Vanity is a charlatan. Pride is silent.

Someone will speak about certain things because of vanity, yet, will keep silent about them because of pride.

By dint of pride, any wealthy person could have in his residence an antique car, possibly from the last century. However, because of vanity, this person would prefer to drive a car of the latest model.

Hurt vanity causes frightful suffering. However, hurt pride can cause death.

When vanity and pride are united, they can perform monstrosities.

Vanity is also accustomed to being disguised with the costume of modesty. A vain painter or writer can appear in public displaying the costume of a beggar.

When an artist is hurt in his vanity, then he is apt to fall into terribly painful situations.

A fruit-bearing olive tree is like the one who works on himself and who trusts in the grace of God for all eternity.

The Lord knows how to pay well the one who trusts in His holy name.

Jesus commendeth Salome

It came to pass then, when Jesus had heard these words which Salome spake, that he said: "Well said, Salome. Amen, amen, I say unto you: I will perfect you in all mysteries of the kingdom of the Light."

The Kingdom of the Light is formed by the conscious circle of the Solar Humanity, which operates over the superior centers of the Being.

Chapter 55

Self-willed aideth his emanations and they again oppress Sophia

And Jesus continued again in the discourse and said unto his disciples: "It came to pass then thereafter, that I drew near unto the chaos, shining very exceedingly, to take away the light from that lion-faced power. As I shone exceedingly, it was in fear and cried out to its Self-willed god, that he should help it. And forthwith the Self-willed god looked out of the thirteenth aeon, and looked down into the chaos, exceedingly wrathful and desiring to help his lion-faced power. And forthwith the lion-faced power, it and all its emanations, surrounded Pistis Sophia, desiring to take away the whole light in Sophia. It came to pass then, when they oppressed Sophia, that she cried to the height, crying unto me that I should help her. It came to pass then, when she looked to the height, that she saw Self-willed exceedingly wrathful, and she was in fear, and uttered the twelfth repentance because of Self-willed and his emanations. She cried on high unto me, saying..."

The power of the lions of the law utilizes the same tenebrous elements in order to punish the sinner.

For example, the great dictators of history were utilized in order to punish the world.

Psychic aggregates that are related with the law of karma exist within every human being.

The lion of the law can utilize those psychic aggregates, which are related with the law of karma in order to punish the delinquent one.

The ego wants to make the initiate (who marches towards the Thirteenth Aeon) fall down.

The power of the lions of the law oppresses Pistis Sophia.

The Self-willed ego and the powers of the darkness mortally hate those who march towards the Thirteenth Aeon.

The twelfth repentance of Sophia

1. *O Light, forget not my praise-singing.*

2. *For Self-willed and his lion-faced power have opened their chops against me and have acted craftily against me.*

3. *They have surrounded me, desiring to take away my power, and have hated me, because I have sung praises unto thee.*

4. *Instead of loving me they slandered me. But I sang praises.*

5. *They plotted a plot to take away my power, because I have sung to thee praises, O Light; and hated me, because I have loved thee.*

6. *Let the darkness come over Self-willed, and let the ruler of the outermost darkness abide at his right hand.*

7. And when thou passes sentence, take from him his power; and the deed which he hath plotted, to take from me my light, —mayest thou take his from him.

8. And may all his powers of his light in him finish, and let another of the three triple-powers receive his sovereignty.

9. May all the powers of his emanations be lightless and may his matter be without any light in it.

10. May his emanations remain in the chaos and not dare to go to their region. May their light in them die away and let them not go to the thirteenth aeon, their region.

11. May the Receiver, the Purifier of the lights, purify all the lights which are in Self-willed, and take them from them.

12. May the rulers of the lower darkness rule over his emanations, and let no one give them shelter in his region; and let no one hearken to the power of his emanations in the chaos.

13. Let them take away the light in his emanations and blot out their name from the thirteenth aeon, yea rather take his name for ever out of that region.

14. And on the lion-faced power let them bring the sin of him who emanated it, before the Light, and not wipe out the iniquity of the matter which hath brought him [sc. Self-willed] forth.

15. And may their sin be altogether before the Light eternally, and may they let them not look beyond [the chaos] and take their names out of all regions;

16. Because they have not spared me and have oppressed him whose light and whose power they have taken away, and also conformably with those who set me therein, they desired to take away my whole light from me.

17. They loved to descend to the chaos; so let them abide therein, and they shall not be brought up [therefrom] from now on. They desired not the region of virtuousness for dwelling-place, and they shall not be taken thither from now on.

18. He put on darkness as a garment, and it entered into him as water, and it entered in into all his powers as oil.

19. Let him wrap himself into the chaos as into a garment, and gird himself with the darkness as with a leathern girdle for ever.

20. Let this befall them who have brought this upon me for the Light's sake and have said: Let us take away her whole power.

21. But do thou, O Light, have mercy upon me for the sake of the mystery of thy name, and save me in the goodness of thy grace.

22. For they have taken away my light and my power; and my power hath inwardly tottered, and I could not stand upright in their midst.

23. I am become as matter which is fallen; I am tossed hither and thither as a demon in the air.

24. My power hath perished, because I possess no mystery; and my matter hath become dwindled because of my light, for they have taken it away.

25. And thy mocked me; they looked at me, nodding at me.

26. Help me according to thy mercy.

"Now, therefore, let him whose spirit is ready, come forward and utter the solution of the twelfth repentance of Pistis Sophia."

Self-willed and the Lion-faced Power always act against Pistis Sophia.

initiates are hated because they sing praises unto the Great Light.

initiates sing praises to the Great Light, although the darkness hates them.

Pistis Sophia is hated because she loves the Great Light.

Let the darkness cover the animal ego.

The administrator of the outermost darkness is the prince of this world, the iniquitous one.

The Antichrist is the iniquitous one.

Whosoever pronounces himself against the inner Christ is the Antichrist.

The false, materialistic science has been created by the mind of the Antichrist.

The Antichrist is the Machiavellian mind of the materialistic scientists who perform miracles and misleading prodigies.

The evil minds of the dwellers of the Earth is the Antichrist.

The Antichrist's humanity, which is this present humanity, will perish between fire and water. Thus, this is how the Antichrist will lose its power.

The same happens within the initiate who wishes to return to the Thirteenth Aeon.

The Antichrist succumbs within the initiate who returns to the Thirteenth Aeon.

All the powers and the false light of the Antichrist will succumb within the initiate.

The initiate gains the crystallization of the superior forces of Nature and the cosmos within himself, replacing the Antichrist and its power.

The three superior forces of Nature and the cosmos are: Holy Affirmation, Holy Negation, and Holy Conciliation.

Positive, negative, and neutral forces.

Father, Son, and Holy Spirit.

The emanations of the prince of this world are the red demons of Seth.

The matter of the prince of this world must remain without any light in it.

The emanations of the prince of this world fall into the inferior chaos.

The lights, or percentages of Essence, which are bottled up within the ego, must be liberated by means of the annihilation of each part of the ego or "I."

The Divine Mother Kundalini must purify all light and take it from within each psychic aggregate.

In the infernal worlds, the Rulers watch the tenebrous ones and do not permit them to leave the abode of Pluto.

Similarly, within each one of ourselves, the Rulers, the superior parts of our Being, must watch over their emanations, which are the red demons of Seth.

The Essence, which is bottled up within the tenebrous ones, can only escape from within them through their supreme death.

The power of the demons in the Chaos must be annulled little by little.

The light which is enclosed within the red demons of Seth must be taken away from them in a revolutionary manner.

The names of the lost ones are erased in the Thirteenth Aeon.

The lion of the law projects the guilt in front of itself in order for it to be known and never erases iniquities from the one who has produced them.

Karma disappears only by patient destruction of psychic aggregates, and through forgiveness, or negotiation.

Nevertheless, the projected guilt continues in Akasa as a movie until we annihilate the Teleoginooras films.

Guilt is always visible and tangible in the Teleoginooras films.

The tenebrous ones must live within the inferior Chaos.

They are not permitted to look beyond the abode of Pluto.

The red demons of Seth have spared no one, but have oppressed every one whose Light and power they have taken away.

The tenebrous ones always desire to take away the light from Pistis Sophia.

The perverse ones defend the inferior Chaos. Therefore, let them continue to abide within Tartarus.

The tenebrous ones never desire the abode of Virtuousness. This is why they continue to dwell in the womb of the Averno.

"Demonius Est Deus Inversus:" The demon is God inverted.

The inferno is the womb of Heaven.

The other face of God is in the Averno.

The Averno is the shadow of light.

The Light of lights must save us with the mystery of His name and the power of His grace.

Pistis Sophia cannot stand until she passes through the Buddhist Annihilation.

Newness comes only through death. If the seed does not die, the plant is not born.

The fallen initiate suffers the unspeakable.

The powers of the initiates decrease when they do not possess the mystery, which means, when they do not work in the Ninth Sphere (sex).

The misterium magnum of the universe resides in its seed, in its Iliaster, and specifically in its limbus magnum.

The misterium of the tree resides in its seed.

The misterium of a human resides in his seed.

Whosoever does not work with the misterium magnum fails in the Great Work.

The [male] initiate who does not have a Hermetic Glass must attain one in order to work in the mysteries.

Understand that the Hermetic Glass is the feminine yoni.

The mysteries of lingam-yoni must be cultivated in secret.

The laws of the number six teach that when an alchemist does not possess a Hermetic Glass that is in good condition, he must then search for another one that will be in a perfect state, in order to work within the laboratory.

Nevertheless, not a single alchemist can successfully use a Hermetic Glass without the will of the Father, who is in secret.

The misterium magnum of sex is terribly divine.

Many are the learned ignoramuses who do not know the rules and procedures of the Sixth Arcanum.

The Pharisee "I" of the learned ignoramuses that do not know the rules and procedures of the Sixth Arcanum calumniate and condemn the alchemist who takes a new Hermetic Glass.

The profane and profaners ignore the mysteries of the Sixth Arcanum.

Foolish are the adepts who renounce their laboratory work by obeying the learned ignoramuses.

The adepts who are bottled up within moral prejudice and ethical codes renounce the use of a Hermetic Glass. Thus, they fail in the Great Work.

A destroyed Hermetic Glass is not useful for laboratory work.

The human matter of Pistis Sophia inevitably languishes because of the lack of light.

An alchemist who abdicates the sexual mysteries of lingam-yoni, as a fact, resigns from being an alchemist. Therefore, such a person fails.

The tenebrous ones mock the sexual abstainers by nodding their heads.

Sexual abstinence originates terribly perverse, malignant Poisoniooskirian vibrations.

The Poisoniooskirian vibrations are terribly malignant.

The Poisoniooskirian vibrations originate the development of the abominable Kundabuffer organ.

The abominable Kundabuffer organ is the sexual fire directed from the coccygeal bone downwards, towards the atomic infernos of the human being.

The abominable Kundabuffer organ is the tail of Satan, the tempting serpent of Eden, the horrible Python serpent that slithered in the mud of the earth and that the irritated Apollo hurt with his darts.

The tempting serpent is the antithesis of the serpent of brass, which is entwined in the generator lingam.

Moses healed the Israelites in the wilderness with the marvellous power of the serpent of brass. Yet, the tempting serpent of Eden has this painful humanity submerged in a fatal, collective, hypnotic state.

The serpent of brass, the serpent that is entwined on the rod of Asclepius, God of Medicine, must awaken us, must take us away from the collective hypnotic state.

Let us then distinguish between Kundalini and Kundabuffer, between the serpent that ascends and the one that descends.

We must never commit the error of attributing all the left and tenebrous powers of the descending serpent (Kundabuffer) to the serpent (Kundalini) that ascends through the medullar spinal canal of the human being.

Only the one who is prepared can understand the twelfth repentance of Pistis Sophia.

Andrew, within us, is the autonomous and self-cognizant part of our own Being, who is occupied with the three factors of the revolution of the consciousness.

These three factors are: to be born, to die, and to sacrifice oneself for humanity.

The cross of Saint Andrew is accustomed to being terribly painful.

The Mercury and the Sulphur must incessantly cross if we long to continue the performance of the Great Work.

The sufferings of the initiate, crucified on the cross of Andrew, are inexpressible.

It is not possible to purify and perfect the Mercurial bodies if we renounce the disintegration of the Dry Mercury.

The Dry Mercury is crystallized as the psychic aggregates, living personifications of our psychological defects.

The disintegration of the psychic aggregates is possible only through conscious works and voluntary sufferings.

There is the need to pass through great emotional crises and intentional sufferings if, we truly want to atomically disintegrate our psychological defects.

/e can better comprehend the inexpressible suffering of ner Andrew.

lessed are they that mourn, for they shall be comforted."

The supreme repentance—necessary in order to disintegrate any psychic aggregates—demands cries and remorse.

It is not possible to disintegrate psychic aggregates without tears, repentance, and supreme pain.

To comprehend Andrew without the transmutation science of "Yesod-Mercury," and without the disintegration of the undesirable psychic elements that we carry in our interior, would be impossible.

Egoic perforation and egoic disintegration is performed within the flaming forge of Vulcan.

The supreme sacrifice of the inner Andrew is urgent, non-delayable, and unpostponable.

The alchemist who does not sacrifice himself for humanity will never become a Bodhisattva.

Only the Bodhisattvas with compassionate hearts, who have given their life for humanity, can incarnate the inner Christ.

We must make a complete differentiation between the Sravakas and Pratyeka Buddhas on one side, and Bodhisattvas on the other.

The Sravakas and Pratyeka Buddhas preoccupy themselves only with their particular perfection, without caring a bit for poor, suffering humanity.

Obviously, the Pratyeka Buddhas and Sravakas can never incarnate Christ.

Only the Bodhisattvas who sacrifice themselves for humanity can incarnate Christ.

The sacred title of Bodhisattva is legitimately attained only by those who have renounced all Nirvanic happiness for the love of this suffering humanity.

Obviously, before the Bodhisattva is born, the Bodhichitta must be formed within us. Furthermore, it is important to clarify the necessity of disintegrating the ego, the "I," in order for the Bodhichitta to emerge.

The Bodhichitta is formed with the merits of love and supreme sacrifice for our fellowmen.

The Bodhisattva is formed within the environment and psychological atmosphere of the Bodhichitta.

We must not mistake the Bodhichitta with the Bodhisattva. The Bodhichitta is the awakened and developed superlative consciousness of the Being.

The Bodhichitta emerges in the aspirant who sacrifices himself for his fellowmen, long before the Mercurial bodies have been created.

We could never convert ourselves into Bodhisattvas without the complete work of the inner Andrew.

Anyone with his Mercurial bodies can be a Sravaka or a Buddha Pratyeka, but this is not sufficient in order to be a Bodhisattva.

Only those who have sacrificed themselves through distinct Mahamanvantaras for the planetary humanities deserve to be called Bodhisattvas.

H. P. B. conventionally referred to Bodhisattva as those who possess the superior existential bodies of the Being, or better said, Mercurial bodies. However, in strict, orthodox Buddhism, only those who have Bodhichitta within themselves and who have renounced all Nirvanic happiness for the love of humanity can qualify themselves as Bodhisattvas.

The cross of Saint Andrew has the form of an "X," which is the extraordinary hieroglyph of the luminous and divergent radiations that emerge from the Creator Logos.

The rose, symbol of the Solar Logos, shines in the center of the cross of Saint Andrew.

The cross of Saint Andrew symbolizes illumination... revelation after frightful sacrifices.

The Greek cross and the cross of Saint Andrew have the same significance in Hermetic science.

It is not irrelevant to remember that the vertical "phallus" within the formal "cteis," forms a cross.

Phallus-uterus, when connected, form a cross.

Nevertheless, the cross as an "X" indicates the complete work in the Great Work.

The work will have victoriously concluded if the rose shines on the cross of Saint Andrew.

The perverse ones use their tongues in order to discredit the initiates.

With words of hatred, the fiendish ones slander the adepts who work in the Great Work of the Father.

Nevertheless, the adepts respond to this infamy with love, and bless those who damn them.

Chapter 56

Andrew interpreteth the twelfth repentance from Psalm CVIII [Modern Psalm 109]

And Andrew came forward and said: "My Lord and Saviour, thy light-power hath prophesied afore time through David concerning this repentance which Pistis Sophia hath uttered, and said in the one-hundred-and-eighth Psalm [Modern Psalm 109]*:*

1. *God, keep not silent at my praise-singing.*

2. *For the mouths of the sinner and crafty have opened their chops against me and with crafty deceitful tongue have talked behind me.*

3. *And they have surrounded me with words of hate and have fought against me without a cause.*

4. *Instead of loving me they have slandered me. But I prayed.*

5. *They showed evil against me for good and hate for my love.*

6. *Set a sinner over him, and let the slanderer stand at his right hand.*

7. When sentence is passed upon him, may he go forth condemned and his prayer become sin.

8. May his days be shortened and another receive his overseership.

9. May his children become orphans and his wife a widow.

10. May his children be carried away and be driven forth and beg; may they be thrown out of their houses.

11. May the money-lender sift out all that he hath, and may strangers plunder all his best efforts.

12. Let there be no man to back him, and no one to take pity on his orphans.

13. May his children be exterminated and his name blotted out in a single generation.

14. Let the sin of his fathers be remembered before the Lord, and the sin of his mother be not blotted out.

15. Let them be ever present to the Lord and his memory be rooted out from the earth;

16. In that he hath not thought of using mercy and hath persecuted a poor and wretched man and hath persecuted a sorry creature to slay him.

17. He loved cursing, —and it shall come unto him. He desired not blessing, —it shall stay far from him.

18. He clothed himself with cursing as with a vesture, and it entered into his bowels as water, and it was as oil in his bones.

19. May it be for him as a garment in which he shall be wrapped, and as a girdle with which he shall ever be girded.

20. This is the work of them who slander [me] before the Lord, and speak unlawfully against my soul.

21. But do thou, O Lord God, be gracious unto me; for thy name's sake save me.

22. For I am poor and I am wretched; my heart is tumult within me.

23. I am carried away in the midst as a shadow which hath sunk down, and I am shaken out as grasshoppers.

24. My knees have become weak from fasting, and my flesh is altered from [lack of] oil.

25. But I have become a mock unto them; they saw me and wagged their heads.

26. Help, O Lord God, and save me according to thy grace.

27. May they know that this is thy hand, and that thou, O Lord, hast fashioned them.

"This is then the solution of the twelfth repentance which Pistis Sophia uttered, when she was in the chaos."

The tenebrous ones pay the noble services with black coins.

These tenebrous sinners are the red demons of Seth, upon whom karma falls.

The sentence falls upon the red demons of Seth.

It is obvious that the lion of the law punishes the red demons of Seth without consideration.

The days are shortened for the red demons of Seth, and others receive their sovereignty.

Obviously, karma is terrible, and often the children of the perverse ones often become orphans and their wives become widows.

The lion of the law is implacable, and many times the children of the fiendish ones are often carried away and driven forth to beg. They are thrown out of their houses.

The money-lenders sift out the money from the perverse ones and strangers plunder all of their best efforts.

No one has mercy for the orphans of perversity, and no man takes pity on them.

The children of the perverse ones will be exterminated and their name will be blotted out in a single generation.

The sin of the father of these children is before the Lord and the sin of their mother is not blotted out. Thus, karma is in action.

The children of perdition will always be present with their sins. However, their memory will be rooted out from the Earth.

The perverse sinner never thought of using mercy for his neighbor and had persecuted the poor wretched man. Therefore, karma will fall upon him.

The perverse one takes no pity on anyone and persecutes the sorry creature in order to slay it.

The fiendish love cursing. Therefore, their cursing will fall upon them as a ray of vengeance.

The perverse ones desire no blessing. Therefore, blessings will always stay far from them.

The perverse ones always clothe themselves with cursing, as with a vesture. Therefore, the curse shall then enter their bowels as water and as oil in their bones.

This disgrace is to the fiendish ones as a garment in which they shall be wrapped and as a girdle with which they shall ever be girded.

This is the fatal work of those who slander Pistis Sophia and who speak unlawfully about the initiates.

These perverse ones are obviously within and outside of ourselves.

Those who are within are the red demons of Seth, living personifications of our psychological defects.

The tenebrous ones who are outside of ourselves are those brothers of the tenebrous fraternity.

Obviously, the tenebrous powers fight against the initiates to death, trying to take them away from the path that leads to the final liberation.

Only the inner Christ can help us.

However, the inner Lord can do nothing without the serpent.

As long as we do not completely die, all of us will be poor, wretched, and miserable.

The heart is tumultuous within those who have their ego alive and strong.

Only the tranquil heart can give us true and legitimate happiness.

The purpose of profound interior meditation is to obtain true tranquility.

It is not possible to obtain the peace of the tranquil heart as long as the psychological factors of non-tranquility exist within us.

We explore the psychological "I" during profound interior meditation.

During profound interior meditation we propose only to integrally comprehend the psychological defect discovered in self-observation.

Each self-observed defect must be previously comprehended through meditation, before proceeding with its elimination.

Prayer and Sexual Magic are indispensable for elimination.

We have to pray during the connection of the "lingam-yoni," in the Ninth Sphere.

In these instances, we will beg the Divine Mother Kundalini to disintegrate and eliminate the psychological aggregate that we have previously comprehended.

Thus, by eliminating the factors of non-tranquility, we will attain complete tranquility.

Only the tranquil heart can reach illumination and omniscience.

When the Bodhisattva reaches illumination, then he prepares himself for omniscience.

It is not possible to reach omniscience unless we previously learn to live between the absolute and the relative, between the mutable and immutable.

Those who have passed beyond the Illuminated Void and the relativity of life experience that which is called Tality.

The Tality is the great Reality of life, free in its movement.

Only those who can wilfully experience Tality receive the power of omniscience.

No one can reach omniscience without having reached the true reality of the tranquil heart.

There is a need to shake out and eliminate the psychic aggregates, as grasshoppers.

The knees of those who have ego tremble and their flesh is altered from lack of oil.

How weak they are, those who have egoic consciousness. They tremble with fear.

The tenebrous ones mock the fallen initiates.

Only the grace of the inner Christ can save the fallen ones.

Only the Lord has formed the hands of the fallen ones, and only He can save us.

The great Buddhist Annihilation is urgent, non-delayable, and unpostponable.

We must die in all the levels of the mind, and pass beyond the Illuminated Void and the existential relativity of the universe.

It is urgent to cease to exist within the heresy of separatism or in the joy of the Illuminated Void.

It is unpostponable to Self-realize within ourselves that which is called Tality.

The Tality is the great Reality beyond perversity and holiness.

The saints can never exist within the womb of the Tality, which is beyond perversity and holiness.

There is nothing in the Tality which can be called holy.

The great Reality is the great Reality, the Tality. The saints and the perverse ones revolve within the great Wheel of Samsara. Therefore, they are very far from the Tality.

Nevertheless, we must be very careful with the psychic aggregate of self-merits.

The psychic aggregate of self-merits causes us to be newly born in Heaven or on Earth.

The psychic aggregate of self-merits removes us far away from the Tality.

We never obtain real merits because the one who performs the entire true work is the Father.

The first principle of the Gnostic doctrine is the Tality or great Reality.

The inner Christ must destroy the psychic aggregate of self-merits within us in order to take us to the Tality.

The Lord raises the fallen ones.

Work with the Woman-Serpent, and the Lord will save you.

Chapter 57

And Jesus continued again in the discourse and said unto his disciples: "It came to pass again thereafter that Pistis Sophia cried unto me, saying:

"'O Light of lights, I have transgressed in the twelve aeons, and have descended from them; wherefor have I uttered the twelve repentances, [one] for each aeon. Now, therefore, O Light of lights, forgive me my transgression, for it is exceedingly great, because I have abandoned the regions of the height and have come to dwell in the regions of the chaos.'

"When then Pistis Sophia had said this, she continued again in the thirteenth repentance, saying..."

Christ is the Light of lights. He, Himself, is one with the Father.

The inner Christ, or Christus-Vishnu, is the Light of lights.

The Light of lights is: Brahma, Vishnu, Shiva; Father, Son, Holy Spirit.

The Twelve Repentances of Pistis Sophia are related with the Twelve Hours of Apollonius, the Twelve Works of Hercules, the Twelve Aeons.

In these Twelve Repentances, the qualification of the eight great Initiations of the Fire take place, as well as four more works following the resurrection of the inner Christ within the Bodhisattva.

It is clear that every fallen Bodhisattva descends from the Thirteenth Aeon and falls into the Chaos.

Undoubtedly, Pistis Sophia must work in the Chaos, in order to reascend to the Thirteenth Aeon.

The Thirteenth Repentance of Pistis Sophia belongs to the Thirteenth Aeon.

Unquestionably, the initiate must work in each one of the Thirteen Aeons, if he wants the final liberation.

The First Aeon is Malkuth, which is here and in the submerged Abyss.

The Second Aeon is Yesod, which is in our sexual organs and in the fourth dimension, within which is the Terrestrial Paradise, the Ethereal World.

The Third Aeon is the Astral World, the Sephirah Hod.

The Fourth Aeon is Netzach, the Mental World.

The Fifth Aeon is Tiphereth, the Causal World.

The Sixth Aeon is Geburah, the Buddhic or Intuitional World.

The Seventh Aeon is the World of Atman, the Ineffable One, the region of Chesed or Gedulah.

The Eight Aeon is Binah, the region of the Holy Spirit, the world of Shiva, the Third Logos.

The Ninth Aeon is Chokmah, the region of the Logos, the Cosmic Christ.

The Tenth Aeon is Kether, the region of the Ancient of Days.

The Eleventh Aeon is the Region of Ain Soph Aur, the Third Great Aspect of the Absolute.

The Twelfth Aeon is the region of Ain Soph, the Second Aspect of the Absolute.

The Thirteenth Aeon is the region of the Ain, the Unmanifested Absolute.

Each one of the Thirteen Aeons must be Self-realized within ourselves.

Based on conscious works and voluntary sufferings, Pistis Sophia must Self-realize herself in these Thirteen Aeons.

The thirteenth repentance of Sophia

1. *Hearken unto me singing praises unto thee, O Light of lights. Hearken unto me uttering the repentance for the thirteenth aeon, the region out of which I have come down, in order that the thirteenth repentance of the thirteenth aeon may be accomplished, those [aeons] which I have overstepped and out of which I have come down.*

2. *Now, therefore, O Light of lights, hearken unto me singing praises unto thee in the thirteenth aeon, my region out of which I have come down.*

3. *Save me, O Light, in thy great mystery and forgive my transgression in thy forgiveness.*

4. *And give unto me the baptism and forgive my sins and purify me from my transgression.*

5. *And my transgression is the lion-faced power, which will never be hidden from thee; for because of it have I gone down.*

6. *And I alone among the invisibles, in whose regions I was, have transgressed, and have gone down into the chaos. Moreover I have transgressed, that thy commandment may be accomplished.*

"This then Pistis Sophia said. Now, therefore, let him whom his spirit urgeth to understand her words, come forward and proclaim her thought."

Martha came forward and said: "My Lord, my spirit urgeth me to proclaim the solution of that which Pistis Sophia hath spoken; thy power hath prophesied afore time concerning it through David in the fiftieth Psalm [Modern Psalm 51], *saying thus..."*

The mystery of the Light is the mystery of the inner Christ.

Only the mystery of Christ can save us.

The inner Christ as a Ruler of the Light must eliminate all of the undesirable psychic elements that we carry in our interior. Only thus can the mystery of the Light be perfected within us.

The baptism is a pact of Sexual Magic.

If someone receives the baptism and does not fulfill the pact, then this one fails completely.

Only the inner Christ can forgive sins.

The Lord also grants this power to the Woman-Serpent.

The Lion-faced Power is the law of karma in action, punishing Pistis Sophia.

Karma must be paid not only for the evil that is done, but also for the good that should have been done, yet was left undone.

The lion of the law is fought with the scale.

When an inferior law is transcended by a superior law, the superior law washes away the inferior law.

Perform good deeds in order to pay your debts.

When we have capital, we do well in negotiations. When we do not have capital, then we must pay with pain.

It is possible to ask the lions of the law for credit.

This credit must be paid with good deeds or with supreme pain.

We must liberate and emancipate ourselves from the law of causality.

We can make the great jump only by awakening and developing the consciousness.

It is necessary for the Bodhichitta, which means the auric embryo, the awakened consciousness, to fall into the Illuminated Void.

Only thus can the Bodhichitta be free from the world of relativity.

The world of relativity is the world of combinations and of duality.

The universal machine of relativity is based on the law of cosmic causality.

The law of cosmic causality is the same as the law of karma.

The law of causality is the same as the law of action and consequence.

We can submerge ourselves in the Illuminated Void by means of the Great Jump.

Thus, and only thus, can we liberate ourselves from the law of karma.

The world of relativity is based on constant dualism and therefore, on the chain of causes and effects.

We must break chains in order to submerge ourselves within the Illuminated Void.

The Illuminated Void is obviously just the antechamber of the Tality, which is the great Reality.

The path that leads to the great Reality is absolutely sexual.

Many degrees of intuition exist. However, the highest degree is only for the mystics or religious philosophers.

Only such people with Prajnaparamita intuition can experience the Tality.

The Lion-faced Power governs in the world of relativity, but not in the Illuminated Void, nor in the great Reality.

Martha interpreteth the thirteenth repentance from Psalm L [Modern Psalm 51]

1. *Be gracious unto me, O God, according to thy great grace; according to the fullness of thy mercy blot out my sin.*

2. *Wash me thoroughly from my iniquity.*

3. *And may my sin be ever present to thee.*

4. *That thou mayest be justified in thy words and prevail when thou judgest me.*

"This is then the solution of the words which Pistis Sophia hath uttered."

Jesus said unto her: "Well said, finely, Martha, blessed [one]."

The inner Christ can blot out sins by granting forgiveness for them.

The inner Christ washes us of all iniquity when forgiving our sins and disintegrating our psychic aggregates.

When a sin is disintegrated it is no longer present before the Lord.

The words of the inner Christ, prevailing in just judgement, radically liberates us.

Chapter 58

Jesus sendeth forth a light-power to help Sophia

And Jesus continued again in the discourse and said unto his disciples: "It came to pass then, when Pistis Sophia had said these words, that the time was fulfilled that she should be led out of the chaos. And of myself, without the First Mystery, I despatched out of myself a light-power, and I sent it down to the chaos, so that it might lead Pistis Sophia forth from the deep regions of the chaos, and lead [her] to the higher regions of the chaos, until the command should come from the First Mystery that she should be led entirely forth out of the chaos. And my light-power led Pistis Sophia up to the higher regions of the chaos. It came to pass then, when the emanations of Self-willed had noticed that Pistis Sophia was led forth into the higher regions of the chaos, that they also sped after her upwards, desiring to bring her again into the lower regions of the chaos. And my light-power, which I had sent to lead up Sophia out of the chaos, shone exceedingly. It came to pass then, when the emanations of Self-willed pursued Sophia, when she had been led into the higher regions of the chaos, that she again sang praises and cried out unto me, saying..."

It is obvious that when Pistis Sophia reaches the Thirteenth Aeon, she must depart from the Chaos.

Rare are the initiates who are capable of knocking on the Thirteenth Gate.

The first gate is in the hall of Malkuth and the last gate is in the hall of Ain.

There have been rare cases in which someone has knocked on the frightful and terrible gate of Ain Soph Aur, the Eleventh Gate.

Those who have knocked on the Eleventh Gate have come close to losing their life.

Many have perished at the Eleventh Gate. Very few are those who reach the Thirteenth Aeon.

High and low regions exist in the inferior Chaos or in the sexual Chaos.

Because the work is performed within the Chaos, there is the need to ascend.

We can only ascend with the help of the inner Christ and by means of the Light-Power.

The command of the First Mystery always arrives to the elevated regions of the Chaos. However, only with the help of the inner Christ and by means of intensive sexual work, is it possible to ascend to the elevated regions.

It is urgent and non-delayable to ascend to the elevated regions of the sexual Chaos, to refine the sexual impulse, to make the sacrament of the church of Rome more perfect.

The metaphysical copulation, the chemical coitus, becomes more refined with the help of the inner Christ.

The tenebrous elements attack, even reaching unto the Thirteenth Aeon. This is terrible.

Nevertheless, the inner Christ defeats the tenebrous ones and liberates Pistis Sophia.

The inner Christ is INRI, the devouring fire, the living fire.

Seven lights emerge from Christ.

It is written that seven lights emerge from one light and from each one of the seven, seven times seven.

There are forty-nine fires that are rooted in Christ.

The forty-nine fires burn within the universe and within the Human Being.

The forty-nine fires are the forty-nine autonomous and Self-independent parts of our own Being.

Our Being has forty-nine independent parts.

Our Being is a college with forty-nine children.

The fire is the most perfect and never adulterated reflection of the single flame. As in Heaven, so on Earth.

The fire originates life and death. The fire is the origin and the end of all things.

Only by means of the fire is it possible to disintegrate the red demons of Seth in order to liberate Pistis Sophia.

Sophia uttereth a song of praise

1. *I will sing praises unto thee, O Light, for I desired to come unto thee. I will sing thee praises, O Light, for thou art my deliverer.*

2. *Leave me not in the chaos. Save me, O Light of the Height, for it is thou that I have praised.*

3. *Thou has sent me thy light through thyself and hast saved me. Thou hast let me to the higher regions of the chaos.*

4. *May the emanations of Self-willed which pursue me, sink down into the lower regions of the chaos, and let them not come to the higher regions to see me.*

5. *And may great darkness cover them and darker gloom come over them. And let them not see me in the light of thy power, which thou hast sent unto me to save me, so that they may not get dominion over me.*

6. *And let not their resolution which they have formed, to take away my power, take effect for them. And as they have spoken against*

me, to take from me my light, take rather from them theirs instead of mine.

7. *And they have proposed to take away my whole light and have not been able to take it, for thy light-power was with me.*

8. *Because they have taken counsel without thy commandment, O Light, therefore have they not been able to take away my light.*

9. *Because I have had faith in the Light, I shall not be afraid; and the Light is my deliverer and I shall not fear.*

"Now, therefore, let him whose power is exalted, speak the solution of the words which Pistis Sophia hath uttered."

And it came to pass, when Jesus had finished speaking these words unto his disciples, that Salome came forward and said: "My Lord, my power constraineth me to speak the solution of the words which Pistis Sophia hath uttered. Thy power hath prophesied afore time through Solomon, saying..."

Christ, the Light, is the deliverer of Pistis Sophia.

The inner Christ can and must take the initiate out of the Chaos.

The intimate Lord can take us to the most elevated zones of the Chaos.

The emanations of the ego are sinking and disintegrating into the inferior Chaos.

The tenebrous ones must submerge themselves into the Abyss and Sophia must make herself invisible to them.

The tenebrous ones fight in order to make the initiate fall, in order to trap him, so that the liberation should not be permitted to him.

Christ can protect the Gnostic ascetic, if this is His will.

The tenebrous powers celebrate reunions in order to plan attacks against Pistis Sophia.

The Gnostic has faith in Christ, and He saves him.

Salome interpreteth the song of Sophia from the Odes of Solomon

1. I will give thanks unto thee, O Lord, for thou art my God.

2. Abandon me not, O Lord, for thou art my hope.

3. Thou hast given me thy vindication for naught, and I am saved through thee.

4. Let them who pursue me, fall down and let them not see me.

5. May a smoke-cloud cover their eyes and an air-mist darken them, and let them not see the day, so that they may not seize me.

6. May their resolution be impotent, and may what they concoct come upon them.

7. They have devised a resolution, and it hath not taken effect for them.

8. And they are vanquished, although they be mighty, and what they have wickedly prepared is fallen upon them.

9. My hope is in the Lord, and I shall not be afraid, for thou art my God, my Saviour.

It came to pass then, when Salome had finished saying these words, that Jesus said unto her: "Well said, Salome: and finely. This is the solution of the Words which Pistis Sophia hath uttered."

The force of gratitude causes the plant to germinate in the orchard of the Gnostic ascetic.

The force of gratitude causes the plant to bear fruit.

The force of cosmic gratitude makes universal life fertile.

In some way, we must express our gratitude to the Creator.

Our Innermost God deserves our eternal gratitude.

All our hope is concerned with the inner Christ.

The one who works on himself has hope in the inner Christ.

Only the inner Christ can give us revindication and save us.

Great is the work of the inner Christ, working in and within us, with immense sacrifice. This is the nature of the *Salvatur Salvandus*.

May the inhuman elements that we carry within and that pursue us as an evil shade fall down.

May the tenebrous elements submerge themselves within the darkness of the Abyss. These are our elements.

These are the living personifications of oneself.

May all the concoctions of those perverse ones who dwell within us fall upon them.

They are the red demons of Seth, the perverse ones and subjective parts of the abominable ego.

May all that which the red demons of Seth have wickedly prepared fall upon them.

Hope is in the inner Christ, in the martyr of Calvary, who must live the complete cosmic drama within the Bodhisattva.

The cosmic drama is never exclusively historic. This drama is a palpitating actuality, and the inner Christ must live it within us, here and now.

The processes of the cosmic drama are written within the Four Gospels of the Lord.

Chapter 59

The power sent by Jesus formeth a light-wreath on Sophia's head

And Jesus continued again in the discourse and said unto his disciples: "It came to pass then, when Pistis Sophia had finished saying these words in the chaos, that I made the light-power, which I had sent to save her, become a light-wreath on her head, so that from now on the emanations of Self-willed could not have dominion over her. And when it had become a light-wreath round her head, all the evil matters in her were shaken and all were purified in her. They perished and remained in the chaos, while the emanations of Self-willed gazed upon them and rejoiced. And the purification of the pure light which was in Pistis Sophia, gave power to the light of my light-power, which had become a wreath round her head.

"It came to pass then moreover, when it surrounded the pure light in Sophia, and her pure light did not depart from the wreath of the power of the light-flame, so that the emanations of Self-willed should not rob it from it, —when then this befell her, the pure light-power in Sophia began to sing praises. And she praised my light-power, which was a wreath round her head, and she sang praises, saying..."

The Light-Power of the inner Christ is found in the christonic substance of the Solar Logos.

This marvellous substance is the sacred sperm.

The crown of the saints, the church of Laodicea, shines on the head of the Christified ones.

Evil matters are disintegrated when the light-wreath of the saints shines on the head of Pistis Sophia.

The evil matters are disintegrated in the Chaos.

The ego, the emanations of the Self-willed, the demons, condemn Pistis Sophia to death, and this sentence is completely fulfilled.

It is worthwhile that the tenebrous ones condemn the initiate to death.

The tenebrous ones rejoice when the ego dies.

It is obvious that the tenebrous ones feel satisfaction when the sentence of the black lodge is fulfilled.

The tribunals of the tenebrous fraternity condemn the initiate to death.

The light of Pistis Sophia must purify itself in order to give power to the light of the Light-Power that converts itself into a light-wreath around the head of the initiate.

The light-wreath of the inner Christ becomes one with the pure light of Pistis Sophia, then it is gold and flame.

The red demons of Seth can do nothing against the gold and the flame.

The light of the initiate and the light of the inner Christ are truly the gold and the flame, inseparable and eternal.

Sophia sings praises to the inner Christ.

Sophia uttereth another song of praise

1. *The Light hath become a wreath round my head; and I shall not depart from it, so that the emanations of Self-willed may not rob it from me.*

2. *And though all the matters be shaken, yet shall I not be shaken.*

3. *And though all my matters perish and remain in the chaos, —those which the emanations of Self-willed see, —yet shall I not perish.*

4. *For the Light is with me, and I myself am with the Light.*

"These words then Pistis Sophia uttered. Now, therefore, let him who understandeth the thought of these words, come forward and proclaim their solution."

The light of the inner Christ and the light of Pistis Sophia form one single, integral, and perfect light.

The multiple undesirable elements of the terrestrial psyche shall not steal the light from Pistis Sophia.

The Christic wreath upon the head of the ineffable Beings can never be stolen.

The Christic wreath upon the head of the wise is found intimately related with the pineal gland.

The lotus of one thousand petals, the chakra Sahasrara, the Diamond Eye, is found where the pineal gland is situated.

Nevertheless, we must remember that the center of intuition, related with the pineal gland, becomes illuminated with Christification.

The pineal gland and the pituitary gland are united by means of a nerve fiber canal, which disappears in the corpse.

The sense of psychological self-observation is located within the pituitary gland.

The marvellous auras of the pituitary and pineal glands gloriously shine, illuminated and integrated upon the head of the Christified ones.

All of the inhuman matters can be shaken. Yet, Christified Pistis Sophia shall not be shaken.

The psychic aggregates will obviously perish in the Chaos.

Obviously, the aggregates will perish in the Chaos.

Some aggregates of the Chaos are only Kabbalistic bark.

The corpses of the Abyss, which are without Essence, are bark.

The corpses or matters of the Chaos are slowly disintegrating.

The Divine Mother Kundalini usually extracts the Essence from within one or another psychic aggregate.

When the Essence is extracted, the psychic aggregate converts itself into a corpse of the Chaos.

These cases are an exception because normally the Divine Mother Kundalini slowly disintegrates the psychic aggregates before extracting the Essence.

The Light of Christ is within Sophia, and she is within Him.

Mary, his mother, asketh and receiveth permission to speak

Then Mary, the mother of Jesus, come forward and said: "My son according to the world, My God and Saviour according to the height, bid me proclaim the solution of the words which Pistis Sophia hath uttered."

And Jesus answered and said: "Thou also, Mary, hast received form which is in Barbelo, according to matter, and hast received likeness which is in the Virgin of Light, according to light, thou and the other Mary, the blessed one; and on thy account the darkness hath arisen, and moreover out of thee did come forth the material body in which I am, which I have purified and refined, —now, therefore, I bid thee proclaim the solution of the words which Pistis Sophia hath uttered."

And Mary, the mother of Jesus, answered and said: "My Lord, thy light-power hath prophesied afore time concerning these words through Solomon in the nineteenth Ode and said...

The Woman-Serpent, Isis, Rhea, Cybele, Adonia, Diana, Marah, Tonantzin, etc. is the Mother of Christ. Nonetheless, She is the daughter of Her Son.

The Woman-Serpent is mother of the Lord, according to the world, and the Lord is Her God and Savior, according to the Height.

The abode of Barbelo is the ocean of the Uncreated Light.

The likeness that the Divine Mother Kundalini has received, according to Light, is that likeness that is in the Virgin of Light.

The Virgin of Light, according to Light, is the Unmanifested Cosmic Mother, whose veil no mortal has lifted.

Rare are those who pass over the threshold of the Temple of the Transparent Walls. Very rare are those who gain entry into the Temple of the Unmanifested Cosmic Mother.

For this, we must pass through the complete Buddhist Annihilation.

Only those who possess the Dharmakaya body, the Law body, the body which is Substance-Being, can enter into the Temple of the Unmanifested Cosmic Mother.

The darkness has arisen by the work of the Woman-Serpent.

The three Marys are fundamental in Gnosis: Isis-Mary, Mary in Nature, and the Unmanifested Cosmic Mother.

Christ shines upon the head of Pistis Sophia.

Mary, mother of Jesus, receives form that is in Barbelo, according to Nature, yet she receives likeness that is in the Virgin of Light.

The Terrestrial Mary and the other Mary, the Blessed One, shine in their essential quality. Thus, thanks to the Woman-Serpent, thanks to Her the darkness has arisen.

The material body of Jesus, the body that was purified and refined, comes forth from the terrestrial Mother.

Mary, his mother, interpreteth the song of Sophia from the XIXth Ode of Solomon

1. The Lord is on my head as a wreath, and I shall not depart from him.

2. The wreath in truth is woven for me; and it hath caused thy twigs to sprout in me.

3. For it is not like unto a wreath withered that sprouteth not. But thou art alive on my head and thou hast sprouted upon me.

4. Thy fruits are full and perfect, filled with thy salvation.

Pistis Sophia rejoices with the crown of Light. She knows what is the flourishing staff of the adept.

The staff of the one who has raised the serpent flourishes. You know this.

The withered wreath is an evident sign of downfall. No buds will sprout from it.

The Lord lives within Pistis Sophia when she has been forgiven.

Truly, Sophia frightfully suffers when she wishes to rise up.

The fruits of the Lord are plethoric and perfect.

Jesus commendeth his mother

It came to pass then, when Jesus had heard his mother Mary say these words, that he said unto her: "Well said, finely. Amen, amen, I say unto thee: They shall proclaim thee blessed from one end of the earth to the other; for the pledge of the First Mystery hath taken up its abode with thee, and through that pledge shall all from the earth and all from the height be saved, and that pledge is the beginning and the end."

Marah, the Woman-Serpent, is always blessed. The pledge of the First Mystery is maintained with Her.

All is maintained with the Woman-Serpent, through the pledges of the First Mystery.

It is obvious that the Divine Mother Kundalini works by the will of the Father.

Chapter 60

The commandment of the First Mystery is fulfillled for taking Sophia entirely out of the chaos

And Jesus continued again in the discourse and said unto his disciples: "It came to pass when Pistis Sophia had uttered the thirteenth repentance, —in that hour was fulfilled the commandment of all the tribulations which were decreed for Pistis Sophia for the fulfilment of the First Mystery, which was from the beginning, and the time had come to save her out of the chaos and lead her out from all the darknesses. For her repentance was accepted from her through the First Mystery; and that mystery sent me a great light-power out of the height, that I might help Pistis Sophia and lead her up out of the chaos. So I looked towards the aeons into the height and saw that light-power which the First Mystery had sent me, that I might save Pistis Sophia out of the chaos."

The Thirteenth Repentance corresponds to the Thirteenth Aeon.

Truly, thirteen are the Aeons and thirteen are the repentances.

Receiving the Eight Initiations is one thing, and qualifying them is another very different thing.

Beyond the eight qualifying Initiations, five more works follow.

The Twelve Works of Hercules, situated in the twelve levels of the Being, are spoken of. However, the thirteenth level also exists.

When Pistis Sophia reaches the Thirteenth Aeon, she is liberated.

Pistis Sophia is lead out from all the darknesses by the fulfillment of the First Mystery, which is contained in the Will of the Father.

The commandment of all the tribulations which were decreed for Pistis Sophia is fulfilled only in the Thirteenth Aeon.

The repentance of the initiate is integrally accepted only through the First Mystery.

The inner Christ receives the Light-Power from the Ancient of Days. By means of this Light-Power, he can help the initiate and lead him up out of the Chaos.

The Lord looks towards the Light-Power that the Father has sent Him and He proceeds to save Pistis Sophia.

The First Mystery and Jesus sent forth two light-powers to help Sophia

"It came to pass, therefore, when I had seen it, coming forth from the aeons and hastening down to me, —I was above the chaos, —that another light-power went forth out of me, that it too might help Pistis Sophia. And the light-power which had come from the height through the First Mystery, came down upon the light-power which had gone out of me; and they met together and became a great stream of light."

When then Jesus had said this unto his disciples, he said: "Understand ye in what manner I discourse with you?"

The Light-Power of the Father is integrated with the Light-Power of the Christ.

A light-stream is formed when the Light-Power of the Father is integrally united with the Light-Power of the Christ.

Mary Magdalene interpreteth the Mystery from Psalm LXXXIV [Modern Psalm 85]

Mary started forward again and said: "My Lord, I understand what thou sayest. Concerning the solution of this word thy light-power hath prophesied afore time through David in the eighty-fourth Psalm [Modern Psalm 85], *saying:*

10. Grace and truth met together, and virtue and peace kissed each other.

11. Truth sprouted forth out of the earth, and virtue looked down from heaven.

"'Grace' then is the light-power which hath come down through the First Mystery; for the First Mystery hath hearkened unto Pistis Sophia and hath had mercy on her in all her tribulations. 'Truth' on the other hand is in the power which hath gone forth out of thee, for that thou hast fulfilled the truth, in order to save her out of the chaos. And 'virtue' again is the power which hath come forth through the First Mystery, which will guide Pistis Sophia. And 'peace' again is the power which hath gone forth out of thee, so that it should enter into the emanations of Self-willed and take from them the lights which they have taken away from Pistis Sophia, —that is, so that thou mayest gather them together into Pistis Sophia and make them at peace with her power. 'Truth' on the other hand is the power which went forth out of thee, when thou wast in the lower regions of the chaos. For this cause thy power hath said through David: 'Truth sprouted out of the earth,' because thou wert in the lower regions of the chaos. 'Virtue' on the other hand which hath 'looked down from heaven,' —it is the power which hath come down from the height through the First Mystery and hath entered into Pistis Sophia."

Grace and Truth meet together. Virtue and Peace are eternally kissing.

Virtue is derived from the syllable VIR, virility.

Sexual virility is urgent in order for the virtues to be born within us.

Sexual potency, virility, is needed in order to work in the Ninth Sphere.

We must disintegrate the psychic aggregates within the flaming forge of Vulcan.

Devi Kundalini Shakti assists us in the Ninth Sphere.

Each time we disintegrate a psychic aggregate with virility, a new virtue is born in its place within us.

Virtue and Peace kiss each other, because the virtues are born with the disintegration of the ego, and fundamental peace arrives.

Truth comes to us when the ego has died.

The ego dies only by descending to the subterranean Tartarus.

The one who wants to ascend must first of all descend.

Every exaltation is preceded by a frightful and terrible humiliation.

Therefore, the Truth must be attained from below, by working in the Ninth Sphere.

Virtue comes from heaven each time an undesirable psychic element is disintegrated.

Grace is the Light-Power, which is known only by the one who receives it.

This Light-Power comes by the will of the First Mystery.

The First Mystery is the Merciful One, the Mercy of the Mercy, who always take pity on the initiate.

The First Mystery is the Ancient of Days, here and now.

Fortunate is the one who receives the Light-Power that comes from the Father.

Grace is the Light-Power.

A conceited, vain, or proud person cannot consciously know how to take advantage of the Grace, the Light-Power that comes from the Father.

Thus, before receiving the Grace of the Ancient of Centuries, we must disintegrate the psychic aggregates of mystical pride, mystical conceit, and mystical vanity.

Let us then make a complete differentiation between mystical pride, mystical conceit, and mystical vanity, and the common and current pride, conceit, and vanity.

Mystical pride, conceit and vanity are related to the initiates, adepts, and simple aspirants.

Common and current pride, conceit and vanity are different. Many people have them.

We must find the Truth-Power within ourselves.

The one who does not find the Truth within himself never finds it outside of himself.

In order to leave the Chaos, we must fulfil the Truth.

The virtues must crystallize within the initiate. These wisely guide him.

Peace emerges within the initiate as a power that penetrates him, in the most difficult regions.

Peace within the initiate makes him invincible.

The initiate discovers the eternal lights contained in the Abyss, by means of Peace.

All the lights of universal wisdom are reuniting within the initiate and make him at peace with his power.

The Truth is that which is, which has always been, and which will always be.

The Truth is the unknowable, from instant to instant.

Within the Abyss, Truth disguises itself with darkness.

Demonius Est Deus Inversus.

The demon is God, but inverted.

The inferno is the womb of Heaven.

The Philosophical Stone, the stone of truth, must be searched for within the inferno.

Lucifer is the best friend that we have.

Now, we comprehend why the Truth is the inferior power that emerges from Pistis Sophia in the Chaos.

Thus, the Truth emerges from the Averno and departs from the monster of the Earth.

Every treasure is found inserted within the womb of the Earth. The Golden Fleece is not an exception.

Chapter 61

It came to pass then, when Jesus had heard these words, that he said: "Well said, Mary, blessed one, who shalt inherit the whole Light-kingdom."

Thereon Mary, the mother of Jesus, also came forward and said: "My Lord and my Saviour give commandment unto me also that I repeat this word."

Jesus said: "Whose spirit is understanding, him I do not prevent, but I urge him on still more to speak the thought which hath moved him. Now, therefore, Mary, my mother according to matter, thou in whom I have sojourned, I bid thee that thou also speak the thought of the discourse."

Marah, Mary, Isis, in Nature, also has the right to speak about the Christic mysteries.

Mary, the mother, further interpreteth the scripture

And Mary answered and said: "My Lord, concerning the word which thy power hath prophesied through David: 'Grace and truth met together, virtue and peace kissed each other. Truth sprouted forth out of the earth, and virtue looked down from heaven,' —thus hath thy power prophesied this word afore time about thee."

Grace and Virtue always meet together and Peace and Virtue kiss each other.

Virtue comes from Heaven, and Truth sprouts from the inferno.

The story of the phantom spirit

"When thou wert little, before the spirit had come upon thee, whilst thou wert in a vineyard with Joseph, the spirit came out of the height and came to me in my house, like unto thee; and I had not known him, but I thought that thou wast he. And the spirit said unto me: 'Where is Jesus, my brother, that I meet with him?' And when he had said this unto me, I was at a loss and thought it as a phantom to try

me. So I seized him and bound him to the foot of the bed in my house, until I went forth to you, to thee and Joseph in the field, and I found you on the vineyard, Joseph propping up the vineyard. It came to pass, therefore, when thou didst hear me speak the word unto Joseph, that thou didst understand the word, wert joyful and saidest: 'Where is he, that I may see him; else I await him in this place.' And it came to pass, when Joseph had heard thee say these words, that he was startled. And we went down together, entered the house and found the spirit bound to the bed. And we looked on thee and him and found thee like unto him. And he who was bound to the bed was unloosed; he took thee in his arms and kissed thee, and thou also didst kiss him. Ye became one.

"This then is the word and its solution. 'Grace' is the spirit which hath come down out of the height through the First Mystery, for it hath had mercy on the race of men and sent its spirit that he should forgive the sins of the whole world, and they should receive the mysteries and inherit the Light-kingdom. 'Truth' on the other hand is the power which hath sojourned with me."

The Spirit must integrate himself with the human being, in order to become one with him and within him.

This integration is not possible as long as we remain asleep.

We must drink the wine of Gnosis and die within ourselves in order to attain the integration.

The vine, the wine, is the result of the miracle of sexual transmutation.

Attaining the radical death of oneself is possible only by working within the flaming forge of Vulcan.

Of the spiritual and material bodies of Jesus

"When it had come forth out of Barbelo, it became material body for thee, and hath made proclamation concerning the region of Truth. 'Virtue' is thy spirit, who hath brought the mysteries out of the height to give them to the race of men. 'Peace' on the other hand is the power which hath sojourned in thy material body according to the world,

which hath baptized the race of men until it should make it stranger unto sin and make it at peace with thy spirit, so that they may be at peace with the emanations of the Light; that is, 'Grace and truth kissed each other.' As it saith: 'Truth sprouted forth out of the earth,' —'truth' is thy material body which sprouted forth out of me according to the world of men, and hath made proclamation concerning the region of Truth. And again as it saith: 'Virtue [looked down] from heaven'—'virtue' is the power which looked out of the height, which will give the mysteries of the Light to the race of men, so that they will become virtuous and good, and inherit the Light-kingdom."

It came to pass then, when Jesus had heard these words which his mother Mary spake, that he said: "Well said, finely, Mary."

The Grace-Power comes from the height, by order of the First Mystery.

The Grace, or better if we say, the Grace-Power, always comes from the height, through the First Mystery.

Christ is the Spirit of Fire, the Fire of the fire, the astral signature of the Fire. Only he can save us.

Only the inner Christ can forgive the karmic debts that we have.

The inner Lord can forgive the initiate when the repentance is true.

All doors are closed for the unworthy, except the one of repentance.

To receive the mysteries and to inherit the Light Kingdom is possible, thanks to the Spirit of Fire.

The Truth-Power is in the inner Christ and within the inner Christ, here and now.

When the inner Christ departs from the abode of Barbelo, the ocean of the great Light, He comes to preach the Truth.

The Truth transforms itself into a real body for the initiate, because he is completely integrated with the Truth.

When the initiate experiences the Truth, he teaches the path that leads to the Truth.

Every true Bodhisattva sacrifices himself for the Truth.

Chapter 62

The other Mary came forward and said: "My Lord, bear with me and be not wroth with me. Yea, from the moment when thy mother spake with thee concerning the solution of these words, my power disquieted me to come forward and likewise to speak the solution of these words."

Virtue is the Spirit of the Fire that brings the mysteries from the Height in order to give them to the human race.

Fundamental peace is possible only by self-exploring the ego in order to totally disintegrate it.

It is stated that the Peace-Power has dwelt in the material body according to the world. This is due to the ego which abides within the body. As long as it continues to thrive, peace will obviously be absent.

We remain at peace with the Spirit by killing the ego.

The greeting in the Initiatic College is, "May peace be with Thee." The reply is, "And also with thy Spirit."

We need to be in peace with the emanation of the Light.

Grace-Power and Truth-Power embrace and kiss each other, thus forming an integral wholeness.

The Truth is the Tality, or totality.

Obviously, the Tality is found in the depth of a Christ or a Buddha.

The Tality is beyond the machinery of relativity, and also beyond the Illuminated Void.

The Tality is that which is beyond the body, the affections, and the mind.

The Tality is that which is far beyond all dualism.

The Tality in Christ, or in Buddha, or in Hermes, is always the same.

Grace emerges from the Tality.

The Truth is that which is, which has always been and which will always be.

The Truth is incarnated only within the body of a Being like Jesus, Buddha, or Hermes, etc.

The temple of all the degenerated people of the Earth is a temple of iniquity and darkness.

The Aryan Race is already degenerated and will soon be destroyed.

The state in which this present humanity is found is useless in order to incarnate the Monad, the Being.

It is not possible for the Divine Monad to incarnate within the physical body because of the way in which it is born, and because of its present condition.

The incarnation of the Divine Monad and the distinct parts of the Being is made possible only by preparing the physical body by means of the work in the Ninth Sphere.

The Ninth Sphere is sex.

Really, only the sexual energy can transform the physical body in order for it to incarnate the Divine Monad.

It is possible to convert the physical body in the temple of the Truth, by means of the sexual creative energy of Shiva, the Holy Spirit.

It is possible to inherit the Light Kingdom only by means of the mysteries of virtue.

Virtues will not be born within us if the ego is not annihilated.

If the virtues do not crystallize in us, we will never possess our Souls.

With patience, you will possess your Soul.

Each time a psychic aggregate is eliminated, we crystallize a virtue in its place.

This is how the Soul crystallizes within us, little by little.

Only by means of virtue can one enter into the mysteries.

The other Mary further interpreteth the same scripture from the baptism of Jesus

Jesus said unto her: "I bid thee speak their solution."

Mary said: "My Lord, 'Grace and truth met together' —'grace' then is the spirit who hath come upon thee, when thou didst receive the baptism from John. 'Grace' then is the godly spirit who hath come upon thee; he hath had mercy on the race of men, hath come down and hath met with the power of Sabaoth, the Good, which is in thee and which hath made proclamation concerning the regions of Truth. It hath said again: 'Virtue and peace kissed each other' —'virtue' then is the spirit of the Light, which did come upon thee and hath brought the mysteries of the height, to give them unto the race of men. 'Peace' on the other hand is the power of Sabaoth, the Good, which is in thee, —he who hath baptized and hath forgiven the race of men, —and it hath made them at peace with the sons of the Light. And moreover as thy power hath said through David: 'Truth sprouted forth out of the earth' —that is the power of Sabaoth, the Good, which sprouted forth out of Mary, thy mother, the dweller on earth. 'Virtue', which 'looked down from heaven,' on the other hand is the spirit in the height who hath brought all mysteries of the height and given them to the race of men; and they have become virtuous and good, and have inherited the Light-Kingdom."

And it came to pass, when Jesus had heard Mary speak these words, that he said: "Well said, Mary, inheritress of the Light."

Grace is the spirit that comes to us in the baptism.

The baptism is a pact of Sexual Magic.

When we fulfill the pact of Sexual Magic, then we reach the Inner Self-realization of the Being.

The power of Sabaoth is the power of the Verb that comes to us as Grace when we fulfill the pact of Sexual Magic.

Virtue is the Spirit of the Light that crystallizes within us when the ego dies.

Virtue initiates us into the great mysteries of life and death.

Without virtues, we are not admitted into the temples of mysteries.

Sabaoth baptizes the human being and makes him at peace with the Children of the Light.

Sabaoth is the Verb, the Word, the intimate Logoi, within each one of us.

Mary is the daughter of Her Son, Her Lord and Savior. Mary, Marah, the Woman-Serpent, is an autonomous and self-cognizant part of our own Being.

Mary, the mother, again further interpreteth the same scripture from meeting of herself with Elizabeth (Isabel), mother of John the Baptizer

And Mary, the mother of Jesus, again came forward, fell down at his feet, kissed them and said: "My Lord, my son and my Saviour, be not wroth with me, but pardon me, that I may once more speak the solution of these words. 'Grace and truth met together' —it is I, Mary, thy mother, and Isabel, mother of John, whom I have met. 'Grace' then is the power of Sabaoth in me, which went forth out of me, which thou art. Thou hast had mercy on the whole race of men. 'Truth' on the other hand is the power in Isabel, which is John, who did come and hath made proclamation concerning the way of Truth, which thou art, —who hath made proclamation before thee. And again, 'Grace and truth met together,' —that is thou, my Lord, thou who didst meet John on the day when thou hadst to receive the baptism. And again thou and John are 'Virtue and peace kissed each other.'"

Sabaoth, the Verb, the Logos, is always the Son of Isis, the Saitic Mother of the great mysteries.

John, who preached the path that leads to the Truth, was the son of Isis and Abel.

This signifies that John, the precursor, was someone who had incarnated the Divine Monad.

Atman, the Divine Spirit of the human being, has two children, two Souls: Isis and Abel.

Isis is Buddhi, the Spiritual Soul, and is feminine.

Abel is the Human Soul and is masculine.

Isabel is a profoundly significant name.

IS-ABEL: ABEL is the gentleman who loves IS, his soul, his Valkyrie.

The Spirit-Soul is the wife of the Causal Man, the real Man.

Therefore, John was someone who had incarnated the Monad.

We must not mistake Isis, the adorable Valkyrie, with the Saitic Mother Kundalini.

ISIS, as a mantra, can be applied to the Valkyrie. Yet, specifically, ISIS must be applied to the Divine Mother Kundalini.

Christ is the path of Truth and life.

Grace and Truth always meet together.

Of the incarnation of Jesus

"'Truth hath sprouted forth out of the earth, and virtue looked down from heaven,' —this is, during the time when thou didst minister unto thyself, thou didst have the form of Gabriel, thou didst look down upon me from heaven and speak with me. And when thou hadst spoken with me, thou didst sprout up in me, —that is the 'truth', that is the power of Sabaoth, the Good, which is in thy material body, that is the 'truth' which 'sprouted up out of the earth."

It came to pass then, when Jesus had heard his mother Mary speak these words, that he said "Well said, and finely. This is the solution of all the words concerning which my light-power hath prophesied afore time through the prophet David."

John and Christ, Grace and Truth, meet together.

John baptizes by Grace and Christ is the Truth.

Virtue and Peace always kiss each other.

Christ, taking the form of Gabriel, looks down from Heaven and speaks with his Divine Mother.

Christ penetrates as the most pure light-stream into the womb of Marah, the Divine Mother Kundalini. Christ is the Truth.

The Truth is unquestionably the power of Sabaoth.

Sabaoth is the incarnated Logos, the truth, the treasure hidden within the womb of the Earth.

The treasure must always be searched for within the profound womb of the Earth.

There is the need to dig within the profundities of the underworld.

The Note of a Scribe

A note by a later hand, copied from another scripture

(Now these are the names which I will give from the Boundless onward. Write them with a sign, that the Sons of God may be revealed from here on.

This is the name of the Immortal: aaa, ooo; *and this is the name of the voice, for the sake of which the Perfect Man hath set himself in motion:* iii. *And these are the interpretations of the names of these mysteries: the first [name], which is* aaa, *its interpretation is* fff; *the second, which is* mmm *or* ooo, *its interpretation is* aaa; *the third, which is* ps ps ps, *its interpretation is* ooo; *the fourth, which is* fff, *its interpretation is* nnn; *the fifth, which is* ddd, *its interpretation is* aaa. *He on the throne is* aaa. *This is the interpretation of the second;* aaa,aaa,aaa; *this is the interpretation of the whole name).*

The Sons of God are exclusively the Christified ones, those who have found the Golden Fleece within the womb of the world.

The ordinary intellectual animals are sons of the devil.

I.A.O. is the sacred name. I.A.O. is the mantra of the Ninth Sphere. I.A.O. is the Dharani of Sexual Magic.

I, reminds us of **Ignis**, the fire.

A, reminds us of **aqua**, the water.

O, reminds us of **origo**, principle, Spirit.

I, **Ignis**, **INRI**, the Sulphur.

A, **aqua**, the Mercury of the secret philosophy.

O, the **Origo**, the principle mediator between Sulphur and Mercury of the secret philosophy.

I, the Perfect Man, is put in movement by *I:* **Ignis**, **INRI**, the fire.

A, **aqua**, the Mercury that is extracted from the brute mineral, the metallic soul of the sacred sperm, the water that does not moisten, is the fountain of immortality.

O, **origo**, is the principle mediator between the Sulphur and the Mercury. It unites the two substances before it dies.

Sulphur and Mercury, united by means of Salt, give origin to the Red Carbuncle, the Philosophical Stone.

We will teach the complete science of Alchemy, which is the unveiled mysteries of the Great Work, in our next book, entitled *The Great Work*.

F, **fire**, **Fohat**. The **A**, which is the pure water of life, the Mercury of the Great Work, can never be elaborated upon without fire.

O, **origo**, principle, Spirit, is the Salt. As a result of it being volatile, it participates with the element air, and because of it being firm it participates with the fire. This must be analyzed.

The Salt is within the **M**, Mercury, sea, water. However, it also participates with the fire, which is the Sulphur.

The Salt is volatile because it participates with the air. However, it also participates with the element earth, as we see in the salt mines.

The Salt is related with **air**, **fire**, **water**, and **earth**.

The Salt is the great mediator between Sulphur and Mercury. The Salt joins these two elements, integrates them, unites them in a single whole.

M or **O** whose interpretation is **A**, is such because it is found in the Chaotic sea of the sacred Mercury. It is the Salt of the great Ocean.

P, **Patar**, **Peter**, sex and its mysteries, cannot function without the origo, the principle, the substance that unites the Sulphur and the Mercury.

S, the sweet and affable hiss (still small voice) that Elijah heard in the desert and that Apollonius utilized in order to wilfully leave the physical body, is profoundly significant.

We very well know that Apollonius was covered with a woollen mantle in order to practice.

While seated, he concentrated on his navel.

He begged his God to send the **S**, the sweet and affable hiss (still, small voice), the subtle voice.

When he had heard the sound that the cricket produces, he wilfully left the physical body.

This fine sound vibrates in the cerebellum, in the head.

In order to hear the subtle voice, quietude and silence of the mind is needed.

S is the ray, the fire that without **O**, **origo**, principle or Spirit, would be impossible to be because **S** is **O**, Spirit.

Thus, **S**, fire, is also **O**, **origo**, the principle Spirit.

The interpretation of **F** is **N**. This is because the three lines that represent the three primary forces of Nature and the cosmos are in the letter **N**.

Without the three primary forces positive, negative, and neutral within us, it would be impossible to light the sacred fire.

Man represents the Holy Affirmation.

Woman represents the Holy Negation.

The Holy Conciliation, the neutral force, conciliates the two forces in order to create and create a new.

If there is a creation by means of Kriya-Shakti, meaning, without spilling Hermes' Glass, just as the Lemurians of the third, fourth, and fifth subraces did it, then the sacred fire will awaken in the aspirant.

Thus the explanation of **F**, **fire**, **Fohat**, is in the letter **N**, with its three forces.

A. Z. F. is the secret key of the Great Arcanum. This is known by the Brahmans.

A, **aqua**, **water**, is the Ens Seminis within which is the Ens Virtutis of the fire.

Without the Mercury of the wise, the Great Work is not possible. This is why the interpretation of **DDD** is **A**.

Even the Gods are sons of the Mercury of the wise.

It is clear that our interior profound God (Deus) also becomes a Son of the Mercury.

The Pistis Sophia Unveiled

The Second Book

Chapter 63

John also came forward and said, "O Lord, bid me also speak the solution of the words which thy light-power hath prophesied afore time through David."

And Jesus answered and said unto John, "To thee too, John, I give commandment to speak the solution of the words which my light-power hath prophesied through David:

10. Grace and truth met together, and virtue and peace kissed each other.

11. Truth hath sprouted forth out of the earth, and virtue looked down from heaven.

John is the Verb within the Being of each one of us.

Christ expressed Himself through the Prophet David.

Solomon, son of David, King of Zion, learned a lot from David.

Truth emerges from the Abyss. Truth is found by the one who discovers the Treasury, the Golden Fleece within the womb of the world.

Virtue comes from the Height, from Heaven, when we eliminate those matters of the Abyss in and within ourselves, here and now.

Each time we disintegrate a psychic aggregate, a virtue, which comes from the Height, from Heaven, crystallizes within our Essence.

It is written that the vital body or the foundation of organic life within each one of us has four ethers.

The chemical ether and the ether of life are related with chemical processes and sexual reproduction.

The chemical ether is a specific foundation for the organic chemical phenomenons.

The ether of life is the foundation of the reproductive and transformative sexual processes of the race.

The two superior ethers, luminous and reflective, have more elevated functions.

The luminous ether is related with the caloric, luminous, perceptive, etc. phenomena.

The reflective ether serves as a medium of expression for willpower and imagination.

By means of initiation the two superior ethers are separated in order to form the Soma Psuchikon.

It is necessary to know that the Soma Psuchikon is the ethereal body of the Heavenly Man.

We can travel through the infinite with the heavenly, ethereal, christified, and stigmatized body.

The heavenly virtues crystallize within the Essence.

The Essence, charged with the virtues, powers, laws, etc., is dressed with the Soma Psuchikon.

The Soul dressed with the Soma Psuchikon is the human being of the Fifth Round, the liberated human.

In the Fifth Round, the Earth will be blue, ethereal, transparent and ineffable.

The ethereal, christified Human, the Man-Christ, can consciously and perfectly enter and depart from the physical body at will.

Truth and virtue have totally united within the Ethereal Man.

The Ethereal Man is the perfect Bodhichitta.

The one who does not possess the Bodhichitta (even when he has created the superior existential bodies of the Being) is still unconscious and absurd.

To visit the Buddhic lands with conscious will is possible only by possessing the Bodhichitta.

The Buddhic lands are the superior worlds.

The Bodhisattvas must first of all create the Bodhichitta.

Fortunate is the Bodhisattva who has the awakened Bodhichitta within his interior.

The one who has the awakened Bodhichitta can see, hear, touch and feel all of the marvels of the Buddhic lands.

The one who possesses the awakened Bodhichitta in his interior can visit the temples of the serpent within the depths of the seas.

The Ethereal Man, the awakened Bodhichitta, can make himself invisible to the sight of his enemies.

The Man-Christ, the conscious Bodhichitta, can make his physical body immortal.

It is written that not even the poison of the Borgias, neither the knife, nor the bullet, can destroy the physical body of the Bodhichitta.

The wildest beasts of Nature are humble in the presence of the Man-Christ.

John further interpreteth the same scripture

And John answered and said: "This is the word which thou hast said unto us afore time: 'I have come out of the Height and entered into Sabaoth, the Good, and embraced the light-power in him.' Now therefore, 'Grace and truth' which 'met together;' — thou art 'grace,' thou who art sent out of the regions of the Height through thy Father, the First Mystery which looketh within, in that he hath sent thee, that thou mayest have mercy on the whole world. 'Truth' on the other hand is the power of Sabaoth, the Good, which bound itself in thee and which thou hast cast forth to the Left, — thou the First Mystery which looketh without. And the little Sabaoth, the Good, took it and cast it forth into the matter of Barbelo, and he made proclamation concerning the regions of Truth to all the regions of those of the Left."

The inner Christ comes out of the Height and enters into Sabaoth the Good, the Ethereal Man, who is the living crystallization of the Heavenly Sabaoth.

Grace, Christ, meet together with Truth, which emerges from the Abyss.

Grace and Truth are found integrated within the Ethereal Man.

Truth is the goal of Sabaoth the Good, the Man-Christ, the awakened Bodhichitta.

Of Sabaoth, Barbelo, Yabraoth and the light-vesture

"That matter of Barbelo then it is which is body for thee today.

"And 'virtue and peace' which 'kissed each other' – 'Virtue' then art thou who didst bring all the Mysteries through thy Father, the First Mystery which looketh within, and hast baptized this power of Sabaoth, the Good; and thou didst go to the region of the rulers and didst give unto them the Mysteries of the Height; they became righteous and good.

"'Peace,' on the other hand, is the power of Sabaoth, that is thy soul, which did enter into the matter of Barbelo, and all the rulers of the six aeons of Yabraoth have made peace with the mystery of the Light.

"And 'truth' which 'sprouted forth out of the earth,' – it is the power of Sabaoth, the Good, which came out of the region of the Right, which lieth outside the Treasury of the Light, and which hath come into the region of those of the Left; it hath entered into the matter of Barbelo, and hath made proclamation concerning the mysteries of the region of Truth.

"'Virtue' on the other hand which 'looked down from heaven,' is thou the First Mystery, which looketh down without, as thou didst come out of the spaces of the Height with the mysteries of the Light-kingdom; and thou didst come down upon the light-vesture which thou didst receive from the hand of Barbelo, which [vesture] is Jesus, our Saviour, in that thou didst come down upon him as a dove."

It came to pass then, when John had brought forward these words, that the First Mystery which looketh without, said unto him: "Well said, John, beloved brother."

The First Mystery sees everything from the interior to the exterior.

The Little Sabaoth, the Man-Christ, who is the living crystallization of the Great Sabaoth, or Secret Elohim, takes the

Truth. He accomplishes It and places It within the Ocean of Light, which is the abode of Barbelo.

Sabaoth-Christ always proclaims that which concerns the Regions of Truth.

The people, the multitudes who always live in the Left, receive the teachings of Sabaoth.

It is obvious that those multitudes who live in the Left are ignorant.

The crowds evolve and devolve incessantly in the valley of Samsara.

The devolving multitudes of the Left enter the infernal worlds.

The involution within the womb of the Earth lasts until the Second Death.

The Essence is free only with the Second Death, which is, the death of the ego within the womb of the Earth.

The Essence that has passed through the Second Death evolves again, beginning with the mineral kingdom.

The evolving Essences pass through the mineral, plant, and animal kingdoms, before reconquering the human state which they had lost.

The Wheel of Samsara rotates three thousand times.

Whosoever wants to be liberated must liberate himself from the laws of evolution and involution.

The final liberation is obtained only by way of the revolution of the Consciousness.

The Wheel of Samsara rotates with the laws of evolution and involution.

The evolving Anubis ascends through the right side of the wheel.

The devolving Typhon descends towards the Abyss through the left side of the wheel.

The devolving multitudes submerge themselves within the womb of the Earth.

Each human cycle has one hundred and eight lives. After the one hundred and eighth life, the soul enters into the Abyss.

Three thousand cycles exist, three thousand rotations of the great wheel.

After the last cycle, the wheel ceases to rotate and all opportunities are lost.

The souls of the last cycle submerge themselves within the Great Alaya of the universe, in an elemental state.

The Ethereal Body of the Man-Christ is the crystallization of the Light that descends from the abode of Barbelo.

Christ is the Virtue. Christ brings all of the mysteries by the command of the Father.

The Father is the First and the Last of the mysteries.

Christ baptizes the power of Sabaoth, the Good.

The inner Christ delivers the mysteries of the Heights to the Rulers.

These Rulers, as we have said, are the distinct autonomous and self-cognizant parts of our own Being.

The power of Sabaoth, as we have said, is the Man-Christ, the Man-Soul, revested with the Ethereal Body.

It is clear that peace is the power of Sabaoth, which is the Soul of the Lord integrated with the Light that descends from Barbelo.

It is not possible to understand the Rulers of the six Aeons of Yabraoth unless we comprehend the laws of the Sixth Mystery.

It is necessary to know that the laws of the Sixth Mystery are contained within the Sixth Arcanum.

The Sixth Mystery is related with the lovers, love, and sex.

The Rulers of the Sixth Mystery have made peace with the mystery of the Light.

The absolute peace with the mystery of the Light is completely sexual and can be attained only through sex.

Whosoever gains innocence will arrive to the mansion of peace.

The Rulers of the Sixth Mystery are within us.

The laws of the Sixth Mystery take us to the resurrection.

Every Resurrected Adept has completely liberated himself from original sin.

Whosoever liberates himself from original sin makes peace with the mystery of the Light.

It is obvious that the Truth, which is obtained within the womb of the world, is the Treasury of Sabaoth, the Good, the Man-Christ.

The Truth is the Treasury which is found within the womb of the world.

The Truth is the Golden Fleece, which is always guarded by a dragon that throws fire and sulphur.

Sabaoth, the Good, departed from the region of Virtue and conquered the Treasury of the Light.

The Man-Christ always comes to the region of the lost in order to help them.

Those who live in the region of the Left devolve within the womb of the world.

The pseudo-esotericists and pseudo-occultists of this valley of tears (who are bottled up within the dogma of evolution) stupidly believe that they can liberate themselves without dissolving the ego.

The fanatics of the dogma of evolution devolve through the path of the left hand.

The path that leads to the Abyss is paved with good intentions.

The Abyss is filled with sincerely mistaken ones.

Fornicators and the enemies of sex are abundant in the infernal worlds.

Homosexuals, lesbians, the henchmen of Lilith, those who sterilize themselves, and women who use contraceptives devolve within the infernal worlds.

The supporters of induced abortion and the women who willfully abort are also seen in the sphere of Lilith.

and I gave unto them the light-stream and let them go down into the chaos to help Pistis Sophia and to take from the emanations of Self-willed the light-powers they had taken from her, and give them to Pistis Sophia.

"And straightaway, when they had brought down the light-stream into the chaos, it shone most exceedingly in the whole of the chaos, and spread itself over all their regions. And when the emanations of Self-willed had seen the great light of that stream, they were terror-stricken one with the other. And that stream drew forth out of them all the light-powers which they had taken from Pistis Sophia, and the emanations of Self-willed could not dare to lay hold of that light-stream in the dark chaos; nor could they lay hold of it with the art of Self-willed, who ruleth over the emanations."

Christ is the power that comes from the Height.

Christ is the Saviour of Pistis Sophia.

Pistis Sophia could not depart from the Chaos if it was not for the inner Christ.

The initiate, filled with Pistis Sophia, departs from the Chaos, thanks to the inner Christ.

The power that comes from Christ is a sunderable part of Christ.

The sunderable part of Christ gives the erotic impulse to the human being.

The sunderable part of Christ, or better said, the living double of Christ, is Lucifer, the Maker of Light.

Thanks to the Maker of Light, Pistis Sophia is liberated.

The powers of Christ are found placed within the double of Christ.

The power that comes from the inner Christ and the Christified Soul of Sabaoth, the Good, are joined, are integrated. They make themselves one single stream of light, a single total.

Thus the Man-Christ, revested with the Soma Psuchikon, is a resplendent whole.

Gabriel, as a regent of the Moon, is one of the planetary Genii.

Yet, the inner Gabriel is something distinct. He is one of the autonomous and conscious parts of our own Being.

The inner Gabriel governs our Psychological Moon.

The Psychological Moon also has two faces, the visible and the hidden.

All of our psychological defects, visible to simple sight are in the visible part of the Psychological Moon.

However, the secret defects are found in the hidden part of our own Psychological Moon.

It is obvious that defects, psychic aggregates and perversities that we do not even remotely suspect, exist in the hidden part of our own Psychological Moon.

Michael in the Sun is an ineffable Archangel. Yet, Michael within us is different. Michael is an independent and conscious part of our own Being.

Our readers must not forget the forty-nine fires.

Obviously, the forty-nine fires are the forty-nine independent and conscious parts of our own Being.

Michael and Gabriel, who symbolize the Sun and the Moon, the Sulphur and the Mercury, serve the alchemist in order to perform the Great Work.

Thanks to the magistracy of the fire, the initiates filled with Pistis Sophia can rescue and take the Light of the consciousness that is imprisoned in the psychic aggregates.

It is clear that the psychic aggregates (within which the Light of the consciousness is imprisoned) are Dry Mercury.

We must annihilate the psychic aggregates and the Arsenic Sulphur.

The arsenic, poisonous Sulphur is an infernal type of fire within the lower animal depths of the human being.

The Arsenic Sulphur is that horrible Python serpent that slithered in the mud of the earth and that the irritated Apollo hurt with his darts. It is the tail of Satan.

We must distinguish between Satan and Lucifer. Satan is the devil, black as coal, the fallen Lucifer.

We must whitewash the devil. This is only possible by practicing Sexual Magic intensely and by disintegrating the ego.

Humanity has converted Lucifer into the devil.

Each one of us must whitewash his particular devil in order to convert him into Lucifer.

When Lucifer shines within ourselves, he converts himself into our particular, individual Moses.

Fortunate is the one who integrates himself with his own Moses.

Moses, descending from Sinai with the luminous horns upon his forehead, deserved to be chiselled by Michelangelo.

The doctrine of Moses is the doctrine of Lucifer.

Christus-Lucifer is our Saviour, the Redeemer of Pistis Sophia.

Christus-Lucifer grasps the scale and the sword as a lord of justice.

Lucifer, integrated with the inner Christ, shines in Sabaoth, the Solar Man.

The Heavenly Sabaoth crystallizes within the Sabaoth-Man, thanks to the inner Moses.

Sabaoth-Moses are totally integrated.

Sabaoth is the internal God who must crystallize in the human person, thanks to the good duties of Lucifer.

The Antichrist, the ego, knows nothing about these things. He merely wants a mechanical man and a universe that was originated by chance, an absurd miracle from a reason without reason.

On the other hand, religion hates Lucifer, and curses Him without knowing that he is the sunderable part of the inner Christ.

The processes of cells and atoms would not be possible without the existence of intelligent, igneous principles. Those who ignore this fact are as ignorant as those religious fanatics who hate Lucifer.

Christus-Lucifer is the Saviour within each one of us.

The light-stream—which means, the Man-Christ—shines in the Chaos and in all regions.

The demons are terrified before the presence of the Man-Christ.

The Man-Christ is revested with all the Light-Powers that the tenebrous ones had taken away from Pistis Sophia.

The tenebrous ones never dare to touch the Man-Christ in the dark Chaos.

The ego, the red demons of Seth, run away from the presence of the Man-Christ in the Chaos.

The light-stream restoreth the light-powers to Sophia

"And Gabriel and Michael led the light-stream over the body of the matter of Pistis Sophia and poured into her all the light-powers which they had taken from her. And the body of her matter became shining throughout, and all the powers in her whose light they had taken away, took light and ceased to lack their light, for they got their light which had been taken from them, because the light was given them through me. And Michael and Gabriel, who ministered and had brought the light-stream into the chaos, will give them the mysteries of the Light; it is they to whom the light-stream was entrusted, which I have given unto them and brought into the chaos. And Michael and Gabriel have taken no light for themselves from the lights of Sophia, which they had taken from the emanations of Self-willed.

"It came to pass then, when the light-stream had ingathered into Pistis Sophia all her light-powers, which it had taken from the emanations of Self-willed, that she became shining throughout; and the light-powers in Pistis Sophia, which the emanations of Self-willed had not taken, became joyful again and filled themselves with light. And the lights which were poured into Pistis Sophia, quickened the body of her matter, in which no light was present, and which was on the point of perishing or perished. And they raised up all her powers which were on the point of being dissolved. And they took unto themselves a light-

power and became again as they were before, and they increased again in their sense of the Light. And all the light-powers of Sophia knew themselves mutually through my light-stream and were saved through the light of that stream."

Mercury and Sulphur are the elements of the Great Work.

Pistis Sophia can reconquer her powers only by means of Mercury and Sulphur.

The initiate personally shines with the powers that divinize.

The powers that had been lost are precisely the forty-nine autonomous and self-cognizant parts of our own Being.

Each one and all of the autonomous and conscious parts of our own Being are precisely the cosmic powers of Pistis Sophia.

Each power is personified by one or another self-cognizant part of our own Being.

Three types of relations exist in the world and in life.

The first one is the relation with the physical body. It is clear that if we do not know how to relate with our physical body, we will become ill.

The second type is the relation with the environment. If we do not know how to relate with people, we undoubtedly create many problems for ourselves.

The third type is the most important relation. It is the relation of the human being dealing with himself, with the distinct, independent, and conscious parts of his own Being.

The powers of the Adept are precisely the autonomous and self-cognizant parts of our own Being.

We can establish correct relations with each one and all of the independent and conscious parts of our own Being, only by passing through the Buddhist Annihilation.

Therefore, to covet psychic powers is absurd.

Those who proceed like this convert themselves into adepts of the Left hand.

It is better to annihilate the ego in order to establish correct relations with the powers that divinize.

The powers that divinize are the forty-nine fires.

The forty-nine fires are the forty-nine independent and self-cognizant parts of our own Being.

It is clear that the initiate, filled with Pistis Sophia, re-conquers the light that the psychic aggregates have taken away from within each one of the forty-nine parts of the Being.

The diverse parts of the Being receive the light through Christ.

Gabriel, the Mercury, and Michael, the Sulphur, permits us to enter into the mysteries of the Light, into the Great Work.

We can receive the light-stream, thanks to Mercury and Sulphur.

Neither the Mercury nor the Sulphur ever plunder the Light of lights of Pistis Sophia.

Rather, Gabriel and Michael take away the light from the Self-willed, the ego, the light that had been stolen by the psychic aggregates.

Pistis Sophia becomes luminous when the light-stream extracts, or liberates the Essence which was bottled up within the emanations of the Self-willed (the ego).

We know very well that the integrated light-stream is Christ-Sabaoth or Lucifer-Sabaoth.

The Light-Powers return to Pistis Sophia when all the undesirable elements of Self-willed have been annihilated.

The Body of Gold, To Soma Heliakon, with which Pistis Sophia is dressed, shines with the lights that have been poured into Pistis Sophia.

It is obvious that when Pistis Sophia lets herself fall, she loses To Soma Heliakon, the Body of Gold of the Solar Man.

The powers of Pistis Sophia are elevated when the ego has been annihilated.

The powers of Pistis Sophia are renewed in the Light and grow towards the Light when the ego has died.

The light stream, having accomplished its purpose, departeth from Sophia

"And my light-stream, when it had taken away the lights from the emanations of Self-willed, which they had taken away from Pistis Sophia, poured them into Pistis Sophia, and turned itself about and went up out of the chaos."

The light-stream, Christus-Lucifer, takes away the lights from within the diverse aggregates, in order to return them to Pistis Sophia.

The light-stream turns itself about and goes up out of the profundity of the Chaos.

The light-stream liberates the powers of Pistis Sophia, and returns them to her interior.

Chapter 65

When then the First Mystery said this to the disciples, that it had befallen Pistis Sophia in the chaos, he answered and said unto them: "Understand ye in what manner I discourse with you?"

Peter came forward and said: "My Lord, concerning the solution of the words which thou hast spoken, thus hath thy light-power prophesied afore time through Solomon in his Odes..."

Peter, within each human being, is the Hierophant of sex, one part of our Being.

Christ also expressed Himself through Solomon, son of David, King of Zion.

It is clear that Christ is the Instructor of the World.

Christ is the Master of most excellence, the venerable, great Master.

In reality, Christ expresses Himself through any Self-realized and perfect human.

This is how Christ has always instructed humanity.

Christ is the Master of Masters.

Within any prepared human being, Christ always lives the same cosmic drama.

This signifies that the Four Gospels are actually always palpitating.

The Four Gospels are not of time.

Christ triumphs over temptations each time He performs the cosmic drama.

Peter interpreteth the narrative from the Odes of Solomon

1. A stream came forth and became a great wide flood.

2. It tore away all to itself and turned itself against the temple.

3. Dams and buildings could not hold it, nor could the art of them who hold the waters.

4. It was led over the whole land and laid hold of all.

5. They who were on the dry sand, drank; their thirst was quieted and quenched, when the draught from the hand of the Highest was given.

6. Blessed are the ministers of that draught, to whom the water of the Lord is entrusted.

7. They have refreshed parched lips; they whose power was taken away, have gotten joy of heart and they have laid hold of souls, having poured in the breath, so that they should not die.

8. They have raised up limbs which were fallen; they have given power to their openness and light unto their eyes.

9. For they all have known themselves in the Lord and are saved through the water of Life eternal.

"Hearken, therefore, my Lord, that I may set forth the word in openness. As thy power hath prophesied through Solomon: 'A stream came forth and became a great flood,' — this is: The light-stream hath

spread itself out in the chaos over all the regions of the emanations of Self-willed.

"And again the word which thy power hath spoken through Solomon: 'It tore away all to itself and led it over the temple.' — that is: It drew all the light-powers out of the emanations of Self-willed, which they had taken from Pistis Sophia, and poured them anew into Pistis Sophia.

"And again the word thy power hath spoken: 'The dams and buildings could not hold it,' — that is: The emanations of Self-willed could not hold the light-stream within the walls of the darkness of the chaos.

"And again the word which it hath spoken: 'It was led over the whole land and filled all,' — that is: When Gabriel and Michael had led it over the body of Pistis Sophia, they poured into her all the lights which the emanations of Self-willed had taken from her, and the body of her matter shone.

"And the word which it hath spoken: 'They who were in the dry sand, drank' — that is: All in Pistis Sophia whose light had before been taken away, got light.

"And the word which it hath spoken: 'Their thirst was quieted and quenched,' — that is: Her powers ceased to lack the light, because their light, which had been taken from them, was given them [again].

"And again as thy power hath spoken: 'The draught through the Highest was given them,' — that is: The light was given unto them through the light-stream, which came forth out of thee, the First Mystery.

"And as thy power hath spoken: 'Blessed are the ministers of that draught,' — this is the word which thou hast spoken: 'Michael and Gabriel, who have ministered, have brought the light-stream into the chaos and also led it forth again. They will give them the mysteries of the Light of the Height, they to whom the light-stream is entrusted.'

"And again as thy power hath spoken: 'They have refreshed parched lips' — that is: Gabriel and Michael have not taken for themselves

from the lights of Pistis Sophia, which they had spoiled from the emanations of Self-willed, but they have poured them into Pistis Sophia.

"And again the word which it hath spoken: 'They whose power was taken away, have gotten joy of heart,' — that is: All the other powers of Pistis Sophia, which the emanations of Self-willed have not taken, are become exceedingly merry and have filled themselves with light from their light-fellows, for these have poured it into them.

"And the word which thy power hath spoken: 'They have quickened souls, having poured in the breath, so that they should not die,' — that is: When they had poured the lights into Pistis Sophia, they quickened the body of her matter, from which they had before taken its lights, and which was on the point of perishing.

"And again the word which thy power hath spoken: 'They have raised up limbs which were fallen, or that they should not fall,' — that is: When they poured into her her lights, they raised up all her powers which were on the point of being dissolved.

"And again as thy light-power hath spoken: 'They have received again their light and have become as they were before;' and again the word which it hath spoken: 'They have given light unto their eyes,' — that is: They have received sense in the Light and known the light-stream, that it belongeth to the Height.

"And again the word which it hath spoken: 'They all have known themselves in the Lord,' — that is: All the powers of Pistis Sophia have known one another through the light-stream.

And again the word which it hath spoken: 'They are saved through water of Life eternal,' — that is: They are saved through the whole light stream.

"And again the word which it hath spoken: 'The light-stream tore all to itself and drew it over the temple,' — that is: When the light-stream had taken all the light-powers of Pistis Sophia and had spoiled them from the emanations of Self-willed, it poured them into Pistis Sophia

and turned itself about and went out of the chaos and came over thee, — thou who art the temple.

"This is the solution of all the words which thy light-power hath spoken through the Ode of Solomon."

It came to pass then, when the First Mystery had heard Peter speak these words, that he said unto him: "Well said, blessed Peter. This is the solution of the words which have been spoken."

The Christic light-stream falls into our interior, provoking a great flood.

Then, the psychological city that we carry in our interior (which is Babylon the great, the mother of all abominations and fornications of the Earth) collapses.

The transmuted Genesiac waters inundate all that which is within our interior.

The Christic light-stream provokes the interior catastrophe.

All crumbles away. The false structures that are created by the psychic aggregates collapse; they cannot resist the Christic light-stream.

The entire Philosophical Earth (our body) is transformed within its interior.

The diverse parts of the Being drink. Their thirst is quieted and quenched when the draught from the hand of the Highest is given.

The ministers of the draught, to whom the mercurial water have been entrusted, are the parts of the Being who are related with the transmutation science of Yesod-Mercury.

The distinct self-cognizant and independent parts of the Being have refreshed their parched lips. They are filled with joy with the waters of life.

All the self-cognizant and independent parts of the Being come to know themselves within the interior, profound Lord, by means of conscious works and voluntary sufferings. They save themselves by means of the Mercurial waters of the wise.

The light-stream penetrates into the Chaos over all the emanations or undesirable elements of the ego.

The inner Christ liberates the Essence, the powers, in order to pour them into the interior of the initiate, by means of the Buddhist Annihilation.

Thus, Christ tears away all that is useless and then directs Himself towards our inner temple.

The emanations of the ego cannot hold the light-stream within the obscurity of the Chaos.

The Sulphur and the Mercury of the wise are represented by Michael, the Solar Spirit, and by Gabriel, the Lunar Angel. They produce a complete transformation. Thanks to them, the luminous powers are recaptured and even the physical body of the initiate converts itself into a vehicle of the Lord.

Thanks to the inner Christ, the distinct self-cognizant and self-independent parts of the Being receive the Light.

Michael and Gabriel (agents and ministers of the Sulphur and the Mercury of the wise) bring the stream of Christic Light to our sexual chaos in order to completely Christify ourselves.

Michael and Gabriel are two self-cognizant and self-independent parts of our own Being, skilled in the science of Alchemy.

As Michael and Gabriel exist within the Macrocosm, so too do they exist within the Microcosmic Human Being.

It is obvious that we always receive the mysteries of the Light of the Height by means of the Sulphur and the Mercury.

Sulphur and Mercury are fundamental in order to receive the light-stream.

Michael and Gabriel carry the stream of Christic Light.

Michael and Gabriel, Sulphur and Mercury, are incessantly crossing themselves in order to give origin to the Philosophical Stone.

The Sulphur and Mercury never steal the Light because these two alchemical substances are the only fundamental elements of the Great Work.

It is obvious that the parts of the Being whose power was taken away by the ego are joyous in their hearts when the Light has been returned to them.

All the other powers of the Being that the ego cannot take away from the initiate are happy with the transcendental achievements.

Within all the parts of the Being, the Light reflects and fills the wholeness of the host with happiness.

The word of Christ strengthens the Souls that suffer.

Michael and Gabriel—Sulphur and Mercury—pour the Light into Pistis Sophia.

The entire body of Pistis Sophia is charged with Light.

All the parts of the Being come to know themselves in the Lord.

Christ dwells in His temple and the powers of Pistis Sophia integrate with the inner Christ.

Peter, the Hierophant of sex, always explains the mysteries.

Those who believe or think that sex is filthy and unworthy insult the Holy Spirit.

Those who pretend to know the mysteries while excluding the power of sex are in fact condemned to the submerged involution of the infernal worlds.

Any pseudo-esoteric knowledge that is far away from the mysteries of sex is absolutely useless, futile, and absurd.

Sex is the real esoteric path that leads to the final liberation.

We advance along the sexual path while we are disintegrating the ego.

Those who have the intention of reaching liberation while abusing or cursing sex are learned ignoramuses, mistaken ones, who are unknowledgeable of the mysteries of Pistis Sophia. They are sincerely mistaken ones who enter into the Abyss.

Chapter 66

The emanations of Self-willed cry aloud to him for help

And the First Mystery continued again in the discourse and said: "It came to pass then, before I had led forth Pistis Sophia out of the chaos, because it was not yet commanded me through my Father, the First Mystery which looketh within, — at that time then, after the emanations of Self-willed had perceived that my light-stream had taken from them the light-powers which they had taken from Pistis Sophia, and had poured them into Pistis Sophia, and when they again had seen Pistis Sophia, that she shone as she had done from the beginning, that they were enraged against Pistis Sophia and cried out again to their Self-willed, that he should come and help them, so that they might take away the powers in Pistis Sophia anew."

The tenebrous ones return to fight against the initiate, even following the recovery of the Light-Powers.

He sendeth forth another more violent power like unto a flying arrow

"And Self-willed sent out of the height, out of the thirteenth aeon, and sent another great light-power. It came down into the chaos as a flying arrow, that he might help his emanations, so that they might take away the lights from Pistis Sophia anew. And when that light-power had come down, the emanations of Self-willed which were in the chaos and oppressed Pistis Sophia, took great courage and again pursued Pistis Sophia with great terror and great alarm. And some of the emanations of Self-willed oppressed her."

The tenebrous forces always want to take away all light from the initiate, even when the initiate has reached the Thirteenth Aeon.

The fashioning of the serpent-, basilisk-, and dragon-powers

"One of them changed itself into the form of a great serpent; another again changed itself also into the form of a seven-headed basilisk; another again changed itself into the form of a dragon. And moreover the first power of Self-willed, the lion-faced, and all his other very numerous emanations, they came together and oppressed Pistis Sophia and led her again into the lower regions of the chaos and alarmed her again exceedingly."

The tempting serpent of Eden, the horrible python, incessantly fights in order to make the initiate fall.

The basilisk of seven heads represents the seven engenders of the inferno: anger, greed, lust, envy, pride, laziness, and gluttony.

The dragon of the mysteries is the guardian of the Great Treasury.

The demon power of Adamas dasheth Sophia down

"It came to pass then that looking down out of the twelve aeons, Adamas, the Tyrant, who also was wroth with Pistis Sophia, because she desired to go to the Light of lights, which was above them all; therefore was he wroth with her. It came to pass then, when Adamas, the Tyrant, had looked down out of the twelve Aaeons, that he saw the emanations of Self-willed oppressing Pistis Sophia, until they should take from her all her lights. It came to pass then, when the power of Adamas had come down into the chaos unto all the emanations of Self-willed, — it came to pass then, when that demon came down into the chaos, that it dashed down Pistis Sophia. And the lion-faced power and the serpent-form and the basilisk-form and the dragon-form and all the other very numerous emanations of Self-willed surrounded Pistis Sophia all together, desiring to take from her anew her powers, and they oppressed Pistis Sophia exceedingly and threatened her. It came to pass then, when they oppressed her and

alarmed her exceedingly, that she cried again to the Light and sang praises, saying..."

Adamas, the great Lord of the Law, and his servants fight against Pistis Sophia. They do not want her final liberation.

The Pratyeka Buddhas and many powerful Gods, lords of the law, do not want the final liberation of Pistis Sophia.

If we want the final liberation, we need to submerge ourselves within the Light of the Light and within the Intelligence of the Intelligence.

When they want their final liberation, the Bodhisattvas must fight against the powers of Light and against the powers of darkness.

The Bodhisattva who has the awakened Bodhichitta in his interior cannot be arrested by the Prince Adamas, nor by the holy Pratyeka Buddhas.

The Bodhisattvas can defeat the Prince Adamas and the Pratyeka Buddhas only by surrendering themselves to the Father, who is in secret.

Adamas fulfills his duty of collecting old debts from Pistis Sophia.

It is necessary to close the final accounts in order to achieve the final liberation.

Ordinary karma exists, but the law of Katancia (superior karma) also exists.

We must close the accounts in the superior tribunals of celestial justice, before achieving the final liberation.

Karmic debts are paid in the tribunals of objective justice.

The Gods and the great initiates must be judged by the judges of the law of Katancia.

The lawyers of the tribunals of celestial justice defend the initiates in front of the cosmic judges.

There are also cosmic executioners who fulfil the terrible commands of the law.

Each one of us carries the police of karma within our consciousness. The police of karma conduce us to the tribunals of the law.

The law of Katancia is not an exception, and the great initiates are conduced to superior tribunals.

The negotiations with Adamas are frightful.

When we have cosmic capital, we pay. Thus, the results are marvellous.

Perform good deeds and perform them in abundance, so that you will have useful deeds as cosmic capital.

The great law, combined with the powers of the Abyss, closes the way of Pistis Sophia.

Adamas and his agents are never evil or perverse. They fulfill the law and nothing more.

The judges of the law are beyond good and evil.

Sophia again crieth to the Light

1. *O Light, it is thou who hast helped me; let thy light come over me.*

2. *For thou art my protector, and I come hence unto thee, O Light, having faith in thee, O Light.*

3. *For thou art my saviour from the emanations of Self-willed and of Adamas, the Tyrant, and thou shalt save me from all his violent threats.*

The negotiations with Adamas and with the law can only be arranged in the Light and for the Light.

Adamas is certainly not a tyrant. He collects what we owe before we escape from this universe, and nothing more.

When it is stated in Pistis Sophia that Adamas is a Tyrant, let us comprehend that the great Kabir Jesus Christ speaks allegorically or symbolically.

Gabriel and Michael and the light-stream again go to her aid

"And when Pistis Sophia had said this, then at the commandment of my Father, the First Mystery which looketh within, I sent again Gabriel and Michael and the great light-stream, that they should help Pistis Sophia. And I gave commandment unto Gabriel and Michael to bear Pistis Sophia in their hands, so that her feet should not touch the darkness below; and I gave them commandment moreover to guide her in the regions of the chaos, out of which she was to be led.

"It came to pass then, when the Angels had come down into the chaos, they and the light-stream, and moreover [when] all the emanations of Self-willed and the emanations of Adamas had seen the light-stream, how it shone very exceedingly and there was no measure for the light about it, that they became terror-stricken and quitted Pistis Sophia. And the great light-stream surrounded Pistis Sophia on all sides of her, on her left and on her right and on all her sides, and it became a light-wreath round her head.

"It came to pass then, when the light-stream had surrounded Pistis Sophia, that she took great courage, and it ceased not to surround her on all her sides; and she was no longer in fear of the emanations of Self-willed which are in the chaos, nor was she any more in fear of the other new power of Self-willed which he had cast down into the chaos as a flying arrow, nor did she any more tremble at the demon power of Adamas which had come out of the aeons."

Pistis Sophia departs from the Chaos with the help of Michael and Gabriel, who are the symbols of the Sulphur and Mercury of the wise.

The tenebrous ones incessantly attack the initiate who is filled with Pistis Sophia, but the Christic light-stream triumphs.

The Christic power triumphs over Adamas and over the tenebrous ones.

The demon power of Adamas, which comes out of the Aeons, is sacred. It is the Law of Katancia.

The First Mystery which looketh within is the Ancient of Days, the Concealed of the Concealed, the Goodness of Goodness, the Mercy of Mercy.

The transfiguration of Sophia

"And moreover by commandment of myself, the First Mystery which looketh without, the light-stream which surrounded Pistis Sophia on all her sides shone most exceedingly, and Pistis Sophia abode in the midst of the light, a great light being on her left and on her right, and on all her sides, forming a wreath round her head. And all the emanations of Self-willed [could] not change their face again, nor could they bear the shock of the great light of the stream, which was a wreath round her head. And all the emanations of Self-willed, — many of them fell at her right, because she shone most exceedingly, and many others fell at her left, and were not able at all to draw nigh unto Pistis Sophia because of the great light; but they fell all one on another, or they all came near one another, and they could not inflict any ill on Pistis Sophia, because she had trusted in the Light."

The completely defeated tenebrous ones fall in the presence of Pistis Sophia.

Jesus, the First Mystery looking without, causeth Sophia to triumph

"And at the commandment of my Father, the First Mystery which looketh within, I myself went down into the chaos, shining most exceedingly, and approached the lion-faced power, which shone exceedingly, and took its whole light and held fast all the emanations of Self-willed, so that from now on they went not into their region, that is the thirteenth aeon, and I took away the power of all the emanations of Self-willed, and they all fell down in the chaos powerless. And I led forth Pistis Sophia, she being on the right of Gabriel and Michael. And the great light-stream entered again into her. And Pistis Sophia beheld with her eyes her foes, that I had taken their light-power from them. And I led Pistis Sophia forth from the chaos, she treading under foot the serpent-faced emanation of Self-willed, and

moreover treading under foot the seven-faced-basilisk emanation, and treading under foot the lion and dragon-faced power. I made Pistis Sophia continue to stand upon the seven-headed basilisk emanation of Self-willed; and it was more mighty than them all in its evil doings. And I, the First Mystery, stood by it and took all the powers in it, and made to perish its whole matter, so that no seed should arise from it from now on."

The inner Christ defeats the lion of the law and the tenebrous ones, the antithesis of the Thirteenth Aeon.

Pistis Sophia, the initiate, elaborates upon the Philosophical Stone with Michael and Gabriel, with the Sulphur and the Mercury.

The light-stream enters Pistis Sophia and she triumphs over the darkness.

She, Pistis Sophia, triumphs over the tempting serpent of Eden, and over the undesirable psychic elements.

Pistis Sophia triumphs over the seven-headed basilisk, the symbol of the seven capital sins.

Pistis Sophia defeats the Lion-faced Power, the law of Katancia, with the help of Christ.

By means of Christ's help, Pistis Sophia defeats the Dragon, the symbol of Lucifer, the one who delivers her to the 'Treasury of the Kings,' the Golden Fleece.

The seven-headed basilisk dies with all of its evil doings, and no seed should arise from it.

Thus, Christ completely liberates the initiate.

The inner Christ is the Lord of the Great Work.

The secret Christ annihilates even the most inner roots of the evil within us.

Chapter 67

And when the First Mystery said this unto his disciples, he answered and said: "Understand ye in what manner I discourse with you?"

James came forward and said: "My Lord, concerning the solution of the words which thou hast said, thus hath thy light-power prophesied thereon afore time through David in the ninetieth Psalm [Modern Psalm 91]*..."*

James is the Holy Master of the Great Work.

We, the Gnostics, are especially interested in our inner James.

Our inner James is one of the autonomous and self-cognizant parts of our own Being.

The blessed Master of the Great Work is our Mercury.

The Father of the Lights teaches us the science of the Great Work through James.

The Apostle James (with his pumpkin hat and a star formed out of a seashell on his forehead) is something profoundly significant.

We know very well that Holy Water was carried within a pumpkin in the Middle Ages.

James's staff, decorated with certain ornaments that makes it look like the Caduceus of Mercury, invites us to reflect.

In his hand, James carried the book of the Great Work (Saint John's The Apocalypse) which is only understood by the alchemist.

The universal Epistle of the Apostle James is fundamental knowledge for the Great Work.

Christ-Light-Power was prophesied through David in the Ninetieth Psalm.

James interpreteth the narrative from Psalm XC [Modern Psalm 91]

1. *Whoso then dwelleth under the help of the Most High, will abide under the shadow of the God of heaven.*

2. *He will say unto the Lord: Thou are my succour and my place of refuge, my God, in whom I trust.*

3. *For he will save me out of the snare of the hunters and from mighty word.*

4. *He will shade thee with his breast, and thou shalt have trust beneath his wings; his truth shall surround thee as a shield.*

5. *Thou wilt not be afraid of terror by night nor of an arrow which flieth by day.*

6. *Of a thing which slinketh in the darkness, of a mischance and a demon at mid-day.*

7. *A thousand will fall on thy left, and ten thousand at thy right hand; but they shall not come nigh thee.*

8. *Nay rather with thine eyes wilt thou behold, thou wilt see the requital of the sinners.*

9. *For thou, O Lord, art my hope. Thou hast established the Most High for thyself as refuge.*

10. *Harm will not come high unto thee; scourge will not come nigh thy dwelling.*

11. *For he will give commandment to his angels on thy behalf that they guard thee on all thy ways.*

12. *And bear thee on their hands, that thou mayest never strike with thy foot against a stone.*

13. *Thou wilt stride over the serpent and basilisk and tread on lion and dragon.*

14. *Because he hath trusted in me, I will save him; I will overshadow him, because he hath known my name.*

15. *He will cry unto me and I shall hearken unto him; I am at his side in his tribulation and will save him and honour him,*

16. *And increase him with many days and show him my salvation.*

"This, my Lord, is the solution of the words which thou hast said. Hearken therefore, that I may say it in openness.

"The word then which thy power hath spoken through David, 'O you who dwelleth under the shelter of the Most High and abide under the protection of the God of heaven,' – that is: When Sophia had trusted in the Light, she abode under the light of the light-stream, which through thee came out of the Height.

"And the word which thy power hath spoken through David, 'I say of the Lord, my stronghold and my place of refuge, my God, in whom I trust,' – it is the word with which Pistis Sophia hath sung praises: 'For thou art my protector, and I come hence unto thee.'

"And again the word which thy power hath spoken, 'He will save you out of the snare of the hunters, and from the mighty word,' – it is what Pistis Sophia hath said: 'O Light, I have faith in three, for thou wilt save me from the emanations of Self-willed and from those of Adamas, the Tyrant, and thou wilt save me also from all their mighty threats.'

"And again the word which thy power hath spoken through David: 'He will shade thee with his breast, and thou shalt have trust beneath His wings,' – that is: Pistis Sophia hath been in the light of the light-stream, which hath come from thee, and hath continued in firm trust in the light, that on her left and that on her right, which are the wings of the light-stream.

"And the word which thy light-power hath prophesied through David: 'Truth will surround thee as a shield,' – it is the light of the light-stream which hath surrounded Pistis Sophia on all her sides as a shield.

"And the word which thy power hath spoken: 'He will not be afraid of terror by night,' – that is: Pistis Sophia hath not been afraid of

the terrors and alarms into which she had been planted in the chaos, which is the 'night.'

"And the word which thy power hath spoken: 'He will not be afraid of an arrow which flieth by day,' — that is: Pistis Sophia hath not been afraid of the power which Self-willed hath sent last of all out of the height, and which hath come into the chaos as it were a flying arrow. Thy light-power therefore hath said, 'Thou wilt not be afraid of an arrow which flieth by day,' — for that power hath come out of the thirteenth aeon, it being that which is lord over the twelve aeons, and which giveth light unto all the aeons; wherefor hath he [David] said 'day.'

"And again the word which thy power hath spoken: 'He will not be afraid of a thing which slinketh in the darkness,' — that is: Sophia hath not been afraid of the Lion-faced emanation, which caused fear for Pistis Sophia in the chaos, which is the 'darkness.'

"And the word which thy power hath spoken, 'He will not be afraid of a mischance and of a demon at mid-day' — that is: Pistis Sophia hath not been afraid of the demon emanation of Tyrant Adamas, which hath cast Pistis Sophia to the ground in a great mischance, and which hath come forth out of Adamas out of the twelfth aeon; wherefor then hath thy power said: 'He wil not be afraid of the demon mischance at midday,' — 'midday' because it hath come out of the twelfth aeon which is 'midday'; and again ['night,' because] it hath come out of the chaos, which is the 'night,' and because it hath come out of the twelfth aeon which is in the midst between both; therefore hath thy light-power said 'midday' because the twelve aeons lie in the midst between the thirteenth aeon and the chaos.

"And again the word which thy light-power hath spoken through David, 'A thousand will fall on his left, and ten thousand at his right hand, but they shall not come nigh him,' — that is: When the emanations of Self-willed, which are exceedingly numerous, could not bear the great light of the light-stream, many of them fell on the left hand of Pistis Sophia and many at her right, and they could not come nigh her, to do her [harm].

"And the word which thy light-power hath spoken through David: 'Nay rather with thine eyes wilt thou behold, and wilt see the requital of the sinners, for thou, O Lord, art my hope,' — that is the word: Pistis Sophia hath with her eyes beheld her foes, that is the emanations of Self-willed, who all have fallen one on another; not only hath she with her eyes beheld this, but thou also thyself, my Lord, the First Mystery, hast taken the light-power which is in the Lion-faced power, and hast moreover taken the power of all the emanations of Self-willed and imprisoned them in that chaos, [so that] from henceforth they have not gone forth to their own region. Therefore then hath Pistis Sophia with her eyes beheld her foes, that is the emanations of Self-willed, in all which David hath prophesied concerning Pistis Sophia, saying: 'Nay rather with thine eyes wilt thou behold, and thou wilt see the requital of the sinners.' Not only hath she with her eyes beheld, how they fall one on another in the chaos, but she hath also seen the requital with which it was requited them. Just as the emanations of Self-willed have thought to take away the light of Sophia from her, so hast thou requited them and repaid them in full, and hast taken the light-power in them instead of the lights of Sophia, who hath had faith in the Light of the Height.

"And as thy light-power hath spoken through David: 'Thou hast established the Most High for thyself as refuge: harm will not come nigh unto thee, scourge will not come nigh thy dwelling,' — that is: When Pistis Sophia had had faith in the Light and was afflicted, she sang praises unto it, and the emanations of Self-willed could not inflict on her any harm, nor could they [injure] her, nor could they at all come nigh her.

"And the word which thy light-power hath spoken through David: 'He will give commandment to his Angels on thy behalf, that they guard thee on all thy ways and bear thee on their hands, that thou mayest never strike thy foot against a stone,' — it is again thy word: Thou hast given commandment to Gabriel and Michael, that they guide Pistis Sophia in all the regions of the chaos, until they lead her forth and that they uplift her on their hands, so that her feet do not

touch the darkness beneath, and [that] on the other hand they of the lower darkness do not seize hold of her.

"And the word which thy light-power hath spoken through David: 'Thou wilt tread on serpent and basilisk and tread on lion and dragon; because he hath trusted in me, I will save him and I will overshadow him, because he hath known my name,' — that is the word: When Pistis Sophia was on the point of coming forth out of the chaos, she trod on the emanations of Self-willed, and she trod on the serpent-faced ones and on the basilisk-faced ones, which have seven heads; and she trod on the lion-faced power and on the dragon-faced one. Because she had had faith in the Light, is she saved from all of them.

"This, my Lord, is the solution of the words which thou hast spoken."

The help of the most High is the inner God of each one of us.

The inner God of each one of us is our succour and our place of refuge.

We must always trust our inner God.

The Ancient of Days will save us from the snare of the hunters and from the voice of the law.

The snares of the hunters are the snares of the tenebrous ones.

The Lord will shade us with His breath and will protect us with His sacred words of Mercury.

The wings of Mercury are opened in the dorsal spine at the height of the heart.

The igneous wings are marvellous. They shine on the Angels.

The Truth protects us. When the Lord was asked, "What is the Truth?" He kept silent.

When the same question was asked of Buddha, he turned his back and walked away.

The Truth is the unknowable from moment to moment.

We can experience that which is beyond the body, affections and the mind, that which is the Truth, only by submerging ourselves into the bosom of the Tality.

Those who live within the machinery of relativity do not know the Truth.

The world of relativity is the painful world in which we live in, the vain world of duality.

The tenebrous arrows fly against the initiate in the terrors of the night.

The enemy forces slink in the darkness.

The initiates of the darkness, as well as the initiates of the Light, fall to the Left and to the Right.

The Path of the Middle (the Eightfold Path of the Bodhisattvas with compassionate hearts) leads us to the port of liberation.

Unfortunately, rare are those who are capable of marching on the Path of the Middle towards the final liberation. Those who do not fall on the tenebrous path of the Left, fall on the path of the Right.

The tenebrous ones descend through the path of the Left within the abode of Pluto.

The saints ascend through the path of the Right, towards the marvellous Kingdom of the Light.

The tenebrous ones as well as the saints rotate within the Wheel of Samsara.

The tenebrous ones pass through the Buddhist Annihilation within the heart of the world.

Posteriorly they enter into the elemental paradises of Nature, after having suffered a great deal.

The journey through the subterranean world is millions of times more bitter than bile.

The saints return to the Valley of Samsara. They reincorporate themselves into a new human organism when the reward is finished.

Neither the human beings with goat skins, nor the human beings with sheep skins achieve the final liberation.

The authentic final liberation is only for the rebels, for those who march on the Path of the Middle.

Difficult is the Eightfold Path of the Bodhisattvas with compassionate hearts.

The limit of good is evil. The limit of evil is good.

The Eightfold Path of the Bodhisattvas with compassionate hearts has nothing to do with good or evil.

All which is good for those who march on the path of the Right is evil for those who descend through the tenebrous Left.

All which is good for the tenebrous of the Averno is evil for the walkers who ascend through the path of the Right.

Demons and saints look with horror and terror at the revolutionary adepts of the Path of the Middle.

No one understands these rebels of the Path of the Middle.

The revolutionary walker of the Eightfold Path (even when surrounded by many people) walks terribly alone.

Hitler, who was terrorized in the presence of an Adept from the Path of the Middle exclaimed: "I know the Super-Man. I have seen him. He is terribly cruel. I, myself, have felt fear."

The path is sexual. We advance by annihilating the ego and sacrificing ourselves for humanity.

The Pratyeka Buddhas (even after having built the existential superior bodies of the Being) are not Bodhisattvas.

Obviously, the Pratyeka Buddhas fell in the path of the Right.

There are also a great deal of Masters who fell on the path of the Left by means of Black Tantra.

The Bodhisattvas with compassionate hearts sacrifice themselves for planetary humanities through successive Mahamanvantaras, and finally, they achieve the incarnation of Christ.

Only the Bodhisattvas of the Path of the Middle achieve the incarnation of Christ within themselves.

The inner Christ is the true refuge of the Bodhisattva of a compassionate heart.

The inner Christ is beyond all evil and all punishment.

The Angels of the Lord help the Bodhisattvas of compassionate hearts.

We need to defeat the tempting serpent of Eden and the horripilating basilisk of evil.

The Bodhisattva of a compassionate heart must confront the lion of the law and defeat the Dragon.

The inner Christ saves those who trust in Him.

The Lord will assist us in the great tribulations.

The Lord will increase us and show us salvation.

Pistis Sophia trusted in the Light and the light-stream came from the Height in order to save her.

The Light of the Light saves the initiate from the emanations of Self-willed and from Adamas, the terrible prince of the great law.

Pistis Sophia drives the forces of the Right and the Left, which are the wings of the light-stream.

Nevertheless, Pistis Sophia marches on the Path of the Middle.

The initiate must learn how to walk with two feet.

It just so happens that some initiates do not know how to use the left foot and they fail.

The Pratyeka Buddhas and their Sravakas aspirants are scared, and they anathematize the Bodhisattva who knows how to walk with his two legs.

The sincere and noble devotees from the path of the Right stone the initiates who learn to sustain themselves in equilibrium over their left leg.

Every initiate who knows how to walk with his two legs terrorizes the noble ones of the Right.

I am speaking in parables; I am speaking of sheep and goats.

Some initiates know how to live with sheep, yet they do not know how to live with goats.

The initiates who are capable of sustaining themselves in complete equilibrium over the left foot are very rare.

Whosoever has understanding, let him understand, for there is wisdom within.

If Christ disguises Himself as the devil in order to descend into the Abyss and save us, why do we not imitate His example?

The devil is whitewashed and transformed into a Maker of Light, that is, into Lucifer; you know this.

I repeat, the initiate must learn how to move himself upon his two legs.

The initiate must learn how to disguise himself and move amongst the devils, not only in the Averno but also here in this world that we live in.

The Light is the shield that protects the initiate.

Every initiate must learn how to dim his light when he descends into the infernal worlds.

If the initiate who descends into the infernal worlds does not learn how to dim his interior light, he will scare the demons; he then cannot help the lost ones.

The initiates must learn how to live serenely and gently within the terrors of the Abyss and the night.

There is the need to learn how to handle the flaming sword.

In the abode of Pluto, the lord of time teaches us how to handle the sword.

The abode of Pluto is the Greek Tartarus, the Roman Averno, the infernal worlds within the interior of the Earth.

The Thirteenth Aeon is the superior Aeon. From it comes the Light of the Twelve Aeons.

Rare—very rare—are those who obtain the arrival to the Thirteenth Aeon.

Pistis Sophia knows what Adamas, the Tyrant is. The law is the law, and the law is fulfilled.

The law of karma is medicine for the Soul.

The law throws us to the floor and punishes us when we deserve it.

Midday is Kabbalistically stated, because it is between the Thirteenth Aeon and the Chaos.

We fear the Lion-faced Power within the darkness, within the Chaos. But in the Light, the fear disappears because we comprehend that the Law of Karma is a great medicine for the Soul.

In complete Midday, which means, between the Thirteenth Aeon and the Chaos, the initiate has no need to fear disgrace or any demon.

It is profoundly significant and Kabbalistic to say one thousand or ten thousand.

One thousand will fall towards the Left, and ten thousand towards the Right.

It is necessary to be two, in order to be one, and to know oneself as two.

This is why the terrible ones of the Right will fall, as well as the horrible ones of the Left.

The enemies of the Left, and the sincerely mistaken ones of the Right fall at the revolutionary step of Pistis Sophia.

The inner Christ, within the initiate, defeats the tenebrous forces and also the law. The Lord defeats the inferior powers and imprisons them in the Chaos.

The tenebrous powers that had tormented Pistis Sophia are submitted to her when she is with faith in the Light of the Height.

Pistis Sophia, guided by Gabriel and Michael, Mercury and Sulphur, cannot be imprisoned.

The initiate must pass over the tempting serpent of Eden, and over the horrendous basilisk of passions.

Furthermore, the initiate must defeat the lion of the law and the Dragon.

The inner Christ is above the law and the Dragon; you know this.

The monsters that personify the ego, the pluralized "I," must die.

Chapter 68

It came to pass then, when the First Mystery had heard these words, that he said: "Well said, James, beloved one."

And the First Mystery continued again in the discourse and said unto his disciples: "It came to pass, when I had led Pistis Sophia out of the chaos, that she cried out again and said..."

In the Chaos, without light, the initiate suffers indescribably.

Sophia singeth a song of praise

1. *I am saved out of the chaos and loosed from the bonds of the darkness. I am come unto thee, O Light.*

2. *For thou wert light on all sides of me, saving me and helping me.*

3. *And the emanations of Self-willed, which fought against me, thou hast hindered through thy light, and they could not come nigh me: for thy light was with me and saved me through thy light-stream.*

4. *Because in sooth the emanations of Self-willed constrained me, they took from me my power and cast me out into the chaos with no light in me. So I became as heavy-weighing matter in comparison with them.*

5. *And thereafter came a light-stream unto me through thee which saved me; it shone on my left and on my right and surrounded me on all sides of me, so that no part of me was without light.*

6. *And thou hast covered me with the light of thy stream and purged from me all my evil matters; and I shall be relieved of all my matters because of thy light.*

7. *And it is thy light-stream which hath raised me up and taken from me the emanations of Self-willed which constrained me.*

8. *And I have become sure-trusting in thy light and purified light in thy stream.*

9. And the emanations of Self-willed which constrained me have withdrawn themselves from me; and I shone in thy great power, for thou savest for ever.

"This is the repentance which Pistis Sophia hath uttered when she came forth out of the chaos and was freed from the bonds of the chaos. Now, therefore, who hath ears to hear, let him hear."

Only the Christic light-stream can save the fallen initiate.

The Christic power illuminates the intelligent rebel who marches on the Path of the Middle.

The Christic light-stream saves us from the Pratyeka Buddhas of the Right and from the tenebrous adepts of the Left.

The evil matters of the undesirable psychic elements that the initiate carries within are eliminated by the Christic light-stream.

The ineffable Isis (the divine and venerable Saitic Mother of ancient Egyptian mysteries) as a light-stream from Her Son Christ, eliminates the compelling emanations of Self-willed.

Isis, whose veil no mortal has lifted, is the daughter of Her Son, the terrific Christic light-stream.

In one of Schillers' poems, a young boy who dared to lift the veil of the Saitic Mother instantaneously fell to death when he saw the naked Truth in the face of the Goddess.

Whosoever has ears to hear, let him hear, and whosoever has understanding, let him understand, for there is wisdom within.

Chapter 69

It came to pass then, when the First Mystery had finished saying these words unto his disciples, that Thomas came forward and said: "My Lord, my light-dweller hath ears and my mind hath understood the words which thou hast said. Now, therefore, give commandment unto me to set forth clearly the solution of the words."

And the First Mystery answered and said unto Thomas, "I give thee commandment to set forth the solution of the song which Pistis Sophia sang unto me."

Thomas, the particular Thomas of each one of us, only accepts the Instructor of the World, the inner Christ within each one of us.

The Thomas that exists within each one of us places his mind in the hands of the inner Christ, and only accepts the inner Christ. The Gospel of Thomas is marvellous.

Whosoever places his mind in the hands of the inner Christ and accepts only the inner Christ marches on the path of final liberation. The demons of the mind will never defeat him.

Thomas is one of the twelve within our own selves, one part of our own Being.

The mind of Thomas exclusively receives the words of Christ.

Thomas interpreteth the song of Sophia from the Odes of Solomon

Thomas answered and said: "My Lord, concerning the song which Pistis Sophia hath uttered, because she was saved out of the chaos, thy light-power prophesied afore time thereon through Solomon, the son of David, in his Odes:

1. *I am saved from the bonds and am fled unto thee, O Lord.*
2. *For thou hast been on my right hand, saving me and helping me.*
3. *Thou hast hindered my adversaries and they have not been revealed, because thy face was with me, saving me in thy grace.*
4. *I was despised in the sight of many and cast out; I have become as lead in their sight.*
5. *Through thee I have gotten a power which helped me; for thou hast set lamps on my right and on my left, so that no side of me may be without light.*

6. Thou hast overshadowed me with the shadow of thy grace, and I was relieved of the coats of skin.

7. It is thy right hand which hath raised me up, and thou hast taken the sickness from me.

8. I have become powerful in thy truth and purified in thy virtue.

9. My adversaries have withdrawn themselves from me, and I am justified by thy goodness, for thy rest endureth unto all eternity.

"This then, my Lord, is the solution of the repentance which Pistis Sophia hath uttered when she was saved out of the chaos. Hearken therefore, that I may say it in openness.

"The word then which thy light-power hath spoken through Solomon: 'I am saved from the bonds and am fled unto thee, O Lord,' — it is the word which Pistis Sophia hath spoken: 'I am loosed from the bonds of the darkness and am come unto thee, O Light.'

"And the word which thy power hath spoken: 'Thou wert on my right hand, saving and helping me,' — it is again the word which Pistis Sophia hath spoken: 'Thou art become a light on all sides of me, [saving me] and helping me.'

"And the word which thy light-power hath spoken: 'Thou hast hindered my adversaries and they have not been revealed,' — it is the word which Pistis Sophia hath spoken: 'And the emanations of Self-willed which fought against me, thou hast hindered through thy light, and they could not come nigh me.'

"And the word which thy power hath spoken: 'Thy face was with me, saving me in thy grace,' — it is the word which Pistis Sophia hath spoken: 'Thy light was with me, saving me in thy light-stream.'

"And the word which thy power hath spoken: 'I was dispised in the sight of many and cast out,' - it is the word which Pistis Sophia hath spoken: 'The emanations of the Self-willed constrained me and took my power from me, and I have been despised before them and cast out into the chaos, with no light in me.'

"And the word which thy power hath spoken: 'I have become as lead in their sight,' — it is the word which Pistis Sophia hath spoken: 'When they had taken my light from me, I became as heavy-weighing matter before them.'

"And moreover the word which thy power hath spoken: 'Through Thee I have gotten a power for me which helped me,' — it is again the word which Pistis Sophia hath spoken: 'And thereafter came a light-power unto me through thee which saved me.'

"And the word which thy power hath spoken: 'Thou hast set lamps on my right and on my left, so that no side of me may be without light,' — it is the word which Pistis Sophia hath spoken: 'Thy power shone on my right and on my left and surrounded me on all sides of me, so that no part of me was without light.'

"And the word which thy power hath spoken: 'Thou hast overshadowed me with the shadow of thy grace,' — it is again the word which Pistis Sophia hath spoken: 'And thou hast covered me with the light of the stream.'

"And the word which thy power hath spoken: 'I was relieved of the coats of skin,' — it is again the word which Pistis Sophia hath spoken: 'And they have purified me of all my evil matters, and I raised myself above them in thy light.'

"And the word which thy power hath spoken through Solomon: 'It is thy right hand which hath raised me up, and hath taken the sickness from me.' — it is the word which Pistis Sophia hath spoken: 'And it is thy light-stream which hath raised me up in thy light and hath taken from me the emanations of Self-willed which constrained me.'

"And the word which thy power hath spoken: 'I have become powerful in thy truth and purified in thy virtuousness,' - it is the word which Pistis Sophia hath spoken: 'I have become powerful in thy light and purified light in thy stream.'

"And the word which thy power hath spoken: 'My adversaries hath withdrawn themselves from me,' — it is the word which Pistis Sophia

hath spoken: 'The emanations of Self-willed which constrained me hath withdrawn themselves from me.'

"And the word which thy power hath spoken through Solomon: 'And I am justified in thy goodness, for thy rest endureth unto all eternity,' — it is the word which Pistis Sophia hath spoken: 'I am saved in thy goodness; for thou savest every one.'

"This then, O my Lord, is the whole solution of the repentance which Pistis Sophia hath uttered when she was saved out of the chaos and loosed from the bonds of the darkness."

The Grace of Christ saves us. However, we must eliminate, coat by coat, the multiple defects of a psychological type.

Obviously, each defect has multiple psychic aggregates that process themselves in the seven and in the forty-nine levels of the Being.

In any case, the seven is multiplied by seven; you know this.

Thomas, in fact, is not comprehended.

Thomas is despised and even condemned by many.

He is judged unjustly as being incredulous and skeptical for the mere fact that he does not accept any thing that does not come directly from the inner Christ.

The power that helps the initiate is the power of the Solar Verb.

We must eliminate the coats of skin. In esotericism, this signifies the elimination of our psychological defects, coat by coat.

The right hand of the inner Christ must clean the leper. It must heal him.

Only the inner Christ will eliminate the filthy leprosy of Lazarus from ourselves.

This is the horrifying leprosy of our abominations.

We need to purify the interior Light in the light-stream of the inner Christ.

Chapter 70

It came to pass then when the First Mystery had heard Thomas say these words, that he said unto him: "Well said, finely, Thomas, blessed one. This is the solution of the song which Pistis Sophia hath uttered."

And the First Mystery continued again and said unto the disciples: "And Pistis Sophia continued and sang praises unto me, saying..."

The First Mystery blesses Thomas and approves the solution of the song of Pistis Sophia.

The secret Christ within the Adept confers to him power in heaven and over the infernos.

Hermes Trismegistus states: "Separate that Spirituous Earth from the Dense or Crude by means of a gentle heat, with much attention. In great measure it ascends from the Earth up to Heaven, and descends again, newborn, on the Earth, and the superior and the inferior are increased in power."

The matter of the Light-Powers is the Mercury of the secret philosophy, the metallic soul of the sacred sperm, a living result of the transmutation science Yesod-Mercury.

The emanations of Self-willed are the psychic aggregates, Dry Mercury, the undesirable psychic elements that we carry within.

Christ liberates us from Adamas, the prince of superior karma.

Sophia singeth another song praise

1. *I sing a song unto thee; through thy commandment hast thou led me down out to the higher aeon which is above, and hast led me up to the regions which are below.*

2. *And again through thy commandment thou hast saved me out of the regions which are below, and through thee hast thou taken there the matter in my light-powers, and I have seen it.*

3. *And thou hast scattered far from me the emanations of Self-willed which constrained me and were hostile to me, and hast bestowed power on me to loose myself from the bonds of the emanations of Adamas.*

4. *And thou hast smitten the basilisk with the seven heads and cast it out with my hands and hast set me above its matter. Thou hast destroyed it, so that its seed may not raise itself up from now on.*

5. *And thou wert with me, giving me power in all this, and thy light surrounded me in all regions, and through thee hast thou made all the emanations of Self-willed powerless.*

6. *For thou hast taken the power of their light from them and made straight my way to lead me out of the chaos.*

7. *And thou hast removed me from the material darknesses and taken from them all my powers, from which the light had been taken.*

8. *Thou hast put into them purified light and unto all my limbs, in which was no light, thou hast given purified light from the Light of the Height.*

9. *And thou hast made straight the way for my limbs, and the light of thy face hath become for me life indestructible.*

10. *Thou hast led me forth above the chaos, the region of the chaos and extermination, in order that all the matters in it which are in that region, might be unloosed and all my powers be renewed in thy light, and thy light be in them all.*

11. *Thou hast deposited the light of thy stream in me and I am become purified light.*

"This again is the second song which Pistis Sophia hath uttered. Whosoever hath understood this repentance, let him come forward and speak it."

The basilisk of seven heads is the ego with its seven capital sins that multiply themselves incessantly within us.

With the help of the inner Christ, we must take the Light away from the darkness.

We have abominable elements within the Abyss, monsters of the inferno, that must be put to death by the inner Christ.

This is how we can take from within those tenebrous abominations the Light that had been stolen from us.

The Light and the divine powers return to the initiate when the infernal aggregates which were created by our errors die.

The powers of the initiate are renewed in the light of the inner Christ.

Chapter 71

It came to pass then, when the First Mystery had finished saying these words, that Matthew came forward and said: "I have understood the solution of the song which Pistis Sophia hath uttered. Now, therefore, give commandment unto me, that I speak it in openness."

And the First Mystery answered and said: "I give commandment unto thee, Matthew, to set forth the interpretation of the song which Pistis Sophia hath uttered."

And Matthew answered and said: "Concerning the interpretation of the song which Pistis Sophia hath uttered, thus thy light-power prophesied afore time thereon through the Ode of Solomon..."

According to science, Matthew speaks scientifically in his Gospel, announcing the times of the end, which we are now in.

Matthew speaks according to the science in Pistis Sophia.

Matthew is one of the autonomous and independent parts of our own Being, the part that is related with pure science.

Pure science is the science of the Being. Distinguish between the science of Christ and the science of the Antichrist.

For these times of worldly crises and bankruptcy of all principles, the science of the Antichrist performs miracles and crooked prodigies.

Every knee is bent in the presence of the Antichrist, because the Antichrist makes atomic bombs, N-bombs, H-bombs, rays of death, and manned spacecraft to the Moon, etc...

The materialistic science of the Antichrist, with all of its rotten theories, absurd utopias, hypothesis and barbarism of all types, is worshipped by the great Harlot.

The number of the great Harlot is 666; you know this.

Mercury causes us to descend from the heights to the Chaos, but it also causes us to part from the Abyss and return to the Thirteenth Aeon.

It is obvious that through sex we descend, fall, or ascend.

Lucifer, the Maker of Light, is within the mysteries of sex.

Lucifer is the stairway to descend. Lucifer is the stairway to ascend.

We must distinguish between a fall and a descent.

Those who follow the Nirvanic Spiral Path, those who do not march on the Eightfold Path, are at the height of the Middle.

Clearly, those of the Spiral suffer less because their triumphs are few.

Those of the Direct Path suffer a great deal because their triumphs are many.

Christ liberates us and confers powers over the bonds in order to loosen them.

The inner Christ smites the horrible Python serpent with seven heads, the tempting serpent of Eden (the abominable Kundabuffer organ). The Lord raises us above the malignant roots of the tempting serpent so we can disintegrate even its seeds, the filthy germs of lust.

Christ helps us and His name illuminates us and all the Aeons.

Matthew interpreteth the song of Sophia from the Odes of Solomon

1. *He who hath led me down out of the higher regions which are above, hath led me up out of the regions which are in the bottom below.*

2. *Who hath there taken those in the Middle, he hath taught me concerning them.*

3. *Who hath scattered my foes and my adversaries, he hath bestowed power on me over the bonds, to unloose them.*

4. *Who hath smitten the serpent with the seven heads with my hands, he hath set me up above its root, that I may extinguish its seed.*

5. *And thou wert with me, helping me; in all regions thy name surrounded me.*

6. *Thy right hand hath destroyed the venom of the slanderer; thy hand hath cleared the way for thy faithful.*

7. *Thou hast freed them out of the tombs and hast removed them from the midst of the corpses.*

8. *Thou hast taken dead bones and hast clothed them with a body and to them who stirred not, hast thou given the activity of life.*

9. *Thy way is become indestructibleness and thy face [also].*

10. *Thou hast let thy aeon above decay, so that they all may be loosed and renewed and thy light become a foundation for them all.*

11. *Thou hast piled thy riches upon them and they have become a holy dwelling-place.*

"This then, my Lord, is the solution of the song which Pistis Sophia hath uttered. Hearken, therefore, that I may say it in openness.

"The word which thy power hath spoken through Solomon: 'Who hath led me down out of the higher regions which are above, he hath also led me up out of the regions which are in the bottom below,' — it

is the word which Pistis Sophia hath spoken: 'I sing praises unto thee; through thy commandment hast thou led me down out of this higher aeon which is above, and hast led me to the regions below. And again through thy commandment thou hast saved me and led me up out of the regions which are below.'

"And the word which thy power hath spoken through Solomon: 'Who hath there taken those in the Middle and hath taught me concerning them,' — it is the word which Pistis Sophia hath spoken: 'And again through thy commandment hast thou caused the matter in the midst of my power to be purified, and I have seen it.'

"And moreover the word which thy power hath spoken through Solomon: 'Who hath scattered my foes and my adversaries,' — it is the word which Pistis Sophia hath spoken: 'Thou hast scattered far from me all the emanations of Self-willed which constrained me and were hostile to me.'

"And the word which thy power hath spoken: 'Who hath bestowed on me wisdom over the bonds, to unloose them,' — it is the word which Pistis Sophia hath spoken: 'And he hath bestowed on me wisdom to loose myself from the bonds of those emanations.'

"And the word which thy power hath spoken: 'Who hath smitten the serpent with the seven heads with my hands, he hath set me up above its root, that I may extinguish its seed,' — it is the word which Pistis Sophia hath spoken: 'And thou hast smitten the serpent with the seven heads through my hands and set me up above its matter. Thou hast destroyed it, so that its seed may not raise itself up from now on.'

"And the word which thy power hath spoken: 'And thou wert with me, helping me,' — it is the word which Pistis Sophia hath spoken: 'And thou wert with me, giving me power in all this.'

"And the word which thy power hath spoken: 'And thy name surrounded me in all regions,' — it is the word which Pistis Sophia hath spoken: 'And thy light surrounded me in all their regions.'

"And the word which thy power hath spoken: 'And thy right hand hath destroyed the venom of the slanderers,' — it is the word which Pistis Sophia hath spoken: 'And through thee the emanations of Self-willed became powerless, for thou hast taken from them the light of their power.'

"And the word which thy power hath spoken: 'Thy hand hath cleared the way for thy faithful,' — it is the word which Pistis Sophia hath spoken: 'Thou hast made straight my way to lead me out of the chaos, because I have had faith in thee.'

"And the word which thy power hath spoken: 'Thou hast freed them out of the tombs and hast removed them from the midst of the corpses,' — it is the word which Pistis Sophia hath spoken: 'Thou hast freed me out of the chaos and removed me out of the material darknesses, that is out of the dark emanations which are in the chaos, from which thou hast taken their light.'

"And the word which thy power hath spoken: 'Thou hast taken dead bones and hast clothed them with a body, and to them who stirred not, thou hast given activity of life,' — it is the word which Pistis Sophia hath spoken: 'And thou hast taken all my powers in which was no light, and hast bestowed on them within purified light, and unto all my limbs, in which no light stirred, thou hast given life-light out of thy Height.'

"And the word which thy power hath spoken: 'Thy way is become indestructibleness, and thy face [also],' — it is the word which Pistis Sophia hath spoken: 'And thou hast made straight thy way for me, and the light of thy face hath become for me life indestructible.'

"And the word which thy power hath spoken: 'Thou hast led thy aeon above decay, so that all might be loosed and renewed,' — it is the word which Pistis Sophia hath spoken: 'Thou hast led me, thy power, up above the chaos and above decay, that all the matters in that region may be loosed and all my powers renewed in the Light.'

"And the word which thy power hath spoken: 'And thy light hath [become] foundation for them all,' — it is the word which Pistis Sophia hath spoken: 'And thy light hath been in them all.'

"And the word which thy light-power hath spoken through Solomon: 'Thou hast put thy riches over him, and he hath become a holy dwelling-place,' — it is the word which Pistis Sophia hath spoken: 'Thou hast stayed the light of thy stream over me, and I have become a purified light.'

"This then, my Lord, is the solution of the song which Pistis Sophia hath uttered."

The slanderers of the Left and also the ones of the Right uselessly drain their defamatory spittle.

They judge the initiate absurdly, because they do not comprehend him.

The initiates of the Eightfold Path of the Buddhas are terribly criticized, because they are not comprehended.

There are many who believe that they comprehend the initiates of the Direct Path, yet they do not comprehend them.

The most difficult part of the matter is that these people do not comprehend that they do not comprehend.

The initiate is removed from the midst of the corpses and is resurrected in the Lord.

The Lord collects the bones of the dead and clothes them and gives them the activity of life.

This must be understood psychologically. It is obvious that we must spiritually resurrect in the Lord.

The path of the Lord is indestructible, as is His face.

The interior, profound Lord within the sanctuary of the Being guides the course of the centuries.

The Light of the inner Christ is always renewed.

Each time that an Avatar is born, the Light of the Lord is renewed.

Every Avatar, whenever the time may be that He appears, is the vehicle of the inner Christ.

Therefore, the inner Christ, the inner profound Lord, is the Master of all Masters.

Therefore, the inner Christ, the Solar Logos, is the single Instructor that the world has.

Verily, in reality, Christ is the single Master.

Christ, the inner Christ, the inner, profound Lord is the Master of all Masters.

Unquestionably and according to Hermetic principles, we must ascend from Earth to heaven and again descend anew in order to ascend again, so that we can attain power over above and below.

This is how we penetrate into all dense matter and how we will dominate all that is subtle.

Whosoever wants to ascend must first of all descend.

Every exaltation is preceded by a frightful and terrible humiliation.

The Mercury must be incessantly purified by means of the transmutation science and the disintegration of the undesirable psychic elements that we carry within our interior.

Christ disperses all the hostile and inhuman emanations that all together constitute the "myself."

The Word of Christ liberates us from the bonds of that which constitutes the ego.

The Word of the inner Christ permits us to disintegrate the interior beast.

The Word of the Lord smites the tempting serpent of Eden.

We eliminate the lustful roots of the horrible serpent with seven heads that slithers in the mud of the earth by means of the secret and philosophical Verb.

We must eliminate even the most intimate roots of that which is called lust.

The Word that the inner Christ utters is the same Word that Pistis Sophia utters. The inner Christ gives strength to the initiate.

The inner Christ utters, and Pistis Sophia repeats His Words.

The Lord destroys the poison of the slanderers.

The Lord takes away the Light of His strength from those who have stolen it from Him. Obviously, the inhuman psychic elements steal the Light.

The Straight Road, the Direct Path, the Eightfold Path, leads us from the darkness to the light.

Those who renounce the happiness of Nirvana for the love of humanity, those who have the Nirmanakaya body or vehicle of solar transformation are the authentic Bodhisattvas who, indeed, walk along the Direct Path and know the Word of the Lord.

The inner Christ takes us out from within the sepulchres and liberates us from the corpses.

This is known by a complete, true Bodhisattva.

The Bodhisattvas know very well what the egoic corpses are and the sepulchres in which they are placed.

Each initiate is an Aeon that the Lord guides above death and destruction.

We will be liberated and renewed in the inner Christ.

The Lord takes us beyond the Chaos and destruction.

The Light is the foundation of the Great Work.

The Light of the inner Christ converts us into purified light.

Chapter 72

It came to pass when the First Mystery had heard Matthew speak these words, that he said: "Well spoken, Matthew, and finely, beloved. This is the solution of the song which Pistis Sophia hath uttered."

The hostile emanations of Self-willed are precisely the irradiations or manifestations of the subjective and inhuman "egoic consciousness."

Sophia continueth to sing

And the First Mystery continued again and said:

1. *I will declare: Thou art the higher Light, for that hast saved me and led me unto thee, and thou hast not let the emanations of Self-willed, which are hostile unto me, take my light.*
2. *O Light of lights, I sing praises unto thee; thou hast saved me.*
3. *O Light, thou hast led up my power out of the chaos; thou hast saved me from them which have gone down into the darkness.*

"These words again hath Pistis Sophia uttered. Now, therefore, whose mind hath become understanding, comprehending the words which Pistis Sophia hath uttered, let him come forward and set forth their solution."

The Light of lights saves us intimately when we work in the Great Work.

They, the tenebrous ones, descend into the darkness of the No-Being and reduce themselves into atomic dust.

Mary, Marah, Isis, Adonia, Tonantzin, is the Divine Mother Kundalini, the Woman-Serpent.

Peter must deny Christ three times; it is written: "Before the cock crows twice, thou shalt deny me thrice."

These are the three purifications based upon iron and fire, before the resurrection of the inner Christ within ourselves.

Peter must descend to the Abyss three times, in order to work in the darkness.

The cock is Gaio, IAO, the Mercury of the secret philosophy.

The triumph of Gaio is the success of the Sulphuric Mercury, the resurrection of the Lord.

Mary is afraid of Peter

It came to pass then, when the First Mystery had finished speaking these words unto the disciples, that Mary came forward and said: "My Lord, my mind is ever understanding, at every time to come forward and set forth the solution of the words which she hath uttered; but I am afraid of Peter, because he threatened me and hateth our sex."

And when she had said this, the First Mystery said unto her: "Every one who shall be filled with the spirit of light come forward and set forth the solution of what I say, — no one shall be able to prevent him. Now, therefore, O Mary, set forth then the solution of the words which Pistis Sophia hath uttered."

Then Mary answered and said unto the First Mystery in the midst of the disciples: "My Lord, concerning the solution of the words which Pistis Sophia hath uttered, thus hath thy light-power prophesied afore time through David..."

> Marah, the Divine Mother Kundalini, knows very well that the Light-Power of the inner Christ was prophesied through David, King of Zion.

Mary interpreteth the Song of Sophia from Psalm XXIX [Modern Psalm 30]

1. *I will exalt thee, O Lord, for thou hast received me, and thou hast not made glad my foes over me.*

2. *O Lord, my God, I cried up unto thee, and thou hast healed me.*

3. *O Lord, thou hast led up my soul out of hell; thou hast saved me from them which have gone down into the pit.*

> The Lord saves us from the infernos. The Lord liberates us from within the womb of the psychic aggregates that have fallen in the infernal worlds.

Chapter 73

And when Mary had said this, the First Mystery said unto her: "Well said, finely, Mary, blessed one."

And he continued again in the discourse and said unto the disciples, "Sophia again continued in this song and said..."

> Sophia says that which the Lord says, because Sophia is the result of the multiple, sunderable divisions of the Lord.

Sophia continueth her song

1. The Light hath become my saviour.

2. And it hath changed my darkness into light, and it has rent the chaos which surrounded me and girded me with light.

It came to pass then, when the First Mystery had finished saying these words, that Martha came forward and said: "My Lord, thy power hath prophesied afore time through David concerning these words..."

> The Light saves Pistis Sophia. Unquestionably, only the Light of lights, the Father of all lights unfolded into the inner Christ can save us.

Martha interpreteth from Psalm XXIX [Modern Psalm 30]

10. The Lord hath become my helper.

11. He hath changed my lamentation into joy; he hath rent my mourning robe and girded me with joy.

And it came to pass when the First Mystery had heard Martha speak these words, that he said: "Well said, and finely, Martha."

And the First Mystery continued again and said unto the disciples: "Pistis Sophia again continued in the song and said..."

> The interior, profound Lord converts lamentations into joy. He tears away the mourning-robe and girds us with joy.

There is too much suffering in the Great Work, but the Lord saved us from the Abyss and fills us with plenitude.

Sophia continueth her song

1. *My power, sing praises to the Light and forget not all the powers of the light which it hath given unto thee.*

2. *And the powers which are in thee, sing praises to the name of his holy mystery;*

3. *Who forgiveth all thy transgression, who saveth thee from all the afflictions with which the emanations of Self-willed have constrained thee;*

4. *Who hath saved thy light from the emanations of Self-willed, which belong to destruction; who hath wreathed thee with light in his compassion, until he saved thee;*

5. *Who hath filled thee with purified light; and thy beginning will renew itself as an invisible of the Height.*

"With these words Pistis Sophia sang praises, because she was saved and remembered all things which I had done unto her."

The Light that has been given to us (the Light that is awarded to us when the ego dies) is the Light of the inner Christ.

The powers of Pistis Sophia, all of the independent parts of the Being, must sing praises to the inner, profound Lord.

Only the inner Christ can forgive us and save us from all bitterness.

Nevertheless, we do not deny that the inner Christ grants the power to pardon sins to His Divine Mother Kundalini, the Woman-Serpent. The emanations of Self-willed restricts us and embitters our lives.

The Lord crowns us with His light and saves us.

The Lord fills us with His purified light.

Our principles, renewed by the Lord, shine gloriously.

Chapter 74

It came to pass then, when the First Mystery had finished setting forth these words unto the disciples, that he said unto them: "Who hath understood the solution of these words, let him come forward and say it in openness."

Mary again came forward and said: "My Lord, concerning these words with which Pistis Sophia hath sung praises, thy light-power prophesied them though David..."

The Light-Power of the Lord was prophesied through David, King of Zion.

David was certainly a great initiate through whom the Light-Power of the inner Christ was expressed.

David achieved the Buddhist Annihilation.

Mary interpreteth from Psalm CII [Modern Psalm 103]

1. My soul, praise the Lord, let all that is in me praise his holy name.

2. My soul, praise the Lord and forget not all his requitals.

3. Who forgiveth all thy iniquities; who healeth all thy sicknesses;

4. Who redeemeth thy life from decay; who wreatheth thee with grace and compassion;

5. Who satisfieth thy longing with good things; thy youth will renew itself as an eagle's.

"That is: Sophia will be as the invisibles who are in the Height; he hath, therefore, said 'as an eagle,' because the dwelling-place of the eagle is in the height, and the invisibles also are in the Height; that is: Pistis Sophia will shine as the invisibles, as she was from her beginning."

It came to pass then, when the First Mystery had heard Mary say these words, that he said: "Well said, Mary, blessed one."

The eternal youth is renewed with the Elixir of Long Life.

Whosoever resurrects in the Lord will enjoy the Elixir of Long Life. Therefore, he will convert himself into a Mutant.

Pistis Sophia, who is the resurrected initiate, enters into the superior order that the Logos has established in Nature.

The immortal members of this secret order, even being visible, become invisible to humanity.

These brothers and sisters form the conscious circle of the Solar humanity that operates upon the superior centers of the Being.

The brothers and sisters of the superior order work intensely, through uncountable centuries, helping humanity.

The brothers and sisters of the superior order are endowed with terribly divine powers.

The brothers and sisters of the superior order are Feathered Serpents. They are eagles of the Spirit.

Sophia is led to a region below the thirteenth aeon and given a new mystery

It came to pass then thereafter, that the First Mystery continued in the discourse and said unto the disciples: "I took Pistis Sophia and led her up to a region which is below the thirteenth aeon, and gave unto her a new mystery of the Light which is not that of her aeon, the region of the invisibles. And moreover I gave her a song of the Light, so that from now on the rulers of the aeons could not [prevail] against her. And I removed her to that region until I should come after her and bring her to her higher region.

"It came to pass then, when I had removed her to that region, that she again uttered this song thus..."

There exists a certain mystery in a region that is below the Thirteenth Aeon, which is known only by the great initiates.

She continueth to sing

1. *In faith have I had faith in the Light; and It remembered me and hearkened to my song.*

2. It hath led my power up out of the chaos and the darkness of the whole matter, and it hath led me up. It hath removed me to a higher and surer aeon, lofty and firm; it hath changed my place on the way which leadeth to my region.

3. And it hath given unto me a new mystery, which is not that of my aeon, and given unto me a song of the Light. Now, therefore, O Light, all the rulers will see what thou hast done unto me, and be afraid and have faith in the Light.

"This song then Pistis Sophia uttered, rejoicing that she had been led up out of the chaos and brought to regions which are below the thirteenth aeon. Now, therefore, let him whom his mind stirreth, so that he understandeth the solution of the thought of the song which Pistis Sophia hath uttered, come forward and say it."

Andrew came forward and said: "My Lord, this is concerning what thy light-power hath prophesied afore time through David."

The mystery of the secret "Daath" is comprehended only by a few.

The inner Andrew of each one of us, with his famous cross in an "X," (which was explained in previous chapters) says, "My Lord, this is concerning what thy light-power hath prophesied afore time through David."

Andrew interpreteth from Psalm XXXIX [Modern Psalm 40]

1. In patience I tarried for the Lord; he hath given heed unto me and ear unto my weeping.

2. He hath led up my soul out of the pit of misery and out of the filthy mire; he hath set my feet on a rock and made straight my steps.

3. He hath put in my mouth a new song, a song of praise for our God. Many will see and be afraid and hope in the Lord.

It came to pass then, when Andrew had set forth the thought of Pistis Sophia, that the First Mystery said unto him: "Well said, Andrew, blessed one."

The living rock of truth is the Philosophical Stone.

Chapter 75

And he continued again in the discourse and said unto the disciples: "These are all adventures which have befallen Pistis Sophia. It came to pass then, when I had led her to the region which is below the thirteenth aeon, and was about to go unto the Light and depart from her, that she said unto me..."

Pistis Sophia passes through terrible adventures along the Eightfold Path.

The conversation of Sophia and the Light

"O Light of lights, thou wilt go to the Light and depart from me. And Tyrant Adamas will know that thou hast departed from me and will know that my saviour is not at hand. And he will come again to this region, he and all his rulers who hate me, and Self-willed also will bestow power unto his lion-faced emanation, so that they all will come and constrain me all together and take my whole light from me, in order that I may become powerless and again without light. Now, therefore, O Light and my Light, take from them the power of their light, so that they may not be able to constrain me from now on."

The road that leads us to the Light of the light is the path of the razor's edge. This way is full of dangers within and without.

The light promiseth to seal the regions of Self-willed

"It came to pass then, when I heard these words which Pistis Sophia had spoken unto me, that I answered her, saying: 'My Father, who hath emanated me, hath not yet given me commandment to take their light from them; but I will seal the regions of Self-willed and of all his rulers who hate thee because thou hast had faith in the Light. And I will also seal the regions of Adamas and of his rulers, so that

none of them may be able to fight with thee, until their time is completed and the season cometh that my Father give me commandment to take their light from them.'"

Christ saves the initiate and protects him from Adamas, the Tyrant, and from the attacks of the tenebrous ones and from the Rulers.

Chapter 76

"And thereafter I said again unto her: 'Hearken that I may speak with thee about the time when this which I have said unto thee will come to pass. It will come to pass when [the] three times are completed.'

"Pistis Sophia answered and said unto me: 'O Light, by what shall I know when the three times will take place, so that I may be glad and rejoice that the time is near for thee to bring me to my region, and moreover rejoice therein that the time is come when thou wilt take the light-power from all them which hate me, because I have had faith in thy light?'

The initiate who wants the final liberation must liberate himself from Adamas, and from the Rulers of the cosmos, and from the vibrations of Self-willed.

In the proper time and hour, the inner Christ within the initiate will settle the affairs with Adamas and the Rulers in order to liberate Pistis Sophia.

Three indicates complete perfection. Only when the three times are completed does the initiate achieve the final liberation.

How Sophia will know that the time of her final deliverance hath come

"And I answered and said unto her: 'If thou seest the gate of the Treasury of the Great Light which is opened after the thirteenth aeon,

and that is the left [one], — when that gate is opened, then are the three times completed.'

"Pistis Sophia again answered and said: 'O Light, by what shall I know, — for I am in this region, — that the gate is opened?'"

> The gate of the Treasury of the Great Light must open beyond the Thirteenth Aeon.
>
> We must pay all at the gate of the Treasury of the Great Light, before the gate of the universe is delivered unto us.
>
> Whosoever has understanding, let him understand, for there is wisdom within.
>
> It is not possible to depart from the universe without having settled all of our affairs at the gate of the Treasury.

What will come to pass at that time

"And I answered and said unto her: 'When that gate is opened, they who are in all the aeons will know because of the Great Light which will obtain in all their regions. But see, I have now settled that they shall venture no ill against thee, until the three times are completed. And thou wilt have the power of going down into their twelve aeons when it pleaseth thee, and also of returning and going into thy region, which is below the thirteenth aeon, and in which thou now art. But thou wilt not have the power of passing through the gate of the Height which is in the thirteenth aeon, so as to enter into thy region whence thou didst come down. Moreover, if then the three times are completed, Self-willed and all his rulers will again constrain thee, to take thy light from thee, being enraged against thee and thinking that thou hast imprisoned his power in the chaos, and thinking that thou hast taken its light from it. He will then be embittered against thee, to take from thee thy light, in order that he may send it down into the chaos and it may get down to that emanation of his, so that it may be able to come up out of the chaos and go to his region. Adamas will attempt this. But I will take all thy powers from him and give them unto thee, and I will come to take them. Now, therefore, if they constrain thee at that time, then sing praises to the Light, and I will not delay to

help thee. And I will quickly come unto thee to the regions which are below thee. And I will come down to their regions to take their light from them. And I will come to this region whither I have removed thee, and which is below the thirteenth aeon, until I bring thee to thy region whence thou art come.'

"It came to pass then, when Pistis Sophia had heard me say these words unto her, that she rejoiced with great joy. But I removed her to the region which is below the thirteenth aeon. I went to the Light and departed from her."

When the gate of the universe is delivered unto us, the Great Light shines in all of the Aeons.

Pistis Sophia is attacked by Adamas and by Self-willed and by the Rulers of the universe, even in the last moment before the gate of the universe is delivered unto us.

The one who writes this has accompanied some twins towards the gate of the universe, and thus can explain this mystery.

Fortunate are those who achieve the departure from this universe in order to enter into the Uncreated Light.

Those who enter into the bosom of the great Reality possess the glorious body of Dharmakaya.

Those who possess the body of Dharmakaya submerge themselves within the joy of life, free in its movement.

Happiness is inexhaustible for those who submerge themselves within the bosom of the great Reality.

Adamas tries to capture Pistis Sophia, but the inner Christ fights against Adamas and defeats him.

Pistis Sophia sings praises unto the Light, and Christ helps her.

The inner profound Lord must take Pistis Sophia to the region of Daath, before finally taking her far beyond the Thirteenth Aeon, the abode of the Light.

Christ takes Pistis Sophia out of the mysterious region of Daath when He considers it to be necessary and He takes her to the region of Daath when it is indispensable.

The region of Daath is absolutely sexual.

The Sephirah Daath is related with the great mysteries of the lingam-yoni.

The great initiates must work for certain periods with the transmutation science of Yesod-Mercury.

When the initiates of midday are working with the transmutation science, the chalice of the temple appears without its metallic cover.

When the initiate is not working with Daath (the mystery that is below the Thirteenth Aeon) then the chalice of the temple shines with its golden cover.

The time for the final deliverance of Sophia is completed

And all these adventures the First Mystery told to the disciples, that they should come to pass for Pistis Sophia. And he sat on the Mount of Olives, narrating all these adventures in the midst of the disciples. And he continued again and said unto them: "And it came to pass again after this, while I was in the world of men and sat in the way, that is in this region which is the Mount of Olives, before my vesture was sent unto me, which I had deposited in the four-and-twentieth mystery from the interior, but the first from the exterior, which is the Great Uncontainable, in which I am enwrapped, and before I had gone to the Height to receive my second vesture, — while I sat with you in this region, which is the Mount of Olives, the time was completed of which I had said to Pistis Sophia: 'Adamas and all his rulers will constrain thee.'"

Christ keeps His vesture in the Four-and-twentieth Mystery, the mystery that works with the laws of the Sixth Mystery.

Only by working in the Great Work with the Rulers of the Sixth Mystery is the Adept able to invest himself with the vesture of glory.

Adamas and the Rulers of the distinct zones of the universe put forth many impediments for the initiate.

Chapter 77

"It came to pass then, when that time came on, — and I was in the world of men, sitting with you in this region, which is the Mount of Olives, — that Adamas looked down out of the twelve aeons and looked down at the regions of the chaos and saw his demon power which is in the chaos, that no light at all was in it, because I had taken its light from it; and he saw it, that it was dark and could not go to his region, that is to the twelve aeons."

Time and time again, Adamas is angry with Pistis Sophia when she takes the Light.

The powers of good and evil fight against the initiate and he must defeat them if he wants the final liberation.

It is urgent to receive the gate of the universe in order to escape from this world of relativity.

Before receiving the final Truth, the war against the power of good and evil is frightful.

In the world of duality, which is within the machinery of relativity, Adamas collects very ancient debts from Pistis Sophia.

Tenebrous and diabolic emanations are found to be related with old karmic debts.

Tenebrous regions within the universal regions are the living result of karma.

The Angels of the Law collect karmic debts from the initiates.

The dark Chaos waits for those who owe.

The one who is paying and is restricted and pursued, remains without Light.

Pistis Sophia, without Light, extremely suffers. Her splendors are eclipsed within the battle of antithesis.

Adamas sendeth forth two emanations of darkness to plague Sophia

"Thereon Adamas again remembered Pistis Sophia and became most exceedingly wroth against her, thinking that it was she who

had imprisoned his power in the chaos, and thinking that it was she who had taken its light from it. And he was exceedingly embittered; he piled wrath on wrath and emanated out of himself a dark emanation, and another chaotic and evil, the violent [one], so as through them to harass Pistis Sophia. And he made a dark region in his region, so as to constrain Sophia therein. And he took many of his rulers; they pursued after Sophia, in order that the two dark emanations which Adamas had emanated might lead her into the dark chaos which he had made, and constrain her in that region and harass her, until they should take her whole light from her, and Adamas should take the light from Pistis Sophia and give it to the two dark violent emanations, and they should carry it to the great chaos which is below and dark, and cast it into his dark power which is chaotic, if perchance it might be able to come to his region, because it had become exceedingly dark, for I had taken its light-power from it.

"It came to pass then, when they pursued after Pistis Sophia, that she cried out again and sang praises to the Light, since I had said unto her: 'If thou shalt be constrained and singest praises unto me, I will come quickly and help thee.' It came to pass then, when she was constrained, — and I sat with you in this region, that is on the Mount of Olives, — that she sang praises to the Light, saying..."

> The initiate who fights in order to depart from the universe of relativity resigns and has faith in the inner Christ. Nevertheless, he is willing to lose his Light and fall into the Chaos if the inner Lord wishes him to do so.

Sophia again singeth a song to the Light

1. *O Light of lights, I have had faith in thee. Save me from all these rulers who pursue after me, and help me.*

2. *That in sooth they may never take from me my light, as the lion-faced power [did]. For thy light is not with me nor thy light-stream to save me. Nay, Adamas is the more enraged against me, saying unto me: 'Thou hast imprisoned my power in the chaos.'*

3. Now, therefore, O Light of lights, if I have done this and have imprisoned it, if I have done any injustice at all to that power,

4. Or if I have constrained it, as it hath constrained me, then let all these rulers who pursue after me, take my light from me and leave me empty;

5. And let my foe Adamas pursue after my power and seize upon it and take my light from me and cast it into his dark power which is in the chaos, and keep my power in the chaos.

6. Now, therefore, O Light, lay hold on me in thy wrath and lift up thy power above my foes who have lifted themselves up against me to the very end.

7. Quicken to me, as thou hast said unto me: 'I will help thee.'

The lion of the law pursues Pistis Sophia, but she has faith in the inner Christ.

Chapter 78

It came to pass then, when the First Mystery had finished saying these words unto the disciples, that he said: "Who hath understood the words which I have spoken, let him come forward and set forth their solution."

James came forward and said: "My Lord, concerning this song which Pistis Sophia hath sung, thus thy light-power hath prophesied afore time through David in the seventh Psalm..."

The resigned initiates bow before the verdict of the law.

James interpreteth the song from Psalm VII

1. O Lord, my God, in Thee have I hoped. Free me from my pursuers and save me,

2. That in sooth he may never steal away my soul as a lion, without any one to deliver and save me.

3. O Lord, My God, if I have done this, if injustice is on my hands,

4. If I have requited those who requite me with evil, then let me fall down empty through my foes.

5. And let the foe pursue after my soul and seize it, and trample my life to the ground and lay my honour in the dust (Selah.)

6. Arise, O Lord, in thy wrath, raise thyself up for the end of my foes.

7. Arise according to the commandment which thou hast commanded.

It came to pass when the First Mystery had heard James speak these words, that he said: "Well said, James, beloved."

James, the blessed Master of the Great Work within ourselves, resigns and awaits the verdict of the Lord.

Chapter 79

And the First Mystery continued again and said unto the disciples: "It came to pass then, when Pistis Sophia had finished uttering the words of this song, that she turned herself back to see whether Adamas and his rulers had turned back to go to their aeon. And she saw them, how they pursued after her. Then she turned unto them and said unto them..."

The Light of the interior profound Lord can liberate the initiate from his persecutors.

Sophia addresseth Adamas and his rulers

1. Why pursue ye after me and say: 'I should not have help, that the Light should save not me from you?'

2. Now, therefore, my vindicator is the Light and a strong one; but it is long-suffering until the time of which it hath said unto me: 'I will come and help thee.' And it will not bring its wrath upon you always. But this is the time of which he hath spoken unto me.

3. *Now, therefore, if ye turn not back and cease not to pursue after me, then will the Light make ready its power, and it will make itself ready in all its powers.*

4. *And in its power hath it made itself ready, so that it may take your lights which are in you, and ye may become dark; and its power hath brought it to pass, so that it may take your power from you and ye go to ground.*

"And when Pistis Sophia had said this, she looked at the region of Adamas and saw the dark and chaotic region which he made, and saw also the two dark exceedingly violent emanations which Adamas had emanated, in order that they might seize Pistis Sophia and cast her down into the chaos which he had made and constrain and harass her in that region, until they should take her light from her. When Pistis Sophia had seen those two dark emanations and the dark region which Adamas had made, that she feared and cried unto the Light, saying..."

Adamas, the law, can collect and cause the initiate to suffer, but the inner Christ helps the Soul who wants to escape from the universe of relativity.

Sophia again singeth to the Light

1. *O Light, lo! Adamas, the doer of violence, is wrathful; he hath made a dark emanation,*

2. *And he hath also emanated another chaos and hath made another dark and chaotic [one] and made it ready.*

3. *Now, therefore, O Light, the chaos which he hath made, in order to cast me down therein and take from me my light-power, take from him his own.*

4. *And the plan which he hath devised, to take my light, — they are to take his own from him; and the injustice which he hath spoken, to take my lights from me, — take then all of his.*

"These are the words which Pistis Sophia hath uttered in her song. Now, therefore, who is sober in spirit, let him come forward and set forth the solution of the words which Pistis Sophia [hath uttered] in her song."

Evil falls upon the heads of those who have done evil.

Chapter 80

Martha again came forward and said: "My Lord, I am sober in my spirit and understand the word which thou sayest. Now, therefore, give me commandment to set forth their solution in openness."

And the First Mystery answered and said unto Martha: "I give thee commandment, Martha, to set forth the solution of the words which Pistis Sophia hath uttered in her song."

And Martha answered and said: "My Lord, these are the words which thy light-power hath prophesied afore time through David in the seventh Psalm, saying..."

If the initiate does not change, if he does not repent, he falls under the arrows of the law.

Martha interpreteth the words of Sophia from Psalm VII

12. *God is a righteous vindicator and strong and long-suffering, who bringeth not his wrath every day.*

13. *If ye turn not, he will whet his sword; he hath bent his bow and made it ready.*

14. *And he hath made ready for him instruments of death; he hath made his arrows for those who will be burnt up.*

15. *Behold, injustice hath been in labour, hath conceived wrong and brought forth iniquity.*

16. It hath digged a pit and hollowed it out. It will fall into the hold which it hath made.

17. Its wrong will return on its own head, and its injustice will come down on its pate.

When Martha had said this, the First Mystery which looketh without, said unto her: "Well said, finely, Martha, blessed [one]."

The instruments of death and the arrows of justice are prepared against the transgressors of the law.

Injustice produces iniquities and the law falls upon the transgressors.

Each one will fall into the hole which he has dug.

Evil will return upon the one who produces it.

Injustice falls upon the one who originates it; this is the law.

Chapter 81

Jesus bringeth Sophia again to the thirteenth aeon

It came to pass then, when Jesus had finished telling his disciples all the adventures which had befallen Pistis Sophia when she was in the chaos, and the way she had sung praises to the Light, that it should save her and lead her out of the chaos, and lead her into the twelve aeons, and also the way it had saved her out of all her afflictions with which the rulers of the chaos had constrained her, because she longed to go to the Light, that Jesus continued again in the discourse and said unto his disciples: "It came to pass then after all this, that I took Pistis Sophia and led her into the thirteenth aeon, shining most exceedingly, there being no measure for the light which was about me. I entered into the region of the four-and-twenty invisibles, shining most exceedingly. And they fell into great commotion; they looked and saw Sophia, who was with me. Her they knew, but me they knew not, who I was, but held me for some sort of emanation of the Light-land.

"It came to pass then, when Pistis Sophia saw her fellows, the invisibles, that she rejoiced in great joy and exulted exceedingly and desired to proclaim the wonders which I had wrought on her below in the earth of mankind, until I saved her. She came into the midst of the invisibles, and in their midst sang praises unto me, saying..."

Only the inner Christ can save the initiate and settle the debts.

This is only possible based on great repentance and profound comprehension.

The region of the twenty-four Elders is the Thirteenth Aeon.

The twenty-four Elders are within us. They are the twenty-four zodiacal parts of our own Being.

The twenty-four Elders know the human soul very well.

The twenty-four Elders know that Christ is the central fire of the Earth.

Christ is I.N.R.I., the central fire of the Earth and of every sun or galaxy.

The living or philosophical fire burns within the nucleus of every cosmic unity.

Sophia singeth the praises of the Light to her fellow-invisibles

1. *I will give thanks unto Thee, O Light, for thou art a Saviour; thou art a deliverer for all time.*

2. *I will utter this song to the Light, for it hath saved me and saved me out of the hand of the rulers, my foes.*

3. *And thou hast preserved me in all the regions, thou hast saved me out of the height and the depth of the chaos and out of the aeons of the rulers of the sphere.*

4. *And when I was come out of the Height, I wandered round in regions in which is no light, and I could not return to the thirteenth aeon, my dwelling-place.*

5. For there was no light in me nor power. My power was utterly weakened.

6. And the Light saved me in all my afflictions. I sang praises unto the Light, and it hearkened unto me, when I was constrained.

7. It guided me in the creation of the aeons to lead me up into the thirteenth aeon, my dwelling-place.

8. I will give thanks unto thee, O Light, that thou hast saved me, and for thy wondrous works unto the race of men.

9. When I failed of my power, thou hast given me power; and when I failed of my light, thou didst fill me with purified light.

10. I was in the darkness and in the shadow of the chaos, bound with the mighty fetters of the chaos, and no light was in me.

11. For I have provoked the commandment of the Light and have transgressed, and I have made wroth the commandment of the Light, because I had gone out of my region.

12. And when I had gone down, I failed of my light and became without light, and no one had helped me.

13. And in my affliction I sang praises unto the Light, and it saved me out of my afflictions.

14. And it hath also broken asunder all my bonds and led me up out of the darkness and the affliction of the chaos.

15. I will give thanks unto thee, O Light, that thou hast saved me and that thy wondrous works have been wrought in the race of men.

16. And thou hast shattered the upper gates of the darkness and the mighty bolts of the chaos.

17. And thou didst let me depart out of the region in which I had transgressed, and my light was taken, because I have transgressed.

18. And I ceased from my mysteries and went down to the gates of the chaos.

19. And when I was constrained, I sang praises to the Light. It saved me out of all my afflictions.

20. Thou sentest thy stream; it gave me power and saved me out of all my afflictions.

21. I will give thanks unto thee, O Light, that thou hast saved me, and for thy wondrous works in the race of men.

"This then is the song which Pistis Sophia hath uttered in the midst of the four-and-twenty invisibles, desiring that they should all of the wondrous works which I had done for her, and desiring that they should know that I have gone to the world of men and have given them the mysteries of the Height. Now, therefore, who is exalted in his thought, let him come forward and say the solution of the song which Pistis Sophia hath uttered."

Christ is the Light and life. Whosoever trusts in Him will never be in darkness.

The enemy Rulers are the agents of the law.

Nevertheless, we must comprehend the significance of the parable. The masters of karma are obliged to administer the law.

Great dangers exist in the Heights, just as in the profundities of the Chaos and out of the Aeons.

The Rulers of the Sphere always call upon us to pay our debts in the tribunals of objective justice.

When the initiate provokes the one who commands the Light and violates the law, then the one who commands the law punishes him.

The inner Christ has to work intensely within the initiated human being in order to disintegrate the undesirable psychic elements and save him.

The violator of the law lives in the regions where the law has transgressed, but the inner Christ, with compassion, allows him to depart from these regions, with the condition of supreme repentance.

The fallen initiate loses his sacred mysteries and falls into the prisons of the Chaos.

The inner Christ descends to the world of men each time when necessary and gives them the mysteries of the Heights.

The Lord always reincarnates Himself when religion decreases and degenerates and when evil takes force.

Chapter 82

It came to pass then, when Jesus had finished saying these words, that Philip came forward and said, "Jesus, my Lord, my thought is exalted, and I have understood the solution of the song which Pistis Sophia hath uttered. The prophet David hath prophesied concerning it afore time in the one-hundred-and-sixth Psalm [Modern Psalm 107], *saying..."*

Within each human being, Philip is one of the self-cognizant parts of our own Being.

Philip must teach the initiate how to travel consciously outside of the physical body.

Philip must practically teach the initiate to place the physical body into the superior dimensions in order to travel within hyperspace.

The great initiates can travel to very remote places of the Earth with their physical body, without the necessity of ships, airplanes, cars, etc.

There exists a clue in order to invoke Philip: "To the little heaven, Philip." This is the clue.

The mystic must go to sleep while concentrating on Philip.

The mystic must submerge himself into meditation while invoking Philip. The mystic must arise from the bed when he feels that his body is in the state of lassitude and he must advance while invoking Philip.

The Lord orientates and helps the initiates who walk in the desert of Life.

In reality, life converts itself into a desert for those who advance along the Eightfold Path of the Buddhas.

Philip interpreteth the song from Psalm CVI [Modern Psalm 107]

1. *Give ye thanks unto the Lord, for he is good, for his grace is eternal.*

2. *Let the delivered of the Lord say this, for it is he who hath delivered them out of the hand of their foes.*

3. *He hath gathered them together out of their lands, from the east and from the west and from the north and from the sea.*

4. *They wandered round in the desert, in a waterless country; they found not the way to the city of their dwelling-place.*

5. *Hungry and thirsty, their soul fainted in them.*

6. *He saved them out of their necessities. They cried unto the Lord and he hearkened unto them in their affliction.*

7. *He led them on a straight way, that they might go to the region of their dwelling-place.*

8. *Let them give thanks unto the Lord for his graciousness and his wondrous works unto the children of men.*

9. *For he hath satisfied a hungering soul; he hath filled a hungering soul with good things,*

10. *Them who sat in darkness and the shadow of death, who were fettered in misery and iron.*

11. *For they had provoked the word of God and made wroth the determination of the Most High.*

12. *Their heart was humbled in their miseries; they become weak and no one helped them.*

13. *They cried unto the Lord in their affliction; he saved them out of their necessities.*

14. *And he led them out of the darkness and the shadow of death and brake their bonds asunder.*

15. Let them give thanks unto the Lord for his graciousness and his wondrous works unto the children of men.

16. For he hath shattered the gates of brass and burst the bolts of iron asunder.

17. He hath taken them unto himself out of the way of their iniquity. For they were brought low because of their iniquities.

18. Their heart abhorred all manner of meat and they were near unto the gates of death.

19. They cried unto the Lord in their affliction and he saved them out of their necessities.

20. He sent his word and healed them and freed them from their miseries.

21. Let them give thanks unto the Lord for his graciousness and his wondrous works unto the children of men.

"This then, my Lord, is the solution of the song which Pistis Sophia hath uttered. Hearken, therefore, my Lord, that I may say it clearly. The word which David hath spoken: 'Give ye thanks unto the Lord, for he is good; his grace is eternal.' — it is the word which Pistis Sophia hath spoken: 'I will give thanks unto thee, O Light, for thou art a Saviour and thou art a deliverer for all time.'

"And the word which hath David spoken: 'Let the delivered of the Lord say this, for he hath delivered them out of the hand of their foes,' - it is the word which Pistis Sophia hath spoken: 'I will utter this song to the Light, for it hath saved me and saved me out of the hand of the rulers, my foes.' And the rest of the Psalm.

"This then, my Lord, is the solution of the song which Pistis Sophia hath uttered in the midst of the four-and-twenty invisibles, desiring that they should know all the wondrous works which thou hast done for her, and desiring that they should know that thou hast given thy mysteries to the race of men."

"It came to pass then, when Jesus had heard Philip say these words, that he said: "Well said, blessed Philip. This is the solution of the song which Pistis Sophia hath uttered."

End of the Story of Pistis Sophia

Those who discover the path of the straight line arrive at the bosom of the great Reality.

The marvellous works of the Lord with the children of men take them to the final Truth.

The Word of the Lord heals the initiates and liberates them from their miseries, but we must perform the Word within ourselves.

Whosoever hears the Word and does not perform It is like a man who looks at himself in front of a mirror and then turns his back and walks away.

Within ourselves, Philip has great wisdom, love, and power.

The Eager Soul, Pistis Sophia, can be liberated only with the help of the Lord.

The inner Christ is Father and Mother at the same time.

The inner Christ conciliates the Macrocosm with the Microcosm within real human beings.

The inner Christ, as a mediator, moves Himself between two spheres, the one from above and the one from below.

The Fire of the fire, Christ, is the living nucleus of every planet, sun, and galaxy.

The inner Christ is the great mediator and the great integrator.

The Father, who is in secret, and our Divine Mother Kundalini are integrated within the inner Christ.

All of the forty-nine autonomous and self-cognizant parts of our Being are integrated within the inner Christ.

In reality, the forty-nine fires are integrated within the inner Christ.

The Human Soul, Pistis Sophia, is saved by Christ.

Pistis Sophia, integrated with the inner Christ, shines gloriously within the Uncreated Light.

The happiness of Pistis Sophia is inexhaustible when she integrates herself with the inner Christ.

This is the Word of the Blessed One. These are the teachings that the Adorable One uttered on the Mount of Olives.

The inner Lord is our profound Saviour.

We have spoken of Pistis Sophia, the Eager Soul, so hated by the Antichrist of the false, materialistic science.

The skeptical Sadducees, enemies of the Eternal One, hate the Christ and Pistis Sophia.

The forever-hypocritical Pharisees (who by misinterpreting the scriptures kill the spirit that vivifies it) those scoundrels of the dead sects who know nothing about Christic esotericism, also hate and condemn Pistis Sophia.

It is written in letters of fire that the sandals of Peter the fisherman will return to Rome.

On one occasion, the Lord told me, "I have always helped you, and I will always help you. I always help those who have passed through the schools of the Baalim."

Verily, verily I say unto you, that neither the materialistic Sadducees nor the hypocritical Pharisees of dead sects know anything about the inner Christ or about Pistis Sophia.

The schools of the Baalim are the materialistic and religious organizations that do not know the inner Christ or Pistis Sophia.

Any materialistic or mystical organization that pronounces itself against the mysteries of sex belongs to the order of the schools of the Baalim.

Verily, verily I say unto you, that sex is the road that leads to the profound bosom of the great Reality.

Chapter 83

Mary questioneth Jesus

It came to pass then again, after all this, that Mary came forward, adored the feet of Jesus and said: "My Lord, be not wroth with me, if I question thee, because we question concerning everything with precision and certainty. For thou hast said unto us afore time: 'Seek that ye may find, and knock that it may be opened unto you. For every one who seeketh shall find, and to every one who knocketh it shall be opened.' Now, therefore, my Lord, who is it whom I shall seek, or who is it at whom we shall knock? Or rather, who is able to give us the decision upon the words concerning which we shall question thee? Or rather, who knoweth the power of the words concerning which we shall question? Because thou in the mind hast given us mind of the Light and hast given us sense and an exceedingly exalted thought; for which cause, therefore, no one existeth in the world of men nor any one in the height of the aeons who can give the decision on the words concerning which we question, save thee alone, who knoweth the universe, who is perfected in the universe; because we do not question in the manner in which the men of the world question, but because we question in the Gnosis of the Height which thou hast given unto us and we question moreover in the type of the excellent questioning which thou hast taught us, that we may question therein. Now, therefore, my Lord, be not wroth with me, but reveal unto me the matter concerning which I shall question thee."

It came to pass, when Jesus had heard Mary Magdalene say these words, that he answered and said unto her, "Question concerning what thou desirest to question, and I will reveal it unto thee with precision and certainty. Amen, amen, I say unto you: Rejoice in great joy and exult most exceedingly. If ye question concerning all with precision, then shall I exult most exceedingly, because ye question concerning all with precision and question in the manner in which it beseemeth to question. Now, therefore, question concerning what thou wouldst question, and I will reveal it unto thee with joy."

It came to pass then, when Mary had heard the Saviour say these words, that she rejoiced in great joy and exulted most exceedingly and said unto Jesus: "My Lord and Saviour, of what manner then are the four-and-twenty invisibles and of what type, or rather of what quality are they, or of what quality is then their light?"

Mary Magdalene can never be absent from the cosmic drama.

Verily, verily, I say unto you that light would first be lacking from the face of the Earth before a Mary Magdalene would be absent from a great initiate's side.

The Solar Logos (reincarnated in a human body) has a Mary Magdalene as a wife and works with her in the Great Work.

Only the inner Christ possesses and knows the power of the words which are concerned with what we are questioning about.

Let us distinguish between the mind, and a mind of Light.

Let us distinguish between subjective reasoning, and objective reasoning.

Objective reasoning is the reasoning of the Being.

Subjective reasoning is the reasoning of the animal ego.

Objective reasoning is possessed only by the one who has passed through the Buddhist Annihilation.

We must know that there are Three Minds that exist: the first is the Sensual Mind, the second is the Intermediate Mind, and the third is the Inner Mind.

In the Sensual Mind, we find the yeast of the Sadducees.

In the Intermediate Mind, we find the yeast of the Pharisees.

Beware of the yeast of the materialistic Sadducees.

Beware of the yeast of the hypocritical Pharisees.

Open up the Inner Mind so that you can enter into the Kingdom of Heaven.

Verily, verily I say unto you that we open the Inner Mind only by awakening the consciousness.

It is impossible to awaken if we have not previously passed through the Buddhist Annihilation.

Only the Inner Mind confers unto us the objective reasoning of the Being.

The objective reasoning is the mind of Light, it is real intelligence, exalted thoughts.

The Four-and-twenty Invisibles exist in the zodiacal macrocosm and in the zodiacal human being.

Chapter 84

Of the glory of the four-and-twenty invisibles

And Jesus answered and said unto Mary: "What is there in this world which is like unto them, or rather what region is there in this world which is comparable to them? Now, therefore, to what am I to liken them, or rather what am I to say concerning them? For nothing existeth in this world to which I shall be able to liken them, and no form existeth in it which is able to be like them. Now, therefore, nothing existeth in this world which is of the quality of the heaven. [But] amen, I say unto you: Every one of the invisibles is nine times greater than the heaven and the sphere above it and the twelve aeons all together, as I have already said unto you at another time. And no light existeth in this world which is more excellent than the light of the sun. Amen, amen, I say unto you: The four-and-twenty invisibles shine ten-thousand times more than the light of the sun which is in this world, as I have already said unto you at another time. For the light of the sun in its shape in truth is not in this world, for its light pierceth through many veils and regions. But the light of the sun in its shape in truth, which is in the region of the Virgin of Light, shineth ten-thousand times more than the four-and-twenty invisibles and the great invisible forefather and also the great triple-powered god, as I have already said unto you at another time.

"Now, therefore, Mary, there is no form in this world, nor any light, nor any shape, which is comparable to the four-and-twenty invisibles, so that I may liken it to them. But yet a little while and I will lead thee and thy brethren and fellow-disciples into all the regions of the

Height and will lead you into the three spaces of the First Mystery, save only the regions of the space of the Ineffable, and ye shall see all their shapes in truth without similitude.

"And if I lead you into the height and ye shall see the glory of them of the height, then will ye be in very great amazement."

In reality, nothing in this world is comparable to the Four-and-twenty Elders, nor is anything similar to them.

Nevertheless, the Four-and-twenty Elders are the Four-and-twenty autonomous and self-cognizant parts of our own inner, profound Being.

We must never forget the seven, the twelve and the twenty-four, etc. within ourselves.

Indeed, the forty-and-nine fires are the forty and nine independent and self-cognizant parts of our real Being.

Each one of the Four-and-twenty Invisibles shines ten thousand times more than the light of the physical sun.

The spiritual light of the invisible Sun penetrates through many veils and suprasensible regions.

The light of the spiritual Sun shines in the region of the Virgin of Light.

The Sun-Christ shines ten thousand times more than the Four-and-twenty Invisibles.

The great invisible Forefather is Aelohim, the Unknowable Divinity.

The great Triple-Powered God is the Demiurge Creator of the universe: Multiple Perfect Unity.

The Creator Logos is the Holy Triamatzikamno, the Verb, the Great Word.

The three spaces of the First Mystery are the regions of the Demiurge Creator.

The regions of the space of the Ineffable are the regions of Aelohim, the Unknowable Divinity.

Of the glory of the Fate

"And if I lead you into the region of the rulers of the Fate, then will ye see the glory in which they are, and because of their overtowering great glory ye will deem this world before you as darkness of darknesses, and ye will look at the whole world of men, how it will have the condition of a speck of dust for you because of the great distance it is far distant from it, and because of the great condition it is considerably greater than it."

In reality, this painful valley of Samsara is the Darkness of darknesses, where only cries and gnashing of teeth are heard.

The Rulers of the Law live in the glory of the Light.

This world is a great speck of dust and ruins, in a dark corner of the universe, very distant from the sacred Absolute Sun.

The Light shines in the Twelve Aeons, but in this valley of Samsara darkness reigns.

Of the glory of the twelve aeons

"And if I lead you into the twelve aeons, then will ye see the glory in which they are: and because of the great glory the region of the rulers of the Fate will count for you as the darkness of darknesses, and it will have for you the condition of a speck of dust because of the great distance it is far distant from it and because of the great condition it is considerably greater than them, as I have already said unto you at another time."

Certainly, the Twelve Aeons are very far away from the Light of lights, and from the sacred Absolute.

Of the glory of the thirteenth aeon

"And if I lead you moreover into the thirteenth aeon, then will ye see the glory in which they are; the twelve aeons will count for you as the darkness of darknesses, and ye shall look at the twelve aeons, how their region will have for you the likeness of a speck of dust because

of the great distance it is far distant from it, and because of the great condition it is considerably greater than the former."

Within the Thirteenth Aeon, there exist splendors that are impossible to define with words.

The Twelve Aeons, or Regions of the Light, result in darkness in spite of their splendors, when they are compared with the luminous radiations of the Thirteenth Aeon.

Of the glory of the Middle

"And if I lead you into the region of those of the Middle, then will ye see the glory in which they are; the thirteen aeons will count for you as the darkness of darknesses. And again ye will look at the twelve aeons and upon the whole Fate and the whole ordering and all the spheres and all the others in which they are; they will have for you the condition of a speck of dust because of the great distance their region is distant from it and because of the great condition it is considerably greater than the former."

The Thirteen Aeons become the Darkness of darknesses for those who are found within the bosom of the Great Reality and the universe of relativity.

A speck of dust are the Twelve Aeons, where the Rulers of the Law, the whole Fate and the sacred order that the Logos has established in Nature dwell.

The whole Fate and the superior order and all the Spheres of the Rulers, and all the Spheres where the agents of the law live are certainly a speck of dust, because they are very far from the Absolute.

Of the glory of the Right

"And if I lead you into the region of those of the Right, then will ye see the glory in which they are; the region of those of the Middle will count for you as the night which is in the world of men. And if ye look at the Middle, it will have for you the condition of a speck of dust

because of the great distance the region of those of the Right is considerably distant from it."

Those from the Right also have a glory of distinct splendors.

The region of the Middle is like the night, which is in the world of men, where there is suffering, renunciation and where the work of the great cause is performed.

Of the glory of the Treasury

"And if I lead you into the Light-land, that is into the Treasury of the Light, and ye see the glory in which they are, then will the region of those of the Right count for you as the light at midday in the world of men, when the sun is not out; and if ye look at the region of those of the Right, it will have for you the condition of a speck of dust because of the great distance the Treasury of the Light is distant from it."

In the Light-land, the Soul of the world (which is in the Treasury of the Light) you will see the glory of the pure Souls.

Then you will have evidence that the Souls of the Right live in the Midday, which means, they develop within the Aeons.

Those of the Right are also found to be very distant from the Treasury of the Light.

Of the glory of the Inheritance

"And if I lead you into the region of those who have received the inheritances and have received the mysteries of the Light, and ye see the glory of the Light in which they are, then the Light-land will count for you as the light of the sun which is in the world of men. And if ye look upon the Light-land, then will it count for you as a speck of dust because of the great distance the Light-land is distant from it, and because of the greatness by which it is considerably greater than former."

Those who have received the lost Inheritances and the mysteries of the Light are in a region that has its glory, its splendors, which is the Light of the Soul of the world, the Solar Light in the world of men.

The Light-land is like the light of the Sun, where those who have received the mysteries and the lost Inheritances dwell.

Nevertheless, the Light-land is like a great speck due to the huge distance that exists between the world and the Absolute.

Chapter 85

It came to pass then, when Jesus had finished speaking these words unto his disciples, that Mary Magdalene started forward and said: "My Lord, be not wroth with me if I question thee, because we question thee concerning all with precision."

And Jesus answered and said unto Mary: "Question concerning what thou desirest to question, and I will reveal it unto thee in openness without similitude, and all concerning which thou questionest, I will say unto thee with precision and certainty. I will perfect you in all power and all fullnesses, from the interior of the interiors to the exterior of the exteriors, from the Ineffable to the darkness of darknesses, so that ye shall be called the fullnesses perfected in all Gnoses.' Now, therefore Mary, question concerning what thou mayest question, and I will reveal it to thee with great joy and great exultation."

Mary again questioneth Jesus

When Mary had heard the Saviour say these words, she rejoiced in exceedingly great joy and exulted, and said: "My Lord, will then the men of the world who have received the mysteries of the Light, be superior to the emanations of the Treasury in thy kingdom? For I have heard thee say, 'If I lead you into the region of those who have received the mysteries of the Light, then will the region of the [emanations of the] Light-land count for you as a speck of dust because of the great distance in which it is distant from it, and because of the great light in which it is,' — that is the Light-land is the Treasury, the region of the emanations, — will therefore then, my Lord, the men who have received the mysteries be superior to the Light-land and superior to those emanations in the kingdom of the Light?"

Let us distinguish between men who have received the mysteries of the Light and the emanations of the Treasury of the Kingdom.

The Light-land is the Treasury. Therefore, men who have certainly received those great mysteries (that are found beyond the Light-land) will be in the regions of the emanations.

Chapter 86

And Jesus answered and said unto Mary: "Finely indeed dost thou question concerning all with precision and certainty. But hearken, Mary, that I may speak with thee about the consummation of the aeon and the ascension of the universe. It will not yet take place; but I have said unto you: 'If I lead you into the region of the inheritances of those who shall receive the Mystery of the Light, then will the Treasury of the Light, the region of the emanations, count for you as a speck of dust only and as the light of the sun by day.'

One day, the Aeon and the Aeons will be consummated, and the universe will reascend towards the Great Light.

Similarly, our interior universe will be consummated in the Aeons in order to reascend towards that which has no name, the region of the cosmic inheritances, of those who will receive the mystery of the Light.

It is unquestionable that the region where we have our divine inheritance is even beyond the Treasury of the Light, the region of the emanations.

Everything is relative, even the Treasury of the Light. The Region of the Emanations becomes pale when in the presence of the ineffable splendors of the Region where we have our divine inheritance.

Of the twelve saviours and their regions in the Inheritance

"I have therefore said, 'This will take place at the time of the consummation and of the ascension of the universe.' The twelve saviours of

the Treasury and the twelve orders of every one of them, which are the emanations of the seven Voices and of the five Trees, they will be with me in the region of the inheritances of the Light; being kings with me in my kingdom, and every one of them being king over his emanations, and moreover every one of them being king according to his glory, the great according to his greatness and the little according to his littleness.

"And the saviour of the emanations of the first Voice will be in the region of the souls of those who have received the first mystery of the First Mystery in my kingdom.

"And the saviour of the emanations of the second Voice will be in the regions of the souls of those who have received the second mystery of the First Mystery.

"In like manner also will the saviour of the emanations of the third Voice be in the region of the souls of those who have received the third mystery of the First Mystery in the Inheritances of the Light.

"And the saviour of the emanations of the fourth Voice of the Treasury of the Light will be in the region of the souls of those who have received the fourth mystery of the First Mystery in the inheritances of the Light.

"And the fifth saviour of the fifth Voice of the Treasury of the Light will be in the regions of the souls of those who have received the fifth mystery of the First Mystery in the inheritances of the Light.

"And the sixth saviour of the emanations of the sixth Voice of the Treasury of the Light will be in the regions of the souls of those who have received the sixth mystery of the First Mystery.

"And the seventh saviour of the emanations of the seventh Voice of the Treasury of the Light will be in the region of the souls of those who have received the seventh mystery of the First Mystery in the Treasury of the Light.

"And the eighth saviour, that is the saviour of the emanations of the first Tree of the Treasury of the Light, will be in the region of the souls

of those who have received the eighth mystery of the First Mystery in the inheritances of the Light.

"And the ninth saviour, that is the saviour of the emanations of the second Tree of the Treasury of the Light, will be in the region of the souls of those who have received the ninth mystery of the First Mystery in the inheritances of the Light.

"And the tenth saviour, that is the saviour of the emanations of the third Tree of the Treasury of the Light, will be in the region of the souls of those who have received the tenth mystery of the First Mystery in the inheritances of the Light.

"In like manner also the eleventh saviour, that is the saviour of the fourth Tree of the Treasury of the Light, will be in the region of the souls of those who have received the eleventh mystery of the First Mystery in the inheritances of the Light.

"And the twelfth saviour, that is the saviour of the emanations of the fifth Tree of the Treasury of the Light, will be in the region of the souls of those who have received the twelfth mystery of the First Mystery in the Inheritances of the Light."

All of this will be a concrete fact in the great consummation.

The Twelve Saviours of the Treasury of the Light, and the Twelve Orders of each one of them, are the emanations of the Seven Voices and the Five Trees.

Unquestionably, the twelve and their Twelve Orders and the Seven Voices and the Five Trees will be absorbed in Christ in the day of "Be with us."

Indubitably, all of them will be kings in Christ, in His Kingdom, and they will be with the Lord in the region of the Inheritances of the Light.

Thus, the kings will be happy with the inner Christ in His Kingdom.

Each one of them will be a king over all the autonomous and conscious parts of their own Being.

In the beginning chapters of Pistis Sophia, we explain what the Seven Voices and the Five Trees and the Twelve Powers are.

There are Twelve Zodiacal Saviours or Twelve Avatars, and also the twelve Stellar Orders within each one of us.

The zodiacal constellation of Leo is the superior order, the order of the lions of fire, the order of the igneous breaths.

Obviously, the Twelve Saviours are found to be related with the Seven Radicals of the fire and with the Five Trees of the law.

Also, it is true and very certain that the Seven Voices are the Seven Spirits before the throne of the Lamb.

There exists a zodiacal flight of steps, which is related with the Twelve Saviours and the twelve zodiacal mysteries.

The Saviour of the emanations of the First Voice, which is related with Gabriel, will be in the regions of the souls of those who have received the First Mystery of the First Mystery.

The Saviour related with the emanations of Raphael will be in the region of the souls who have received the Second Mystery of the First Mystery.

The Saviour of the emanations of Uriel will be in the region of the souls of those who have received the Third Mystery of the First Mystery, in the Inheritances of the Light.

The Saviour of the emanations of the Fourth Voice of Michael, in the Treasury of the Light, will be in the region of the souls of those who have received the Fourth Mystery of the First Mystery, in the Inheritances of the Light.

Samael, the Fifth Saviour, Fifth Voice in the Treasury of the Light, will be in the region of the souls of those who have received the Fifth Mystery of the First Mystery, in the region of the Inheritances of the Light.

The Sixth Saviour of the emanations of the Sixth Voice of the Treasury of the Light, named Zachariel, will be in the region of the souls of those who have received the Sixth Mystery of the First Mystery.

Oriphiel, the Seventh Saviour of the emanations of the Treasury of the Light will be in the region of the souls of those who have received the Seventh Mystery of the First Mystery of the Light.

Before continuing, we must not forget the Seven Radicals within ourselves.

This invites us to think upon the seven mysteries related with the seven grades of the power of the fire.

Obviously, the seven exist within the human being. I want to emphatically refer to the seven autonomous and self-cognizant parts of our own Being.

I must now explain that the First Mystery is always the Ancient of Days and His Son.

Now that this has been explained we will say that there exist seven Planetary Regions related with the seven mysteries.

We pass from mystery to mystery only by means of the advancement of the igneous serpent of our magical powers.

We will now continue explaining the words of the great Kabir Jesus.

There exist Five Trees of the great Treasury of the Light.

The Eighth Saviour (who is the Saviour of the emanations of the first Tree of the Treasury of the Light) will obviously be in the region of the souls of those initiates who have received the Eighth Mystery.

Unquestionably, the Eighth Mystery is found to be related to the First Mystery of the Inheritances of the Light.

We already know that the First Mystery is the Father, who is in secret.

All of the mysteries correspond to the Lord and to His Son.

The Ninth Saviour is the Saviour of the second Tree of the Treasury of the Light. Obviously, he must be in the region of the souls of those who have received the Ninth Mystery of the First Mystery, in the Inheritances of the Light.

The Tenth Saviour is the Saviour of the emanations of the third Tree of the Treasury of the Light. Unquestionably, he is always in the region of the souls of those who have received the Tenth Mystery of the First Mystery, in the Inheritances of the Light.

The Eleventh Saviour, who is the Saviour of the fourth Tree of the Treasury of the Light, will always be in the region of the souls of those who have received the Eleventh Mystery of the First Mystery, in the Inheritances of the Light.

The Twelfth Saviour, who is the Saviour of the emanations of the fifth Tree of the Treasury of the Light, will always be in the region of the souls of those who have received the Twelfth Mystery of the First Mystery, in the Inheritances of the Light.

Without commentaries we have repeated what the great Kabir Jesus Christ has said, precisely in order to emphasize and reflect.

The Twelve Saviours, or twelve Christified Ones, are related with the twelve zodiacal signs and with the twelve planets of the solar system that rotate around the Sun.

In the beginning of this book, we have stated that our solar system is composed of the Sun and the twelve planets.

We spoke clearly of the thirteen heavens and of their relations with the thirteen worlds and the thirteen Aeons.

Twelve worlds rotate around the Sun, and each one of them has its corresponding planetary genie.

It is clear that the twelve are also within ourselves.

It is obvious that the Twelve Powers within the Macrocosm, as well as in the Microcosmic human being, are related with the twelve mysteries.

Each one of the twelve mysteries is always related with the First Mystery.

The twelve mysteries are situated in the twelve fundamental parts of the Being.

Let us think about the twelve Sephiroth, or Twelve Aeons within ourselves. Thus, we will comprehend the twelve mysteries by Kabbalistic relation.

The Thirteenth Mystery is the most secret of all the mysteries.

Of the ascension of those of the Treasury into the Inheritance

"And the seven Amens and the five Trees and the three Amens will be on my right, being kings in the inheritances of the Light. And the Twin-Saviour, that is the Child of the Child, and the nine guards will abide also at my left, being kings in the inheritances of the Light."

All of this related with the Seven Amens and the Five Trees and the Three Amens, has been previously explained, as well as the Twin Saviour.

Of their ranks in the kingdom

"And every one of the saviours will rule over the orders of his emanations in the inheritances of the Light as they did also in the Treasury of the Light.

"And the nine guards of the Treasury of the Light will be superior to the saviours in the inheritances of the Light. And the Twin-saviours will be superior to the nine guards in the kingdom. And the three Amens will be superior to the Twin-saviours in the kingdom. And the five Trees will be superior to the three Amens in the inheritances of the Light."

The reader must read the first chapters where I speak about all of this.

Obviously, each one of the Twelve Saviours will rule over the Orders that are found to be related with their own essences, lives, zodiacal Monads. It is clear that each one of the twelve is related with a zodiacal sign.

We have explained that twelve zodiacal orders exist. Leo is the superior order, being governed by the lions of life, or lions of fire.

Now our devotees will comprehend the power of the Twelve Saviours over the forces, Essences, and prodigies of the twelve zodiacal constellations.

The Nine Guardians of the Treasury of the Light are within the Microcosmic human being and within the Macrocosm.

Obviously, the Nine Guardians are found to be related with the Mercury of the wise and with the transmutation science of Yesod-Mercury.

It is clear that the nine are superior to the twelve in the Inheritances of the Light, for the Gods are the children of the Mercury of the wise.

Let us understand very well that the Twelve Saviours reached the exalted state in which they are in, thanks to the mystery of the Ninth Sphere.

The sexual mysteries are found in the Ninth Sphere.

The Twin Saviour is found in the Sixth Aeon. He is the Causal Man with the incarnated Christ.

It is amazing that Christ descended from the kingdom of Chokmah in order to manifest himself in Tiphereth.

The Lord is born from the womb of the Divine Mother Kundalini.

The Lord is conceived by the work and grace of the Holy Spirit.

The Lord incarnates in the Causal Man.

Therefore, the Causal Man is the Child of the Child.

The Lord only incarnates within the true Bodhisattvas. This is the reason why it is said that Christ is the Bodhisattva.

Christ is the Multiple Perfect Unity.

Christ is the Platonic Logos.

Christ is the Demiurge Architect of the universe.

Christ is our Lord Quetzalcoatl.

Quetzalcoatl is the Feathered Serpent, the Multiple Perfect Unity.

The Twin Saviour is superior to the Nine Guardians in the kingdom, due to the fact that he made himself Master of the mysteries of the Ninth Sphere.

The Three Amens—Holy Affirmation, Holy Negation, and Holy Conciliation—are superior to the Twin Saviour in the Kingdom.

It is evident, that the Twin Saviour is such, due to the crystallization of the three primordial forces of Nature and the cosmos in himself.

Without these three forces, the Twin Saviour never would have become what he is. This is why these three primordial forces are superior to the Twin Saviour.

The Five Trees of the great law govern the cosmos and they are superior to the Three Amens in the Inheritances of the Light.

Obviously, every Christified One must settle his accounts and present himself before the cosmic treasury, before receiving the gate of the universe.

Of the powers of the Right, and their emanation and ascension

"And Yew and the guard of the veil of the Great Light, and the receiver of Light and the two great guides and the great Sabaoth, the Good, will be kings in the first saviour of the first Voice of the Treasury of the Light, [the saviour] who will be in the region of those who have received the first mystery of the First Mystery. For in sooth Yew and the guard of the region of those of the Right and Melchisedec, the great receiver of the Light, and the two great guides have come forth out of the purified and utterly pure light of the first Tree up to the fifth.

"Yew in sooth is the overseer of the Light, who hath come forth first out of the pure light of the first Tree; on the other hand, the guard of the veil of those of the Right hath come forth out of the second Tree; and the two guides again have come forth out of the pure and utterly purified light of the third and fourth Trees of the Treasury of the Light; Melchisedec again hath come forth out of the fifth Tree; on the other hand Sabaoth, the Good, whom I have called my father, hath come forth out of Yew, the overseer of the Light.

"These six then by command of the First Mystery the last Helper hath caused to be in the region of those of the right, for the economy of the ingathering of the upper light out of the aeons of the rulers and

out of the worlds and all races in them, — of every one of whom I will tell you the employment over which he hath been set in the expansion of the universe. Therefore, because of the importance of the employment over which they have been set, they will be fellow-kings in the first saviour of the first Voice of the Treasury of the Light, who will be in the region of the souls of those who have received the first mystery of the First Mystery."

Yew, prince of the faces, guardian of the veil of the great Light, and the receiver of Light, and the great guides of the great Sabaoth, the Good, independent and self-cognizant, transcendental parts of our own Being, will be kings with the First Saviour.

The First Saviour is related with the First Voice of the Treasury of the Light.

Obviously, the First Saviour has received the First Mystery of the First Mystery.

Those who have received the First Mystery of the First Mystery have their Saviour.

The Ancient of Days is indeed the First Mystery of the First Mystery.

Yew, Angel of faces, and the guard of the region of those of the Right, and Melchisedek, the Genie of the Earth who is the Great Receiver of the Light, and the two great guides, have come forth from the purified Light.

The divine hierarchies that exist in the Macrocosm and in the Microcosm emanate from the Five Trees of the great law.

Yew, prince of the faces, always obedient to the Ancient of Days, is the overseer, which means, he is the splendor, the Life of the great Light.

Yew emanates from the pure Light of the First Tree of the great law. He is the same law within ourselves, here and now.

It is written that the Guard of the Veil has emanated from the Second Tree.

The two great guides emanate from the pure Light of the Third and Fourth Trees of the great treasury.

Melchisedec, the regent of the planet Earth, who dwells in the region of Agarthi within the interior of the World, has emanated from the Fifth Tree of the great law.

Sabaoth, the Good, emanates from Yew, the prince of the faces, the overseer, the splendor of the Light.

These six are in reality six self-cognizant and independent parts of our own Being.

The economy of the ingathering of the Light is something transcendental.

To talk about the ingathering of the Light is something tremendous.

We know very well that the intellectual animal is not a human being.

If we place the intellectual animal and the human being face to face, we will find physical similarities. However, the psychological processes of each one of them are completely different.

At the time of the end of the Lemurian continent (which in the past was situated in the Pacific Ocean) some real humans who fell into animal generation became degenerated and mixed themselves with beasts of Nature.

Obviously, this is the origin of the Atlantean root race.

The present human root race descended from the trunk of Atlantis.

Therefore, this present root race that now lives on the face of the Earth is the outcome of the fatal mixture of humans and beasts.

Unquestionably, it is necessary to create the human being. The intellectual animal is not a human being.

Fortunately, the intellectual mammal bears the germs of the human being in his sexual glands.

Nevertheless, the availability of becoming a human is needed.

The Sun is performing a tremendous experiment at this moment, in the test tube of Nature. The Sun wants to create human beings.

In the time of Abraham, the prophet, the sun achieved the creation of a good number of humans.

During the first eight centuries of Christianity, a good ingathering of Solar Men was also achieved.

In these present times of the twentieth century, the Sun is making tremendous efforts in the test tube of Nature.

The Sun wants a new harvest of light for the Light.

Nevertheless, a revolution of the grain, of the seed, is needed, a conscious cooperation with the Sun.

The sexual reproductive system that the animals use, including the intellectual mammal mistakenly called man (human), is useless in order to create the human being.

The human being can never be created by means of the exclusively animal sexual reproductive system.

If the human being wants to be created, it is necessary to utilize the sexual system of human reproduction.

The power of Kriya-Shakti, (through which the Solar Men reproduce themselves) is the single power that, indeed, can create human beings.

Unfortunately, the intellectual animals mortally hate the power of Kriya-Shakti. This is because the power of Kriya-Shakti totally excludes the sexual orgasm, the animal spasm, which is the seminal spilling of the irrational and intellectual beasts. Seminal ejaculation is exclusively animal, never human.

Human creation within ourselves is achieved only by avoiding the seminal ejaculation.

However, the intellectual animal rejects the reproduction of Kriya-Shakti due to the fact that the beast only knows how to reproduce itself by means of the system of animal generation.

Unquestionably, when the intellectual animal admits the Solar and human reproductive system of the great power of Kriya-Shakti, then he converts himself into a true human.

It is clear that by means of the power of Kriya-Shakti, the germs of the true Man (which are within the organism) are developed. This is how the true Man is born within ourselves.

The Sun wants a harvest of Solar Men.

In an Anahuac codex, I found a phrase which states: "The Gods made men from wood, and then they fused them with Divinity." I then found another phrase which states: "Not all men achieve the fusion with Divinity."

Men made from wood: this reminds us of the Masters of carpentry, such as Joseph the carpenter, the terrestrial father of Jesus—in other words, the workers of the Great Work.

Unquestionably, the true Man can be born within the human organism, based on conscious works and voluntary sufferings. Nevertheless, it is written that not all men achieve the fusion with Divinity.

The real Man (human being) must convert himself into a Bodhisattva, in order to completely fuse himself with Divinity.

Obviously, only the Bodhisattvas with compassionate hearts can incarnate Christ.

It has always been said, and for good reason, that Christ is the Bodhisattva.

Solar Men are truly the ingathering of the supreme Light of the Aeons.

The Sun now wants a new harvest of Solar Men and it deserves it, due to the great work performed with organic life.

The Sun has worked intensely in this delicate thin covering of organic life, placed over the geological crust of the Earth.

Now, the Sun wants to see the result of its work.

The Sun wishes to have a new harvest of Solar Men at once.

Every race of humanoids serves the solar experiment.

Nevertheless, when a race is becoming too lunar, mechanical and materialistic, the Sun destroys it, because it is no longer useful for its experiment.

Such is the case of this present Aryan root race, which has become vulgar, crude, atheistic, and frightfully materialistic.

This is the reason why this present root race will be destroyed in the "Thirteenth Katun" of the Mayas.

Nevertheless, before the great catastrophe (which is approaching) the Sun will obtain a small harvest of Solar Men.

Truly, the Sun will harvest only a few solar, exemplary individuals in this epoch.

It is clear that this present root race of humanoids (which populates the face of the Earth) presents no hope what so ever.

This Aryan root race has reached maximum degeneration. Therefore, it will suddenly be destroyed.

Fortunate are those who live in the region of the souls who have received the First Mystery of the First Mystery.

Verily, they will be fellow-kings with the First Saviour of the First Voice of the Treasury of the Light.

Of the powers of the Middle and their ascension

"And the Virgin of Light and the great guide of the Middle, whom the rulers of the aeons are wont to call the Great Yew after the name of the great ruler who is in their region, — he and the Virgin of Light and his twelve ministers, from whom ye have received your shape and from whom ye have received the power, they all will be kings with the first saviour of the first Voice in the region of the souls of those who will receive the first mystery of the First Mystery in the Inheritances of the Light.

"And the fifteen helpers of the seven virgins of the Light who are in the Middle, they will expand themselves in the regions of the twelve saviours, and the rest of the angels of the Middle, every one of them according to his glory, will rule with me in the inheritances of the Light. And I shall rule over them all in the inheritances of the Light."

The Virgin of Light is our Divine Mother Kundalini.

The great Guide of the Middle is the prince of the faces, the great Yew.

All of this is within ourselves. They are the distinct parts of our own Being.

The Rulers of the Aeons know very well the prince of the faces, the splendid Yew.

The marvellous Ruler who is in his region is a very excellent part of our own Being.

He and the Virgin of Light and the twelve potencies within our own Being have endowed us with our celestial shape.

The celestial zodiacal shape that we carry within our Being was inherited from the twelve potencies.

All of them will be kings with the First Saviour of the First Voice, in the region of the souls that will receive the First Mystery of the First Mystery, in the Inheritances of the Light.

Typhon Baphomet, Lucifer-Prometheus, is the best of the helpers of the Divine Mother Kundalini in the work of the Great Work.

There exists seven degrees of the power of the fire that we must develop within ourselves. These are the Seven Radicals. These are the seven serpents, two groups of three, with the sublime coronation of the seventh tongue of fire that unites us with the One, with the Law, with the Father.

These are the seven "Woman-Serpents," the Seven Virgins.

All of these Fiery Helpers and the Seven Virgins always expand themselves in the regions of the Twelve Zodiacal Saviours.

The rest of the distinct parts of the Being, each one according to His glory, integrated with the inner Christ, will govern with Him in the Inheritances of the Light. The Lord will govern over them all, in the Inheritances of the Light.

But this shall not take place till the consummation of the aeon

"All this then which I have said unto you will not take place at this time, but it will take place at the consummation of the aeon, that is at the ascension of the universe; that is at the dissolution of the universe

and at the total ascension of the numbering of the perfect souls of the inheritances of the Light.

"Before the consummation, therefore, this which I have said unto you will not take place, but every one will be in his own region into which he hath been set from the beginning, until the numbering of the ingathering of the perfect souls is completed.

"The seven Voices and the five Trees and the three Amens and the Twin-saviours and the nine guards and the twelve saviours and those of the region of the Right and those of the region of the Middle, every one will abide in the region in which they have been set, until the numbering of the perfect souls of the inheritances of the Light shall be raised up all together.

"And also all the rulers who have repented, they also will abide in the region into which they have been set, until the numbering of the souls of the light shall be raised up all together."

All of this, which the great Kabir Jesus has said will be carried out in the consummation of the Aeon, at the end of the Mahamanvantara.

At the end of the great Cosmic Day, the words of the Lord will be consummated. Obviously, the universe will ascend from octave to octave before its total dissolution.

The perfect souls of the Inheritances of the Light will ascend with the universe, from octave to octave. In the end, they will become submerged within the bosom of the Absolute. They will then enjoy an inexhaustible joy.

When the universe is dissolved, the joy of the great Pralaya arrives. The great Pralaya is the profound Cosmic Night.

When the ingathering of the perfect souls is completed, the Mahapralaya, the Cosmic Night arrives. The Cosmic Night arrives when the ingathering of the perfect souls is completed.

Truthfully, the quantities of years assigned to a Cosmic Day are symbolic. The Cosmic Night arrives when the ingathering of the perfect souls is complete, which means, when the Cosmic Day is absolutely perfected.

The Seven Voices, or Verbs in the Macrocosm and in the Microcosmic man, and the Three Amens, which means the three forces, and the Twin Saviour, and the nine guardians of the mysteries of sex and the Twelve Saviours of the zodiacal belt of the Macrocosm and of the Microcosmic man, and the ones from the Right, and the ones from the Middle, will remain in their region.

All of them, each one of them, will abide in their respective sphere, and all of the repented Rulers will abide in their regions until the end of the great Cosmic Day.

Certainly, all of them are autonomous and self-cognizant parts of our own individual Being.

At the end of the Mahamanvantara, all the parts are integrated with the inner Christ, and the profound night of the great Pralaya arrives.

As for the Twin Saviour, it is unquestionable that Ce-Acatl is the twin of Quetzalcoatl, the Mexican Christ.

Ce-Acatl burned himself in the blazing fire. He sacrificed himself for Quetzalcoatl.

Ce-Acatl is the other part of the Being of Quetzalcoatl, reincarnated in another body.

Thus, the Christified Adept, who has his twin, lives simultaneously in distinct times and places.

The transactional passing of all the self-cognizant and independent parts of our own Being, during the final integration, inwardly occurs. Each part sinks into another. Each part receives the Gnostic Unction and the seal of its mystery. Each one, which means, each part is suitable for its sphere and for its ministry.

All of the parts integrated with the inner Christ submerge themselves within the Inheritances of the Light.

The order in which the great Kabir Jesus describes the process of the final integration (in the man and within the man) is marvellous.

Of the ascension of the souls of the perfect

"[The souls] will all come, every one at the time when he will receive the mysteries; and all the rulers who have repented will pass through and come into the region of the Middle. And those of the Middle will baptize them and give unto them the spiritual unction and seal them with the seals of their mysteries. And they will pass through those of all the regions of the Middle, and they will pass through the region of the Right and the interior of the region of the nine guards and the interior of the region of the Twin-saviours and the interior of the region of the three Amens and of the twelve saviours and the interior of the five Trees and of the seven Voices. Every one giveth unto them his seal of his mystery, and they pass into the interior of them all and go to the region of the inheritances of the Light; and every one bideth in the region up to which he hath received mysteries in the inheritances of the Light."

Of the rank of the souls of the perfect

"In a word, all the souls of men who shall receive the mysteries of the Light will precede all the rulers who have repented, and they will precede all those of the region of the Middle and those of the whole region of the Right, and they will precede those of the whole region of the Treasury of the Light. In a word, they will precede all those of the region of the Treasury, and they will precede all those of the regions of the first Commandment, and they will pass into the interior of them all and go into the inheritance of the Light up to the region of their mystery; and every one abideth in the region up to which he hath received mysteries. And those of the region of the Middle and of the Right and those of the whole region of the Treasury, every one abideth in the region of the order into which he hath been set from the beginning on, until the universe shall be raised up. And every one of them accomplisheth his economy to which he hath been set, in respect of the ingathering of the souls who have received the mysteries, in respect of this economy, so that they may seal all the souls who will receive the mysteries and who will pass through their interior towards the inheritance of the Light.

"Now, therefore, Mary, this is the word concerning which though dost question me with precision and certainty. For the rest now then, who hath ears to hear, let him hear."

The souls who receive the mysteries of the Light precede the repented Rulers in the valuable work of integration.

The Archons precede those of the region of the Middle in the work of human and solar integration.

They will precede the ones of the Middle, and the ones of the region of the Right always precede the ones of the region of the Treasury of the Light.

In a word, all of them who work in the work of individual integration will precede to all the ones of the Treasury of the Light.

In reality, all of them will precede all those of the region of the First Commandment.

We already know that the First Commandment is in the Ancient of Days.

In the process of final integration, they will pass towards the interior, one inside of the other, unto the Inheritance of the Light, and posteriorly to the region of their mystery.

Thus, each one of those of the region of the Middle and of the Right and each one of those of the complete region of the Treasury, will remain within their corresponding region until the future Cosmic Day.

Each one of the parts of the Being that is integrated will keep his qualities until the beginning of the new Mahamanvantara.

All the souls must receive the Inheritance of the Light. The arrival to the Inheritances of the Light is accomplished from interior to interior.

Each part of the Being must complete his values for the integration.

In Gnosis, if the diverse, autonomous and self-cognizant parts of the Being were unknown, then the work of the solar and human integration would not be understood.

In all of this, there is a process described by the great Kabir Jesus. Whosoever has understanding, let him understand, for there is wisdom within.

This is how Mary, the Woman-Serpent, receives the teaching of Jesus.

Chapter 87

Mary interpreteth the discourse from the scriptures

"It came to pass then, when Jesus had finished speaking these words, that Mary Magdalene started forward and said:

"My Lord, my indweller of light hath ears and I comprehend every word which thou sayest. Now, therefore, my Lord, on account of the word which thou hast spoken, 'All the souls of the race of men who shall receive the mysteries of the Light, will go into the inheritance of the Light before all the rulers who will repent, and before those of the whole region of the Right and before the whole region of the Treasury of the Light,' — on account of this word, my Lord, thou hast said unto us afore time: 'The first will be last and the last will be first,' — that is, the 'last' are the whole race of men which will enter into the Light-kingdom sooner than all those of the region of the Height, who are the 'first.' On this account, therefore, my Lord, hast thou said unto us, 'Who hath ears to hear, let him hear,' — that is thou desirest to know whether we comprehend every word which thou speakest. This, therefore, is the word, my Lord."

It came to pass then, when Mary had finished saying these words, that the Saviour was greatly astonished at the definitions of the words which she spake, for she had become pure spirit utterly. Jesus answered again and said unto her: "Well said, spiritual and pure Mary. This is the solution of the word."

The soul is valuable. It is a precious gem that goes into the Inheritance of the Light before all; before the Rulers and before the ones of the Right and before the complete region of the Treasury of the Light.

The Man-Soul, the Man-Being, will enter the region of the Inheritance of the Light before the other parts of the Being.

It is written that the first will be the last and the last will be the first.

The suffering man will be the first in the Inheritance of the Light, then all the other parts of the Being will follow.

At the same time that the races of Solar Men are being collected, they will enter the region of the Inheritance of the Light before the Beings that live in the Ineffable regions.

Chapter 88

It came to pass then again after all these words, that Jesus continued in the discourse and said unto his disciples: "Hearken, that I may discourse with you concerning the glory of those of the Height, how they are, according to the manner in which I discoursed with you unto this day."

The Last Helper is, indeed, Adhi-Buddha. Obviously, Adhi-Buddha is the Father of the Father, the Unmanifested in the Unknowable. Unquestionably, the Unknowable Unmanifested is the Buddha of the Buddha.

When entering the bosom of the Absolute, the Ancient of Days must integrate himself with Adhi-Buddha.

Of the last Helper

"Now, therefore, if I lead you into the region of the last Helper, who surroundeth the Treasury of the Light, and if I lead you into the region of that last Helper and ye see the glory in which he is, then will the region of the inheritance of the Light count for you only for the size of a city of the world, because of the greatness in which the last Helper is, and because of the great light in which he is."

That the regions beyond the Helpers are indescribable

"And thereafter I will discourse with you also concerning the glory of the Helper who is above the little Helper. But I shall not be able to discourse with you concerning the regions of those who are above all Helpers; for there existeth no form in this world to describe them, for there existeth in this world no likeness which is like unto them, that I may compare them therewith, nor greatness nor light which is like unto them, not only in this world, but they also have no likeness with those of the Height of Justice from their region upwards. On this account, therefore, there existeth in fact no manner of describing them in this world because of the great glory of those of the Height and because of the great immeasurable greatness. On this account, therefore, there existeth no manner to describe it in this world."

It came to pass then, when Jesus had finished speaking these words unto his disciples, that Mary Magdalene came forward and said unto Jesus, "My Lord, be not wroth with me if I question thee, because I trouble repeatedly. Now, therefore, my Lord, be not wroth with me if I question thee concerning all with precision and certainty. For my brethren will herald it among the race of men, so that they may hear and repent and be saved from the violent judgements of the evil rulers and go to the Height and inherit the Light-kingdom; because, my Lord, we are compassionate not only towards ourselves, but compassionate towards the whole race of men, so that they may be saved from all the violent judgements. Now, therefore, my Lord, on this account we question concerning all with certainty, for my brethren herald it to the whole race of men, in order that they may escape the violent rulers of the darkness and be saved out of the hands of the violent receivers of the outer-most darkness."

It came to pass, when Jesus had heard Mary say these words, that the Saviour answered in great compassion towards her and said unto her, "Question concerning what thou desirest to question, and I will reveal it unto thee with precision and certainty and without similitude."

The violent judgements of the evil Archons fall upon those who violate the law.

The terms good and evil are very discussable. Something is good when it is suitable for us, and evil when it is not suitable for us.

Evil Rulers must be understood in esoteric form. No one can enjoy the violent judgements of the lords of karma. This is why they are symbolically denominated as evil Archons.

We need to be saved from the Archons or violent Rulers of darkness and also from the violent receivers of the outermost darkness.

In the Averno there exists the darkness, and also the Darkness of the darkness. The Averno is found situated within the nine submerged, mineral infra-dimensions. These nine infra-dimensions are within the interior of the planet Earth.

Nevertheless, do not confuse the nine submerged infra-dimensions with the merely physical geological part of the world Earth.

It is useful to clarify that the merely physical geological part of the world Earth is hollow.

Let us remember the survivors of Lemuria, Atlantis, etc.. They still live in Agarthi, the interior part of the Earth.

They keep their archaic, powerful civilizations, and they even have cosmic ships in which they travel with through the unalterable Infinite.

The divine humanity of Agarthi works and lives under the personal direction of Melchisedek, the King of the World. Multiple entrances lead to the Kingdom of Agarthi. Some of these entrances are guarded by fierce tribes.

Nine superior dimensions also exist within the interior geological part of the world.

The secret temples of the conscious circle of the solar humanity (which operates upon the superior centers of the Being) are found situated within the nine superior dimensions.

Creatures and terribly divine forces operate in the nine superior dimensions of the planet Earth.

The violent receivers of the darkness of the darknesses dwell in the infra-infernos of the world Earth.

Let us then distinguish between what is the merely geological, physical, and tri-dimensional part of the Earth, and what are the superior dimensions and infra-dimensions of the interior of the Earth.

The mineral mass Earth then has three absolutely different aspects that the Gnostic must study.

Woe to those who fall in the Tartarus, in the Darkness of the darknesses governed by the violent receivers of the Abyss!

Chapter 89

Mary further questioneth Jesus

It came to pass then, when Mary had heard the Saviour say these words, that she rejoiced with great joy and exulted exceedingly and said unto Jesus, "My Lord, by how much greatness then is the second Helper greater than the first Helper? By how much distance is he distant from him, or rather how many times more does he shine than the latter?"

The Second Helper and the First Helper are autonomous and self-cognizant parts of our own Being.

Jesus explained all of this very well, so there is no need to comment about it.

Of the second Helper

Jesus answered and said unto Mary in the midst of the disciples: "Amen, amen, I say unto you: The second Helper is distant from the first Helper in great immeasurable distance in regard to the height above and the depth below and the length and the breadth. For he is exceedingly distant from him in great immeasurable distance through the angels and all the archangels and through the gods and all the invisibles. And he is very considerably greater than the latter in an incalculable measure through the angels and archangels and through the gods and all the invisibles. And he shineth more than the latter in an utterly immeasurable measure, there being no measure for the light in which he is, and no measure for him through angels and archangels and through the gods and all the invisibles, as I have already said unto you at another time."

It is clear that the distance from the Second Helper to the First Helper is an immeasurable, intimate distance in regards to the divine height above, and the depth below, and the length and breadth. People do not understand these immeasurable, psychological distances. Thus, the Second Helper is considerably much greater and psychologically exalted than the First.

Of the third, fourth, and fifth Helpers

"In like manner also the third Helper and fourth and fifth Helper, — one is greater than the other ...and shineth more than the latter and is distant from fim in a great immeasurable distance through the angels and archangels and the gods and all the invisibles, as I have already said unto you at another time. And I will tell unto you also the type of every one [of them] at their expansion."

The Third, Fourth, and Fifth Helpers shine marvelously. In the depth, these Five Helpers are: Gabriel, Raphael, Uriel, Michael, Samael. It is clear that these five have their exponents in the Human Soul of every living creature.

Chapter 90

Mary again questioneth Jesus

It came to pass then, when Jesus had finished saying these words unto his disciples, that Mary Magdalene came forward again, continued and said unto Jesus: "My Lord, in what form will be those who have received the Mystery of the Light, in the midst of the last Helper?"

Of those who receive the mystery of the last Helper

And Jesus answered and said unto Mary in the midst of the disciples: "They who have received the mystery of the Light, if they come out of the body of the matter of the rulers, then will every one be in his order according to the mystery which he hath received. Those who have received the higher mysteries will abide in the higher order; those who have received the lower mysteries will be in the lower orders. In a word, up to what region every one hath received mysteries, there will he abide in his order in the inheritance of the Light. For which cause I have said unto you afore time, 'Where your heart is, there will your treasure be,' — that is up to what region every one hath received Mysteries, there shall he be."

It came to pass when Jesus had finished saying these words unto his disciples, that John came forward and said unto Jesus: "My Lord and my Saviour, give me also commandment that I discourse before thee, and be not wroth with me if I question concerning all with precision and certainty; for thou, my Lord, hast promised me to make relevation unto us of all concerning which I shall question thee. Now, therefore, my Lord, hide nothing from us at all in the matter on which we shall question thee."

And Jesus answered in great compassion and said unto John: "To thee also, blessed John, and beloved, I give commandment to speak the word which pleaseth thee, and I will reveal it unto thee face to face without similitude, and I will say unto thee all on which thou wilt question me with precision and certainty."

These words of the great Kabir Jesus are so clear that an explanation is unnecessary.

John questioneth Jesus

And John answered and said unto Jesus: "My Lord, will then every one abide in the region up to which he hath received the mysteries, and hath he no power to go into other orders which are above him; and hath he no power to go into the orders which are below him?"

It is clear that the one who receives the mysteries in one region, continues in this region until he receives more elevated mysteries.

Chapter 91

And Jesus answered and said unto John: "Finely indeed do ye question on all with precision and certainty. But now, therefore, John, hearken that I may discourse with thee. Every one who hath received mysteries of the Light will abide in the region up to which every one hath received mysteries, and he hath not the power to go into the height into the orders which are above him."

The Verb, the Word, speaks with precision and certainty.

Of the first Commandment

"So that he who hath received mysteries in the first Commandment hath the power to go into the orders which are below him, that is into all the orders of the third space; but he hath not the power to go into the height to the orders which are above him."

Of the first space

"And he who shall receive the mysteries of the First Mystery, which is the four-and-twentieth mystery from without and the head of the first space which is without, — he hath the power to go into all the orders which are without him; but he hath not the power to go into the regions which are above him or to pass through them."

It is obvious that the one who has received mysteries in the First Commandment has power to go to the orders which are below him, which means, to all of the orders of the third Space. However, he can never go to the orders which are above him.

The mysteries of the First Mystery are terribly divine. It is clear that the work of the Great Work is contained in the Four-and-twentieth Mystery. All the mysteries of the First Mystery are found in the Four-and-twentieth Mystery. The one who performs the Great Work has the right to enter all of the orders above and below.

It is easy to understand that the entire beginning and the end of the Great Work is in the Four-and-twentieth Mystery.

Of the second space

"And of those who have received the mysteries in the order of the four-and-twenty mysteries, every one will go into the region in which he hath received mysteries, and he will have the power to pass through all the orders and spaces which are without him; but he hath not the power to go into the higher orders which are above him or to pass through them."

It is clear that those who have received mysteries in the orders of the Four-and-twentieth Mysteries have the right to live in the regions where they received the mysteries. However, they cannot pass through orders or spaces that are above them. The orders of the First Mystery always correspond to the Ancient of Days.

We, Samael Aun Weor,
tell ye, in the name
of the First Mystery
of Pistis Sophia
and the Saviour
of the world,
that I will unveil
the remaining part
of the Gnostic Bible
in the half of the half
of the time.

Of the third space

"And he who hath received mysteries in the orders of the First Mystery which is in the third space, hath the power to go into all the lower orders which are below him and to pass through all; but on the other hand he hath not the power to go into the regions which are above him or to pass through them."

Of the Thrice-spiritual

"And he who hath received mysteries of the first Thrice-spiritual, which ruleth over the four-and-twenty mysteries all together which rule over the space of the First Mystery, of whose region at the expansion of the universe I will tell you — he, therefore, who shall receive the mystery of that Thrice-spiritual, hath the power to go down into all orders which are below him; but he hath not the power to go into the height into the orders which are above him, that is into all the orders of the space of the Ineffable.

"And he who hath received the mystery of the second Thrice-spiritual, hath the power to go into all the orders of the first Thrice-spiritual and to pass through them all and all their orders which are in them: but he hath not the power to go into the higher orders of the third Thrice-spiritual.

"And he who hath received the mystery of the third Thrice-spiritual, which ruleth over the three Thrice-spirituals and the three spaces of the First Mystery all together, [hath the power to go into all the orders which are below him]; but he hath not the power to go into the height into the orders which are above him, that is into the orders of the space of the Ineffable."

Of the master-mystery

And he who hath received the master-mystery of the First Mystery of the Ineffable, that is the twelve mysteries of the First Mystery all together, which rule over all the spaces of the First Mystery, — he, therefore, who shall receive that mystery, hath the power to pass through all the orders of the spaces of the three Thrice-spirituals and the three spaces of the First Mystery and all their orders, and hath the power to pass through all the orders of the inheritances of the Light, to pass through them from without within and from within without and from above below and from below above and from the height to the depth and from the depth to the height and from the length to the breadth and from the breadth to the length; in a word, he hath the power to pass through all the regions of the inheritances of the Light, and he hath the power to bide in the region where he pleaseth, in the Inheritance of the Light-kingdom.

"And amen, I say unto you: That man will at the dissolution of the world be king over all the orders of the Inheritance of the Light. And he who shall receive that mystery of the Ineffable which I am,—"

Of the gnosis of the master-mystery

"That mystery knoweth why the darkness hath arisen and why the light hath arisen.

"And that mystery knoweth why the darkness of the darknesses hath arisen and why the light of the lights hath arisen.

"And that mystery knoweth why the chaos hath arisen and why the treasury of the light hath arisen.

"And that mystery knoweth why the judgments have arisen and why the light-land and the region of the inheritances of the light have arisen.

"And that mystery knoweth why the chastisements of the sinners have arisen and why the rest of the kingdom of the light hath arisen.

"And that mystery knoweth why the sinners have arisen and why the inheritances of the light have arisen.

"And that mystery knoweth why the impious have arisen and why the good have arisen.

"And that mystery knoweth why the chastisements and judgments have arisen and why all the emanations of the light have arisen.

"And that mystery knoweth why the sins have arisen and why the baptisms and the mysteries of the light have arisen.

"And that mystery knoweth why the fire of chastisement hath arisen and why the seals of the light, so that the fire should not harm them, have arisen.

"And that mystery knoweth why wrath hath arisen and why peace hath arisen.

"And that mystery knoweth why slander hath arisen and why songs of the light have arisen.

"And that mystery knoweth why the prayers of the light have arisen.

"And that mystery knoweth why cursing hath arisen and why blessing hath arisen.

"And that mystery knoweth why knavery hath arisen and why deceit hath arisen.

"And that mystery knoweth why the slaying hath arisen and why the quickening of the souls hath arisen.

"And that mystery knoweth why adultery and fornication have arisen and why purity hath arisen.

"And that mystery knoweth why intercourse have arisen and why continence hath arisen.

"And that mystery knoweth why insolence and boasting have arisen and why humbleness and meekness have arisen.

"And that mystery knoweth why tears have arisen and why laughter hath arisen.

"And that mystery knoweth why slander hath arisen and why good report hath arisen.

"And that mystery knoweth why appreciation hath arisen and why disdain of men hath arisen.

"And that mystery knoweth why murmuring hath arisen and why innocence and humbleness have arisen.

"And that mystery knoweth why sin hath arisen and why purity hath arisen.

"And that mystery knoweth why strength hath arisen and why weakness hath arisen.

"And that mystery knoweth why motion of body hath arisen and why its utility hath arisen.

"And that mystery knoweth why poverty hath arisen and why wealth hath arisen.

"And that mystery knoweth why the freedom of the world hath arisen and why slavery hath arisen.

"And that mystery knoweth why death hath arisen and why life hath arisen."

Chapter 92

It came to pass then, when Jesus had finished saying these words unto his disciples, that they rejoiced in great joy and exulted when they heard Jesus say these words.

And Jesus continued again in the discourse and said unto them: "Hearken, therefore, now still further, O my disciples, so that I discourse with you concerning the whole gnosis of the mystery of the Ineffable."

Of the gnosis of the mystery of the Ineffable

"That mystery of the Ineffable knoweth why unmercifulness hath arisen and why mercifulness hath arisen.

"And that mystery knoweth why ruin hath arisen and why everlasting eternity hath arisen.

"And that mystery knoweth why the reptiles have arisen and why they will be destroyed.

"And that mystery knoweth why the wild beasts have arisen and why they will be destroyed.

"And that mystery knoweth why the cattle have arisen and why the birds have arisen.

"And that mystery knoweth why the mountains have arisen and why the precious stones therein have arisen.

"And that mystery knoweth why the matter of gold hath arisen and why the matter of silver hath arisen.

"And that mystery knoweth why the matter of copper hath arisen and why the matter of iron and of stone hath arisen.

"And that mystery knoweth why the matter of lead hath arisen.

"And that mystery knoweth why the matter of glass hath arisen and why the matter of wax hath arisen.

"And that mystery knoweth why herbs, that is the vegetables, have arisen and why all matters have arisen.

"And the mystery knoweth why the waters of the earth and all things in them have arisen and why also the earth hath arisen.

"And that mystery knoweth why the seas and the waters have arisen and why the wild beasts in the seas have arisen.

"And that mystery knoweth why the matter of the world hath arisen and why it [the world] will be utterly destroyed."

Chapter 93

Jesus continued again and said unto his disciples: "Yet further, O my disciples and companions and brethren, let every one be sober in the spirit which is in him, let him understand and comprehend all the words which I shall say unto you; for from now on will I begin to discourse with you concerning all the gnoses of that Ineffable.

"That mystery knoweth why the west hath arisen and why the east hath arisen.

"And that mystery knoweth why the south hath arisen and why the north hath arisen.

"Yet further, O my disciples, hearken and continue to be sober and hearken to the total gnosis of the mystery of the Ineffable.

"That mystery knoweth why the demons have arisen and why mankind hath arisen.

"And that mystery knoweth why the heat hath arisen and why the pleasant air hath arisen.

"And that mystery knoweth why the stars have arisen and why the clouds have arisen.

"And that mystery knoweth why the earth became deep and why the water came thereon.

"And that mystery knoweth why the earth became dry and why the water came thereon.

"And that mystery knoweth why famine hath arisen and why superfluity hath arisen.

"And that mystery knoweth why the hoar-frost hath arisen and why the healthful dew hath arisen.

"And that mystery knoweth why the dust hath arisen and why the delightsome freshness hath arisen.

"And that mystery knoweth why the hail hath arisen and why the pleasant snow hath arisen.

"And that mystery knoweth why the west wind hath arisen and why the east wind hath arisen.

"And that mystery knoweth why the fire of the height hath arisen and why the waters have arisen.

"And that mystery knoweth why the east wind hath arisen.

"And that mystery knoweth why the south wind hath arisen and why the north wind hath arisen.

"And that mystery knoweth why the stars of the heaven and the disks of the light-givers have arisen and why the firmament with all its veils hath arisen.

"And that mystery knoweth why the rulers of the spheres have arisen and why the sphere with all its regions hath arisen.

"And that mystery knoweth why the rulers of the aeons have arisen and why the aeons with their veils have arisen.

"And that mystery knoweth why the tyrant rulers of the aeons have arisen and why the rulers who have repented have arisen.

"And that mystery knoweth why the servitors have arisen and why the decans have arisen.

"And that mystery knoweth why the angels have arisen and why the archangels have arisen.

"And that mystery knoweth why the lords have arisen and why the gods have arisen.

"And that mystery knoweth why the jealousy in the height hath arisen and why concord hath arisen.

"And that mystery knoweth why hate hath arisen and why love hath arisen.

"And that mystery knoweth why discord hath arisen and why concord hath arisen.

"And that mystery knoweth why avarice hath arisen and why renunciation of all hath arisen and love of possessions hath arisen.

"And that mystery knoweth why love of the belly hath arisen and why satiety hath arisen.

"And that mystery knoweth why the paired have arisen and why the unpaired have arisen.

"And that mystery knoweth why impiety have arisen and why fear of God have arisen.

"And that mystery knoweth why the light-givers have arisen and why the sparks have arisen.

"And that mystery knoweth why the thrice-powerful have arisen and why the invisibles have arisen.

"And that mystery knoweth why the forefathers have arisen and why the purities have arisen.

"And that mystery knoweth why the great Self-willed have arisen and why his faithful have arisen.

"And that mystery knoweth why the great triple-powerful hath arisen and why the great invisible forefather hath arisen.

"And that mystery knoweth why the thirteenth aeon hath arisen and why the region of those of the Middle hath arisen.

“”And that mystery knoweth why receivers of the Middle hath arisen and why the virgins of the light hath arisen.

"And that mystery knoweth why the ministers of the Middle have arisen and why the angels of the Middle have arisen.

"And that mystery knoweth why the light-land hath arisen and why the great receiver of the light hath arisen.

"And that mystery knoweth why the guards of the region of the Right have arisen and why the leaders of them have arisen.

"And that mystery knoweth why the gate of life hath arisen and why Sabaoth, the Good, hath arisen.

"And that mystery knoweth why the region of the Right hath arisen and why the light-land, which is the treasury of the light, hath arisen.

"And that mystery knoweth why the emanations of the light have arisen and why the twelve saviours have arisen.

"And that mystery knoweth why the three gates of the treasury of light have arisen and why the nine guards have arisen.

"And that mystery knoweth why the twin saviours have arisen and why the three Amens have arisen.

"And that mystery knoweth why the five Trees have arisen and why the seven Amens have arisen.

"And that mystery knoweth why the Mixture which existeth not, hath arisen and why it is purified."

Chapter 94

And Jesus continued again and said unto his disciples: "Still further, O my disciples, be sober and let every one of you bring hither the power of sensing the Light before him, that ye may sense with sureness. For from now on I will discourse with you concerning the whole region in truth of the Ineffable and concerning the manner, how it is."

The disciples lose courage

It came to pass then, when the disciples had heard Jesus utter these words, that they gave way and let go entirely.

Then Mary Magdalene came forward, threw herself at the feet of Jesus, kissed them and wept aloud and said: "Have mercy upon me, my Lord, for my brethren have heard and let go of the words which thou saidest unto them. Now, therefore, my Lord, concerning the gnosis of all the things which thou hast said, that they are in the mystery of the Ineffable; but I have heard thee say unto me: 'From now on I will begin to discourse with you concerning the total gnosis of the mystery of the Ineffable,' — this word, therefore, which thou saidest, thou hast not gone forward to complete the word. For this cause, therefore, my brethren have heard and have let go and ceased to sense in what manner thou discoursest with them. Concerning the word which thou saidest unto them, now, therefore, my Lord, if the gnosis of all this is in that mystery, where is the man who is in the world, who hath the ability to understand that mystery with all its gnoses and the type of all these words which thou hast spoken concerning it?"

Chapter 95

It came to pass then, when Jesus had heard Mary say these words and knew that the disciples had heard and had begun to let go, that he encouraged them and said unto them: "Grieve no more, my disciples, concerning the mystery of the Ineffable, thinking that ye will not understand it. Amen, I say unto you: That mystery is yours, and every one's who will give ear unto you, so that they renounce this whole world and the whole matter therein and renounce all the evil thoughts therein and renounce all the cares of this aeon."

Jesus explaineth that that mystery is really simpler than all mysteries

"Now, therefore, I say unto you: For every one who will renounce the whole world and all therein and will submit himself to the godhead, that mystery is far easier than all the mysteries of the Light-kingdom and it is sooner to understand than them all and it is easier than them all. He who reacheth unto the gnosis of that mystery, renounceth this whole world and all the cares therein.

"For this cause have I said to you afore time: 'All ye who are heavy under your burden, come hither unto me, and I will quicken you. For my burden is easy and my yoke is soft.' Now, therefore, he who will receive that mystery, renounceth the whole world and the cares of all the matter therein. For this cause, therefore, my disciples, grieve not, thinking that ye will not understand that mystery. Amen, I say unto you: That mystery is far sooner to understand than all mysteries. And amen, I say unto you: That mystery is yours and every one's who will renounce the whole world and the whole matter therein.

"Now, therefore, hearken, my disciples and my companions and my brethren, that I may urge you onto the gnosis of the mystery of the Ineffable concerning which I discourse with you, because I have in sooth gotten as far as to tell you the whole gnosis at the expansion of the universe; for the expansion of the universe is its gnosis.

"But now then hearken that I may discourse with you progressively concerning the gnosis of that mystery."

Of the rending asunder and emanation of the powers of the universe

"That mystery knoweth wherefor the five Helpers have rent themselves asunder and wherefor they have come forth from the Fatherless [pl.].

"And that mystery knoweth wherefor the great Light of lights hath rent itself asunder and wherefor it hath come forth from the Fatherless.

"And that mystery knoweth wherefor the first Commandment hath rent itself asunder and wherefor it hath divided itself into the seven mysteries and wherefor it is named the first Commandment and wherefor it hath come forth from the Fatherless.

"And that mystery knoweth wherefor the Great Light of the Impressions of the Light hath rent itself asunder and wherefor it hath

set itself up without emanations and wherefor it hath come forth from the Fatherless.

"And that mystery knoweth wherefor the First Mystery, that is the four-and-twentieth mystery from without, hath rent itself asunder and wherefor it imitated in itself the twelve mysteries according to the number of the numbering of the Uncontainables and Boundless and wherefor it hath come forth from the Fatherless."

Of those of the second space of the Ineffable

"And that mystery knoweth wherefor the twelve Immoveables have rent themselves asunder and wherefor they have set themselves with all their orders and wherefor they have come forth from the Fatherless.

"And that mystery knoweth wherefor the Unwaverables have rent themselves asunder and wherefor they have set themselves up, divided into twelve orders, and wherefor they have come forth from the Fatherless, which belong to the orders of the space of the Ineffable.

"And that mystery knoweth wherefor the Incomprehensibles, which pertain to the second space of the Ineffable, have rent themselves asunder and wherefor they have come forth from the Fatherless.

"And that mystery knoweth wherefor the twelve Undesignatables have rent themselves asunder and wherefor they have set themselves up after all the orders of the Unindicatables, themselves being uncontainable and boundless, and wherefor they have come forth from the Fatherless.

"And that mystery knoweth wherefor these Unindicatables have rent themselves asunder, — [they] who have not indicated themselves nor brought themselves into publicity according to the economy of the One and Only, the Ineffable, and wherefor they have come forth from the Fatherless.

"And that mystery knoweth wherefor the Superdeeps have rent themselves asunder and wherefor they have distributed themselves, being a single order, and wherefor they have come forth from the Fatherless.

"And that mystery knoweth wherefor the twelve orders of the Unspeakables have rent themselves asunder and wherefor they have divided themselves, being three portions, and wherefor they have come forth from the Fatherless.

"And that mystery knoweth wherefor all the Imperishables, being their twelve orders, have rent themselves asunder and wherefor they have settled themselves, being expanded in a single order, and wherefor they have divided themselves and formed different orders, being uncontainable and boundless, and wherefor they have come forth from the Fatherless.

"And that mystery knoweth wherefor the Impassables have rent themselves asunder and wherefor they have set themselves up, being twelve boundless spaces, and have settled themselves, being three orders of spaces, according to the economy of the One and Only, the Ineffable, and wherefor they have come forth from the Fatherless.

"And that mystery knoweth wherefor the twelve Uncontainables, which belong to the orders of the One and Only, the Ineffable, have rent themselves asunder and wherefor they have come forth from the Fatherless, until they were brought to the space of the First Mystery, which is the second space.

"And that mystery knoweth wherefor the four-and-twenty myriads of Praise-singers have rent themselves asunder and wherefor they have extended themselves outside the veil of the First Mystery, which is the twin-mystery, that which looketh within and without, the One and Only, the Ineffable, and wherefor they have come forth from the Fatherless.

"And that mystery knoweth wherefor all the Uncontainables have rent themselves asunder — [those], which I have just named, which are in the regions of the second space of the Ineffable, which is the

space of the First Mystery, and wherefor those Uncontainables and Boundless have come forth from the Fatherless.

Of those of the first space of the Ineffable

"And that mystery knoweth wherefor the four-and-twenty mysteries of the first Thrice-spiritual have rent themselves asunder and wherefor they are called the four-and-twenty spaces of the first Thrice-spiritual and wherefor they have come forth from the second Thrice-spiritual.

"And that mystery knoweth wherefor the four-and-twenty mysteries of the second Thrice-spiritual have rent themselves asunder and wherefor they have come forth from the third Thrice-spiritual.

"And that mystery knoweth why the four-and-twenty mysteries of the third Thrice-spiritual — that is the four-and-twenty spaces of the third Thrice-spiritual have rent themselves asunder and wherefor they have come forth from the Fatherless.

"And that mystery knoweth wherefor the five Trees of the first Thrice-spiritual have rent themselves asunder and wherefor they have extended themselves, standing one behind the other and moreover bound one to the other with all their orders, and wherefor they have come forth from the Fatherless.

"And that mystery knoweth wherefor the five Trees of the second Thrice-spiritual have rent themselves asunder and wherefor they have come forth from the Fatherless.

"And that mystery knoweth wherefor the five Trees of the third Thrice-spiritual have rent themselves asunder and wherefor they have come forth from the Fatherless.

"And that mystery knoweth why the Fore-uncontainables of the first Thrice-spiritual have rent themselves asunder and wherefor they have come forth from the Fatherless.

"And that mystery knoweth wherefor the Fore-uncontainables of the second Trispiritual have rent themselves asunder and wherefor they have come forth from the Fatherless.

"And that mystery knoweth wherefor all the Fore-uncontainables of the third Thrice-spiritual have rent themselves asunder and wherefor they have come forth from the Fatherless.

"And that mystery knoweth wherefor the first Thrice-spiritual from below — those who belong to the orders of the One and Only, the Ineffable — hath rent itself asunder and wherefor it hath come forth from the second Thrice-spiritual.

"And that mystery knoweth wherefor the third Thrice-spiritual — that is the first Thrice-spiritual from above — hath rent itself asunder and wherefor it have come forth from the twelfth Pro-thrice-spiritual, which is in the last region of the Fatherless.

"And that mystery knoweth wherefor all the regions which are in the space of the Ineffable, and all those in them, have expanded themselves, and wherefor they have come forth from the last Limb of the Ineffable.

"And that mystery knoweth itself, wherefor it hath rent itself asunder to come forth from the Ineffable, — that is from That which ruleth them all and which expanded them all according to their orders."

Chapter 96

Jesus promiseth to explain further all in detail

"Of all these then will I speak unto you at the expansion of the universe — in a word, all those whom I have spoken of unto you: those who will arise and those who will come, those who emanate, and those who come forth, and those who are without over them, and those who are implanted in them, those who will contain the region of the First Mystery and those who are in the space of the Ineffable — of these will I speak unto you, because I will reveal them unto you, and

I will speak of them unto you according to every region and according to every order, at the expansion of the universe. And I will reveal unto you all their mysteries which rule over them all, and their Prothrice spirituals and their Super-thrice-spirituals which rule over their mysteries and their orders."

Of the mystery succinctly

"Now, therefore, the mystery of the Ineffable knoweth wherefor all these have arisen of whom I have spoken unto you in openness, and through which all these have arisen. It is the mystery which is in them all; and it is the out-going of them all, and it is the up-going of them all, and it is the setting-up of them all.

"And the mystery of the Ineffable is the mystery which is in all these of whom I have spoken unto you, and of whom I will speak unto you at the expansion of the universe. And it is the mystery which is in them all, and it is the one only mystery of the Ineffable and the gnosis of all these of whom I have spoken unto you, and of whom I will speak unto you, and of whom I have not spoken. Of these will I speak unto you at the expansion of the universe and of their total gnosis one with another, wherefor they have arisen. It is the one and only word of the Ineffable.

"And I will tell you the expansion of all mysteries and the types of every one of them and the manner of their completion in all their figures. And I will tell you the mystery of the One and Only, the Ineffable, and all its types, all its figures and its whole economy, wherefor it hath come forth from the last Limb of the Ineffable. For that mystery is the setting-up of them all."

Of the one and only word of the Ineffable

"And that mystery of the Ineffable is more-over also a one and only word, which existeth in the speech of the Ineffable, and it is the economy of the solution of all the words which I have spoken unto you.

"And he who will receive the one and only word of that mystery which I shall now say unto you, and all its types and all its figures, and the manner of accomplishing its mystery, — for ye are perfect and all - perfect and ye will accomplish the whole gnosis of that mystery with its whole economy, for unto you all mysteries are entrusted, — hearken, therefore, now, that I may tell you that mystery, which is [...?]"

Of the ascension of the soul of him who shall receive the one and only mystery

"He then, who shall receive the one and only word of that mystery, which I have told you, if he cometh forth out of the body of the matters of the rulers, and if the retributive receivers come and free him from the body of matter of the rulers, — that is those [receivers] who free from the body all out-going souls, — when, therefore, the retributive receivers free the souls which hath received this one and only mystery of the Ineffable, which I have just told you, then will it straightway, if it be set free from the body of matter, become a great light-stream in the midst of those receivers, and the receivers will be exceedingly afraid of the light of that soul, and the receivers will be made powerless and fall down and desist altogether for fear of the great light which they have seen.

"And the soul which receiveth the mystery of the Ineffable, will soar into the height, being a great light-stream, and the receivers will not be able to seize it and will not know how the way is fashioned upon which it will go. For it becometh a great light-stream and soareth into the height, and no power is able to hold it down at all, nor will they be able to come nigh it at all.

"But it will pass through all the regions of the rulers and all the regions of the emanations of the Light, and it will not give answers in any region, nor giveth it any apologies, nor giveth it any tokens; neither will any power of the rulers nor any power of the emanations of the Light be able to come nigh that soul. But all the regions of the rulers and all the regions of the emanations of the Light, — every

one singeth unto it praises in their regions, in fear of the light of the stream which envelopeth that soul, until it passeth through them all, and goeth to the region of the inheritance of the mystery which it hath received, — that is to the mystery of the One and Only, the Ineffable, — and until it becometh one with its Limbs. Amen, I say unto you: It will be in all the regions in the time a man shooteth an arrow."

Of the rank of such a soul

"Now, therefore, amen, I say unto you: Every man who will receive that mystery of the Ineffable and accomplish it in all its types and all its figures, - he is a man in the world, but he towereth above all angels and will tower still more above them all.

"He is a man in the world, but he towereth above all archangels and will tower still more above them all.

"He is a man in the world, but he towereth above all tyrants and will raise himself above them all.

"He is a man in the world, but he towereth above all lords and will raise himself above them all.

"He is a man in the world, but he towereth above all gods and will raise himself above them all.

"He is a man in the world, but he towereth above all light-givers and will raise himself above them all.

"He is a man in the world, but he towereth above all pure [ones] and will raise himself above them all.

"He is a man in the world, but he towereth above all triple-powers and will raise himself above them all.

"He is a man in the world, but he towereth above all forefathers and will raise himself above them all.

"He is a man in the world, but he towereth above all invisibles and will raise himself above them all.

"He is a man in the world, but he towereth above the great invisible forefather and will raise himself above him.

"He is a man in the world, but he towereth above all those of the Middle and will raise himself above them all.

"He is a man in the world, but he towereth above the emanations of the Treasury of the Light and will raise himself above them all.

"He is a man in the world, but he towereth above the Mixture and will raise himself entirely above it.

"He is a man in the world, but he towereth above the whole region of the Treasury and will raise himself entirely above it.

"He is a man in the world, but he will rule with me in my kingdom.

"He is a man in the world, but he is king in the Light.

He is a man in the world, but he is not one of the world.

"And amen, I say unto you: that man is I and I am that man."

Such souls are one with the First Mystery

"And at the dissolution of the world, that is when the universe will be raised up and when the numbering of the perfect souls will be raised up all together, and when I am king in the midst of the last Helper, being king over all the emanations of the Light and king over the seven Amens and the five Trees and the three Amens and the nine guards, and being king over the Child of the Child, that is the Twin-saviours, and being king over the twelve saviours and over the whole numbering of the perfect souls who shall receive the mysteries in the Light, — then will all men who shall receive the mysteries in the Ineffable, be fellow-kings with me and will sit on my right and on my left in my kingdom.

"And amen, I say unto you: Those men are I, and I am they.

"On this account have I said unto you afore time:

"Ye will sit on your thrones on my right and on my left in my kingdom and will rule with me.'

"On this account, therefore, I have not hesitated nor have I been ashamed to call you my brethren and my companions, because ye will be fellow-kings with me in my kingdom. This, therefore, I say unto you, knowing that I will give you the mystery of the Ineffable; that is: That mystery is I, and I am that mystery."

Of the dignity of the thrones in the kingdom

"Now, therefore, not only will ye reign with me, but all men who shall receive the mystery of the Ineffable, will be fellow-kings with me in my kingdom. And I am they, and they are I. But my throne will tower over them. [And] because ye will suffer sorrows in the world beyond all men, until ye herald forth all the words which I shall speak unto you, your thrones shall be joined to mine in my kingdom.

"On this account I have said unto you afore time: 'Where I shall be there will be also my twelve ministers.' But Mary Magdalene and John, the virgin, will tower over all my disciples and over all men who shall receive the mysteries in the Ineffable. And they will be on my right and on my left. And I am they, and they are I.

"And they will be like unto you in all things save that your thrones will tower over theirs, and my throne will tower over yours."

Of the gnosis of the word of the Ineffable

"And all men who will find the word of the Ineffable, — Amen, I say unto you: The men who shall know that word, will know the gnosis of all these words which I have spoken unto you, both those of the depth and those of the height, those of the length and those of the breadth; in a word, they will know the gnosis of all these words which I have spoken unto you and which I have not yet spoken unto you, which I will speak unto you, region by region and order by order, at the expansion of the universe.

"And amen, I say unto you; They will know in what manner the world is established, and they will know in what type all those of the height are established, and they will know out of what ground the universe hath arisen."

Chapter 97

When then the Saviour had said this, Mary Magdalene started forward and said: "My Lord, bear with me and be not wroth with me, if I question on all things with precision and certainty. Now, therefore, my Lord, is then another the word of the mystery of the Ineffable and another the word of the whole gnosis?"

The Saviour answered and said: "Yea, another is the mystery of the Ineffable and another the word of the whole gnosis."

And Mary answered again and said unto the Saviour: "My Lord, bear with me, if I question thee, and be not wroth with me. Now, therefore, my Lord, unless we live and know the gnosis of the whole word of the Ineffable, shall we not be able to inherit the Light-kingdom?"

Of the distinction between the gnosis of the universe and the mysteries of the Light

And the Saviour answered and said unto Mary: "Surely; for every one who shall receive a mystery of the Light-kingdom, will go and inherit up to the region up to which he hath received mysteries.

"But he will not know the gnosis of the universe, wherefor all this hath arisen, unless he knoweth the one and only word of the Ineffable, which is the gnosis of the universe. And again in openness: I am the gnosis of the universe. And moreover it is impossible to know the one and only word of the gnosis, unless a man first receive the mystery of the Ineffable. But all the men who shall receive mysteries in the Light, — every one will go and inherit up to the region up to which he hath received mysteries.

"On this account I have said unto you afore time: 'He who hath faith in a prophet, will receive a prophet's reward, and he who have faith in a righteous [man] will receive a righteous [man's] reward', — that is: Every one will go to the region up to which he hath received mysteries. He who receiveth a lesser mystery, will inherit the lesser mystery, and he who receiveth a higher mystery, will inherit the higher regions. And every one will abide in his region in the light of my kingdom, and every one will have power over the orders which are below him, but he will not have the power to go to the orders which are above him; but he will abide in the regions of the Inheritance of the Light of my kingdom, being in a great light immeasurable for the gods and all the invisibles, and he will be in great joy and great jubilation.

"But now, therefore, hearken, that I may discourse with you concerning the grandeur of those who shall receive the mysteries of the First Mystery.

Of the ascension of the souls of those who receive the twelve mysteries of the First Mystery

"He, therefore, who shall receive the [first] mystery of that First Mystery, and it shall be at the time that he cometh out of the body of the matter of the rulers, — then the retributive receivers come and lead the soul of that man out of the body. And that soul will become a great light-stream in the hands of the retributive receivers; and those receivers will be afraid of the light of that soul. And that soul will go upwards and pass through all the regions of the rulers and all the regions of the emanations of the Light. And it will not give answers nor apologies nor tokens in any single region of the Light nor in any single region of the rulers; but it will pass through all the regions and cross over them all, so that it goeth and ruleth over all the regions of the first saviour.

"In like manner also he who shall receive the second mystery of the First Mystery and the third and fourth, until he shall receive the twelfth mystery of the First Mystery, if it shall be at the time that he

cometh out of the body of the matter of the rulers, — then the retributive receivers come and lead the soul of that man out of the body of matter. And those souls will become a great light-stream in the hands of the retributive receivers; and those receivers will be afraid of the light of those souls and will become powerless and fall on their faces. And those souls will straightway soar upwards and cross over all the regions of the rulers and all the regions of the emanations of the Light. They will not give answers nor apologies nor token in any single region; but they will pass through all the regions and will cross over them all and rule over all the regions of the twelve saviours, so that they who receive the second mystery of the First Mystery, will rule over all the regions of the second saviour in the inheritances of the Light.

"In like manner also those who receive the third mystery of the First Mystery and the fourth and fifth and sixth up to the twelfth, — every one will rule over all the regions of the saviour up to whom he hath received the mystery.

"And he who shall receive in sequence the twelfth mystery of the First Mystery, that is the master-mystery concerning which I discourse with you, — and he who, therefore, shall receive those twelve mysteries which belong to the First Mystery, if he goeth forth out of the world, will pass through all the regions of the rulers and all the regions of the Light, being a great light-stream, and he will moreover rule over all the regions of the twelve saviours, but they will not be able to be like unto those who receive the one and only mystery of the Ineffable. But he who shall receive those mysteries will abide in those orders, because they are exalted, and he will abide in the orders of the twelve saviours."

Chapter 98

Mary again questioneth Jesus

It came to pass, when Jesus had finished speaking these words unto his disciples, that Mary Magdalene came forward, kissed the feet of Jesus and said unto him: "My Lord, bear with me and be not wroth with me, if I question thee, but have mercy upon us, my Lord, and reveal unto us all things on which we shall question thee. Now, therefore, my Lord, how doth the First Mystery possess twelve mysteries, [and] the Ineffable possess a one and only mystery?"

Of the three mysteries and five mysteries

Jesus answered and said unto her: "Indeed it possesseth a one and only mystery, yet that mystery constituteth three mysteries, although it is the one and only mystery; but the type of every one of them is different. And moreover it constituteth five mysteries, although it is a one and only [one]; but the type of every one is different. So that these five mysteries are alike with one another in the mystery of the kingdom in the inheritances of the Light; but the type of each of them is different. And their kingdom is higher and more exalted than the whole kingdom of the twelve mysteries together of the First Mystery; but they are not alike in the kingdom [with the one and only mystery] of the First Mystery in the Light-kingdom.

"In like manner also the three mysteries are not [?] alike in the Light-kingdom; but the type of every one of them is different. And they themselves also are not alike in the kingdom with the one and only mystery of the First Mystery in the Light-kingdom; and the type of every one of the three of them, and the type of the configuration of each of them, is different from one another."

Of the first mystery

"The first [mystery of the First Mystery], — if thou accomplishest its mystery altogether and standest and accomplishest it finely in all its

figures, then does thou come straightway out of thy body, become a great light-stream and pass through all the regions of the rulers and all of the regions of the Light, while all are in fear of that soul, until it cometh to the region of its kingdom."

Of the second mystery

"The second mystery of the First Mystery, on the other hand, — if thou accomplishest it finely in all its figures, — the man, therefore, who shall accomplish its mystery, if he speaketh that mystery over the head of any man who goeth forth out of the body, and he speaketh it into his two ears, if indeed the man who goeth forth out of the body hath received mysteries for the second time and is sharing in the word of truth, — amen, I say unto you: That man, if he goeth forth out of the body of matter, then will his soul become a great light-stream and pass through all the regions, until it cometh to the kingdom of that mystery."

Of its efficacy for the uninitiated

"But if that man hath received no mysteries and is not sharing in the words of truth, — if he who accomplisheth that mystery, speaketh that mystery over the head of a man who cometh forth out of the body and who hath received no mysteries of the Light, and shareth not in the words of truth, — amen, I say unto you; That man, if he cometh forth out of the body, will be judged in no region of the rulers, nor can he be chastised in any region at all, nor will the fire touch him, because of the great mystery of the Ineffable which is with him.

"And they will hasten quickly and hand him over one to another in turn and lead him from region to region and from order to order, until they bring him before the Virgin of Light, while all the regions are in fear of the mystery and the sign of the kingdom of the Ineffable which is with him.

"And if they bring him before the Virgin of Light, then the Virgin of Light will see the sign of the mystery of the kingdom of the Ineffable

which is with him; the Virgin of Light marvelleth and proveth him, but suffereth them not to bring him to the Light, until he accomplisheth the total citizenship of the light of that mystery, that is the purities of the renunciation of the world and also of the total matter therein.

"The Virgin of Light sealeth him with a higher seal, which is this [...?], and letteth him in that month in which he hath come out of the body of matter, light down into a body which will be righteous and find the godhead in truth and the higher mysteries, so that he may inherit them and inherit the Light eternal, which is the gift of the second mystery of the First Mystery of the Ineffable.

Of the third mystery and its efficacy

"The third mystery of that Ineffable on the other hand, — the man indeed who shall accomplish that mystery, not only if he [himself] cometh forth out of the body, will he inherit the kingdom of the mystery, but if he complete that mystery and accomplish it with all its figures, that is if he go through with that mystery and accomplish it finely and pronounce the name of that mystery over a man who cometh forth out of the body and hath known that mystery, — let the former have delayed or rather not have delayed, — one who is in the dire chastisements of the rulers and in their dire judgments and their manifold fires, — amen, I say unto you: The man who hath come forth out of the body, — if the name of this mystery is pronounced on his behalf, they will hasten quickly to bring him over and hand him over to one another, until they bring him before the Virgin of Light. And the Virgin of Light will seal him with a higher seal, which is this [...?], and in that month will she let him light down into the righteous body which will find the godhead in truth and the higher mystery, so that he inherit the Light-kingdom. This, therefore, is the gift of the third mystery of the Ineffable."

Of the three and five mysteries

"Now, therefore, every one who shall receive one of the five mysteries of the Ineffable, — if he cometh forth out of the body and inheriteth up to the region of that mystery, then is the kingdom of those five mysteries higher than the kingdom of the twelve mysteries of the First Mystery, and it is higher than all the mysteries which are below them. But those five mysteries of the Ineffable are alike with one another in their kingdom yet are they not alike with the three mysteries of the Ineffable.

"He on the other hand who receiveth of the three mysteries of the Ineffable, if he cometh forth out of the body, will inherit up to the kingdom of that mystery. And those three mysteries are alike with one another in the kingdom and they are higher and more exalted than the five mysteries of the Ineffable in the kingdom, but they are not alike with the one and only mystery of the Ineffable."

Of the mysteries of the three spaces

"He on the other hand who receiveth the one and only mystery of the Ineffable, will inherit the region of the whole kingdom according to its whole glory, as I have already told you at another time. And every one who shall receive the mystery which is in the space of the universe of the Ineffable, and all the other mysteries which are united in the Limbs of the Ineffable, concerning which I have not yet spoken unto you, and concerning their expansion and the manner of their setting-up and the type of every one, how it is and wherefor it is named the Ineffable or wherefor it standeth expanded with all its Limbs and how many Limbs are in it and all its economies, of which I will not tell you now, but when I come to the expansion of the universe I will tell you all severally, — to wit, its expansions and its description, how it is, and the aggregation [?] of all its Limbs, which belong to the economy of the One and Only, the unapproachable God in truth, up to what region, therefore, every one shall receive the mysteries in the space of the Ineffable, up to that region will he inherit up to which he hath received. And those of the whole region of the space of that

Ineffable give no answers in that region, nor give they apologies, nor give they tokens, for they are without tokens and they have no receivers, but they pass through all the regions, until they come to the region of the kingdom of the mystery which they have received.

"In like manner also those who shall receive mysteries in the second space, they have no answerers nor apologies, for they are without tokens in that world, which is the space of the first mystery of the First Mystery.

"And those of the third space, which is without, which is the third space from without [? within], — every region in that space hath its receivers and its explanations and its apologies and its tokens, which I will one day tell you when I come to speak of that mystery, that is when I shall have told you of the expansion of the universe."

Of the reign of a thousand years of the Light

"Albeit at the dissolution of the universe, that is when the number of the perfect souls is completed and the mystery [through] which the universe altogether hath risen, is completed, I will pass a thousand years according to the years of the Light, being king over all the emanations of the Light and over the whole number of the perfect souls who have received all mysteries."

Chapter 99

It came to pass, when Jesus had finished speaking these words unto his disciples, that Mary Magdalene came forward and said: "My Lord, how many years of the years of the world is a year of the Light?"

What is a year of the Light

Jesus answered and said unto Mary: "A day of the Light is a thousand years in the world, so that thirty-six myriads of years and a half myriad of years of the world are a single year of the Light.

"I shall, therefore, pass a thousand years of the Light being king in the midst of the last Helper, and being king over all the emanations of the Light and over the whole number of the perfect souls who have received the mysteries of the Light."

Of those of the first space in the kingdom of the thousand years

"And ye, my disciples, and every one who shall receive the mystery of the Ineffable, will abide with me on my right and on my left, being kings with me in my kingdom.

"And they who shall receive the three mysteries of that Ineffable, will be fellow-kings with you in the Light-kingdom; but they will not be alike with you and with those who receive the mystery of the Ineffable, but they will rather abide behind you, being kings.

"And they who receive the five mysteries of the Ineffable, will also abide behind the three mysteries, being also kings.

"And moreover they who receive the twelfth mystery of the First Mystery, will also again abide behind the five mysteries of the Ineffable, being also kings according to the order of every one of them.

"And all who receive of the mysteries in all the regions of the space of the Ineffable, will also be kings and abide before those who receive the mystery of the First Mystery, expanded according to the glory of every one of them, so that those who receive the higher mysteries, will abide in the higher regions, and those who receive the lower mysteries, will abide in the lower regions, being kings in the light of my kingdom.

"These alone are the allotment of the kingdom of the first space of the Ineffable."

Of those of the second space

"They on the other hand who receive all the mysteries of the second space, that is of the space of the First Mystery, will again abide in the light of my kingdom, expanded according to the glory of every one of them, and every one of them being in the mystery up to which he hath received. And those who receive the higher mysteries, will also abide in the higher regions, and those who receive the lower mysteries, will abide in the lower regions in the light of my kingdom.

"This is the allotment of the second king for those who receive the mystery of the second space of the First Mystery."

Of those of the third space, the first from without

"Those on the other hand who receive the mysteries of the third space, that is of the first space from without, those again will abide behind the second king, expanded in the light of my kingdom, according to the glory of every one of them, every one abiding in the region up to which he hath received mysteries, so that those who receive the higher mysteries, will abide in the higher regions, and those who receive the lower mysteries, will abide in the lower regions.

"These are the three allotments of the Light-kingdom.

"The mysteries of these three allotments of the Light are exceedingly numerous. Ye shall find them in the two great Books of Yew. But I will give you and tell you the great mysteries of every allotment, those which are higher than every region, that is the heads according to every region and according to every order which will lead the whole race of men into the higher regions, according to the space of the Inheritance."

Of the Books of Yew

"Of the rest of the lower mysteries, therefore, ye have no need; but ye will find them in the two Books of Yew, which Enoch hath written

whilst I spake with him out of the tree of gnosis and out of the tree of life in the paradise of Adam.

"Now, therefore, when I shall have explained unto you the whole expansion, I will give you and tell you the great mysteries of the three allotments of my kingdom, that is the heads of the mysteries which I will give you and tell you in all their figures and all their types and their ciphers and the seals of the last space, that is the first space from without. And I will tell you the answers and the apologies and the tokens of that space.

"The second space which is within, possesseth no answers nor apologies nor tokens nor ciphers nor seals; but it possesseth only types and figures."

Chapter 100

When the Saviour had finished saying all this unto his disciples, Andrew came forward and said: "My Lord, be not wroth with me, but have mercy upon me and reveal unto me the mystery of the word concerning which I shall question thee, for it hath been hard for me and I have not understood it."

The Saviour answered and said unto him: "Question concerning that on which thou desirest to question, and I will reveal it unto thee face to face without similitude."

Andrew questioneth Jesus

And Andrew answered and said: "My Lord, I am astonished and marvel exceedingly, how the man who are in the world and in the body of this matter, if they come forth out of this world, will pass through these firmaments and all these rulers and all lords and all gods and all these great invisibles and all those of the region of the Middle and those of the whole region of the Right and all the great [ones] of the emanations of the Light, and enter into them all and inherit the Light-kingdom. This matter, therefore, is hard for me."

That the disciples and the powers are all from the same Mixture

When then Andrew had said this, the spirit of the Saviour was roused in him; he cried out and said: "How long am I to endure you? How long am I to bear with you? Have ye then not even yet understood and are ye ignorant? Know ye then not and do ye not understand that ye and all angels and all archangels and the gods and the lords and all the rulers and all the great invisibles and all those of the Middle and those of the whole region of the Right and all the great [ones] of the emanations of the Light and their whole glory, — that ye all one with another are out of one and the same paste and the same matter and the same substance, and that ye all are out of the same Mixture.

"And at the commandment of the First Mystery the Mixture was constrained, until all the great [ones] of the emanations of the light and all their glory purified themselves, and until they purified themselves from the Mixture. And they have not purified themselves of themselves, but they have purified themselves by necessity according to the economy of the One and Only, the Ineffable.

"They indeed have not at all suffered and have not at all changed themselves in the regions, nor at all torn themselves asunder nor poured themselves into bodies of different kinds and from one into another, nor have they been in any affliction at all."

Of transcorporation and purification

"Ye then in particular are the refuse of the Treasury and ye are the refuse of the region of the Right and ye are the refuse of the region of those of the Middle and ye are the refuse of all the invisibles and of all the rulers; in a word, ye are the refuse of all these. And ye are in great sufferings and great afflictions in your being poured from one into another of different kinds of bodies of the world. And after all these sufferings ye have struggled of yourselves and fought, having renounced the whole world and all the matter therein; and ye have

not left off seeking, until ye found all the mysteries of the kingdom of the Light, which have purified you and made you into refined light, exceedingly purified, and ye have become purified light.

"For this cause have I said unto you afore time: 'Seek, that ye may find.' I have, therefore, said unto you: Ye are to seek after the mysteries of the Light, which purify the body of matter and make it into refined light exceedingly purified."

Of the purifying mysteries

"Amen, I say unto you: For the sake of the race of men, because it is material, I have torn myself asunder and brought unto them all the mysteries of the Light, that I may purify them, for they are the refuse of the whole matter of their matter; else would no soul of the total race of men have been saved, and they would not be able to inherit the kingdom of the Light, if I had not brought unto them the purifying mysteries.

"For the emanations of the Light have no need of the mysteries, for they are purified; but it is the race of men which hath need of them, because they all are material refuse [pl.]. For this cause, therefore, have I said unto you afore time: 'The healthy have no need of the physician, but the sick,' — that is: Those of the Light have no need of the mysteries, for they are purified lights; but it is the race of men which hath need of them, for [they] are material refuse [pl.].

"For this cause, therefore, herald to the whole race of men, saying: Cease not to seek day and night, until ye find the purifying mysteries; and say unto the race of men: Renounce the whole world and the whole matter therein. For he who buyeth and selleth in the world and he who eateth and drinketh of its matter and who liveth in all its cares and in all its associations, amasseth other additional matters to the rest of is matter, because this whole world and all therein and all its associations are material refuse [pl.] and they will make enquiry of every one concerning his purity.

"For this cause, therefore, I have said unto you afore time: Renounce the whole world and the whole matter therein, that ye may not amass other additional matter to the rest of your matter in you. For this cause, therefore, herald it to the whole race of men, saying: Renounce the whole world and all its associations, that ye may not amass additional matter to the rest of your matter in you; and say unto them: Cease not to seek day and night and remit not yourselves until ye find the purifying mysteries which will purify you and make you into a refined light, so that ye will go on high and inherit the light of my kingdom."

That all who are purified will be saved

"Now, therefore, Andrew and all thy brethren thy co-disciples, because your renunciations and all your sufferings which ye have endured in every region, and because of your changes in every region and of your being poured from one into another of different kinds of bodies and because of all your afflictions, and after all this ye have received the purifying mysteries and are become refined light exceedingly purified, — for this cause, therefore, ye will go on high and penetrate into all the regions of all the great emanations of the Light and be kings in the Light-kingdom for ever.

That finally they will be higher than all powers

"But if ye come forth out of the body and come on high and reach unto the region of the rulers, then will all the rulers be seized with shame before you, because ye are the refuse of their matter and have become light more purified than them all. And if ye reach unto the region of the Great Invisible and unto the region of those of the Middle and of those of the Right and unto the regions of all the great emanations of the light, then will ye be revered among them all, because ye are the refuse of their matter and are became light more purified than them all. And all the regions will sing praises before you, until ye come to the region of the kingdom.

"This is the answer to the words on which ye question. Now, therefore, Andrew, art thou still in unfaith and unknowing?"

Jesus pardoneth the ignorance of Andrew

When then the Saviour said this, Andrew knew clearly, not only he but also all the disciples knew with precision that they should inherit the Light-kingdom. They all threw themselves down together at Jesus' feet, cried aloud, wept and besought the Saviour, saying: "Lord, forgive our brother the sin of unknowing."

The Saviour answered and said: "I forgive and will forgive; for this cause, therefore, hath the First Mystery sent me, that I may forgive every one his sins."

[Sub-scription:]

A portion of the books of the saviour

[The conclusion of another book]

Chapter 101

Of the Limbs of the Ineffable

"And those who are worthy of the mysteries which abide in the Ineffable, which are those which have not gone forth, — these exist before the First Mystery, and to use a likeness and similitude, that ye may understand it, they are as the Limbs of the Ineffable. And every one existeth according to the dignity of its glory: the head according to the dignity of the head and the eye according to the dignity of the eyes and the ear according to the dignity of the ears and the rest of the Limbs [in like fashion]; so that the matter is manifest: There is a multitude of limbs but one only body. Of this indeed have I spoken in a pattern and similitude and likeness, but not in a form in truth; nor have I revealed the word in truth, but the mystery [only] of the Ineffable."

The Saviour is their treasury

"And all the Limbs which are in it, — according to the word with which I have made comparison, — that is, those which abide on the mystery of the Ineffable, and those which abide in it, and also the three spaces which are after them according to the mysteries, — of all these in truth and verity I am their treasury beside whom there is no other treasury, who hath not his like in the world, but there are still words and mysteries and other regions."

Of the dignity of those who have receive the mysteries

"Now, therefore, blessed is he who hath found the [words of the] mysteries [of the first space] which is from without; and he is a god who hath found these words of the mysteries of the second space, which is in the midst; and he is a saviour and an uncontainable who hath found the words of the mysteries of the third space, which is within, and he is more excellent than the universe and like unto those who are in that third space. Because he hath found the mystery in which they are and in which they stand, — for this cause, therefore, is he like unto them. He on the other hand who hath found the words of the mysteries which I have described unto you according to a likeness, that they are the Limbs of the Ineffable, — amen, I say unto you: That man who hath found the words of these mysteries in divine truth, is the first in truth and like unto him [sc. the First, i.e., the Ineffable], for through those words and mysteries... and the universe itself standeth through that First. For this cause he who hath found the words of those mysteries is like unto the First. For it is the gnosis of the gnosis of the Ineffable concerning which I have discoursed with you this day."

"Renounce the whole world and the whole matter therein and all its cares and all its sins, in a word all its associations which are in it, that ye may be worthy of the mysteries of the Light..."

ENGRAVING BY GUSTAVE DORÉ

THE PISTIS SOPHIA UNVEILED

A Third Book

Chapter 102

Of the proclamation of the disciples

Jesus continued again in the discourse and said unto his disciples: "When I shall have gone into the Light, then herald it unto the whole world and say unto them: Cease not to seek day and night and remit not yourselves until ye find the mysteries of the Light-kingdom, which will purify you and make you into refined light and lead you into the Light-kingdom."

What men should renounce

"Say unto them: Renounce the whole world and the whole matter therein and all its cares and all its sins, in a word all its associations which are in it, that ye may be worthy of the mysteries of the Light and be saved from all the chastisements which are in the judgments.

"Say unto them: Renounce murmuring, that ye may be worthy of the mysteries of the Light and be saved from the fire of the dog-faced [one].

"Say unto them: Renounce eavesdropping [?], that ye may [be worthy of the mysteries of the Light] and be saved from the judgments of the dog-faced [one].

"Say unto them: Renounce litigiousness [?], that ye may be worthy of the mysteries of the Light and be saved from the chastisements of Ariel.

"Say unto them: Renounce false slander, that ye may be worthy of the mysteries of the Light and be saved from the fire-rivers of the dog-faced [one].

"Say unto them: Renounce false witness, that ye may be worthy of the mysteries of the Light and that ye may escape and be saved from the fire-rivers of the dog-faced [one].

"Say unto them: Renounce pride and haughtiness, that ye may be worthy of the mysteries of the Light and be saved from the fire-pits of Ariel.

"Say unto them: Renounce belly-love, that ye may be worthy of the mysteries of the Light and saved from the judgments of Amente.

"Say unto them: Renounce babbling, that ye may be worthy of the mysteries of the Light and be saved from the Amente.

"Say unto them: Renounce craftiness, that ye may be worth of the mysteries of the Light and be saved from the chastisements which are in Amente.

"Say unto them: Renounce avarice, that ye may be worthy of the mysteries of the Light and be saved from the fire-rivers of the dog-faced [one].

"Say unto them: Renounce love of the world, that ye may be worthy of the mysteries of the Light and be saved from the pitch and fire-coats of the dog-faced [one].

"Say unto them: Renounce pillage, that ye may be worthy of the mysteries of the Light and be saved from the fire-rivers of Ariel.

"Say unto them: Renounce evil conversation, that ye may be worthy of the mysteries of the Light and be saved from the chastisements of the fire-rivers...

"Say unto them: Renounce wickedness, that ye may be worthy of the mysteries of the Light and be saved from the fire-seas of Ariel.

"Say unto them: Renounce pitilessness, that ye may be worthy of the mysteries of the Light and be saved from the judgments of the dragon-faced [ones].

"Say unto them: Renounce wrath, that ye may be worthy of the mysteries of the Light and be saved from the fire-rivers of the dragon-faced [ones].

"Say unto them: Renounce cursing, that ye may be worthy of the mysteries of the Light and be saved from the fire-seas of the dragon-faced [ones].

"Say unto them: Renounce thieving, that ye may be worthy of the mysteries of the Light and be saved from the bubbling seas of the dragon-faced [ones.]

"Say unto them: Renounce robbery, that ye may be worthy of the mysteries of the Light and be saved from Yaldabaoth.

"Say unto them: Renounce slandering, that ye may be worthy of the mysteries of the Light and be saved from the fire-rivers of the lion-faced [one].

"Say unto them: Renounce fighting and strife, that ye may be worthy of the mysteries of the Light and be saved from the seething rivers of Yaldabaoth.

"Say unto them: Renounce all unknowing, that ye may be worthy of the mysteries of the Light and be saved from the servitors of Yaldabaoth and the fire-seas.

"Say unto them: Renounce evil doing, that ye may be worthy of the mysteries of the Light and be saved from all the demons of Yaldabaoth and all his judgments.

"Say unto them: Renounce sloth, that ye may be worthy of the mysteries of the Light and be saved from the seething pitch-seas of Yaldabaoth.

"Say unto them: Renounce adultery, that ye may be worthy of the mysteries of the Light-kingdom and be saved from the sulphur and pitch-seas of the lion-faced [one].

"Say unto them: Renounce murder, that ye may be worthy of the mysteries of the Light and be saved from the crocodile-faced ruler, — this one who is in the cold, is the first chamber of the outer darkness.

"Say unto them: Renounce pitilessness and impiety, that ye may be worthy of the mysteries of the Light and be saved from the rulers of the outer darkness.

"Say unto them: Renounce atheism, that ye may be worthy of the mysteries of the Light and be saved from the howling and grinding of teeth.

"Say unto them: Renounce [magic] potions, that ye may be worthy of the mysteries of the Light and be saved from the great cold and hail of the outer darkness.

"Say unto them: Renounce blasphemy, that ye may be worthy of the mysteries of the Light and be saved from the great dragon of the outer darkness.

"Say unto them: Renounce the doctrines of error, that ye may be worthy of the mysteries of the Light and be saved from all the chastisements of the great dragon of the outer darkness.

"Say unto those who teach the doctrines of error and to every one who is instructed by them: Woe unto you, for, if ye do not repent and abandon your error, ye will go into the chastisements of the great dragon and of the outer darkness, which is exceedingly evil, and never will ye be cast [up] into the world, but will be non-existent until the end.

"Say unto those who abandon the doctrines of truth of the First Mystery: Woe unto you, for your chastisement is sad compared with [that of] all men. For ye will abide in the great cold and ice and hail in the midst of the dragon and of the outer darkness, and ye will never from this hour on be cast [up] into the world, but ye shall be frozen up [?] in that region and at the dissolution of the universe ye will perish and become non-existent eternally."

The boundaries of the ways of the worthy

"Rather, say to the men of the world: Be calm, so ye may receive the mysteries of the Light and go on high into the Light-kingdom.

"Say to them: Be ye loving-unto-men, so ye may be worthy of the mysteries of the Light and go on high into the Light-kingdom.

"Say to them: Be ye gentle, so ye may receive the mysteries of the Light and go on high into the Light-kingdom.

"Say to them: Be ye peaceful, so ye may receive the mysteries of the Light and go on high into the Light-kingdom.

"Say to them: Be ye merciful, so ye may receive the mysteries of the Light and go on high into the Light-kingdom.

"Say to them: Give ye alms, so ye may receive the mysteries of the Light and go on high into the Light-kingdom.

"Say to them: Minister unto the poor and the sick and distressed, so ye may receive the mysteries of the Light and go on high into the Light-kingdom.

"Say to them: Be ye loving-unto-God, so ye may receive the mysteries of the Light and go on high into the Light-kingdom.

"Say to them: Be ye righteous, so ye may receive the mysteries of the Light and go on high into the Light-kingdom.

"Say to them: Be good, so ye may receive the mysteries of the Light and go on high into the Light-kingdom.

"Say to them: Renounce all, so ye may receive the mysteries of the Light and go on high into the Light-kingdom.

"These are all the boundaries of the ways for those who are worthy of the mysteries of the Light."

Unto whom are the mysteries of the Light to be given

"Unto such, therefore, who have renounced in this renunciation, give the mysteries of the Light and hide them not from them, even though they are sinners and have been in all the sins and all the iniquities of the world, all of which I have recounted unto you, in order that they may turn and repent and be in the submission which I have

just recounted unto you. Give unto them the mysteries of the Light-kingdom and hide them not from them, for it is because of sinfulness that I have brought the mysteries into the world, that I may forgive all their sins which they have committed from the beginning on."

The mysteries are for the forgiveness of sins

"For this cause I said unto you afore time: 'I am not come to call the righteous.' I have brought the mysteries that their sins may be forgiven for every one and they be received into the Light-kingdom. For the mysteries are the gift of the First Mystery, that he may wipe out the sins and iniquities of all sinners."

Chapter 103

Mary questioneth the Saviour

When Jesus had finished saying these words unto his disciples, Mary came forward and said to the Saviour: "My Lord, will then a virtuous man who is perfected in all virtues, who hath no sin at all, be tormented in the chastisements and judgments or not? Or will rather that man be brought into the kingdom of heaven?"

Of the soul of the righteous man who hath not received the mysteries at death

And the Saviour answered and said unto Mary, "A virtuous man who is perfected in all virtues and who hath never committed any sin of any kind, and who never hath received mysteries of the Light, if the time is at hand when he goeth forth out of the body, then straightway come the receivers of one of the great triple-powers, — those among whom there is a great [one], — to snatch away the soul of that man from the hands of the retributive receivers and spend three days circling with it in all the creatures of the world. After three days they lead it down into the chaos, so as to lead it into all the chastisements of the judgments and to dispatch it to all the judgments. The fires of the chaos do not trouble it greatly; but they will trouble it partly for a short time.

"And with haste they take pity on it, to lead it up out of the chaos and lead it on the way of the Middle through all the rulers. And the rulers do not chastise it in their harsh judgments, but the fire of their regions troubleth it partly. And if it shall be brought into the region of Yachthanabas, the pitiless, then will he indeed not be able to chastise it in his evil judgments, but he holdeth it fast a short time, while the fire of his chastisements troubleth it partly.

"And again they take pity on it quickly, and lead it up out of their regions and they do not bring it into the aeons, so that the rulers of the aeons do not carry it away ravishingly; they bring it on the way of the sun and bring it before the Virgin of Light. She proveth it and findeth that it is pure of sins, but letteth them not bring it to the Light, because the sign of the kingdom of the mystery is not with it. But she sealeth it with a higher seal and letteth it be cast down into the body into the aeons of virtuousness, — that body which will be good to find the signs of the mysteries of the Light and inherit the Light-kingdom forever.

"If on the contrary he hath sinned once or twice or thrice, then he will be cast back into the world again according to the type of sins which he hath committed, the type of which I will tell you when I tell you of the expansion of the universe.

"But amen, amen, I say unto you: Even if a righteous man hath committed no sins at all, he cannot possibly be brought into the Light-kingdom if the sign of the kingdom of the mysteries is not with him. In a word, it is impossible to bring souls into the Light without the mysteries of the Light-kingdom."

Chapter 104

John questioneth Jesus

It cam to pass then, when Jesus had finished saying these words unto his disciples, John came forward and said: "My Lord, suppose a sinning and law-breaking man is replete in all iniquities, and he hath ceased from these for the sake of the kingdom of heaven and renounced the whole world and the whole matter therein, and we give him from the beginning onwards the mysteries of the Light which are in the first space from without, and if he receiveth the mysteries, and after a little while again if he returneth and transgresseth, and thereafter again if he turneth and ceaseth from all sins and turneth and renounceth the whole world and the whole matter therein, so that he cometh again and is in great repentance, and if we know in truth that he longeth after God, so that we give him the second mystery of the first space which is from without — in like manner if he turneth anew and transgresseth and is again in the sins of the world, and again if he thereafter turneth and ceaseth from the sins of the world and again renounceth the whole world and the whole matter therein and again is in great repentance, and we know it with certainty that he is not a play-actor, so that we turn and give him the mysteries of the beginning, which are in the first space from without: — in like manner, if he turneth again and sinneth and is in every type of sin, desirest thou that we forgive him unto seven times and give him the mysteries which are in the first space from without, unto seven times or not?"

The disciples are to forgive many times seven times

The Saviour answered again and said unto John: "Not only forgive him unto seven times, but amen, I say unto you: Forgive him unto many times seven times, and every time give him the mysteries from the beginning onwards which are in the first space from without. Perchance ye win the soul of that brother and he inheriteth the Light-kingdom.

"For this cause, therefore, when ye questioned me afore time, saying: 'If our brother sin against us, desirest thou that we forgive him unto seven times?' — I answered and spoke unto you in similitude, saying: 'Not only unto seven times, but unto seventy times seven.'

"Now, therefore, forgive him many times and every time give him the mysteries which are in the first space which is from without. Perchance ye win the soul of that brother and he inheriteth the Light-kingdom."

Of the reward of the savers of souls

"Amen, amen, I say unto you: He who shall keep in Life and save only one soul, beside the dignity which he possesseth in the Light-kingdom, he will receive yet another dignity from the soul which he hath saved, so that he who shall save many souls, besides the dignity which he possesseth in the Light, he will receive many other dignities for the souls which he hath saved."

Chapter 105

John continueth his questioning

When then the Saviour had said this, John started forward and said: "My Lord, bear with me if I question thee, for from now on I will begin to question thee on all things concerning how we are to herald it to mankind.

"If, therefore, I give that brother a mystery out of the mysteries of the beginning which are in the first space from without, and if I give him many mysteries and he doeth not what is worthy of the kingdom of heaven, — desirest thou that we let him pass through the mysteries of the second space? Perchance we win the soul of that brother, and he turneth, repenteth and inheriteth the Light-kingdom. Desirest thou that we let him pass through to the mysteries [which are in the second space] or not?"

The mysteries shall be given again unto a repentant brother even up to the three of the second space

And the Saviour answered and said unto John: "If it is a brother who is not play-acting, but in truth longeth after God, if ye have given him many times the mysteries of the beginning and because of the necessity of the elements of the Fate he hath not done what is worthy of the mysteries of the Light-kingdom, then forgive him, let him pass through and give him the first mystery which is in the second space. Perhaps ye win the soul of that brother.

"And if he hath not done what is worthy of the mysteries of the Light and have committed transgression and diverse sins, and thereafter hath turned again and been in great repentance and hath renounced the whole world and ceased from all the sins of the world, and ye know with certainty that he doth not play-act but in truth longeth after God, then turn ye anew, forgive him, let him pass on through and give him the second mystery in the second space of the First Mystery. Perchance ye win the soul of that brother and he inheriteth the Light-kingdom.

"And again if he hath not done what is worthy of the mysteries, but hath been in transgression and diverse sins, and thereafter again hath turned and been in great repentance and hath renounced the whole world and the whole matter therein and ceased from the sins of the world, so that ye know truly that he is not play-acting but longeth truly after God, then turn ye anew, forgive him and receive his repentance, because the First Mystery is compassionate and merciful-minded; let also that man pass through and give him the three mysteries together which are in the second space of the First Mystery."

The limit of the power of the disciples to forgive sins

"If that man [then] transgresseth and is in diverse sins, from that moment onwards ye are not to forgive him nor to receive his repentance; but let him be among you as a stumbling-block and as a transgressor.

"For, amen, I say unto you: Those three mysteries will be witnesses for his last repentance, and he hath not repentance from this moment onwards. For, amen, I say unto you: The soul of that man will not be cast back into the world above from this moment onwards, but will be in the abodes of the dragon of the outer darkness."

A former saying explained

"For regarding the souls of such men I have spoken unto you afore time in a similitude, saying, 'If thy brother sinneth against thee, bring him over between thee alone and him. If he hearkeneth unto thee, thou wilt win thy brother; if he hearkeneth not unto thee, take with thee yet another. If he hearkeneth not unto thee and the other, bring him to the assembly. If he hearken not unto the others, let him be for you as a transgressor and as a stumbling-block.' — That is: If he is not usable in the first mystery, give him the second; and if he is not usable in the second give him the three, assembled together, which is 'the assembly'; and if he is not usable in the third mystery, let him be for you as a stumbling-block and as a transgressor."

Of the master-mystery of the forgiveness of sins

"And the word which I have spoken unto you afore time: 'So that through two to three witnesses every word may be established,' — it is this: Those three mysteries will witness his last repentance. And amen, I say unto you: If that man repenteth, no mystery can forgive him his sins, nor can his repentance be received, nor can he at all be hearkened to through any mystery, save through the first mystery of the First Mystery and through the mysteries of the Ineffable. It is these alone which will receive the repentance of that man and forgive his sins; for those mysteries are always compassionate, merciful-minded and forgiving."

Chapter 106

John continueth his questioning

When then the Saviour had said this, John continued again and said to the Saviour: "My Lord, suppose an exceedingly sinful brother who hath renounced the whole world and the whole matter therein and all its sins and all its cares, and we shall prove him and know that he is not in deceit and play-acting but in uprightness and in truth he longeth [after God], and we know that he hath become worthy of the mysteries of the second space or of the third, — desirest thou that we give him of the mysteries of the second space and of the third, before he hath at all received mysteries of the Inheritance of the Light or not? Desirest thou that we give or not?"

Further of the forgiveness of sins

And the Saviour answered and said unto John in the midst of the disciples: "If ye know with certainty that the man hath renounced the whole world and all its cares and all its associations and all its sins, and if ye know in truth that he is not in deceit, neither that he was play-acting nor that he was curious to know the mysteries, how they are brought to pass, but that he longeth after God in truth, hide them not from him, but give him of the mysteries of the second and third space and try even of what mystery he is worthy; and that of which he is worthy, give him and hide it not from him, for if ye hide it from him, ye may be guilty of a great condemnation.

"If ye give him once [of the mysteries] of the second space or of the third and he turneth again and sinneth, ye are to continue again the second time up to the third time. If he still sinneth, ye shall not continue to give him, for those three mysteries will be witnesses unto him for his last repentance. And amen, I say unto you: He who shall give that man anew mysteries of the second space or of the third, is guilty of a great condemnation. But let him be for you as a transgressor and as a stumbling-block.

"Amen, I say unto you: The soul of that man cannot be cast back into the world from this moment onwards; but his habitation is in the midst of the jaws of the dragon of the outer darkness, the region of howling and grinding of teeth. And at the dissolution of the world his soul will be frozen up [?] and perish in the violent cold and exceedingly violent fire and will be non-existent eternally.

"Even if he yet again turneth and renounceth the whole world and all its cares and all its sins, and he is in great citizenship and great repentance, no mystery can receive from him his repentance nor can it hearken unto him, to have mercy upon him and receive his repentance and forgive his sins, save the mystery of the First Mystery and the mystery of the Ineffable. It is these alone which will receive the repentance of that man and forgive his sins; for those mysteries are always compassionate, merciful-minded and forgiving of sins."

Chapter 107

John continueth his questioning

And when the Saviour had said this, John continued again and said: "My Lord, bear with me, if I question thee, and be not wroth with me, for I question concerning all things with surety and certainty for knowledge of the manner how we are to herald it to the men of the world."

And the Saviour answered and said unto John: "Question concerning all things on which thou questionest, and I will reveal them unto thee, face to face in openness without similitude, or with surety."

And John answered and said: "My Lord, if we go forth and herald it and come into a city or a village, and if the men of that city come forth to meet us without our knowing who they are, and if they receive us unto themselves in great deceit and great play-acting and bring us into their house, desiring to make trial of the mysteries of the Light-kingdom, and if they play-act with us in submission and we suppose that they long after God, and we give them the mysteries of the Light-kingdom, and if we thereafter know that they have not done what is worthy of the mystery, and we know that they have play-acted with us, and have been deceitful against us and that they have also made a show of the mysteries region by region, making trial of us and also of our mysteries, — what is then the thing which will befall such?"

Of pretenders who receive the mysteries

And the Saviour answered and said unto John: "If ye come into a city or a village, where ye enter into the house and they receive you unto themselves, give them a mystery. If they are worthy, ye will win their souls and they will inherit the Light-kingdom; but if they are not worthy but are deceitful against you, and if they also make a show of the mysteries, making trial of you and also of the mysteries, then invoke the first mystery of the first mystery which hath mercy on everyone, and say: Thou mystery, which we have given unto these impious and iniquitous souls who have not done what is worthy of thy mystery but have made a show of us, turn back [then] the mystery unto us and make them forever strangers to the mystery of thy kingdom. And shake ye off the dust of your feet as a witness against them, saying: May your souls be as the dust of your house. And amen, I say unto you: In that hour all the mysteries which ye have given unto them will return unto you, and all the words and all the mysteries of the region up to which they have received figures will be taken from them."

A former saying explained

"Concerning such men, therefore, have I afore time spoken unto you in similitude, saying: 'Where ye enter into a house and are received, say unto them: Peace be with you. And if they are worthy, let your peace come upon them; and if they are not worthy, let your peace return unto you.' — that is: If those men do what is worthy of the mysteries and in truth long after God, give them the mysteries of the Light-kingdom; but if they play-act with you and are deceitful against

you, without your having known it, and if ye give them the mysteries of the Light-kingdom, and again thereafter they make a show of the mysteries and they also make trial of you and of the mysteries, then perform the first mystery of the First Mystery, and it will turn back unto you all the mysteries which ye have given unto them, and it will make them strangers to the mysteries of the Light forever.

"And such men will not be led back to the world from this moment onwards; but amen, I say unto you: Their dwelling is in the midst of the jaws of the dragon of the outer darkness. And if they still at a time of repentance renounce the whole world and the whole matter therein and all the sins of the world, and they are in entire submission to the mysteries of the Light, no mystery can hearken unto them nor forgive their sins, save this same mystery of the Ineffable, which hath mercy on everyone and forgiveth every one his sins."

Chapter 108

Mary again questioneth Jesus

When Jesus had finished saying these words unto his disciples, Mary adored the feet of Jesus and kissed them. Mary said: "My Lord, bear with me, if I question thee, and be not wroth with me."

The Saviour answered and said unto Mary: "Question concerning what thou desirest to question, and I will reveal it unto thee in openness."

And Mary answered and said: "My Lord, suppose a good and excellent brother whom we have filled with all the mysteries of the Light, and that brother hath a brother or kinsman, in a word he hath in general any man, and this man is a sinner and impious or better he is no sinner, and such a man hath gone out of the body, and the heart of the good brother is grieved and mourneth over him, that he is in judgments and chastisements, — now, therefore, my Lord, what are we to do to remove him out of the chastisements and harsh judgments?"

And the Saviour answered and said unto Mary: "Concerning this word, therefore, I have already spoken unto you at another time, but hearken that I may say it again, so that ye may be perfected in all mysteries and be called 'the perfected in every fullness.'

How the souls of those who have come out of the body may be helped by those on earth

"Now, therefore, all men, sinners or better who are no sinners, not only if ye desire that they be taken out of the judgments and violent chastisements, but that they be removed into a righteous body and which will find the mysteries of the godhead, so that it goeth on high and inheriteth the Light-kingdom, — then perform the third mystery of the Ineffable and say: Carry ye the soul of this man of whom we think in our hearts, carry him out of all the chastisements of the rulers and haste ye quickly to lead him before the Virgin of Light; and in every month let the Virgin of Light seal him with a higher seal, and in every month let the Virgin of Light cast him into a body which will be righteous and good, so that it goeth on high and inheriteth the Light-kingdom.

"And if ye say this, amen, I say unto you: All who serve in all the orders of the judgments of the rulers hasten to hand over that soul from one to the other, until they lead it before the Virgin of Light. And the Virgin of Light sealeth it with the sign of the kingdom of the Ineffable and handeth it over to her receivers, and the receivers will cast it into a body which will be righteous and find the mysteries of the Light, so that it will be good and goeth on high and inheriteth the Light-kingdom. Lo, this is it on which ye question me."

Chapter 109

Mary continueth her questioning

And Mary answered and said: "Now, therefore, my Lord, hast thou then not brought mysteries into the world that man may not die through the death which is appointed him by the rulers of the Fate, — be it that it is appointed one to die by the sword or die by the waters or through tortures and torturings and acts of violence which are in the law, or through any other evil death, — hast thou then not brought mysteries into the world that man may not die with them through the rulers of the Fate, but that he may die by a sudden death, so that he endure no sufferings through such kinds of death? For they are exceedingly numerous who persecute us because of thee, and numerous those who persecute us because of thy name, in order that, if they torture us, we may speak the mystery and straightway go out of the body without having endured any sufferings at all."

How he who possesseth the mysteries can come forth out of the body without suffering

The Saviour answered and said unto all his disciples: "Concerning this word on which ye question me, I have spoken unto you at another time; but hearken again that I may say it unto you anew: Not only ye, but every man who will accomplish that first mystery of the First Mystery of the Ineffable, — he who, therefore, shall perform that mystery and accomplish it in all its figures and all its types and all its stations, in performing it, he will not come out of the body; but after he hath accomplished that mystery in all its figures and all its types, thereafter then at every time when he shall speak the name of that mystery, he will save himself from all that which is appointed him by the rulers of the Fate. And in that hour he will come forth out of the body of the matter of the rulers, and his soul will become a great light-stream, so that it soareth on high and penetrateth all the regions of the rulers and all the regions of the Light, until it reacheth the region of its kingdom. Neither giveth it answers nor apologies in any region at all, for it is without tokens."

Chapter 110

When then Jesus had said this, Mary continued, threw herself at Jesus' feet, kissed them and said: "My Lord, still will I question thee. Reveal [it] unto us and hide [it] not from us."

Jesus answered and said unto Mary: "Question on what ye question, and I will reveal [it] unto you in openness without similitude."

Mary continueth her questioning

Mary answered and said: "My Lord, hast thou then not brought mysteries into the world because of poverty and riches, and because of weakness and strength, and because of... and healthy bodies, in a word because of all such, so that, if we go into the regions of the land, and they do not have faith in us and they hearken not unto our words, and we perform any such mysteries in those regions, they may know in truth that we herald the words [of the God] of the universe?"

The Saviour answered and said unto Mary in the midst of the disciples: "Concerning this mystery on which ye question me, I have given it unto you at another time; but I will repeat it and speak the word unto you."

The mystery of the raising of the dead

"Now, therefore, Mary, not only ye, but every man who shall accomplish the mystery of the raising of the dead, — that which healeth the demons and all pains and all sicknesses and the blind and the lame and the maimed and the dumb and the deaf, which I have given unto you afore time, — he who shall receive [that] mystery and accomplish it, thereafter then, if he asks for all things, for poverty and riches, for weakness and strength, for ... and healthy body, and for all healings of the body and for the raising of the dead and for healing the lame and the blind and the deaf and the dumb and all sicknesses and all pains, — in a word, he who shall accomplish that mystery and ask for all the things which I have just said, then will they quickly come to pass for him."

The disciples became frenzied at the sublimity of the prospect

When then the Saviour had said this, the disciples came forward, cried out all together and said: "O Saviour, thou hath made us very exceedingly frenzied because of the great deeds of which thou tellest us; and because thou hast borne up our souls, they have pressed to go forth out of us unto thee, for we issue from thee. Now, therefore, because of these great deeds of which thou tellest us, our souls have become frenzied and they have pressed very exceedingly, yearning to go forth out of us on high to the region of thy kingdom."

Chapter 111

How the disciples shall make proclamation

When then the disciples had said this, the Saviour continued again and said unto his disciples: "If ye go into cities or kingdoms or countries, proclaim first unto them, saying: Search ever and cease not, until ye find the mysteries of the Light which will lead you into the Light-kingdom. Say unto them: Beware of the doctrines of error. For many will come in my name and say: It is I. And it is not I, and they will lead many astray."

What mysteries they shall give

"Now, therefore, unto all men who come unto you and have faith in you and hearken unto your words and do what is worthy of the mysteries of the Light, give the mysteries of the Light and hide them not from them. And unto him who is worthy of the higher mysteries, give them, and to him who is worthy of the lower mysteries, give them, and hide not anything from anyone."

The mystery of the raising of the dead not to be given to any

"The mystery of the raising of the dead and of the healing of the sick, on the other hand, give unto no one nor give instruction in it, for that mystery belongeth to the rulers, it and all its namings. For this cause, therefore, give it unto no one, nor give instruction in it until ye establish the faith in the whole world, in order that, if ye come into cities or into countries, and they do not receive you unto themselves, and do not have faith, and do not hearken unto your words, ye may raise the dead in those regions and heal the lame and the blind and manifold of sicknesses in those regions. And through all such they will have faith in you, that ye herald the God of the universe, and will have faith in all your words. For this cause, therefore, have I given unto you that mystery, until ye establish the faith in the whole world."

When then the Saviour had said this, he continued again in the discourse and said unto Mary: "Now, therefore, hearken, Mary, concerning the word on which thou hast question me: Who constraineth the man until he sinneth? Now, therefore, hearken..."

Of the constitution of man

"When the babe is born, the power is feeble in it, and the soul is feeble in it, and also the counterfeiting spirit is feeble in it; in a word, the three together are feeble, without any one of them sensing anything, whether good or evil, because of the load of forgetfulness which is very heavy. Moreover the body also is feeble. And the babe eateth of the delights of the world of the rulers; and the power draweth into itself from the portion of the power which is in the delights; and the soul draweth into itself from the portion of the soul which is in the delights; and the counterfeiting spirit draweth into itself from the portion of the evil which is in the delights and in its lusts. And on the other hand the body draweth into itself the matter which senseth not, which is in the delights. The destiny on the contrary taketh nothing from the delights, because it is not mingled with them, but it departeth again in the condition in which it cometh into the world.

"And little by little the power and the soul and the counterfeiting spirit grow, and every one of them senseth according to its nature: The power senseth to seek after the light of the height; the soul on the other hand senseth to seek after the region of righteousness which is mixed, which is the region of the commixture; the counterfeiting spirit on the other hand seeketh after all evils and lusts and all sins; the body on the contrary senseth nothing unless it taketh up force out of the matter.

"And straightway the three develop sense, every one according to its nature. And the retributive receivers assign the servitors to follow them and be witnesses of all the sins which they commit, with a view to the manner and method how they will chastise them in the judgments."

Of the counterfeiting spirit

"And after this the counterfeiting spirit contriveth and senseth all sins and the evil which the rulers of the great Fate have commanded for the soul, and it maketh them for the soul.

"And the inner power stirreth the soul to seek after the region of the Light and the whole godhead; and the counterfeiting spirit leadeth away the soul and compelleth it continually to do all its lawless deeds, all its mischiefs and all its sin, and is persistently allotted to the soul and is hostile to it, and making it do all this evil and all these sins.

"And it goadeth on the retributive servitors, so that they are witnesses in all the sins which it will make it do. Moreover also if it will rest in the night or by day, it stirreth it in dreams or in lusts of the world, and maketh it to lust after all the things of the world. In a word, it driveth it into all the things which the rulers have commanded for it and it is hostile to the soul, making it do what pleaseth it not.

"Now, therefore, Mary, this is in fact the foe of the soul, and this compelleth it until it doeth all sins."

The state of the sinful soul after death

"Now, therefore, if the time of that man is completed, first cometh forth the destiny and leadeth the man unto death through the rulers and their bonds with which they are bound through the Fate.

"And thereafter the retributive receivers come and lead that soul out of the body. And thereafter the retributive receivers spend three days circling round with that soul in all the regions and dispatch it to all the aeons of the world. And the counterfeiting spirit and the destiny follow that soul; and the power returneth to the Virgin of Light.

"And after three days the retributive receivers lead down that soul to the Amente of the chaos; and when they bring it down to the chaos, they hand it over to those who chastize. And the retributive receivers return unto their own regions according to the economy of the works of the rulers concerning the coming-forth of the souls.

"And the counterfeiting spirit becometh the receiver of the soul, being assigned unto it and transferring it according to the chastisement because of the sins which it hath made it commit, and is in great enmity to the soul.

"And when the soul hath finished the chastisements in the chaos according to the sins which it hath committed, the counterfeiting spirit leadeth it forth out of the chaos, being assigned unto it and transferring it to every region because of the sins which it hath committed; and it leadeth it forth on the way of the rulers of the Middle. And when it reacheth them, the rulers question it on the mysteries of the destiny; and if it hath not found them, they question their destiny. And those rulers chastise that soul according to the sins of which it is guilty. I will tell you the type of their chastisements at the expansion of the universe."

How a sinful soul is brought back to birth

"When, therefore, the time of the chastisements of that soul in the judgments of the rulers of the Middle shall be completed, the counterfeiting spirit leadeth the soul up out of all the regions of the rulers

of the Middle and bringeth it before the light of the sun according to the commandment of the First Man, Yew, and bringeth it before the judge, the Virgin of Light. And she proveth that soul and findeth that it is a sinning soul, and casteth her light-power into it for its standing-upright and because of the body and the community of sense, — the type of which I will tell you at the expansion of the universe. And the Virgin of Light sealeth that soul and handeth it over to one of her receivers and will have it cast into a body which is suitable to the sins which it hath committed.

"And amen, I say unto you: They will not discharge that soul from the changes of the body until it hath yielded its last circuit according to its merit. Of all these then will I tell you their type and the type of the bodies into which it will be cast according to the sins of each soul. All this will I tell you when I shall have told you the expansion of the universe."

Chapter 112

Of the ascension after death of the good soul that hath received the mysteries

Jesus continued again in the discourse and said: "If on the contrary it is a soul which hath not hearkened unto the counterfeiting spirit in all its works, but hath become good and hath received the mysteries of the Light which are in the second space or even those which are in the third space which is within, when the time [of the coming-forth] of that soul out of the body is completed, then the counterfeiting spirit followeth that soul, it and the destiny; and it followeth it on the way on which it will go above.

"And before it removeth itself above, it uttereth the mystery of the undoing of the seals and all the bonds of the counterfeiting spirit with which the rulers have bound it to the soul; and when it is uttered, the bonds of the counterfeiting spirit undo themselves, and it ceaseth to come into that soul and releaseth the soul according to the command-

ments which the rulers of the great Fate have commanded it, saying: 'Release not this soul until it tell thee the mystery of the undoing of all the seals with which we have bound thee to the soul.'

"If then the soul shall have uttered the mystery of the undoing of the seals and of all the bonds of the counterfeiting spirit, and if it ceaseth to come into the soul and ceaseth to be bound to it, then it uttereth in that moment a mystery and releaseth the destiny to its region to the rulers who are on the way of the Middle. And it uttereth the mystery and releaseth the counterfeiting spirit to the rulers of the Fate to the region in which it was bound to it.

"And in that moment it becometh a great light-stream, shining exceedingly, and the retributive receivers who have led it forth out of the body are afraid of the light of that soul and fall on their faces. And in that moment that soul becometh a great light-stream, it becometh entirely wings of light, and penetrateth all the regions of the rulers and all the orders of the Light, until it reacheth the region of its kingdom up to which it hath received mysteries."

Of the state after death of one who hath received the mysteries, and yet hath transgressed

"If on the other hand it is a soul which hath received mysteries in the first space which is without, and if after it hath received the mysteries it hath accomplished them, it [then] turneth and committeth sin after the accomplishing of the mysteries, and if the time of the coming-forth of that soul is completed, then the retributive receivers come to lead that soul out of the body.

"And the destiny and the counterfeiting spirit follow that soul. Because the counterfeiting spirit is bound to it with the seals and the bonds of the rulers, it followeth thus that soul which travelleth on the ways with the counterfeiting spirit.

"It uttereth the mystery of the undoing of all the bonds and all the seals which the rulers have bound the counterfeiting spirit to the soul. And when the soul uttereth the mystery of the undoing of the seals,

straightway the bonds of the seals which are bound in the counterfeiting spirit to the soul undo themselves. And when the soul uttereth the mystery of the undoing of the seals, straightway the counterfeiting spirit undoeth itself and ceaseth to be assigned to the soul. And in that moment the soul uttereth a mystery and restraineth the counterfeiting spirit and the destiny and dischargeth them which follow it. But no one of them is in its power; but it is in their power.

"And in that moment the receivers of that soul come with the mysteries which it have received, come and snatch that soul out of the hands of the retributive receivers, and the [latter] receivers go back to the works of the rulers for the purpose of the economy of the leading-forth of the souls.

"And the receivers of that soul on the other hand who belong to the Light, become wings of light for that soul and become vestures of light for it and they do not lead it into the chaos, because it is not lawful to lead into the chaos souls which have received mysteries, but they lead it on the way of the rulers of the Middle. And when it reacheth the rulers of the Middle, those rulers meeth the soul, they being in great fear and violent fire and with different faces, in a word in great immeasurable fear."

The apology of the rulers of the ways of the Middle

"And in that moment the soul uttereth the mystery of their apology. And they are exceedingly afraid and fall on their faces, being in fear of the mystery which it hath uttered, and of their apology. And that soul surrendereth their destiny, saying unto them: Take your destiny! I come not to your regions from this moment onwards. I have become a stranger unto you for ever, being about to go unto the region of my inheritance."

The apology of the rulers of the Fate

"And when the soul shall have said this, the receivers of the Light fly with it on high and lead it into the aeons of the Fate, it giving every

region its apology and its seals, — which I will tell you at the expansion of the universe. And it giveth the counterfeiting spirit to the rulers and telleth them the mystery of the bonds with which it is bound to it, and sayeth unto them: There have ye your counterfeiting spirit! I come not to your region from this moment onwards. I have become a stranger unto you for ever. And it giveth every one his seal and his apology."

Of the ascension of that soul into the Inheritance

"And when the soul shall have said this, the receivers of the Light fly with it on high and lead it out of the aeons of the Fate and lead it up into all the Aeons [above], it giving to every region its apology and the apology of all the regions and the seals to the tyrants of the king, Adamas. And it giveth the apology of all the rulers of all the regions of the Left, — whose collective apologies and seals I will one day tell you when I shall tell you the expansion of the universe.

"And moreover those receivers lead that soul to the Virgin of Light and soul giveth the Virgin of Light and seals and the glory of the songs of praise. And the Virgin of Light and also the seven other Virgins of the Light together prove that soul and find together their signs in it and their seals and their baptisms and their chrism. And the Virgin of Light sealeth that soul and the receivers of the Light baptize that soul and give it the spiritual chrism; and every one of the Virgins of the Light sealeth it with her seals.

"And moreover the receivers of the Light hand it over to the great Sabaoth, the Good, who is at the gate of the Life in the region of those of the Right, who is called 'Father.' And that soul giveth him the glory of his songs of praise and his seals and his apologies. And Sabaoth the Great and Good sealeth it with his seals. And the soul giveth its science and the glory of the songs of praise and the seals to the whole region of those of the Right. They all seal it with their seals; and Melchisedec, the great Receiver of the light who is in the region of those of the Right, sealeth that soul and all the receivers of Melchisedec seal that soul and lead it into the Treasury of the Light.

"And it giveth the glory and the honour and the laud of the songs of praise and all the seals of all the regions of the Light. And all those of the region of the Treasury of the Light seal it with their seals and it goeth unto the region of the Inheritance."

Chapter 113

When then the Saviour had said this unto his disciples he said unto them: "Understand ye in what manner I discourse with you?"

Mary interpreteth from former sayings

And Mary again started forward and said: "Yea my Lord, I understand in what manner thou dost discourse with me, and I will comprehend them all [sc. thy words]. Now, therefore, concerning these words which thou sayest, my mind hath brought forward four thoughts in me and my light-man hath led me and exulted and seethed, desiring to come forth out of me and enter into thee. Now, therefore, my Lord, hearken that I may tell thee the four thoughts which have arisen in me."

The piece of money which was brought unto Jesus

"The first thought hath arisen in me concerning the word which thou hast spoken: 'Now, therefore, the soul giveth the apology and seal unto all the rulers who are in the region of the king, the Adamas, and giveth the apology and the honour and the glory of all their seals and the songs of praise to the region of the Light.' — Concerning this word then thou hast spoken unto us afore time, when they brought thee the piece of money and thou didst see that it was of silver and copper and didst ask: 'Whose is this image?' They said: 'The king's.' And when thou sawest that it was of silver and copper mixed, thou saidst: 'Give therefore the king's unto the king and God's unto God,' — that is: If the soul receiveth mysteries, it giveth the apology to all the rulers and to the region of the king, the Adamas; and the soul giveth the honour and the glory to all those of the region of the Light. And the word: 'It

hath glistened, when thou didst see that it is made up of silver and copper,' — it is the type thereof, that in it [sc. the soul] is the power of the Light, which is the refined silver, and that in it is the counterfeiting spirit, which is the material copper. This, my Lord, is the first thought."

A saying of Paul

"The second thought, on the other hand, is that which thou hast just said unto us concerning the soul which receiveth the mysteries: 'If it cometh into the region of the rulers of the way of the Middle, they come forth to meet it in exceedingly great fear and they are afraid of it. And the soul giveth the mystery of the fear unto them and they are afraid before it. And it giveth the destiny to its region, and it giveth the counterfeiting spirit to its own region, and it giveth the apology and the seals to every one of the rulers who are on the ways, and it giveth the honour and the glory and the laud of the seals and the songs of praise to all those of the region of the Light.' Concerning this word, my Lord, thou hast spoken afore time through the mouth of our brother Paul: 'Give tax to whom tax is due, give fear to whom fear is due, give tribute to whom tribute is due, give honour to whom honour is due, and give laud to whom laud is due, and owe not any other anything,' — that is, my Lord: The soul which receiveth mysteries giveth apology to all regions. This, my lord, is the second thought."

The foes of one's own house

"The third thought on the other hand concerning the word which thou hast afore time spoken unto us, 'The counterfeiting spirit is hostile to the soul, making it do all sins and all mischiefs, and it transferreth it in the chastisements because of all the sins which it hath made it commit; in a word, it is hostile to the soul in every way,' — concerning this word, therefore, thou hast said unto us afore time: 'The foes of the man are the dwellers in his house,' — that is; The dwellers in the house of the soul are the counterfeiting spirit and the destiny, which

are hostile to the soul the whole time, making it commit all sin and all iniquities. Lo this, my Lord, is the third thought."

A former saying concerning rebirth

"The fourth thought on the other hand concerning the word which thou hast said, 'If the soul goeth forth out of the body and travelleth on the way with the counterfeiting spirit, and if it hath not found the mystery of the undoing of all the bonds and the seals which are bound to the counterfeiting spirit, so that it may cease to haunt or be assigned to it, — if it then hath not found it, the counterfeiting spirit leadeth the soul to the Virgin of Light, the judge; and the judge, the Virgin of Light, proveth the soul and findeth that it hath sinned and, as she also hath not found the mysteries of the Light with it, she handeth it over to one of her receivers, and her receiver leadeth it and casteth it into the body, and it cometh not out of the changes of the body before it hath yielded its last circuit.' Concerning this word, then my Lord, thou hast said unto us afore time: 'Be reconciled with thy foe as long as thou art on the way with him, lest perchance thy foe hand thee over to the judge and the judge hand thee over to the servant and the servant cast thee into prison, and thou shalt not come forth out of that region till thou hast yielded the last farthing.'

"Because of this manifestly is thy word: Every soul which cometh forth out of the body and travelleth on the way with the counterfeiting spirit and findeth not the mystery of the undoing of all the seals and all the bonds, so that it may undo itself from the counterfeiting spirit which is bound to it, — that soul which hath not found mysteries of the Light and hath not found the mysteries of detachment from the counterfeiting spirit which is bound to it, — if then it hath not found it, the counterfeiting spirit leadeth that soul to the Virgin of Light, and the Virgin of Light, yea that judge, handeth over that soul to one of her receivers, and her receiver casteth it into the sphere of the aeons, and it cometh not out of the changes of the body before it hath yielded the last circuit which is appointed for it. This then, my Lord, is the fourth thought."

Chapter 114

It came to pass when Jesus heard Mary say these words, he said: "Well spoken, all-blessed Mary, spiritual [one]. These are the solutions of the words which I have spoken."

Mary continueth to question Jesus

Mary answered and said: "Still, my Lord, do I question thee, because from now on I will begin to question thee on all things with sureness. For this cause, therefore, my Lord, be patient with us and reveal unto us all things on which we shall question thee for the sake of the manner how my brethren are to herald it to the whole race of men."

And when she had said this to the Saviour, the Saviour answered and said unto her in great compassion towards her: "Amen, amen, I say unto you: Not only will I reveal unto you all things on which ye shall question me, but from now on I will reveal unto you other things on which ye have not thought to question, which have not entered into the heart of man, and which also all the Gods, who are below man, know not. Now, therefore, Mary, question on what thou mayest question, and I will reveal it unto thee face to face without similitude."

Chapter 115

And Mary answered and said, "My Lord, in what type then do the baptisms forgive sins? I heard thee say: 'The retributive servitors follow the soul, being witnesses to it for all the sins which it committeth, that they may convict it in the judgments.' Now, therefore, my Lord, do the mysteries of the baptisms wipe out the sins which are in the hands of the retributive servitors so that they forget them? Now, therefore, my Lord, tell unto us the type, how they forgive sins; nay we desire to know it with sureness."

Of the retributive servitors

And the Saviour answered and said unto Mary: "Finely hast thou spoken. The servitors indeed are they who bear witness to all sins, but they abide in the judgments, seizing the souls and convicting all the souls of sinners who have received no mysteries; and they keep them fast in the chaos, chastizing them. And those retributive receivers cannot overstep the chaos to reach the orders which are above the chaos, and convict the souls which come forth out of those regions. Now then it is not lawful to use force on the souls which receive mysteries, and lead them into the chaos, so that the retributive servitors may convict them. But the retributive servitors convict the souls of the sinners and they keep fast those who have received no mysteries which may lead them out of the chaos. The souls on the other hand which receive mysteries, — they have no power of convicting them, because they do not come forth out of their regions, and also, if they come forth into their regions, they are not able to obstruct them; nay, they cannot lead them into that chaos."

How the soul of the sinner is stamped with his sins

"Hearken moreover that I may tell you the word in truth, in what type the mystery of baptism forgiveth sins. Now, therefore, if the souls sin when they are still in the world, the retributive servitors indeed come and are witnesses of all the sins which the soul committeth, lest in sooth they should come forth out of the regions of the chaos, in order that they may convict them in the judgments which are outside the chaos. And the counterfeiting spirit becometh witness of all the sins which the soul shall commit, in order that it may convict it in the judgments which are outside the chaos, not only that it may bear witness of them, but — all the sins of the souls — it sealeth the sins and maketh them fast on to the soul, in order that all the rulers of the chastisements of the sinners may recognize it, that it is a sinning soul, and that they may know of the number of sins which it hath committed, by the seals which the counterfeiting spirit hath made fast on to it, so that it shall be chastized according to the number of sins which it hath committed. This do they with all sinning souls."

How the baptisms purify sins

"Now, therefore, he who shall receive the mysteries of the baptisms, then the mystery of them becometh a great, exceedingly violent, wise fire and it burneth up the sins and entereth into the soul secretly and consumeth all the sins which the counterfeiting spirit hath made fast on to it."

The separation of the portions by the mystery of baptism

"And when it hath finished purifying all the sins which the counterfeiting spirit hath made fast on to the soul, it entereth into the body secretly and pursueth all the pursuers secretly and separateth them off on the side of the portion of the body. For it pursueth the counterfeiting spirit and the destiny and separateth them off from the power and from the soul and putteth them on the side of the body, so that it separateth off the counterfeiting spirit and the destiny and the body into one portion; the soul and power on the other hand it separateth into another. The mystery of baptism on the contrary remaineth in the midst of the two, continually separating them from one another, so that it maketh them clean and purifieth them, in order that they may not be stained by matter.

"Now, therefore, Mary, this is the way in which the mysteries of the baptisms forgive sins and all iniquities."

Chapter 116

When then the Saviour had said this, he said unto his disciples: "Understand ye in what manner I discourse with you?"

Mary interpreteth the same from a former saying

Then Mary started forward and said: "Yea, my Lord, in truth I enquire closely into all the words which thou sayest. Concerning the word then of the forgiveness of sins thou hast spoken unto us in simili-

tude afore time, saying: 'I am come to cast fire on the earth,' and again: 'What will I that it burn?' And again thou hast distinguished it clearly, saying: 'I have a baptism, to baptize in it; and how shall I endure until it is accomplished? Think ye I am come to cast peace on the earth? Nay, but I am come to cast division. For from now on five will be in one house; three will be divided against two, and two against three.' This, my Lord, is the word which thou hast spoken clearly.

"The word indeed which thou hast spoken: 'I am come to cast fire on the earth, and what will I that it burn?' — That is, my Lord: Thou hast brought the mysteries of the baptisms into the world, and thy pleasure is that they should consume all the sins of the soul and purify them. And thereafter again thou hast distinguished it clearly, saying: 'I have a baptism, to baptize in it; and how shall I endure until it is accomplished.' That is: Thou wilt not remain in the world until the baptisms are accomplished and purify the perfect souls.

"And moreover the word which thou hast spoken unto us afore time: 'Think ye I am come to cast peace on the earth? Nay, but I am come to cast division. For from now on five will be in one house; three will be divided against two, and two against three.' That is: Thou hast brought the mystery of the baptisms into the world, and it hath effected a division in the bodies of the world, because it hath separated the counterfeiting spirit and the body and the destiny into one portion; the soul and the power on the other hand it hath separated into another portion; — that is: Three will be against two, and two against three."

And when Mary had said this, the Saviour said: "Well said, thou spiritual and light-pure Mary. This is the solution of the word."

Chapter 117

Mary further questioneth Jesus

Mary answered again and said: "My Lord, I will still continue to question thee. Now, therefore, my Lord, bear with me questioning thee. Lo, in openness have we known the manner in which the baptisms forgive sins. Now on the other hand the mystery of these three spaces and the mysteries of this First Mystery and the mysteries of the Ineffable, in what manner do they forgive sins? Do they forgive in the form of baptisms, or not?"

Of the forgiveness of sins according to the higher mysteries

The Saviour answered again and said: "Nay, but all the mysteries of the three spaces forgive the soul in all the regions of the rulers all the sins which the soul hath committed from the beginning onwards. They forgive it, and moreover they forgive the sins which it thereafter will commit, until the time up to which every one of the mysteries shall be effective, — the time up to which every one of the mysteries shall be effective I will tell you at the expansion of the universe.

"And moreover the mystery of the First Mystery and the mysteries of the Ineffable forgive the soul in all the regions of the rulers all the sins and all the iniquities which the soul hath committed; and not only do they forgive it all, but they impute unto it no sin from this hour unto all eternity, because of the gift of that great mystery and its prodigiously great glory."

Chapter 118

When then the Saviour had said this, he said unto his disciples: "Understand ye in what manner I speak with you?"

Mary interpreteth the same from Psalm XXXI [Modern Psalm 32]

And Mary answered again and said: "Yea my Lord, already have I seized on all the words which thou sayest. Now, therefore, my Lord, concerning the word that thou sayest: 'All the mysteries of the three spaces forgive sins and cover their [sc. the souls'] iniquities,' — David, the prophet, then hath prophesied afore time concerning this word, saying: 'Blessed are they whose sins are forgiven and whose iniquities are covered.'

"And the word which thou hast spoken: 'The mystery of the First Mystery and the mystery of the Ineffable forgive all men who shall receive those mysteries, not only the sins which they have committed from the beginning onwards, but also they impute them not to them from this hour unto all eternity.' Concerning this word David hath prophesied afore time, saying: 'Blessed are those to whom the Lord God will not impute sins.' — that is: Sins will not be imputed from this hour to those who have received the mysteries of the First Mystery and who have received the mystery of the Ineffable."

He said: "Well said, Mary, thou spiritual and light-pure Mary. This is the solution of the word."

And Mary continued again and said: "My Lord, if the man receiveth mysteries from the mysteries of the First Mystery and again turneth and sinneth and transgresseth, and if he thereafter again turneth and repenteth and prayeth in any [mystery] of his mystery, will it be forgiven him, or not?"

Of the forgiveness even unto twelve times of those who have received the mysteries of the First Mystery

The Saviour answered and said unto Mary: "Amen, amen, I say unto you: Every one who shall receive the mysteries of the First Mystery, if he again turneth and transgresseth twelve times and again twelve times repenteth, praying in the mystery of the First Mystery, it will be forgiven.

"But if after the twelve times he again transgresseth and turneth and transgresseth, it will not be forgiven him forever, so that he should turn himself to any [mystery] of this mystery; and this [man] hath not repentance unless he receiveth the mysteries of the Ineffable, which have compassion at every time and forgive at every time."

Chapter 119

Mary continued again and said: "My Lord, but if on the other hand they who have received the mysteries of the First Mystery turn and transgress, and if they come out of the body before they have repented, will they inherit the kingdom or not, because indeed they have received the gift of the First Mystery?"

Of such initiated who sin and die without repentance

The Saviour answered and said unto Mary: "Amen, amen, I say unto you: Every man who hath received mysteries in the First Mystery, having transgressed for the first and second and the third time, and if he cometh out of the body before he hath repented, his judgment is far sorer than all the judgments; for his dwelling is in the midst of the jaws of the dragon of the outer darkness, and at the end of all this he will be frozen up [?] in the chastisements and perish for ever, because he hath received the gift of the First Mystery and hath not abided in it [sc. the gift]."

Of the unending forgiveness of those who have received the mystery of the Ineffable

Mary answered and said: "My Lord, all men who shall receive the mysteries of the mystery of the Ineffable, and have turned again, have transgressed and have ceased in their faith, and again thereafter, when they are still in life, have turned and have repented, how many times will it be forgiven them?"

The Saviour answered and said unto Mary: "Amen, amen, I say unto you: To every man who shall receive the mysteries of the Ineffable, not only if he transgresseth once, turneth again and repenteth, will it be forgiven, but if at any time he transgresseth, and if, when still in life, he turneth again and repenteth, without play-acting, and again if he turneth and repenteth and prayeth in any of his mysteries, then will it be forgiven him, because he hath received of the gift of the mysteries of the Ineffable, and moreover because those mysteries are compassionate and forgive at every time."

And Mary answered again and said unto Jesus: "My Lord, those who shall receive the mysteries of the Ineffable, and have again turned, have transgressed and have ceased in their faith and are moreover come out of the body before they have repented, what will befall such?"

Of such initiated who sin and die without repentance

And the Saviour answered and said unto Mary: "Amen, Amen, I say unto you: All men who shall receive the mysteries of the Ineffable, — blessed indeed are the souls which shall receive of those mysteries; but if they turn and transgress and come out of the body before they have repented, the judgment of those men is sorer than all the judgments, and it is exceedingly violent, even if those souls are new and it is their first time for coming into the world. They will not return to the changes of the bodies from that hour onwards and will not be able to do anything, but they will be cast out into the outer darkness and perish and be non-existent forever."

Chapter 120

Mary interpreteth the same from a former saying

And when the Saviour had said this, he said unto his disciples: "Understand ye in what manner I speak with you?"

Mary answered and said: "I have seized on the words which thou hast said. Now, therefore, my Lord, this is the word which thou hast said: 'They who shall receive the mysteries of the Ineffable, — blessed indeed are those souls; but if they turn, transgress, and cease in their faith, and if they go forth out of the body without having repented, they are no more fit from this hour onwards to return to the changes of the body, nor for anything at all, but they are cast out into the outer darkness, they will perish in that region and be non-existent for ever,' — concerning [this] word thou hast spoken unto us afore time, saying: 'Salt is good; but if the salt becometh sterile, with what are they to salt it? It is fit neither for the dunghill nor for the earth; but they throw it away.' That is: Blessed are all the souls which shall receive of the mysteries of the Ineffable; but if they once transgress, they are not fit to return to the body henceforth from this hour onwards nor for anything at all, but they are cast into the outer darkness and perish in that region."

And when she had said this, the Saviour said: "Well spoken, thou spiritual light-pure Mary. This is the solution of the word."

And Mary continued again and said: "My Lord, all men who have received the mysteries of the First Mystery and the mysteries of the Ineffable, those who have not transgressed, but whose faith in the mysteries was in sincerity, without play-acting, — they then have again sinned through the compulsion of the Fate and have again turned and repented and again prayed in any of the mysteries, how often will it be forgiven them?"

Of the unending compassion of the great mysteries for the repentant

And the Saviour answered and said unto Mary in the midst of his disciples: "Amen, amen, I say unto you: All men who shall receive the mysteries of the Ineffable and moreover the mysteries of the First Mystery, sin every time through the compulsion of the Fate, and if they, when they are still in life, turn and repent and abide in any of their mysteries, it will be forgiven them at every time, because those mysteries are compassionate and forgiving for all time. For this cause then have I said unto you before: Those mysteries will not only forgive them their sins which they have committed from the beginning onwards, but they do not impute them to them from this hour onwards, — of which I have said unto you that they receive repentance at any time, and that they also will forgive the sins which they commit anew."

Of the unrepentant

"If on the other hand those who shall receive mysteries of the mystery of the Ineffable and of the mysteries of the First Mystery turn and sin and come out of the body without having repented, then they will be even as those will be who have transgressed and not repented. Their dwelling also is in the midst of the jaws of the dragon of the outer darkness and they will perish and be non-existent for ever. For this cause have I said unto you: All men who shall receive the mysteries, if they knew the time when they come out of the body, would watch themselves and not sin, in order that they may inherit the Light-kingdom for ever."

Chapter 121

When then the Saviour had said this unto his disciples, he said unto them, "Understand ye in what manner I speak with you?"

Mary interpreteth from a former saying

Mary answered and said: "Yea, my Lord, with precision have I precisely followed all the words which thou hast said. Concerning this word then thou hast spoken unto us afore time: 'If the householder knew at what hour in the night the thief cometh to break into the house, he would keep awake and not suffer the man to break into his house."

When then Mary had said this, the Saviour said, "Well said, thou spiritual Mary. This is the word."

The Saviour continued again and said unto his disciples: "Now, therefore, herald ye unto all men who shall receive mysteries in the light, and speak unto them, saying: Keep watch over yourselves and sin not, lest ye heap evil on evil and go out of the body without having repented and become strangers to the Light-kingdom for ever."

When the Saviour had said this, Mary answered and said, "My Lord, great is the compassion of those mysteries which forgive sins at every time."

If even men on earth are compassionate, how much more then the highest mysteries?

The Saviour answered and said unto Mary in the midst of the disciples, "If today a king who is a man of the world giveth a gift to men of his like, and also forgiveth murderers and those who have intercourse with males, and the rest of the very grievous sins which are deserving of death, — if it becometh him who is a man of the world, to have done this, much more then have the Ineffable and the First Mystery, who are the lords of the universe, the authority to act in all things as it pleaseth them, that they forgive every one who shall receive mysteries.

"Or if on the other hand a king today investeth a soldier with a royal vesture and sendeth him into foreign regions, and he committeth murders and other grievous sins which are deserving of death, then they will not impute them to him, and are not able to do him any evil because he is invested with the royal vesture, — how much more then those who wear the mysteries of the vestures of the Ineffable and those of the First Mystery, who are lords over all those of the height and all those of the depth!"

Chapter 122

Jesus trieth Peter

Thereafter Jesus saw a woman who came to make repentance. He had baptized her three times, and yet she had not done what was worthy of the baptisms. And the Saviour desired to try Peter, to see if he was compassionate and forgiving, as he had commanded them. He said unto Peter: "Lo, three times have I baptized this soul, and yet at this third time she hath not done what is worthy of the mysteries of the Light. Wherefor then doth she make her body good for nothing? Now, therefore, Peter, perform the mystery which cutteth off the souls from the Inheritances of the Light; perform that mystery in order that it may cut off the soul of this woman from the inheritance of the Light."

When then the Saviour had said this, he tried [Peter] to see whether he was compassionate and forgiving.

When then the Saviour had said this, Peter said: "My Lord, let her yet this time, that we may give her the higher mysteries; and if she is fit, then hast thou let her inherit the Light-kingdom, but if she is not fit, then hast thou [to] cut her off from the Light-kingdom."

When then Peter had said this, the Saviour knew that Peter was compassionate as he and forgiving.

When then all this was said, the Saviour said unto his disciples, "Have ye understood all these words and the type of this woman?"

Mary interpreteth the incident from a former saying

Mary answered and said, "My Lord, I have understood the mysteries of the things which have fallen to this woman's lot. Concerning the things then which have fallen to her lot, thou hast spoken unto us afore time in similitude, saying: 'A man owned a fig-tree in his vineyard; and he came to look for its fruit, and he found not a single one on it. He said to the vine-dresser: Lo, three years do I come to look for fruit on this fig-tree, and I have not any produce at all from it. Cut it down then; why doth it make the ground also good for nothing? But he answered and said unto him: My lord, have patience with it still this year, until I dig round it and give it dung; and if it beareth in another year, thou hast let it, but if thou dost not find any fruit at all, then hast thou [to] cut it down.' Lo, my Lord, this is the solution of the word."

The Saviour answered and said unto Mary: "Well said, spiritual [one]. This is [the solution of] the word."

Chapter 123

Mary continued again and said unto the Saviour: "My Lord, a man who hath received mysteries and hath not done what is worthy of them but he hath turned and hath sinned, thereafter he hath again repented and hath been in great repentance, — is it then lawful for my brethren to renew for him the mystery which he hath received, or rather give him a mystery out of the lower mysteries, — is it lawful, or not?"

In the case of the repentance only higher mysteries than those previously received can remit sins

The Saviour answered and said unto Mary: "Amen, amen, I say unto you: Neither the mystery which he hath received nor the lower hearken unto him can forgive his sins; but it is the mysteries which are higher than those which he hath received, which hearken unto him and forgive his sins. Now, therefore, Mary, let thy brethren give him the mystery which is higher than that which he hath received, and they are to accept his repentance from him and forgive his sins, — the latter indeed because he hath received it once more, and the former, because he hath towered over the lower mysteries upward, — the latter indeed hearkeneth not unto him to forgive his sin; but it is the mystery which is higher than that which he hath received, that forgiveth his sins. But if on the other hand he hath received the three mysteries in the two spaces or in the third from within, and he hath turned and transgressed, no mystery hearkeneth unto him to help him in his repentance, neither the higher nor the lower, save the mystery of the First Mystery and the mysteries of the Ineffable, — it is they which hearken unto him and accept his repentance from him."

Mary answered and said: "My Lord, a man who hath received mysteries up to two or three in the second or third space and he hath not transgressed, but is still in his faith in uprightness and without play-acting, what will befall him?"

There is no limit to the number of mysteries the faithful may receive

And the Saviour answered and said unto Mary: "Every man who hath received mysteries in the second and in the third space and hath not transgressed, but is still in his faith without play-acting, it is lawful for such an one to receive mysteries in the space which pleaseth him, from the first to the last, because they have not transgressed."

Chapter 124

Mary continued again and said, "My Lord, a man who hath known the godhead and hath received of the mysteries of the Light, and hath turned and transgressed and done lawlessly and hath not turned to repent, and a man on the other hand who hath not found the godhead nor known it, and that man is sinner and moreover impious, and they both have come out of the body, — which of them will get more suffering in the judgments?"

The fate of the Gnostic who sinneth is more terrible than that of the ignorant sinner

The Saviour answered again and said unto Mary: "Amen, amen, I say unto thee: The man who hath known the godhead and hath received the mysteries of the light, and sinned and hath not turned to repent, he will get suffering in the chastisements of the judgments in great sufferings and judgments exceedingly far more in comparison with the impious and law-breaking man who hath not know the godhead. Now, therefore, who hath ears to hear, let him hear."

Mary interpreteth the same from a former saying

When then the Saviour had said this, Mary started forward and said, "My Lord, my light-man hath ears, and I have understood the whole word which thou hast spoken. Concerning this word then thou hast spoken unto us in a similitude: 'The slave who knew the will of his lord and made not ready nor did the will of his lord, will receive great blows; but he who knew not and did not, will be deserving of less. For from every one to whom more is entrusted, of him will more be demanded, and to whom much is handed over, of him much is required.' That is, my Lord: He who knew the godhead and hath found the mysteries of the Light and hath transgressed will be chastized in a far greater chastisement than he who hath not known the godhead. This, my Lord, is the solution of the word."

Chapter 125

Mary continued again and said unto the Saviour, "My Lord, if the faith and the mysteries shall have revealed themselves, — now, therefore, if souls come into the world in many circuits and are neglectful of receiving mysteries, hoping that, if they come into the world at any other circuit, they will receive them, will they not then be in danger of not succeeding in receiving the mysteries?"

Of those who procrastinate, saying they have many births before them

The Saviour answered and said unto his disciples: "Herald unto the whole world and say unto men: Strive thereafter that ye may receive the mysteries of the light in this time of affliction and enter into the Light-kingdom. Join not one day to another, or one circuit to another, hoping that ye may succeed in receiving the mysteries if ye come into the world in another circuit.

"And these know not when the number of the perfect souls will be at hand; for if the number of the perfect souls shall be at hand, I will now shut the gates of the Light, and no one from this hour onwards will enter in, nor will any one hereafter go forth, for the number of the perfect souls is completed, and the mystery of the First Mystery is completed, for the sake of which the universe hath arisen, — that is: I am that mystery."

Of the time of the completion

"And from this hour onwards no one will be able to enter into the Light and no one be able to go forth. For at the completion of the time of the number of the perfect souls, before I have set fire to the world, in order that it may purify the aeons and the veils and the firmaments and the whole earth and also all the matters which are on it, mankind will be still existing."

Those who procrastinate are excluded from the Light

"At that time then the faith will reveal itself still more and the mysteries in those days. And many souls will come by means of the circuits of the changes of the body, and coming back into the world are some of those in this present time who have hearkened unto me, how I taught, who at the completion of the number of the perfect souls will find the mysteries of the Light and receive them and come to the gates of the Light and find that the number of the perfect souls is complete, which is the completion of the First Mystery and the Gnosis of the universe. And they will find that I have shut the gates of the Light and that it is impossible that any one should enter in or that any one should go forth from this hour."

Their entreaties at the gates of Light

"Those souls then will knock at the gates of the Light, saying: Lord, open unto us! And I will answer unto them: I know you not, whence ye are. And they will say unto me: We have received of thy mysteries and fulfilled thy whole teaching and thou hast taught us on the high ways. And I will answer and say unto them: I know you not, who ye are, ye who are doers of iniquity and of evil even unto now. Wherefore go into the outer darkness. And from that hour they will go into the outer darkness, there where is howling and grinding of teeth.

"For this cause then, herald unto the whole world and say unto them: 'Strive thereafter, to renounce the whole world and the whole matter therein, that ye may receive the mysteries of the Light before the number of the perfect souls is completed, in order that they may not make you stop before the gates of the Light and lead you away into the outer darkness.'

"Now, therefore, who hath ears to hear, let him hear."

Mary interpreteth the same

When then the Saviour had said this, Mary started forward again and said: "My Lord, not only hath my light-man ears, but my soul hath heard and understood all the words which thou sayest. Now, therefore, my Lord, concerning the word which thou hast spoken: 'Herald unto the men of the world and say unto them: Strive thereafter, to receive the mysteries of the Light, in this time of affliction, that ye may inherit the Light-kingdom..."

[A CONSIDERABLE LACUNA HERE OCCURS IN THE TEXT.]

"The chaff indeed he will consume with unquenchable fire, but the wheat he will gather into his barn."

ENGRAVING BY GUSTAVE DORÉ.

THE PISTIS SOPHIA UNVEILED

A Fourth Book

Chapter 126

And Mary continued again and said unto Jesus: "In what form is the outer darkness; or rather how many regions of chastisement are within it?"

Of the dragon of the outer darkness

And Jesus answered and said unto Mary: 'The outer darkness is a great dragon, whose tail is in his mouth, outside the whole world and surrounding the whole world. And there are many regions of chastisement within it. There are twelve mighty chastisement-dungeons with a ruler in every dungeon, and the face of each ruler is different, one from another."

About the rulers of the twelve dungeons and their names

"And the first ruler, who is in the first dungeon, hath a crocodile's face, and his tail is in his mouth. And out of the jaws of the dragon cometh all ice and all dust and all cold and all different diseases. This is he who is called with his authentic name in his region 'Enchthonin.'

"And the ruler who is in the second dungeon, — a cat's face is his authentic face. This is he who is called in his region 'Charachar.'

"And the ruler who is in the third dungeon, — a dog's face is his authentic face. This is he who is called in his region 'Archaroch.'

"And the ruler who is in the fourth dungeon, — a serpent's face is his authentic face. This is he who is called in his region 'Achrochar.'

"And the ruler who is in the fifth dungeon, — a black bull's face is his authentic face. This is he who is called in his region 'Marchur.'

"And the ruler who is in the sixth dungeon, — a wild boar's face is his authentic face. This is he who is called in his region 'Lamchamor.'

"And the ruler who is in the seventh dungeon, — a bear's face is his authentic face. This is he who is called in his region with his authentic name 'Luchar.'

"And the ruler of the eighth dungeon, — a vulture's face is his authentic face, whose name in his region is called 'Laraoch.'

"And the ruler of the ninth dungeon, — a basilisk's face is his authentic face, whose name in his region is called 'Archeoch.'

"And in the tenth dungeon is a multitude of rulers, and every one of them hath seven dragon's heads in his authentic face. And he who is over them all is in his region with his name called 'Xarmaroch.'

"And in the eleventh dungeon is a multitude of rulers, — and every one of them hath seven cat-faced heads in his authentic face. And the great one over them is called in his region 'Rochar.'

"And in the twelfth dungeon is an exceedingly great multitude of rulers, and every one of them hath seven dog-faced heads in his authentic face. And the great one over them is called in his region 'Chremaor.'

"These rulers then of these twelve dungeons are inside the dragon of the outer darkness, each and every one of them hath a name every hour, and every one of them changeth his face every hour."

The doors of the dungeons

"And moreover every one of these dungeons hath a door opening upwards, so that the dragon of the outer darkness hath twelve dark dungeons, and every dungeon hath a door opening upwards."

The angels who watch the doors

"And an angel of the height watcheth each of the doors of the dungeons, — whom Yew, the First Man, the overseer of the Light, the envoy of the First Commandment, hath established as watchers of the dragon, so that the dragon and the rulers of his dungeons which are in him, may not mutiny."

Chapter 127

When the Saviour had said this, Mary Magdalene answered and said: "My Lord, will the souls which shall be led into that region be led through these twelve doors of the dungeons, every one according to the judgment of which it is deserving?"

What souls pass into the dragon, and how

The Saviour answered and said unto Mary: "No soul at all will be led into the dragon through these doors. But the souls of the blasphemers and of those who are in the doctrines of error and of all who teach doctrines of error, and of those who have intercourse with males, and of those stained and impious men and of atheists and murderers and adulterers and sorcerers, — all such souls then, if while still in life they do not repent but remain persistently in their sin, and all the souls which have stayed behind without, — that is those which have had the number of circuits which are appointed them in the sphere, without having repented, — well, at their last circuit will those souls, they and all the souls of which I have just told you, be led out of the jaws of the tail of the dragon into the dungeons of the outer darkness. And when those souls have been led into the outer darkness into the jaws of his tail, he turneth his tail into his own mouth and shutteth them in. Thus will the souls be led into the outer darkness."

The nature of the names of the dragon

"And the dragon of the outer darkness hath twelve authentic names on his doors, a name on every one of the doors of the dungeons. And these twelve names are different one from another; but the twelve are one in the other, so that he who speaketh one name, speaketh all. These then will I tell you at the expansion of the universe. Thus then is fashioned the outer darkness, — that is the dragon."

When then the Saviour had said this, Mary answered and said unto the Saviour: "My Lord, are the chastisements of that dragon far more terrible compared with all the chastisements of the judgments?"

Of the severity of the chastisements of the dragon

The Saviour answered and said unto Mary, "Not only are they more painful compared with all the chastisements of the judgments, but all the souls which are led into that region, will be frozen up [?] in the violent cold and the hail and exceedingly violent fire which is in that region, but also at the dissolution of the world, that is at the ascension of the universe, those souls will perish through the violent cold and the exceedingly violent fire and be non-existent for ever."

Mary answered and said: "Woe unto the souls of sinners! Now, therefore, my Lord, is the fire in the world of mankind fiercer, or the fire in Amente?"

Of the degrees of the fires of the chastisements

The Saviour answered and said unto Mary: "Amen, I say unto thee: The fire in Amente is nine times fiercer than the fire in mankind.

"And the fire in the chastisements of the great chaos is nine times more violent than that in Amente.

"And the fire in the chastisements of the rulers who [are] on the way of the Middle is nine times more violent than the fire of the chastisements in the great chaos.

"And the fire in the dragon of the outer darkness and in all the chastisements in him is seventy times more violent than the fire in all the chastisements and in all the judgments of the rulers who [are] on the way of the Middle."

Chapter 128

The disciples bewail the fate of sinners

And when the Saviour had said this unto Mary, she smote her breast, she cried out and wept, she and all the disciples together, and said:

"Woe unto sinners, for their chastisements are exceedingly numerous!"

Mary came forward, she fell down at the feet of Jesus, kissed them and said: "My Lord, bear with me if I question thee, and be not wroth with me, that I trouble thee oft; for from now on I will begin to question thee on all things with determination."

The Saviour answered and said unto Mary: "Question concerning all things on which thou desirest to question, and I will reveal them unto thee in openness without similitude."

Mary further questioneth Jesus

Mary answered and said: "My Lord, if a good man hath accomplished all the mysteries and he hath a kinsman, in a word he hath a man, and that man is an impious one who hath committed all sins and is deserving of the outer darkness, and he hath not repented, or he hath completed his number of circuits in the changes of the body, and that man hath done nothing useful, and he hath come out of the body, and we have known certainly of him, that he hath sinned and is deserving of the outer darkness, — what are we to do with him, to save him from the chastisements of the dragon of the outer darkness, and that he may be removed into a righteous body which shall find the mysteries of the Light-kingdom, in order that it may be good and go on high and inherit the Light-kingdom?"

How to save the souls of sinners

The Saviour answered and said unto Mary: "If a sinner is deserving of the outer darkness, or hath sinned according to the chastisements of the rest of the chastisements and hath not repented, or a sinning man who hath completed his number of circuits in the changes of the body and hath not repented, — if then these men of whom I have spoken shall come out of the body and be led into the outer darkness, now, therefore, if ye desire to remove them out of the chastisements of the outer darkness and all the judgments and to remove them into a righteous body which shall find the mysteries of the Light, that it may go on high and inherit the Light-kingdom, — then perform this same mystery of the Ineffable which forgiveth sins at every time, and when ye have finished performing the mystery then say..."

A summary of the formulae

"The soul of such or such a man of whom I think in my heart, — if it is in the region of the chastisements of the dungeons of the outer darkness, or if it is in the rest of the chastisements of the dungeons of the outer darkness and in the rest of the chastisements of the dragons, — then is it to be removed out of them all. And if it hath completed its number of its circuits of the changes, then is it to be led before the Virgin of Light, and the Virgin of Light is to seal it with the seal of the Ineffable and cast it down in whatever month into a righteous body which shall find the mysteries of the Light, so that it may be good, go on high and inherit the Light-kingdom. And moreover if it hath completed the circuits of changes then is that soul to be led before the seven Virgins of the Light who are set over the baptisms, and they are to apply them to the soul and seal it with the sign of the kingdom of the Ineffable and lead it into the order of the Light.

"This then will ye say when ye perform the mystery.

"Amen, I say unto you: The soul for which ye shall pray, if it indeed is in the dragon of the outer darkness, he will draw his tail out of his mouth and let go that soul. And moreover if it is in all the regions of the judgments of the rulers, amen, I say unto you: The receivers of Melchisedec will with haste snatch it away, whether the dragon let it go or it is in the judgments of the rulers; in a word, the receivers of Melchisedec will snatch it away out of all the regions in which it is, and will lead it into the region of the Middle before the Virgin of Light, and the Virgin of Light proveth it and seeth the sign of the kingdom of the Ineffable which is on that soul.

"And if it hath not yet completed its number of circuits in the changes of the soul, or [in the changes] of the body, the Virgin of Light sealeth it with an excellent seal and hasteth to have it cast down in any

month into a righteous body which shall find the mysteries of the Light, be good and go on high into the Light-kingdom.

"And if that soul hath had its number of circuits, then the Virgin of Light proveth it, and doth not have it chastized, because it hath had its number of circuits, but handeth it over to the seven Virgins of the Light. And the seven Virgins of the light prove that soul, baptize it with their baptisms and give it the spiritual chrism and lead it into the Treasury of the Light and put it in the last order of the Light until the ascension of all the perfect souls. And when they prepare to draw apart the veils of the region of those of the Right, they cleanse that soul anew and purify it and put it in the orders of the first Saviour who is in the Treasury of the Light."

Chapter 129

It came to pass then, when the Saviour had finished speaking these words unto his disciples, that Mary answered and said unto Jesus: "My Lord, I have heard thee say: 'He who shall receive of the mysteries of the Ineffable or who shall receive of the mysteries of the First Mystery, — they become flames of light-beams and light-streams and penetrate all the regions until they reach the region of their inheritance.'"

Of the light-beams and light-streams

The Saviour answered and said unto Mary: "If they receive the mystery when still in life, and if they come out of the body, they become light-beams and light-streams and penetrate all the regions until they reach the region of their inheritance.

"But if they are sinners and are come out of the body and have not repented, and if ye perform for them the mystery of the Ineffable, in order that they may be removed out of all the chastisements and be cast into a righteous body, which is good and inheriteth the Light-kingdom or is brought into the last order of the Light, then they will not be able to penetrate the regions, because they do not perform

the mystery [themselves]. But the receivers of Melchisedec follow them and lead them before the Virgin of Light. And the servitors of the judges of the rulers make frequent haste to take those souls and hand them over from one to the other until they lead them before the Virgin of Light."

Chapter 130

Mary pleadeth for those who have neglected the mysteries

And Mary continued and said unto the Saviour: "My Lord, if a man hath received the mysteries of the Light which [are] in the first space from without, and when the time of the mysteries up to which they reach is completed, and if that man continueth anew to receive mysteries of the mysteries which [are] within the mysteries which he hath already received, and moreover that man hath become negligent, not having prayed in the prayer which taketh away the evil of the victuals which he eateth and drinketh, and through the evil of the victuals he is bound to the axle of the Fate of the rulers and through the necessity of the elements he hath sinned anew after the completion of the time up to which the mystery reacheth, — because he hath become negligent and hath not prayed in the prayer which taketh away the evil of the souls and purifieth them, — and that man is come out of the body before he hath repented anew and anew received the mysteries of the mysteries which [are] within the mysteries which he hath already received, — those which accept repentance from him and forgive his sins, — and when he came forth out of the body and we knew with certainty that they have carried him into the midst of the dragon of the outer darkness because of the sins which he committed, and that man hath no helper in the world nor any one compassionate, that ye should perform the mystery of the Ineffable until he should be removed out of the midst of the dragon of the outer darkness and led into the Light-kingdom, — now, therefore, my Lord, what will befall him until he save himself from the chastisements of the dragon of the outer darkness? By no means, O Lord, abandon him, because he hath endured sufferings in the persecutions and in the whole godhood in which he is.

"Now, therefore, O Saviour, have mercy with me, lest one of our kinsmen should be in such a manner, and have mercy with all the souls which shall be in this manner; for thou art the key which openeth the door of the universe and shutteth the door of the universe, and thy mystery comprehendeth them all. Have then mercy, O Lord, with such souls. For they have called on the name of thy mysteries, were it but for one single day, and have truly had faith in them and were not in play-acting. Give them then, O Lord, a gift in thy goodness and give them rest in thy mercy."

When then Mary had said this, the Saviour called her most exceedingly blessed because of the words which she had spoken. And the Saviour was in great compassion and said unto Mary: "Unto all men who shall be in this type of which thou hast spoken, unto them while they [are] still in life, give ye the mystery of one of the twelve names of the dungeons of the dragon of the outer darkness, — those which I will give you when I have ended explaining unto you the universe from within outward and from without inward."

Of the efficacy of the names of the twelve angels

"And all men who shall find the mystery of one of the twelve names of that dragon of the outer darkness, and all men even if they are very great sinners, and they have first received the mysteries of the Light and thereafter have transgressed, or they have performed no mystery at all, then if they have completed their circuits in the changes, and if such men go forth out of the body without having repented anew, and if they are led into the chastisements which are in the midst of the dragon of the outer darkness, and remain in the circuits and remain in the chastisements in the midst of the dragon, — these, if they know the mystery of one of the twelve names of the angels while they are in life and are in the world, and if they speak one of their names while they are in the midst of the chastisements of the dragon,

— then, at the hour when they shall speak it, the whole dragon will be tossed about and most exceedingly convulsed, and the door of the dungeon in which the souls of those men are openeth itself upward, and the ruler of the dungeon in which those men are casteth the souls of those men out of the midst of the dragon of the outer darkness, because they have found the mystery of the name of the dragon."

The souls who know the names escape and are taken to Yew

"And when the ruler casteth out souls, straightaway the angels of Yew, the First Man, who watch the dungeons of that region, hasten to snatch away those souls to lead them before Yew, the First Man, the Envoy of the First Commandment. And Yew, the First Man, seeth the souls and proveth them; he findeth that they have completed their circuits and that it is not lawful to bring them anew into the world, for it is not lawful to bring anew into the world all souls which are cast into the outer darkness. But if they have not yet completed their number of circuits in the changes of the body, the receivers of Yew keep them with them until they perform for them the mystery of the Ineffable, and remove them into a good body which shall find the mysteries of the Light and inherit the Light-kingdom."

Of their subsequent fate

"But if Yew proveth them and findeth that they have completed their circuits and that it is not lawful to return them anew to the world, and that also the sign of the Ineffable is not with them, then Yew hath compassion upon them and leadeth them before the seven Virgins of the Light. They baptize them with their baptisms, but they do not give them the spiritual chrism. And they lead them into the Treasury of the Light, but they do not put them in the orders of the Inheritance, because no sign and no seal of the Ineffable is with them. But they save them from all chastisements and put them into the light of the Treasury, separated and apart by themselves alone until the ascension of the universe. And at the time when they will draw apart the

veils of the Treasury of the Light, they cleanse those souls anew and purify them most exceedingly and give them anew mysteries and put them in the last order which is in the Treasury, and those souls will be saved from all the chastisements of the judgments."

And when the Saviour had said this, he said unto his disciples: "Have ye understood in what manner I discourse with you?"

Mary interpreteth the same from a former saying

Mary then answered and said, "My Lord, this is the word which thou hast spoken unto us afore time, in a similitude, saying: 'Make to yourselves a friend out of the Mamon of unrighteousness, so that if ye remain behind, he may receive you into everlasting tents.' Who then is the Mamon of unrighteousness, if not the dragon of the outer darkness? This is the word: He who shall understand the mystery of one of the names of the dragon of the outer darkness, if he remaineth behind in the outer darkness or if he hath completed the circuits of the changes, and speaketh the name of the dragon, he will be saved and go up out of the darkness and be received into the Treasury of the Light. This is the word, my Lord."

The Saviour answered again and said unto Mary: "Well said, spiritual and pure [one]. This is the solution of the word."

Chapter 131

Mary continued again and said: "My Lord, doth the dragon of the outer darkness come into this world or doth he not come?"

Of the light of the sun and the darkness of the dragon

The Saviour answered and said unto Mary: "When the light of the sun is outside [?above the world], he covereth the darkness of the dragon; but if the sun is below the world, then the darkness of the dragon abideth as veiling of the sun and the breath of the darkness cometh into the world in form of a smoke in the night, — that is, if the sun withdraweth into himself his rays, then indeed the world is not able to endure the darkness of the dragon in its true form; otherwise would it be dissolved and go to ruin withal."

When the Saviour had said this, Mary continued again and said unto the Saviour: "My Lord still do I question thee, and hide it not from me. Now, therefore my Lord, who compelleth then the man until he sinneth?"

The Saviour answered and said unto Mary: "It is the rulers of the Fate who compel the man until he sinneth."

Mary answered and said unto the Saviour: "My Lord, surely the rulers do not come down to the world and compel the man until he sinneth?"

Of the cup of forgetfulness

The Saviour answered and said unto Mary, 'They do not come down in this manner into the world. But the rulers of the Fate, when an old soul is about to come down through them, then the rulers of that great Fate who [are] in the regions of the head of the aeons, – which is that region which is called the region of the kingdom of Adamas, and which is that region which is in face of the Virgin of Light, – then the rulers of the region of that head give the old soul a cup of forgetfulness out of the seed of wickedness, filled with all the different desires and all forgetfulness. And straightway, when that soul shall drink out of the cup, it forgetteth all the regions to which it hath gone, and all the chastisements in which it hath travelled."

Of the counterfeiting spirit

"And that cup of the water of forgetfulness becometh body outside the soul, and it resembleth the soul in all [its] figures and maketh [itself] like it, – which is what is called the counterfeiting spirit."

Of the fashioning of a new soul

"If on the other hand it is a new soul which they have taken out of the sweat of the rulers and out of the tears of their eyes, or far rather out of the breath of their mouths, — in a word, if it is one of the new souls or one of such souls, if it is one out of the sweat, then the five great rulers of the great Fate take up the sweat of all the rulers of their aeons, knead it together withal, portion it and make it into a soul. Or far rather if it is refuse of the purification of the Light, then Melchisedec taketh it up from the rulers. The five great rulers of the great Fate knead the refuse together, portion it and make it into different souls, so that every one of the rulers of the aeons, every one of them putteth his portion into the soul. For this cause they knead it jointly, so that all may partake of the soul.

"And the five great rulers, if they portion it and make it into souls, bring it out of the sweat of the rulers. But if it is one out of the refuse and of the purification of the Light, then Melchisedec, the great Receiver of the Light, taketh the refuse up from the rulers, or far rather if it is out of the tears of their eyes or out of the breath of their mouth, — in a word, out of such souls, when the five rulers portion it and make it into different souls, — or far rather if it is an old soul, then the ruler who is in the head of the aeons, himself mixeth the cup of forgetfulness with the seed of wickedness, and he mixeth it with every one of the new souls at the time when he is in the region of the head. And that cup of forgetfulness becometh the counterfeiting spirit for that soul, and bideth outside the soul, being a vesture for it and resembling it in every way, being envelope as vesture outside it."

Of the inbreathing of the power

"And the five great rulers of the great Fate of the aeons and the ruler of the disk of the sun and the ruler of the disk of the moon inbreathe within into that soul, and there cometh forth out of them a portion out of my power which the last Helper hath cast into the Mixture.
"And the portion of that power remaineth within the soul, unloosed and existing on its own authority for the economy unto which it hath

been inset, to give sense unto the soul, in order that it may seek after the works of the Light of the Height always.

"And that power is like the species of the soul in every form and resembleth it. It cannot be outside the soul, but remaineth inside it, as I have commanded it from the beginning. When I willed to cast it into the First Commandment, I gave it commandment to remain outside [? inside] the souls for the economy of the First Mystery."

Jesus promiseth to reveal all in detail

"And so I will tell you at the expansion of the universe all these words concerning the power and also concerning the soul, after what type they are fashioned, or what ruler fashioneth them, or what are the different species of the souls. And so will I tell you at the expansion of the universe how many fashion the soul. And I will tell you the name of all of them who fashion the soul. And I will tell you the manner, how the counterfeiting spirit and the destiny have been prepared. And I will tell you the name of the soul before it is purged, and moreover its name when it hath been purged and become pure. And I will tell you the name of the counterfeiting spirit; and I will tell you the name of the destiny. And I will tell you the name of all the bonds with which the rulers bind the counterfeiting spirit to the soul. And I will tell you the name of all the decans who fashion the soul in the bodies of the soul in the world; and I will tell you in what manner the souls are fashioned. And I will tell you the type of every one of the souls; and I will tell you the type of the souls of the men and of those of the birds and of those of the wild beasts and of those of the reptiles. And I will tell you the type of all the souls and of those of all the rulers which are sent into the world, in order that ye may be completed in all Gnosis. All this will I tell you at the expansion of the universe. And after all this I will tell you wherefore all this hath come to pass."

Of the light-power and the counterfeiting spirit

"Hearken, therefore, that I may discourse with you concerning the soul according as I have said: The five great rulers of the great Fate

of the Aeons and the rulers of the disk of the sun and the rulers of the disk of the moon breathe into that soul, and there cometh out of them a portion of my power, as I have just said. And the portion of that power remaineth within the soul, so that the soul can stand. And they put the counterfeiting spirit outside the soul, watching it and assigned to it; and the rulers bind it to the soul with their seals and their bonds and seal it to it, that it may compel it always, so that it continually doeth its mischiefs and all its iniquities, in order that it may be their slave always and remain under their sway always in the changes of the body; and they seal it to it that it may be in all the sin and all the desires of the world."

The parents we are to abandon

"For this cause, therefore, have I in this manner brought the mysteries into this world which undo all the bonds of the counterfeiting spirit and all the seals which are bound to the soul, — those which make the soul free and free it from its parents the rulers, and make it into refined light and lead it up into the kingdom of its father, the first Issue, the First Mystery, for ever.

"For this cause therefore, have I said unto you afore time: 'He who doth not abandon father and mother and come and follow after me is not worthy of me.' I have, therefore, said at that time, ye are to abandon your parents the rulers, that I may make you sons of the First Mystery for ever."

Chapter 132

Salome is in doubt

And when the Saviour had said this, Salome started forward and said: "My Lord, if our parents are the rulers, how standeth it written in the Law of Moses, 'He who shall abandon his father and his mother, let him die the death?' Hath not thus the Law made statement thereon?"

And when Salome had said this, the light-power in Mary Magdalene bubbled up in her and she said to the Saviour, "My Lord, give commandment unto me that I discourse with my sister Salome to tell her the solution of the word which she hath spoken."

It came to pass then, when the Saviour had heard Mary say these words, then he called her most exceedingly blessed. The Saviour answered and said unto Mary: "I give commandment unto thee, Mary, that thou speak the solution of the word which Salome hath spoken."

Mary removeth the doubt of Salome

And when the Saviour had said this, Mary started forward to Salome, embraced her and said unto her: "My sister Salome, concerning the word which thou hast spoken: It standeth written in the Law of Moses: 'He who shall abandon his father and his mother, let him die the death.' Now, therefore, my sister Salome, the Law hath not said this concerning the soul nor concerning the body nor concerning the counterfeiting spirit, for all these are sons of the rulers and are out of them. But the Law hath said this concerning the power which hath came forth out of the Saviour, and which is the light-man within us today. The Law hath moreover said: Every one who shall remain without the Saviour and all his mysteries, his parents, will not only die the death but go to ruin in destruction."

When then Mary had said this, Salome started forward to Mary and embraced her anew. Salome said: "The Saviour hath power to make me understanding like thyself."

It came to pass, when the Saviour had heard the words of Mary, that he called her most exceedingly blessed. The Saviour answered and said unto Mary in the midst of his disciples: "Hearken, therefore, Mary, who it is who compelleth the man until he sinneth."

Of the charge given to the counterfeiting spirit

"Now, therefore, the rulers seal the counterfeiting spirit to the soul, [but] so that it doth not agitate it every hour, making it do all sins and all iniquities. And they give commandment moreover unto the counterfeiting spirit, saying, 'If the soul cometh out of the body, do not agitate it, being assigned to it and transferring it to all the regions of the judgments, region by region, on account of all the sins which thou hast made it do, in order that it may be chastized in all the regions of the judgments, so that it may not be able to go on high to the Light and return into changes of the body.'

"In a word, they give commandment to the counterfeiting spirit, saying, 'Do not agitate it at all at any hour unless it doth not speak mysteries and undo all the seals and all the bonds with which we have bound thee to it. [But] if it sayeth the mysteries and undoeth all the seals and all the bonds and [sayeth] the apology of the region, and if it cometh, then let it go forth, for it belongeth to those of the Light of the Height and hath become a stranger unto us and unto thee, and thou wilt not be able to seize it from this hour onwards. If on the contrary it sayeth not the mysteries of the undoing of thy bonds and of thy seals and of the apologies of the region, then seize it and let it not out; thou shalt transfer it to the chastisements and all the regions of the judgments on account of all the sins which thou hast made it do. After this lead [such souls] before the Virgin of Light, who sendeth them once more into the circuit."

The command given to the servitors

"The rulers of the great Fate of the aeons hand these over to the counterfeiting spirit; and the rulers summon the servitors of their aeons, to the number of three-hundred-and-sixty-and-five, and give them the soul and the counterfeiting spirit, which are bound to one another. The counterfeiting spirit is the without of the soul, and the compound of the power is the within of the soul, being within both of them, in order that they may be able to stand, for it is the power which keepeth the two up-right. And the rulers give commandment to the servitors,

saying unto them, 'This is the type which ye are to put into the body of the matter of the world.' They say unto them indeed, 'Put the compound of the power, the within of the soul, within them all, that they may be able to stand, for it is their up-rightness, and after the soul put the counterfeiting spirit."

About conception

"Thus they give commandment to their servitors, that they may deposit it into the bodies of the antitype. And following this fashion the servitors of the rulers bring the power and the soul and the counterfeiting spirit down to the world, and pour them out into the world of the rulers of the Middle. The rulers of the Middle look after the counterfeiting spirit; and the destiny, whose name is Moira, leadeth the man until it hath him slain through the death appointed unto him, which the rulers of the great Fate have bound to the soul. And the servitors of the sphere bind the soul and the power and the counterfeiting spirit and the destiny. And they portion them all and make them into two portions and seek after the man and also after the woman in the world to whom they have given signs, in order that they may send them into them. And they give one portion to the man and one portion to the woman in a victual of the world or in a breath of the air or in water or in a kind which they drink.

"All this I will tell unto you and the species of every soul and the type, how they enter into the bodies, whether of men or of birds or of cattle or of wild beasts or reptiles or of all the other species in the world, I will tell you their type. I will tell you their type, in what type they enter into men; I will tell it you at the expansion of the universe."

The compulsion of the parents

"Now, therefore, when the servitors of the rulers cast the one portion into the woman and the other into the man in the fashion which I have told you, then the servitors secretly compel them, even if they are removed at very great distance from one another, so that they concert to be in a concert of the world. And the counterfeiting spirit which

is in the man cometh to the portion which is entrusted to the world in the matter of his body, and lifteth it and casteth it down into the womb of the woman [into the portion] which is entrusted to the seed of wickedness."

The process of gestation

"And in that hour the three-hundred-and-sixty-and-five servitors of the rulers go into her womb and take up their abode in it. The servitors bring the two portions the one to the other, and moreover the servitors withhold the blood of all the food of the woman which she will eat and which she will drink, and they withhold [it] in the womb of the woman up to forty days. And after forty days they knead the blood of the power of all the food and knead it well in the woman's womb.

"After forty days they spend another thirty days in building its members in the image of the body of the man; each buildeth a member. I will tell you of the decans who will build it [sc. the body]; I will tell them you about them at the expansion of the universe."

Of the incarnation of the soul

"If then after this the servitors shall have completed the whole body and all its members in seventy days, after this the servitors summon into the body which they have built, — first indeed they summon the counterfeiting spirit; and thereafter they summon the soul within them; and thereafter they summon the compound of the power into the soul; and the destiny they put outside them all, as it is not blended with them but following them and accompanying them."

Of the sealing of the plasm

"And after this the servitors seal them one to the other with all the seals which the rulers have given them. [And] they seal the day on which they have taken up their abode in the womb of the woman, — they seal [it] on the left hand of the plasm; and they seal the day

on which they have completed the body, on the right hand; and they seal the day on which the rulers have handed it over to them on the middle of the skull of the body of the plasm; and they seal the day on which the soul hath come forth out of the rulers, they seal it on the [left of] the skull of the plasm; and they seal the day on which they kneaded the members and separated them for a soul, they seal it on the right of the skull of the plasm; and the day on which they have bound the counterfeiting spirit to it [the soul], they seal on the back of the skull of the plasm; and the day on which the rulers have breathed the power into the body, they seal on the brain which is in the midst of the head of the plasm and also on the inside [? the heart] of the plasm; and the number of years which the soul will spend in the body, they seal on the forehead which is on the plasm. And so they seal all those seals on the plasm. I will tell you the names of all these seals at the expansion of the universe; and after the expansion of the universe I will tell you wherefor all hath come to pass. And, if ye could understand it, I am that mystery.

"Now, therefore, the servitors complete the whole man. And of all these seals with which they have sealed the body, the servitors carry the whole peculiarity and bring it to all the retributive rulers who [are] over all the chastisements of the judgments; and these hand it over to their receivers, in order that they may lead their souls out of the bodies, — they hand over to them the peculiarity of the seals, in order that they may know the time when they are to lead the souls out of the bodies, and in order that they may know the time when they are to bring to birth the body, so that they may send their servitors in order that they may draw near and follow the soul and bear witness of all the sins it shall do, — they and the counterfeiting spirit, — on account of the manner and way, how they shall chastise it in the judgment."

Of the destiny

"And when the servitors have given the peculiarity of the seals to the retributive rulers, they withdraw themselves to the economy of their occupations which is appointed unto them through the rulers of the

great Fate. And when the number of months of the birth of the babe is completed, the babe is born. Small in it is the compound of the power, and small in it is the soul; and small in it is the counterfeiting spirit. The destiny on the contrary is large, as it is not mingled into the body for their economy, but followeth the soul and the body and the counterfeiting spirit, until the time when the soul shall come forth out of the body, on account of the type of death by which it shall slay it [the body] according to the death appointed for it by the rulers of the great Fate."

Of how a man cometh by his death

"Is he to die by a wild beast, the destiny leadeth the wild beast against him until it slay him; or is he to die by a serpent, or is he to fall into a pit by mischance, or is he to hang himself, or is he to die in water, or through such [kinds of death], or through another death which is worse or better than this, — in a word, it is the destiny which forceth his death upon him. This is the occupation of the destiny, and it hath no other occupation but this. And the destiny followeth every man until the day of his death."

Chapter 133

Mary answered and said: 'To all men then who are in the world, will all which is appointed them through the Fate, whether good or bad or sin or death or life, — in a word, will all which is appointed them through the rulers of the Fate, have to come unto them?"

There is no escape from the destiny

The Saviour answered and said unto Mary, "Amen, I say unto you: All which is appointed unto every one through the Fate, whether all good or all sins, — in a word, all which is appointed them, cometh unto them."

Of the keys of the mysteries

"For this cause, therefore, have I brought the keys of the mysteries of the kingdom of heaven; otherwise no flesh in the world would be saved. For without mysteries no one will enter into the Light-kingdom, be he righteous or a sinner.

"For this cause, therefore, have I brought the keys of the mysteries into the world, that I may free the sinners who shall have faith in me and hearken unto me, so that I may free them from the bonds and the seals of the aeons of the rulers and bind them to the seals and the vestures and the orders of the Light, in order that he whom I shall free in the world from the bonds and the seals of the aeons of the rulers may be freed in the Height from the bonds and seals of the aeons of the rulers, and in order that he whom I shall bind in the world to the seals and the vestures and the orders of the Light may be bound in the Light-land to the orders of the inheritances of the Light.

"For the sake of sinners, therefore, have I torn myself asunder at this time and have brought them the mysteries, that I may free them from the aeons of the rulers and bind them to the inheritances of the Light, and not only the sinners, but also the righteous in order that I may give them the mysteries and that they may be taken into the Light, for without mysteries they cannot be taken into the Light."

The mysteries are for all men

"For this cause, therefore, I have not hidden it, but I have cried it aloud clearly. And I have not separated the sinners but I have cried it aloud and said it unto all men, unto sinners and righteous saying, 'Seek that ye may find, knock that it may be opened unto you; for every one who seeketh in truth, will find, and who knocketh, to him it will be opened.' For I have said unto all men: They are to seek the mysteries of the Light-kingdom which shall purify them and make them refined and lead them into the Light."

A prophecy of John the Baptizer

"For this cause, therefore, hath John the Baptizer prophesied concerning me, saying: 'I indeed have baptized you with water unto repentance for forgiveness of your sins. He who cometh after me is stronger than me. Whose fan is in his hand, and he will purify his floor. The chaff indeed he will consume with unquenchable fire, but the wheat he will gather into his barn.' The power in John hath prophesied concerning me, knowing that I would bring the mysteries into the world and purify the sins of the sinners who shall have faith in me and hearken unto me, and make them into refined light and lead them into the Light."

Chapter 134

When then Jesus had said this, Mary answered and said: "My Lord, if men go to seek and they come upon the doctrines of error, whence then are they to know whether they belong to thee or not?"

The Saviour answered and said unto Mary: "I have said unto you afore time: 'Be ye as skilful money-changers. Take the good, throw the bad away.'"

The criterion of orthodoxy

"Now, therefore, say unto all men who would seek the godhead, 'If north wind cometh, then ye know that there will be cold; if south wind cometh, then ye know that there will be burning and fervent heat.' Now, therefore, say unto them, 'If ye have known the face of the heaven and of the earth from the winds, then know ye exactly, if then any come now unto you and proclaim unto you a godhead, whether their words have harmonized and fitted with all your words which I have spoken unto you through two up to three witnesses, and whether they have harmonized in the setting of the air and of the heavens and of the circuits and of the starts and of the light-givers and of the whole earth and all on it and of all waters and all in them.' Say unto them: 'Those who shall come unto you, and their words

fit and harmonize in the whole Gnosis with that which I have said unto you, I will receive as belonging unto us.' This is what ye shall say unto men, if ye make proclamation unto them in order that they may guard themselves from the doctrines of error."

The Books of Yew

"Now, therefore, for the sake of sinners have I rent myself asunder and am come into the world, that I may save them. For even for the righteous, who have never done any evil and have not sinned at all, it is necessary that they should find the mysteries which are in the Books of Yew, which I have made Enoch write in Paradise, discoursing with him out of the tree of the Gnosis and out of the tree of the Life. And I made him deposit them in the rock Ararad, and set the ruler Kalapatauroth, who is over Skemmut, on whose head is the foot of Yew, and who surroundeth all aeons and Fates, — I set up that ruler as watcher over the Books of Yew on account of the flood, and in order that none of the rulers may be envious of them and destroy them. These will I give you, when I shall have told you the expansion of the universe."

When then the Saviour had said this, Mary answered and said: "My Lord, who now then is the man in the world who hath not sinned at all, who is pure of iniquities? For if he is pure of one, he will not be able to be pure of another, so that he may find the mysteries which are in the Books of Yew? For I say: A man in this world will not be able to be pure of sins; for if he is pure of one, he will not be able to be pure of another."

Few only will accomplish the mystery of the First Mystery

The Saviour answered and said unto Mary: "I say unto you: They will find one in a thousand and two in ten-thousand for the accomplishment of the mystery of the First Mystery. This will I tell unto you when I have explained to you the expansion of the universe. For this cause, therefore, I have rent myself asunder and have brought the mysteries into the world, because all are under sin and all are in need of the gift of the mysteries."

Chapter 135

Mary answered and said unto the Saviour: "My Lord, before thou didst come to the region of the rulers and before thou didst come down into the world, hath no soul entered into the Light?"

No soul had entered into the Light before the coming of the First Mystery

The Saviour answered and said unto Mary: "Amen, amen, I say unto you: Before I did come into the world, no soul hath entered into the Light. And now, therefore, when I am come, I have opened the gates of the Light and opened the ways which lead to the Light. And now, therefore, let him who shall do what is worthy of the mysteries receive the mysteries and enter into the Light."

Mary continued and said, "But, my Lord, I have heard that the prophets have entered into the Light."

Of the prophets

The Saviour continued and said unto Mary, "Amen, amen, I say unto you: No prophet hath entered into the Light; but the rulers of the aeons have discoursed with them out of the aeons and given them the mystery of the aeons. And when I came to the regions of the aeons, I have turned Elias and sent him into the body of John the Baptizer, and the rest also I turned into righteous bodies, which will find the mysteries of the Light, go on high and inherit the Light-kingdom."

Of the patriarchs

"Unto Abraham on the other hand and Isaac and Jacob I have forgiven all their sins and their iniquities and have given them the mysteries of the Light in the aeons and placed them in the region of

Yabraoth and of all the rulers who have repented. And when I go into the Height and am on the point of going into the light, I will carry their souls with me into the Light. But, amen, I say unto you, Mary: They will not go into the Light before I have carried thy soul and those of all thy brethren into the Light."

About the souls of the righteous from Adam to Jesus

"The rest of the patriarchs and of the righteous from the time of Adam unto now, who are in the aeons and all the orders of the rulers, when I came to the region of the aeons, I have through the Virgin of Light made to turn into bodies which will all be righteous, — those which will find the mysteries of the light, enter in and inherit the Light-kingdom."

Mary answered and said: "Blessed are we before all men because of these splendours which thou hast revealed unto us."

The Saviour answered and said unto Mary and all the disciples: "I will still reveal unto you all the splendours of the Height, from the interiors of the interiors to the exteriors of the exteriors, that ye may be perfected in all Gnosis and in all fullness and in the height of the heights and the depths of the depths."

The disciples know of a surety that Jesus is the Great Initiator

And Mary continued and said to the Saviour: "Lo, my Lord, we have openly, exactly and clearly known that thou hast brought the keys of the mysteries of the Light-kingdom, which forgive souls sins and purify them and make them into refined light and lead them into the Light."

[Sub-scription:]

A PORTION OF THE BOOKS OF THE SAVIOUR

"O Light of all lights, which is in the boundless lights, remember us and purify us."

ENGRAVING BY GUSTAVE DORÉ

The Pistis Sophia Unveiled

A Fifth Book

Chapter 136

The disciples gather round Jesus

It came to pass then, when Jesus our Lord had been crucified and had risen from the dead on the third day, that his disciples gathered round him, adored him and said: "Our Lord, have mercy upon us, for we have abandoned father and mother and the whole world and have followed thee."

The invocation of Jesus

At that time Jesus stood with his disciples on the water of the Ocean and made invocation with this prayer, saying: "Hear me, my Father, father of all fatherhood, boundless Light: aeeiouo iao aoi oia psinother thernops nopsither zagoure pagoure nethmomaoth nepsiomaoth marachachtha thobarrabau tharnachachan zorokothora ieou [=Yew] sabaoth."

The grouping of the disciples

And while Jesus said this, Thomas, Andrew, James and Simon the Cananite were in the west with their faces turned towards the east, and Philip and Bartholomew were in the south turned towards the north, and the rest of the disciples and the women-disciples stood back of Jesus. But Jesus stood at the altar.

The interpretation is IAO

And Jesus made invocation, turning himself towards the four corners of the world with his disciples, who were all clad in linen garments, and saying: "IAO IAO IAO." This is its interpretation: iota, because the universe hath gone forth; alpha, because it will turn itself back again; omega, because the completion of all the completeness will take place.

He continueth to make invocation

And when Jesus had said this, he said: "iaphtha iaphtha mounaer mounaer ermanouer ermanouer," *That is: "O father of all fatherhood of the boundless [spaces], hear me for the sake of my disciples whom I have led before thee, that they may have faith in all the words of thy truth, and grant all for which I shall invoke thee; for I know the name of the father of the Treasury of the Light."*

The apocalypse of the heavens

Again did Jesus, — that is Aberamentho, — make invocation, speaking the name of the father of the Treasury of the Light, and said: "Let all the mysteries of the rulers and the authorities and the angels and the archangels and all powers and all things of the invisible god Agrammachamarei and Barbelo draw near the Leech [Bdella] on one side and withdraw to the right."

And in that hour all the heavens went to the west, and all the Aeons and the sphere and their rulers and all their powers flew together to the west to the left of the disk of the sun and the disk of the moon.

The figures of the disk of the sun and of the moon

And the disk of the sun was a great dragon whose tail was in his mouth and who reached to seven powers of the Left and whom four powers in the form of white horses drew.

And the base of the moon had the type of a ship which a male and a female dragon steered and two white bulls drew. The figure of a babe was on the stern of the moon who guided the dragons who robbed the light from the rulers. And on its prow was a cat's face.

And the whole world and the mountains and the seas fled together to the west to the left.

Jesus and the disciples are transported to the ways of the Middle

And Jesus and his disciples remained in the midst in an aery region on the ways of the way of the Middle, which lieth below the sphere. And they came to the first order of the way of the Middle. And Jesus stood in the air of its region with his disciples.

The disciples of Jesus said unto him, "What is this region in which we are?"

Of the repentant and unrepentant rulers

Jesus said: "These are the regions of the way of the Middle. For it came to pass, when the rulers of Adamas mutinied and persistently practised congress, procreating rulers, archangels, angels, servitors and decans ,that Yew, the father of my father, came forth from the Right and bound them to a Fate-sphere.

"For there are twelve aeons; over six Sabaoth, the Adamas, ruleth, and his brother Yabraoth ruleth over the other six. At that time then Yabraoth with his rulers had faith in the mysteries of the light and was active in the mysteries of the Light and abandoned the mystery of congress. But Sabaoth, the Adamas, and his rulers have persisted in the practice of congress.

"And when Yew, the father of my father, saw that Yabraoth had faith, he carried him and all the rulers who had had faith with him, took him unto himself out of the sphere and led him into a purified air in face of the light of the sun between the regions of those of the Middle and between [?] the regions of the invisible god. He posted him there with the rulers who had had faith in him.

"But he carried Sabaoth, the Adamas, and his rulers who had not been active in the mysteries of the Light, but have been persistently active in the mysteries of congress, and inbound them into the sphere."

Of the hierarchies of the unrepentant rulers and the names of their five regents

"He bound eighteen-hundred rulers in every aeon, and set three-hundred and sixty over them, and he set five other great rulers as lords over the three-hundred-and-sixty and over all the bound rulers, who in the whole world of mankind are called with these names: The first is called Kronos, the second Ares, the third Hermes, the fourth Aphrodite, the fifth Zeus."

Chapter 137

Of the powers which Yew bound into the five regents

Jesus continued and said: "Hearken then, that I may tell you their mystery. It came to pass when Yew had thus bound them, that he drew forth a power out of the great Invisible and bound it to him who is called Kronos. And he drew another power out of Ipsantachounchainchoucheoch, who is one of the three triple-powered Gods, and bound it to Ares. And he drew a power out of Chainchoooch, who also is one of the three triple-powered Gods, and bound it to Hermes. Again he drew a power out of the Pistis, the Sophia, daughter of Barbelo, and bound it to Aphrodite."

Of the functions of Zeus, the chief regent

"And moreover he perceived that they needed a helm to steer the world and the aeons of the sphere, so that they might not wreck the world in their wickedness. He went into the Middle, drew forth a power out of the little Sabaoth, the Good, him of the Middle, and bound it to Zeus, because he is a good regent, so that he may steer them in his goodness. And he set thus established the circling of his order, that he should spend thirteen [? three] months in every aeon, confirming [it], so that he may set free all the rulers over whom he cometh, from the evil of their wickedness. And he gave him two aeons, which are in face of those of Hermes, for his dwelling."

The incorruptible names of the regents

"I have told you for the first time the names of these five great rulers with which the men of the world are wont to call them. Hearken now then that I may tell you also their incorruptible names, which are: Orimouth correspondeth to Kronos; Mounichounaphor correspondeth to Ares; Tarpetanouph correpondeth to Hermes; Chosi correspondeth to Aphrodite; Chonbal correspondeth to Zeus. These are their incorruptible names."

Chapter 138

And when the disciples had heard this, they fell down, adored Jesus and said: "Blessed are we beyond all men, because thou hast revealed unto us these great wonders."

They continued, besought him and said, "We beseech thee, reveal unto us: What are then these ways?"

Mary questioneth Jesus on the ways of the Middle

And Mary drew nigh unto him, fell down, adored his feet and kissed his hands and said: "Yea, my Lord, reveal unto us: What is the use of the ways of the Middle? For we have heard from thee that they are set over great chastisements. How then, my Lord, will we remove or escape from them? Or in what way do they seize the souls? Or how long a time do they spend in their chastisements? Have mercy upon us, our Lord, our Saviour, in order that the receivers of the judgments of the ways of the Middle may not carry off our souls and judge us in their evil judgments, so that we ourselves may inherit the Light of thy father and not be wretched and destitute of thee."

Of the mysteries which Jesus will give unto his disciples

When then Mary said this weeping, Jesus answered in great compassion and said unto them: "Truly, my brethren and beloved, who have abandoned father and mother for my name's sake, unto you will I give all mysteries and all gnoses.

"I will give you the mystery of the twelve aeons of the rulers and their seals and their ciphers and the manner of invocation for reaching their regions.

"I will give you moreover the mystery of the thirteenth aeon and the manner of invocation for reaching their region, and I will give you their ciphers and their seals.

"And I will give you the mystery of the baptism of those of the Middle and the manner of invocation for reaching their regions, and I will announce unto you their ciphers and their seals.

"And I will give you the baptism of those of the Right, our region, and its ciphers and its seals and the manner of invocation for reaching thither.

"And I will give you the great mystery of the Treasury of the Light and the manner of invocation for reaching thither.

"I will give you all the mysteries and all the gnoses, in order that ye may be called 'children of the fullness, perfected in all the gnoses and all the mysteries.' Blessed are ye beyond all men on earth, for the children of the Light are come in your time."

Chapter 139

Of the constitution of the way of the Middle

Jesus continued in the discourse and said: "It came to pass thereafter that the father of my father, - that is Yew, — came and took other three-hundred-and-sixty rulers from the rulers of Adamas who had not had faith in the mystery of the Light, and bound them into these aerial regions, in which we are now, below the sphere. He established another five great rulers over them, — that is these who are on the way of the Middle."

Of Paraplex

"The first ruler of the way of the Middle is called Paraplex, a ruler with a woman's shape, whose hair reacheth down to her feet, under whose authority stand five-and-twenty archdemons which rule over a multitude of other demons. And it is those demons which enter into men and seduce them, raging and cursing and slandering; and it is they which carry of hence and in ravishment the souls and dispatch them through their dark smoke and their evil chastisements."

Mary said: "I shall behave badly to question thee. Be not wroth with me if I question on all things."

Jesus said: "Question what thou wilt."

Mary said: "My Lord, reveal unto us in what manner they carry off hence the souls in ravishment, that also my brethren may understand it."

Of Yew and Melchisedec

Jesus, — that is Aberamentho, — said: "Since indeed the father of my father, — that is Yew,— is the foreminder of all the rulers, Gods and powers who have arisen out of the matter of the Light of the Treasury, and Zorokothora Melchisedec is the envoy to all the lights which are purified in the rulers, leading them into the Treasury of the Light, — these two alone are the great Lights, and their ordinance is that they down go to the rulers and purify them, and that Zorokothora Melchisedec carrieth away the purification of the lights which they have purified in the rulers and leadeth them into the Treasury of the Light, — when the cipher and the time of their ordinance cometh, that they go down to the rulers and oppress and constrain them, carrying away the purification from the rulers.

"But straightway when they shall cease from the oppressing and constraining and return to the regions of the Treasury of the Light, it cometh to pass that, if they reach the regions of the Middle, Zorokothora Melchisedec carrieth off the lights and leadeth them unto the gate of those of the Middle and leadeth them into the Treasury of

the Light, and that Yew withdraweth himself into the regions of those of the Right."

How the demon rulers carry off souls

"Up to the time of the cipher for them to come forth again, the rulers mutiny through the wrath of their wickedness, going straightway up to the lights, because they [Yew and Melchisedec] are not with them at that time, and they carry off the souls which they may be able to snatch away in ravishment, and destroy them through their dark smoke and their evil fire."

The chastisements of Paraplex

"At that time then this authority, with name Paraplex, along with the demons which stand under her, carrieth off the souls of the violently passionate, of cursers and of slanderers and dispatcheth them through the dark smoke and destroyeth them through her evil fire so that they begin to be undone and dissolved. One-hundred-and-thirty-and-three years and nine months do they spend in the chastisements of her regions, while she tormenteth them in the fire of her wickedness.

"It cometh to pass then after all these times, when the sphere turneth itself and the little Sabaoth, Zeus, cometh to the first of the aeons of the sphere, which is called in the world the Ram of Boubastis, that is of Aphrodite; and when she [Boubastis] cometh to the seventh house of the sphere, that is to the Balance, then the veils which are between those of the Right and those of the Left draw themselves aside, and there looketh from the height out of those of the Right and great Sabaoth, the Good; and the whole world and the total sphere [become alarmed] before he hath looked forth. And he looketh down on the regions of Paraplex, so that her regions may be dissolved and perish. And all the souls which are in her chastisements, are carried and cast back [up] into the sphere anew, because they are ruined in the chastisements of Paraplex."

Chapter 140

Of Ariouth the AEthiopian

"He continued in the discourse and said: "The second order is called Ariouth the AEthiopian, a female ruler, who is entirely black, under whom stand fourteen other [arch] demons which rule over a multitude of other demons. And it is those demons which stand under Ariouth the Aethiopian, that enter into strife-seekers until they stir up wars and murders arise, and they harden their heart and seduce it to wrath in order that murders may arise.

"And the souls which this authority will carry off in ravishment, pass one-hundred-and-thirteen years in her regions, while she tormenteth them through her dark smoke and her wicked fire, so that they come nigh unto destruction.

"And thereafter, when the sphere turneth itself, and the little Sabaoth, the Good, who is called in the world Zeus, cometh, and he cometh to the fourth aeon of the sphere, that is the Crab, and Boubastis, who is called in the world Aphrodite, cometh into the tenth aeon of the sphere which is called the Goat, at that time the veils which are between those of the Left and those of the Right, draw themselves aside, and Yew looketh forth to the right; the whole world becometh alarmed and is agitated together with all the aeons of the sphere. And he looketh on the dwellings of Ariouth the AEthiopian, so that her regions are dissolved and ruined, and all the souls which are in her chastisements are carried off and cast back into the sphere anew, because they are ruined through her dark smoke and her wicked fire."

Of Triple-faced Hekate

He continued further in this discourse and said: "The third order is called Triple-faced Hekate, and there are under her authority seven-and-twenty [arch] demons, and it is they which enter into men and seduce them to perjuries and lies and to covet that which doth not belong to them.

"The souls then which Hekate beareth hence in ravishment, she handeth over to her demons which stand under her, in order that they may torment them through her dark smoke and her wicked fire, they being exceedingly afflicted through the demons. And they spend one-hundred-and-five years and six months, being chastized in her wicked chastisements; and they begin to be dissolved and destroyed.

"And thereafter, when the sphere turneth itself, and the little Sabaoth, the Good, he of the Middle, who is called in the world Zeus, cometh, and he cometh to the eighth aeon of the sphere which is called the Scorpion, and when Boubastis, whom they call Aphrodite, cometh, and she cometh to the second aeon of the sphere which is called the Bull, then the veils which are between those of the Right and those of the Left draw themselves aside and Zorokothora Melchisedec looketh out of the height; and the world and the mountains are agitated and the aeons become alarmed. And he looketh on all the regions of Hekate, so that her regions are dissolved and destroyed, and all the souls which are in her chastisements, are carried off and cast back anew into the sphere, because they are dissolved in the fire of her chastisements."

Of Parhedron Typhon

He continued and said, "The fourth order is called Parhedron Typhon, who is a mighty ruler, under whose authority are two-and-thirty demons. And it is they which enter into men and seduce them to lusting, fornicating, adultery and to the continual practice of intercourse. The souls then which this ruler will carry off in ravishment pass one-hundred-and-twenty-and-eight years in his regions, while his demons torment them through his dark smoke and his wicked fire, so that they begin to be ruined and destroyed.

"It cometh to pass then, when the sphere turneth itself and the little Sabaoth, the Good, he of the Middle, who is called Zeus, cometh, and when he cometh to the ninth aeon of the sphere which is called the

Archer, and when Boubastis, who is called in the world Aphrodite, cometh, and she cometh to the third aeon of the sphere which is called the Twins, then the veils which are between those of the Left and those of the Right, draw themselves aside, and there looketh forth Zarazaz, whom the rulers call with the name of a mighty ruler of their regions 'Maskelli,' and he looketh on the dwellings of Parhedron Typhon, so that his regions are dissolved and destroyed. And all the souls which are in his chastisements are carried and cast back anew into the sphere, because they are reduced through his dark smoke and his wicked fire."

Of Yachthanabas

Again he continued in the discourse and said unto his disciples: "The fifth order, whose ruler is called Yachthanabas, is a mighty ruler under whom standeth a multitude of other demons. It is they which enter into men and bring it about that they have respect of persons, — treating the just with injustice, and favour the cause of sinners, taking gifts for a just judgment and perverting it, forgetting the poor and needy, — they [the demons] increasing the forgetfulness in their souls and the care for that which bringeth no benefit, in order that they may not think of their life, so that when they come out of the body, they are carried in ravishment.

"The souls then which this ruler will carry off in ravishment, are in his chastisements one-hundred-and-fifty years and eight months, and he destroyeth them through his dark smoke and his wicked fire, while they are exceedingly afflicted through the flames of his fire.

"And when the sphere turneth itself and the little Sabaoth, the Good, who is called in the world Zeus, cometh, and he cometh to the eleventh aeon of the sphere which is called the Water-man, and when Boubastis cometh to the fifth aeon of the sphere which is called the Lion, then the veils which are between those of the Left and those of the Right, draw themselves aside, and there looketh out of the height the great IAO, the Good, he of the Middle, on the regions of Yachthanabas, so that his regions are dissolved and destroyed. And all

the souls which are in his chastisements are carried off and cast back anew into the sphere, because they are ruined in his chastisements.

"These then are the doings of the ways of the Middle concerning which ye have questioned me."

Chapter 141

The disciples beseech Jesus to have mercy upon sinners

And when the disciples had heard this, they fell down, adored him and said: "Help us now, Lord, and have mercy upon us, in order that we may be preserved from these wicked chastisements which are prepared for the sinners. Woe unto them, woe unto the children of men! For they grope as the blind in the darkness and see not. Have mercy upon us, O Lord, in this great blindness in which we are. And have mercy upon the whole race of men; for they have lain in wait for their souls, as lions for their prey, making the prey ready as food for the rulers' chastisements because of the forgetfulness and unknowing which is in them. Have mercy upon us, our Lord, our Saviour, have mercy then upon us and save us in this great stupefaction."

Jesus encourageth his disciples

Jesus said unto his disciples: "Be comforted and be not afraid, for ye are blessed, because I will make you lords over all these and put them in subjection under your feet. Remember that I have already said unto you before I was crucified: 'I will give you the keys of the kingdom of heaven.' Now, therefore, I say unto you: I will give them unto you."

Jesus and his disciples ascend higher

When then Jesus said this, he chanted a song of praise in the great name. The regions of the ways of the Middle hid themselves, and Jesus and his disciples remained in an air of exceedingly strong light.

He breatheth into their eyes

Jesus said unto his disciples, "Draw near unto me." And they drew near unto him. He turned himself towards the four corners of the world, said the great name over their heads, blessed them and breathed into their eyes.

Jesus said unto them: "Look up and see what ye may see."

Their eyes are opened

And they raised their eyes and saw a great, exceedingly mighty light, which no man in the world can describe.

He said unto them anew: "Look away out of the light and see what ye may see."

They said: "We see fire, water, wine and blood."

Jesus explaineth the vision of fire and water, and wine and blood

Jesus, — that is Aberamentho, — said unto his disciples, "Amen, I say unto you: I have brought nothing into the world when I came, save this fire, this water, this wine and this blood. I have brought the water and the fire out of the region of the Light of the lights of the Treasury of the Light; and I have brought the wine and the blood out of the region of Barbelo. And after a little while my father sent me the Holy Spirit in the form of a dove.

"And the fire, the water and the wine are for the purification of all the sins of the world. The blood on the other hand was for a sign unto me because of the human body which I received in the region of Barbelo, the great power of the invisible god. The breath on the other hand advanceth towards all souls and leadeth them unto the region of the Light."

The same explained from former sayings

"For this cause have I said unto you: 'I am come to cast fire on the earth,' — that is: I am come to purify the sins of the world with fire.

"And for this cause have I said to the Samaritan woman: 'If thou knewest of the gift of God, and who it is who saith unto thee: Give me to drink, — thou wouldst ask, and he would give thee living water, and there would be in thee a spring which welleth up for everlasting life.'

"And for this cause I took also a cup of wine, blessed it and give it unto you and said, 'This is the blood of the covenant which will be poured out for you for the forgiveness of your sins.'

"And for this cause they have also thrust the spear into my side, and there came forth water and blood.

"And these are the mysteries of the Light which forgive sins; that is to say, these are the namings and the names of the Light."

Jesus and his disciples descended to earth

It came to pass then thereafter that Jesus gave command: "Let all the powers of the Left go to their regions." And Jesus with his disciples remained on the Mount of Galilee. The disciples continued and besought him, "For how long then hast thou not let our sins which we have committed, and our iniquities be forgiven and made us worthy of the kingdom of thy father?"

Jesus promiseth to give them the mystery of the forgiveness of sins

And Jesus said unto them: "Amen, I say unto you: Not only will I purify your sins, but I will make you worthy of the kingdom of my father. And I will give you the mystery of the forgiveness of sins, in order that to him whom ye shall forgive on earth, it will be forgiven in heaven, and he whom ye shall bind on earth, will be bound in heaven. I will give you the mystery of the kingdom of heaven, in order that ye yourselves may perform the mysteries for men."

Chapter 142

The mystic offering

And Jesus said unto them: "Bring me fire and vine branches." They brought them unto him. He laid out the offering, and set down two wine-vessels, one on the right and the other on the left of the offering. He disposed the offering before them, and set a cup of water before the wine-vessel on the right and set a cup of wine before the wine-vessel on the left, and laid loaves according to the number of the disciples in the middle between the cups and set a cup of water behind the loaves.

The invocation

Jesus stood before the offering, set the disciples behind him, all clad with linen garments, and in their hands the cipher of the name of the father of the Treasury of the Light, and he made invocation thus, saying: "Hear me, O Father, father of all fatherhood, boundless Light: iao iouo iao aoi oia psinother theropsin opsither nephthomaoth nephiomaoth marachachtha marmarachtha ieana menaman amanei (of heaven) israi amen amen soubaibai appaap amen amen deraarai (behind) amen amen sasarsartou amen amen koukiamin miai amen amen iai iai touap amen amen amen main mari marie marei amen amen amen.

"Hear me, O Father, father of all fatherhood. I invoke you yourselves, ye forgivers of sins, ye purifiers of iniquities. Forgive the sins of the souls of these disciples who have followed me, and purify their iniquities and make them worthy to be reckoned with the kingdom of my father, the father of the Treasury of the Light, for they have followed me and have kept my commandments.

"Now, therefore, O Father, father of all fatherhood, let the forgivers of sins come, whose names are these: siphirepsnichieu zenei berimou sochabricher euthari na nai (have mercy upon me) dieisbalmerich meunipos chirie entair mouthiour smour peucher oouschous minionor isochobortha.

"Hear me, invoking you, forgive the sins of these souls and blot out their iniquities. Let them be worthy to be reckoned with the kingdom of my father, the father of the Treasury of the Light.

"I know thy great powers and invoke them: auer bebro athroni e oureph e one souphen knitousochreoph mauonbi mneuor souoni chocheteoph choche eteoph memoch anemph.

"Forgive [sing.] the sins of these souls, blot out their iniquities which they have knowingly and unknowingly committed, which they have committed in fornication and adultery unto this day; forgive them then and make them worthy to be reckoned with the kingdom of my father, so that they are worthy to receive of this offering, holy Father.

"If thou then, Father, hast heard me and forgiven the sins of these souls and blotted out their iniquities, and hast made them worthy to be reckoned with thy kingdom, mayest thou give me a sign in this offering."

And the sign which Jesus had said [? besought] happened.

The rite is consummated

Jesus said unto his disciples: "Rejoice and exult, for your sins are forgiven and your iniquities blotted out, and ye are reckoned with the kingdom of my father."

And when he said this, the disciples rejoiced in great joy.

Directions as to the future use of the rite

Jesus said unto them: "This is the manner and way and this is the mystery which ye are to perform for the men who have faith in you, in whom is no deceit and who hearken unto you in all good words. And their sins and their iniquities will be blotted out up to the day on which ye have performed for them this mystery. But hide this mystery and give it not unto all men, but unto him who shall do all the things which I have said unto you in my commandments.

"This then is the mystery in truth of the baptism for those whose sins are forgiven and whose iniquities are blotted out. This is the baptism of the first offering which showeth the way to the region of Truth and to the region of the Light."

Chapter 143

Of three other mystic rites

Thereafter his disciples said unto him, "Rabbi, reveal unto us the mystery of the Light of thy father, since we heard thee say: 'There is still a fire-baptism and there is still a baptism of the Holy Spirit of the Light, and there is a spiritual chrism; these lead the souls into the Treasury of the Light.' Tell us, therefore, their mystery, so that we ourselves may inherit the kingdom of thy father."

Of the highest mysteries and of the great name

Jesus said unto them: "There is no mystery which is more excellent than these mysteries on which ye question, in that it will lead your souls into the Light of the lights, into the regions of Truth and Goodness, into the region of the Holy of all holies, into the region in which there is neither female nor male, nor are there forms in that region, but a perpetual indescribable Light. Nothing more excellent is there, therefore, than these mysteries on which ye question, save only the mystery of the seven Voices and their nine-and-forty powers and their ciphers. And there is no name which is more excellent then them all, the name in which are all names and all lights and all powers."

Of the efficacy of that name

"Who then knoweth that name, if he cometh out of the body of matter, nor smoke nor darkness nor authority nor ruler of the Fate-sphere nor angel or archangel nor power can hold down the soul which knoweth that name; but if it cometh out of the world and sayeth that name to the fire, it is quenched and the darkness withdraweth.

"And if it sayeth it to the demons and to the receivers of the outer darkness and their rulers and their authorities and their powers, they will all sink down and their flame will burn and they will cry out, 'Holy, holy are thou, most holy of all holies.'

"And if on sayeth that name of the receivers of the wicked chastisements and their authorities and all their powers and also to Barbelo and the invisible god and the three triple-powered Gods, straightway if on will say this name in those regions, they will all fall one on another, will be undone and destroyed and cry out, 'O Light of all lights, which is in the boundless lights, remember us and purify us.'"

And when Jesus had finished saying these words, all his disciples cried out, wept with loud sobbing, saying:....

[Lacuna of eight leaves]

"Thereafter they lead it into fire-rivers and boiling fire-seas, to take vengeance on it therein another eleven months and twenty-and-one-days."

Engraving by Gustave Doré

THE PISTIS SOPHIA UNVEILED

A Sixth Book

Chapter 144

Of the chastisement of the curser

"...[and lead them forth to the fire-rivers and fire-seas] and take vengeance on it therein for another six months and eight days. Thereafter they lead it up on the way of the Middle, and every one of the rulers of the way of the Middle chastiseth it in his chastisements another six months and eight days. Thereafter they lead it to the Virgin of Light, who judgeth the good and the evil, that she may judge it. And when the sphere turneth itself, she handeth it over to her Receivers, that they may cast it into the Aeons of the sphere. And their servitors of the sphere lead it forth to a water which is below the sphere; and it becometh a seething fire and eateth into it, until it purifieth it utterly.

"And then cometh Yaluham, the receiver of Sabaoth, the Adamas, who handeth the souls the cup of forgetfulness, and he bringeth a cup filled with the water of forgetfulness and handeth it to the soul, and it drinketh it and forgetteth all regions and all the regions to which it hath gone. And they cast it down into a body which will spend its time continually troubled in its heart.

"This is the chastisement of the curser."

Of the chastisement of the slanderer

Mary continued and said: "My Lord, the man who persistently slandereth, if he cometh out of the body, whither shall he get or what is his chastisement?"

Jesus said: "A man who persistently slandereth, if his time is completed through the sphere, that he cometh out of the body, then Abiout and Charmon, the receivers of Ariel, come, lead his soul out of the body and spend three days going round with it and instructing it concerning the creatures of the world.

"Thereafter they lead it below into Amente before Ariel, and he chastiseth it in his chastisements eleven months and twenty-and-one-days.

"Thereafter they lead it into the chaos before Yaldabaoth and his forty-and-nine demons, and every one of his demons fall upon it another eleven months and twenty-and-one days, scourging it with fiery whips.

"Thereafter they lead it into fire-rivers and boiling fire-seas, to take vengeance on it therein another eleven months and twenty-and-one-days.

"And thereafter they carry it on to the way of the Middle, and every one of the rulers on the way of the Middle chastiseth it in his chastisements another eleven months and twenty-and-one days.

"Thereafter they carry it to the Virgin of Light, who judgeth the righteous and the sinners, that she may judge it. And when the sphere turneth itself, she handeth it over to her receivers, that they may cast it into the aeons of the sphere. And the servitors of the sphere will lead it to a water which is below the sphere; and it becometh a seething fire and eateth into it until it purifieth it utterly.

"And Yaluham, the receiver of Sabaoth, the Adamas, bringeth the cup of forgetfulness and handeth it to the soul, and it drinketh it and forgetteth all regions and all things and all the regions through which it hath gone. And they deliver it unto a body which will spend its time being afflicted.

"This is the chastisement of the slanderer."

Mary said, "Woe, woe, unto sinners!"

Chapter 145

Of the chastisement of the murderer

Salome answered and said: "My Lord Jesus, a murderer who hath never committed any sin but murdering, if he cometh out of the body, what is his chastisement?"

Jesus answered and said: "A murderer who hath never committed any sin but murdering, if his time is completed through the sphere, that he cometh out of the body, the Receivers of Yaldabaoth come and lead his soul out of the body and bind it by its feet to a great demon with a horse's face, and he spendeth three days circling round with it in the world.

"Thereafter they lead it into the regions of the cold and of the snow, and they take vengeance on it there three years and six months.

"Thereafter they lead it down into the chaos before Yaldabaoth and his forty-and-nine demons, and every one of his demons scourgeth it another three years and six months.

"Thereafter they lead it down into the chaos before Persephone and take vengeance on it with her chastisements another three years and six months.

"Thereafter they carry it on to the way of the Middle, and every one of the rulers of the way of the Middle taketh vengeance on it with the chastisements of its regions another three years and six months.

"Thereafter they lead it unto the Virgin of Light, who judgeth the righteous and the sinners, that she may judge it. And when the sphere turneth itself, she commandeth that it shall be cast into the outer darkness until the time when the darkness of the Middle shall be upraised; it [the soul] will be destroyed and dissolved.

"This is the chastisement of the murderer."

Chapter 146

Peter protesteth against the women

Peter said: "My Lord, let the women cease to question, in order that we also may question."

Jesus said unto Mary and the women: "Give opportunity to your men brethren, that they also may question."

Of the chastisement of the thief

"Peter answered and said: "My Lord, a robber and thief, whose sin is this persistently, when he cometh out of the body, what is his chastisement?"

Jesus said: "If the time of such an one is completed through the sphere, the receivers of Adonis come after him, and lead his soul out of the body, and they spend three days circling round with it and instructing it concerning the creatures of the world.

"Thereafter they lead it down into the Amente before Ariel, and he taketh vengeance on it in his chastisements three months, eight days and two hours.

"Thereafter they lead it into the chaos before Yaldabaoth and his forty-and-nine demons, and every one of his demons taketh vengeance on it another three months, eight days and two hours.

"Thereafter they lead it on to the way of the Middle, and every one of the rulers of the way of the Middle taketh vengeance on it through his dark smoke and his wicked fire another three months, eight days and two hours.

"Thereafter they lead it up unto the Virgin of Light, who judgeth the righteous and the sinners, that she may judge it. And when the sphere turneth itself, she handeth it over to her receivers, that they may cast it into the aeons of the sphere. And they lead it forth into a water which is below the sphere; and it becometh a seething fire and eateth into it until it purifieth it utterly.

"Thereafter cometh Yaluham, the receiver of Sabaoth, the Adamas, bringeth the cup of forgetfulness and handeth it unto the soul; and it drinketh it and forgetteth all things and all the regions to which it had gone. And they cast it into a lame, halt and blind body.

"This is the chastisement of the thief."

Of the chastisement of the arrogant

Andrew answered and said: "An arrogant, overweening man, when cometh out of the body, what will happen to him?"

Jesus said, "If the time of such an one is completed through the sphere, the receivers of Ariel come after him and lead out his soul [out of the body] and spend three days travelling round in the world [with it] and instructing it concerning the creatures of the world.

"Thereafter they lead it down into the Amente before Ariel; and he taketh vengeance on it with his chastisements twenty months.

"Thereafter they lead it into the chaos before Yaldabaoth and his forty-and-nine demons; and he and his demons, one by one, take vengeance on it another twenty months.

"Thereafter they carry it on to the way of the Middle; and every one of the rulers of the way of the Middle taketh vengeance on it another twenty months.

"And thereafter they lead it unto the Virgin of Light, that she may judge it. And when the sphere turneth itself, she handeth it over to her receivers, that they may cast it into the aeons of the sphere. And the servitors of the sphere lead it into a water which is below the sphere; and it becometh a seething fire and eateth into it until it purifieth it.

"And Yaluham, the receiver of Sabaoth, the Adamas, cometh and bringeth the cup with the water of forgetfulness and handeth it to the soul; and it drinketh and forgetteth all things and all the regions to which it had gone. And they cast it up into a lame and deformed body, so that all despise it persistently.

"This is the chastisement of the arrogant and over-weening man."

Of the chastisement of the blasphemer

Thomas said: "A persistent blasphemer, what is his chastisement?"

Jesus said: "If the time of such an one is completed through the sphere, the receivers of Yaldabaoth come after him and bind him by his tongue to a great demon with a horse's face; they spend three days travelling round with him in the world, and take vengeance on him.

"Thereafter they lead him into the region of the cold and of the snow, and take vengeance on him there eleven years.

"Thereafter they lead him down into the chaos before Yaldabaoth and his forty-and-nine demons, and every one of his demons taketh vengeance on him another eleven years.

"Thereafter they lead him into the outer darkness until the day when the great ruler with the dragon's face who encircleth the darkness, shall be judged. And that soul becometh frozen up[?] and destroyed and dissolved.

"This is the judgment of the blasphemer."

Chapter 147

Of the chastisement of homosexuals

Bartholomew said: "A man who hath intercourse with a male, what is his vengeance?"

Jesus said, "The measure of the man who hath intercourse with males and of the man with whom he lieth, is the same as that of the blasphemer.

"When then the time is completed through the sphere, the receivers of Yaldabaoth come after their soul, and he with his forty-and-nine demons taketh vengeance on it eleven years.

"Thereafter they carry it to the fire-rivers and seething pitch-seas, which are full of demons with pigs' faces. They eat into them and take vengeance on [?] them in the fire-rivers another eleven years.

“Thereafter they carry them into the outer darkness until the day of judgment when the great darkness is judged; and then they will be dissolved and destroyed.”

Of the chastisement of a foul act of sorcery

Thomas said: “We have heard that there are some on the earth who take the male seed and the female monthly blood, and make it into a lentil porridge and eat it, saying, ‘We have faith in Esau and Jacob.’ Is this then seemly or not?”

Jesus was wroth with the world in that hour and said unto Thomas: “Amen, I say: This sin is more heinous than all sins and iniquities. Such men will straight way be taken into the outer darkness and not be cast back anew into the sphere, but they shall perish, be destroyed in the outer darkness in a region where there is neither pity nor light, but howling and grinding of teeth. And all the souls which shall be brought into the outer darkness will not be cast back anew, but will be destroyed and dissolved.”

Of the after-death state of the righteous man who hath not been initiated

John answered [and said]: “A man who hath committed no sin, but done good persistently, but hath not found the mysteries to pass through the rulers, when he cometh out of the body, what will happen unto him?”

Jesus said: “If the time of such an one is completed through the sphere, the receivers of Bainchoooch, who is one of the triple-powered Gods, come after his soul and lead his soul with joy and exultation and spend three days circling round with it and instructing it concerning the creations of the world with joy and exultation.

“Th[illegible]ter they lead it down into the Amente and instruct it con-[illegible]e instruments of chastisement in the Amente; but they [illegible]ke vengeance on it therewith. But they will only instruct

it concerning them, and the smoke of the flame of the chastisements catcheth it only a little.

"Thereafter they carry it up unto the way of the Middle and instruct it concerning the chastisements of the ways of the Middle, the smoke from the flame catching it a little.

"Thereafter they lead it unto the Virgin of Light, and she judgeth it and depositeth it with the little Sabaoth, the Good, him of the Middle, until the sphere turneth itself, and Zeus and Aphrodite come in face of the Virgin of Light, while Kronos and Ares come behind her.

"At that hour she taketh that righteous soul and handeth it over to her receivers, that they may cast it into the aeons of the sphere. And the servitors of the sphere lead it forth into a water which is below the sphere; and a seething fire ariseth and eateth into it until it purifieth it utterly.

"Thereafter cometh Yaluham, the receiver of Sabaoth, the Adamas, who giveth the cup of forgetfulness unto the souls, and he bringeth the water of forgetfulness and handeth it to the soul; [and it drinketh it] and forgetteth all things and all the regions to which it had gone."

Of the cup of wisdom

"Thereafter there cometh a receiver of the little Sabaoth, the Good, him of the Middle. He himself bringeth a cup fulled with thoughts and wisdom, and soberness is in it; [and] he handeth it to the soul. And they cast it into a body which can neither sleep nor forget because of the cup of soberness which hath been handed unto it; but it will whip its heart persistently to question about the mysteries of the Light until it find them, through the decision of the Virgin of Light, and inherit the light for ever."

Chapter 148

A sinner suffereth for each separate sin

Mary said: "A man who hath committed all sins and all iniquities and hath not found the mysteries of the light, will he receive the chastisements for them all at once?"

Jesus answered: "Yea, he will receive it; if he hath committed three sins, he will receive chastisement for three."

Even the greatest of sinners, if he repent, shall inherit the kingdom

John said: "A man who hath committed all sins and all iniquities, but at last hath found the mysteries of the light, is it possible for him to be saved?"

Jesus said: "Such a man who hath committed all sins and all iniquities, and he findeth the mysteries of the Light, and performeth and fulfilleth them and ceaseth not nor doeth sins, will inherit the Treasury of the Light."

Of the time favourable for the birth of those who shall find the mysteries

Jesus said unto his disciples: "When the sphere turneth itself, and Kronos and Ares come behind the Virgin of Light and Zeus and Aphrodite come in face of the Virgin, they being in their own aeons, then the veils of the Virgin draw themselves aside and she falleth into joy in that hour when she seeth these two light-stars before her. And all the souls which she shall cast at that hour into the circuit of the aeons of the sphere, that they may come into the world, will be righteous and good and find at this time the mysteries of the Light; she sendeth them anew that they may find the mysteries of the Light.

"If on the other hand Ares and Kronos come in face of the Virgin and Zeus and Aphrodite behind her, so that she seeth them not, then

all the souls which she shall cast in that hour into the creatures of the sphere, will be wicked and wrathful and do not find the mysteries of the Light."

The disciples beseech Jesus to have mercy upon them

When then Jesus said this unto his disciples in the mist of the Amente, the disciples cried and wept: "Woe, woe unto sinners, of whom the negligence and the forgetfulness of the rulers lie until they come out of the body and are led to these chastisements! Have mercy upon us, have mercy upon us, son of the Holy one, and have compassion with us, that we may be saved from these chastisements and these judgments which are prepared for the sinners; for we also have sinned, our Lord and our Light."

[A Later Postscript]

The proclamation of the apostles

...the righteous [man]. They went forth three by three to the four zones of heaven and they proclaimed the goodness of the kingdom in the whole world, the Christ inworking with them through the words of confirmation and the signs and the wonders which followed them. And thus was known the kingdom of God on the whole earth and in the whole world of Israel as a witness for all the nations which are from the rising unto the setting [of the sun].

[Two Lines Erased]

Epilogue of the Original Spanish Edition

We, the Forty-two Judges of Karma, re-united in full council with just authorization of the Hierarchy, and with complete power over the life and death of human beings of this planet, deliver this present work, The Pistis Sophia Unveiled, by Samael Aun Weor, the venerable Master of the White Fraternity. The complete unveiling will be completed at its proper time, hour, and space.

It is urgent to organize the world salvation army, based on the living church, the chosen people, and perfect matrimonies, that work intensely in the three revolutionary factors, in order for the new Celestial Jerusalem to be founded.

Study and practice all the lessons with patience, temperance, loyalty, and obedience to our Divine Mother and to our Divine Father, as well as to the sacred mysteries of our holy church.

Drink the wisdom of the crystalline waters of immaculate whiteness. They contain the tree of philosophers, wise ones, scientists, and religious ones. The waters contain the non-plus-ultra, the summum matter, the Magnus Opus, the Elixir of Longevity, the origin of the body, of the Soul, of the Innermost, and of life; the word and the sexual force, the gleaming Dragon of Wisdom, the Alpha and the Omega, the inner Christ, the internal God, the beginning and the end, the Solar force that the intellectual humanoid needs to incarnate with himself. All these will not be found in any other place.

The fountain of the water of life shall be granted by the grace of the Holy Spirit to the one who thirsts for it. Fortunate is the one who knows how to drink of the pure waters in the perfect matrimony, for such a one will never again be thirsty. Igneous, Aqua, Origo, IAO.

However, to the unrepentant, tenebrous ones, abominable killers, fornicators, sorcerers, idolaters, liars, their part will be in the burning Avitchi, with fire and sulphur. This is the Second Death.

Answer, be sincere with yourselves, place your hand over your heart, ask your Divine Mother Kundalini for advice, and answer with sincerity. Have you Self-realized yourself? Will your theories or doctrines convert you into Angels? What have you gained?

What have you obtained from the many theories and doctrines? Never in the history of the centuries has anyone been known to have christified himself without the perfect matrimony, without seminal transmutation, and without the help of the Divine Mother Kundalini. With Her, you can raise the three scales of imagination, inspiration, and intuition, so that you can enter into the Celestial Jerusalem that follows the great cataclysm.

Woe to the one who adds or takes away words from this book and its unveiling, for we verily warn that the Eternal will place the most horrible grief upon such a rebel.

Those who testify these things say, surely we come quickly. Amen, so be it.

Inverential Peace.

Tradux: D. of the I.G. and of the F.B.

Elohim Agni Tao M.S.T.

Index